MILLBROOK

MILLBROOK
A Narrative of the Early Years of American Psychedelianism

by ART KLEPS

Original Kleptonian
Neo-American Church

Copyright © 1975, 1977, 1992, 1994, 1997

by Arthur J. Kleps, the Original Kleptonian Neo-American Church

Revised and republished copyright © 2005, 2024

by the Original Kleptonian Neo-American Church

Library of Congress cataloging information:

(1) Millbrook (2) Kleps, Arthur (3) Neo-American Church (4) LSD

(5) solipsistic nihilism (6) Leary, Timothy Francis

ISBN 978-0-96003-884-8

All rights reserved. No part of this book may be reproduced in any form, except for brief quotations, without permission in writing from the OKNeoAC.

Portions of this book that we have uploaded to the Internet may be downloaded and copied for personal use, but all commercial use of such material is prohibited.

Thanks to Michael Green for drawing the church seal. Cover map and back cover illustrations by Art Kleps.

This book is dedicated to everyone who helped liberate the working people of Tibet from the oppressive tyranny of the Dalai Lama.

All words mean whatever the chief boo hoo says they mean. For example, when I refer to "sense impressions," or to "appearances," or employ other conventional terms of the kind, I mean *phantasiai* as that term was used by Sextus Empiricus.

Philosophers are so far from rejecting the opinion of a continued existence upon rejecting that of our sensible perceptions, that tho' all sects agree in the latter sentiment, the former, which is, in a manner, its necessary consequence, has been peculiar to a few extravagant skeptics; who after all maintained that opinion in words only, and were never able to bring themselves sincerely to believe it.

— David Hume, *A Treatise of Human Nature*

PREFACE

It is, of course, a thing which ought to be settled, and I am not going to have anything particular to do next winter anyway.

The following narrative is a veracious[1] representation of my recollection of events and what I have to say about the character of persons and places is a veracious representation of my opinion of those persons and places, as in the following veracious sentence:

"Any person who questions my veracity is a filthy swine."

Some quotations are exact. Most are approximations. None are deliberately misleading. I have changed the names and identifying characteristics of a few peripheral figures but most of the names given here are the names which I recall being used at the time.

One will not read far in *Millbrook* without encountering hyperbolic idioms and extended rhetorical metaphors. I have made a considerable effort to be factual but no effort at all to write my history in a plonking style.

The mental strain produced by attempting to separate style from content under such circumstances may be too much for some people. They are left in the lurch. The lurch, however, is

---

[1] See reviews of the 1977 edition, at the back of this printing.

well-provisioned. Take a bearing on the planet Saturn and paddle like crazy.

I hope readers who find factual errors will write to me about them.

The chapter headings and quotations thereunder are taken from *A Connecticut Yankee in King Arthur's Court* by Mark Twain and are in the original order.

CONTENTS

A Word of Explanation   1
1968: Timothy Leary threatens to "go over to Tommy's side" if he doesn't get Maynard Ferguson's furniture back from the Buddha of the Future.

1. **Camelot**   9
   1963: JFK is assassinated. William and Thomas Mellon Hitchcock finance and promote Psychedelianism on their 2,500-acre estate at Millbrook, New York. Teenage queens fail to behave in a manner to which the author has become accustomed.

2. **King Arthur's Court**   13
   1960: Patchogue, Long Island. The author, in his fifth year as a school and clinical psychologist, takes half a gram of mescaline sulfate, with the usual consequences.

3. **Knights of the Table Round**   22
   1963: First visit to the Mellon Hitchcock estate. IFIF. The Castalia Foundation. The Tibetan Book of the Dead. Drs. Leary, Metzner and Alpert, and the supporting cast of the early days. A professor of art from Cornell loses track of which side is which.

4. **Sir Dinadan the Humorist**   42
   1964: Cambridge. IFIF. Lisa Bieberman. The Psychedelic Review. A eulogy for Aldous Huxley. The author gets stoned and loaded with Alan Watts.

5. **An Inspiration**   47
   Easter vacation at Millbrook. Lost in a meditation closet.

6. **The Eclipse**   54
   Solipsism and synchronicity. Enlightenment is a gas. Ideas of reference are where it's at.

7. **Merlin's Tower**   60
   Dick Alpert's photos of co-educational shit-ins. A trip with Tim aborted by Susans who think I'm bananas. Did Herman Hesse smoke edelweiss or what?

8. **The Boss**   63
   A candle explodes, threatening universal urination. The Zmms; Snazzm, Fazzm and McPozzm are introduced and defined. William Mellon Hitchcock hopes to use LSD to make more money on the stock market. Tim says the author is having a bad trip.

9. The Tournament　　　　　　　　　　　　　　　　80
   Fired by a Person person. The hidden hand at work. A visit from the Federal Bureau of Investigation. A refusal to love shit, despite Tim's glowing recommendation.

10. Beginnings of Civilization　　　　　　　　　　86
    Morning Glory Lodge on Cranberry Lake. The Neo-American Church, foundation and former and present doctrines and practices of. Peyote to the people.

11. The Yankee in Search of Adventure　　　　　94
    Millbrook. Tim's in Nepal with a Swedish model of aristocratic lineage. The author finds it hard to believe that "Poughkeepsie" means "Place of Overflowing Shitholes" in the language of the Iroquois. Hollingshead twirls. Ralph pulls out joints. The author reads a sermon on digestion to paying visitors in bed sheets. A Psychedelian PTA meeting.

12. Slow Torture　　　　　　　　　　　　　　　　103
    Millbrook. Bombed with 1,000 mics. The Kundalini experience.

13. Freemen!　　　　　　　　　　　　　　　　　　114
    1965-66: Summer at Cranberry Lake. Winter in Miami. Back to the lake. Visitors, including Jack Kerouac, appear for sugar cubes and conversation. In Texas, a Sado-Judeo-Paulinian (these people are not "Christians") punishment freak sentences Tim to thirty years in prison because hemp was discovered in his daughter's pants.

14. "Defend Thee, Lord!"　　　　　　　　　　　152
    Fun and games in the palaces of the ruling Sado-Judeo-Paulinian serial killers and mass murderers of Washington, D.C. A territorial dispute with a hireling of the American Medical Association, who has a point, sort of.

15. Sandy's Tale　　　　　　　　　　　　　　　　162
    Meat Hook Baird, M.D., tells the Senate of the United States that acid heads are skinny, bespectacled, hedonistic runts with covert and overt homosexual conflicts, pugnacious noses, receding chins and marked "gratification complexes." The author, front page news, causes Bobby Kennedy to foam at the mouth.

16. Morgan le Fay　　　　　　　　　　　　　　　193
    Stabbed in the back on the home front.

17. **A Royal Banquet**   197
    Marijuana goddesses galore. Bill Haines and the Sri Ram Ashrama are introduced to Timothy Leary and the League for Spiritual Discovery. Hired by a funny farm in New Jersey, but there are blackbirds on the left.

18. **In the Queen's Dungeons**   206
    Really stabbed in the back on the home front. Billy Hitchcock tries to help, but Tim thinks I should go to Alabama.

19. **Knight-Errantry as a Trade**   209
    The author, a cockeyed optimist, finds something good to say about delirium tremens.

20. **The Ogre's Castle**   211
    How not to live over a white-lightning run. Jailed in Florida. Back to Millbrook. You're as good a man as I am, Bali Ram.

21. **The Pilgrims**   216
    January, 1967: Tim's in California. Haines is in charge of the Big House. All present are accounted for. The author recovers.

22. **The Holy Fountain**   230
    Under the benign tyranny of William Haines, a.k.a. "Sri Sankara," a fun time is had in the Big House by Leaguers and Ashramites alike.

23. **Restoration of the Fountain**   241
    Bob Ross, goat lover vs. the author and Otto H. Baron von Albenesius, sheep herders.

24. **A Rival Magician**   245
    A crazed dentist disgraces the Neo-American Church on the West Coast, but the author excommunicates the rotten bastard. A sociable trip in the Meditation House.

25. **A Competitive Examination**   253
    Tim decides to return, despite a deal he made with the despots of the Place of Overflowing Shitholes to never do so. He demands that we evict Rudy and Jackie first.

26. **The First Newspaper**   256
    They are driven forth and the author gets their room. The Bombardment and Annihilation of the Planet Saturn and Divine Toad Sweat: Bloated House Organ of the Church. The Mysterium Tremendum on $5 a day.

27. **The Yankee and the King Travel Incognito**   262
   The view from that room was lovely when snow was falling, a hushed surround both brilliant and subdued, which, for all its detail, gave little hint of what century or country we were in.

28. **Drilling the King**   275
   Barefoot Michael Green, Bill Haines and the author are invited to the Bungalow for drinks. Then Bali Ram (shod in gold slippers), Bill Haines and the author are invited to the Bungalow for a trip.

29. **The Smallpox Hut**   281
   Suzanne and Aurora are fixing the drinks?

30. **The Tragedy of the Manor House**   283
   "The needle leaked. Tee hee." Oh well, in for a dime, in for a dollar.

31. **Marco**   285
   Holy shit!

32. **Dowley's Humiliation**   288
   "What do you think this is, Sham? The Calcutta bazaar?" Wendy's offer to strip is accepted, on a trial basis.

33. **Sixth-Century Political Economy**   297
   Tim returns, but too late. Things have changed. Is "Victory Over Horseshit!" a "gentle love message"? Does Tim have enough clout with the Hitchcocks to evict the Ashram? No, to both questions.

34. **The Yankee and the King Sold As Slaves**   306
   Peggy Hitchcock throws a "psychedelic seder" at her town house in New York. Bill Haines and author prepare the punch for this celebration of mass racist infanticide. An Episcopal priest sees the light. The Neo-American Church gets the Gatehouse.

35. **A Pitiful Incident**   322
   The Kriya Press of the Sri Ram Ashrama prints 2,000 copies of the Neo-American Church Catechism and Handbook. Tim's "review" thereof. Moonlight madness and the Mellon millions.

36. **An Encounter in the Dark**   351
   Billy Hitchcock and the author, now boon companions, do not entirely succeed in resisting the artful wiles of ruthless adventuresses who seek to enmesh our souls in the toils of carnality.

37. **An Awful Predicament**   362
   Egalitarian primitivists are all over the place. Tord moves in. The author appears on the Alan Burke Show. It becomes clear Tim would rather rule in Hell than share Heaven with the likes of us.

38. **Sir Launcelot and Knights to the Rescue**   370
   The great Fourth of July party of 1967. Champagne Charlie Rumsey, Joe Gross, M.D., Huntington Hartford and daughter, Cathy, dedicated missionary bee hee. A fast forward to a contrasting, occultist kind of party in California in '68. Tim evicts an East Village, freeloading, female freak from the Bungalow.

39. **The Yankee's Fight with the Knights**   384
   The author is the sanest person on the property? According to Tim and a public poll, yes. Tim pronounces himself a charlatan. Susan is upset, but a Virginian Mellon of Pennsylvania, or vice versa, is delighted to hear it. Capitalism in action.

40. **Three Years Later**   394
   An editorial incident. Back to 1967. Wendy and author tie the knot. So do Howie and Betsy, with Pat O'Neill dancing naked on the Big House roof at the reception. The repetition compulsion is bad news.

41. **The Interdict**   426
   The Sado-Judeo-Paulinian Voodoo-Papist gang lords of the Place of Overflowing Shitholes order their minions to assault us, women and children first.

42. **War!**   430
   Tommy deeds territory to all three persecuted sects. Tim invites the author to take over the Big House.

43. **The Battle of the Sand Belt**   447
   Little Billy takes Orange Sunshine. Suzanne is accused of indecent exposure. The author barfs on a limo, and other mopping-up operations.

44. **A Postscript by Clarence**   488
   The author claims to have loved every minute of it, even when he was barfing on the limo.

Final P.S. by M.T.   497
   Have some solipsistic nihilism with a little Snazzm, Fazzm and McPozzm on the side.

A WORD OF EXPLANATION

Begin here—I've already told you what goes before.

Millbrook, early spring, 1968

"Well, where's that flunky Rumsey and the Mad Scientist?" Bill Haines growled as he stomped into the press room. He was followed, in close formation, by Howie, Betsy and Thorin Druck, a trio commonly and derisively referred to by those of us who knew and loved them as "The Holy Family."

There were at least thirty people in the converted garage of the old farmhouse which had sheltered Haines' Sri Ram Ashram since Tim Leary, "the Mad Scientist," had expelled the Ashram from the fifty-room Big House down the hill, in April of '67, almost exactly a year before. Now we were all being ejected, not only from our dwellings, but from the 2,500-acre Dutchess County estate entirely. Tim, Haines and I had been served with eviction notices from the Hitchcock Cattle Corporation, signed by Tommy and Billy Hitchcock, ordering us and all the members of Tim's League for Spiritual Discovery, Haines' Sri Ram Ashram and my Neo-American Church to be off the property by May 22.

It promised to be a dramatic meeting. My wife Wendy and I, the Ashram members, and those Leaguers who had survived the winter were present out of immediate, if not desperate, self-interest. But the mixed bag of Vassar girls, freaks from Woodstock across the Hudson and visitors from New York who happened to be hanging around that day clearly expected to be entertained. Except for a few rooms, the Big House had been closed for most of the preceding winter and Tim, who hated cold weather, had been in California.

"Tim's somewhere on the property," I replied. "I don't know where Rumsey is. Maybe they're having a little advance meeting up at the Bungalow, or something, ho, ho."

The "Bungalow" had been built in 1913, as a gift from Charles Dieterich to his son, Alfred. Rumsey, a non-practicing lawyer, was an old school chum of William and Thomas Mellon Hitchcock, who were twin brothers and bi-products of several generations of venereal congress between members of America's most bloated plutocratic dynasties. The handsome twins had inherited enormous trust funds in their early twenties, purchased the estate in 1963, and then offered the "Big House," a nineteenth-century extravaganza which had been the residence of the original owner, to Tim Leary, Dick Alpert and Ralph Metzner, as a "psychedelic research center."

Why? The super-rich do not ordinarily do things like this, or anything remotely resembling anything like this, nor does anyone in any other economic bracket very often do anything like this, for that matter. Youthful folly? Courage of Psychedelian conviction? Sympathy and generosity? Boredom? Innocence? Arrogance? Curiosity? Lecherous anticipation of variegated choirs of marijuana goddesses? The hypnotic spell of Timothy Leary? Did the coup d'état of 1963 have anything to do with it?

I asked Billy about his and Tommy's original motivations one time, after the whole project had been beaten into the ground by the powers that were.

"It was the only game in town," he replied, which was a very Billyish kind of thing to say, and not inconsistent with any or all of the above.

Anyway, this magnificently generous, reckless and astonishing offer, for which both of them, and their wives as well, deserve the eternal gratitude of mankind and the perpetual forgiveness of sins, was made shortly after Tim, Dick and Ralph had been kicked out of Harvard and then Mexico because of their Psychedelian activities. They were desperately searching for a suitable locale and powerful patronage. They took one look at the Big House, two looks at the twins and, as Billy laughingly told a reporter during the latter days of the place, "promptly accepted."

The combined wealth of the then resident Hitchcocks: Billy, the prime mover; Tommy, who was always somewhat reluctant; and their sister Peggy, always an enthusiastic participant, was well over one zillion dollars, or something like that, on tap and on order, and raining down from above in refreshing, timely showers. Their father had died in an airplane crash early in WWII, and their mother, who had never remarried, lived in New York City in a Gracie Square apartment overlooking the mayor's house and the East River, and rarely visited her children's private playground.

Under the circumstances, at once so desperate and so grandiose, I think my speculation about a little advance meeting was immediately understood by my fellow residents as meaning what I intended; that possibly one more Byzantine twist was about to occur and the grand master himself would sell us all down the river.

"Let's not get paranoid, Kleps," Haines said. "It's too early in the day."

There was a titter from the audience. Our visitors seemed a little stunned to hear such cynical and jocular discourse between the chief boo hoo and the guru of the Ashram. They usually came, drawn by media images, rarely to see Haines or me, but to look the place over in a general kind of way and perhaps catch a glimpse of Tim in action, possibly levitating over hill and dale, or distributing iridescent capsules to the rest of us, whom they assumed to be his faithful and devoted disciples. They usually ended up at the Ashram because the rest of us customarily sent them there. Even if they read the local papers, it was always extremely difficult for visitors to understand what was going on and, very often, not much easier for those of us who lived there and were deeply involved in what was going on to understand what was going on.

Haines sat down on a ratty old couch facing the open garage door. He was in full regalia: yellow robes, sandals, beads, heavy cane to poke the female members of the Ashram in the crotch with if he felt they were "asking for it," so to speak.

The air was balmy again and full of bird song, the view delightful; gardens, fields, woods, winding roads leading off towards "my" Gatehouse and Millbrook, town of, beyond.

All of us were feeling a lot of plain, old-fashioned grief at the prospect of being driven from this earthly paradise but, just like Adam and Eve, what we talked about was how to make as good a deal as possible with the landlord.

"I hope you're prepared to explain why you let Marlowe take the furniture?" Haines asked.

"Yeah, Kleps," Howie Druck added. Howie, head of The Holy Family, was twenty-six. His wife, Betsy, was twenty-three, and her son by prior alliance, Thorin, the only human being Haines seemed able to relate to without intermittent torrents of abuse, was three.

"Why didn't you stop him?" I asked Haines.

"I am a man of peace. I keep telling you, Kleps, that one of the principles of yoga is non-violence, but you don't seem to believe me."

I sighed. The day before, an excited Howie had appeared at the Gatehouse with a story about how Allan Marlowe was up at the Big House loading a U-Haul trailer with articles of furniture that most definitely didn't belong to him. Tim was away lecturing and couldn't be reached. Marlowe, Howie reported, had said Rosemary (Rosemary Woodruff, Tim's constant companion at the time) had given him permission to take the stuff. Haines had asked him to wait until Tim returned but he refused. According to Howie, Marlowe was crazy. The secret League name he had given himself was Maitreya, the Buddha of the Future and, because he had once thrown a dinner plate at Bill during an argument over vegetarianism, he was "violent." It was time for SPIN to go into action.

Frequently, when there was a crisis of this sort on the

property, Haines would phone or dispatch a messenger to urge me to "send SPIN into action." SPIN, the Society for the Prevention of Injustice to Neo-Americans, was not exactly operational, as Haines knew full well. Once again I regretted ever inventing the damn thing. I drove to the Big House and found Marlowe, assisted by a confederate I didn't recognize, struggling in the main hall with a ten-foot-high oval mirror in a gilded frame we later found out belonged to Maynard Ferguson, the band leader. Just being in the Big House depressed me. Most of the electricity and water was off, the remaining Leaguers were camped out in the woods in tents, and the mansion was inhabited only by rats and cats and phantasmagorical images of cherished people and weird scenes now long gone.

Marlowe had a wild look in his eyes, which showed he was feeling normal, I suppose. Yes, Rosemary had given him permission. His conduct was none of my business since I was not a member of the League and he wasn't a member of the Church.

In a way, I was half a member of the League, since Tim had started to initiate me the previous fall when we were both half crocked and he was trying to abandon Rosemary to my keeping while he took off for Las Vegas. Rosemary had reminded him he was violating the bylaws of the League by acting without consultation with the rest of the group and, after remarking that such shit cut no ice with him, he had desisted.

No, Marlowe had said, he couldn't wait. The U-Haul was rented for only one day. I shrugged and left. The police, Tim had said, should never be called under any circumstances. Although I thought this a reasonable general rule, I had violated it by calling the state police, not the local county thugs, on two occasions without evil consequences.

"I don't see how he can get pissed off at us," I said.

"I'm afraid I do," said Haines, puffing on his pipe (strictly tobacco; Haines rarely smoked the Lesser Sacrament, although he enjoyed it in edible form every now and then) and assuming an air of confident but burdensome insight into the minds of men not granted to lesser mortals. Bill's forecasts of Tim's conduct were almost always for stormy weather in the near future, and I had to admit he usually had Tim's moves "psyched out" better than I did, but to predict trouble over a few pieces of furniture, however fancy, at a time like this didn't make much sense to me.

For weeks Tim had been preaching to Bill and me that our response to the eviction order would determine the fate of the psychedelic movement and world history for eons to come, so we should all defy that spoiled rich brat Tommy at the risk of imprisonment if necessary. Passive resistance, of course. Caves in the hills. TV crews would flock. The hypocrisy of the Republicrat bosses of Dutchess County, who had been raiding the estate repeatedly to harass any one of us they felt like harassing, while treating the owners and rulers of the place as if they were invisible, would be revealed for all to see. Tim's pitch made sense, sort of.

He told us how he had visited Tommy at his apartment in New York, gotten drunk, and ranted and raved at him for hours to no avail. Tommy was determined to play the "aristocrat-serf" game, Tim said. Billy was pretending Tommy was forcing him to go along by invoking hitherto unmentioned rules of their cattle farm corporation, which held title to the property.

Tim assumed, and so did we, that Billy had become as eager as Tommy to throw us to the wolves in order to avoid getting fanged himself and stuck with all the bills for bail and fines. This was only natural, but Tim took a very adversarial position, at least in his speeches to us. Billy and Tommy were playing "money and power games" but we should not allow ourselves to be seduced by mere gold when such high principles were at stake.

Although Bill and I now had our own arrangements with the landlords, including deeds of a sort, complete with a map which had been published in the local weekly, Tim had been the instrument of both our original entries. We had come in under his wing. I felt that if Tim wanted to put up a fight, some kind of primal fealty obliged me to stand with him, and I said so.

It seems absurd at the time of this writing, but those were strange times and Millbrook was a very strange place.

When Bill also accepted Tim's strategy I was astonished. It

was the first time in a long time all three of us had agreed to act in concert about anything important and it was a refreshing change. Although we had not distinguished ourselves as models of amicability during times of peace, when it is only natural to go your own way if no great harm is done by it, we were now united in defiance of a common foe.

Charlie Rumsey was probably authorized to offer a few thousand if we would leave quietly; Tim would tell him we were staying no matter what; Haines would declare, once again, that if he went to jail "Tommy and Billy will be in the cell right next to me"; and I would, what? Probably tell Charlie, keep it simple, that I was simply following Tim's lead as I had promised.

When Tim and Rosemary walked in everyone brightened up a bit, even though Tim looked tired and grim. They sat down in a very unrelaxed way, in chairs which two polite visitors gave up for them. No, Rumsey hadn't arrived yet. Yes, the lecture had gone well, as usual. Awkward silence. Tim was obviously displeased by the large number of people present. Oh well, I thought, we can always move upstairs.

Me: "Tim, did you hear about Allan Marlowe taking some furniture from the Big House yesterday?"

Tim: "What? Marlowe took my furniture? Why didn't you stop him?"

Haines: "He said Rosemary gave him permission. What the hell were we supposed to do?"

Tim jumped up and left followed by Rosemary. Fifteen minutes passed during which Haines moodily examined the floor at his feet, employing the tip of his cane as a probe. I closely examined the picturesque landscape framed by the open garage doors.

Tim and Rosemary returned, faces rigid. Tim pointed an accusing finger at Haines and me and said (exact words):

"OK, YOU GUYS. IF YOU DON'T GET MY FURNITURE BACK BY MONDAY, I'M GOING OVER TO TOMMY'S SIDE."

They left without waiting for a reply. The next day a moving van appeared and loaded up all their remaining possessions.

There never was a meeting with Charlie, or any other kind of general landlord/tenant meeting. Except for the documents mentioned in this book, nothing was ever spelled out, much less resolved.

I didn't see Tim again until fall, when Billy and I went to visit him in the hillside house in Berkeley none of us at Millbrook knew he owned until it was all over. He was sprawled out on a wooden deck overlooking the bay, surrounded by "White Panthers" and others of similar persuasion, who were telling stories about blowing up power stations and other acts of wanton destruction, as was then the fashion. The presence of William Mellon Hitchcock, a capitalist if there ever was one, didn't faze these guys a bit. Were they aware Tim held stock in New England Nuclear, and that they were suggesting that he destroy his own property? Probably not, but it wasn't impossible some of them owned stock in New England Nuclear themselves, such were the bizarre mores of Berkeley in 1968.

Had he ever gotten his furniture back? "No," Tim replied with the utmost blanditude, "as a matter of fact, most of it belonged to Maynard." Then he showed me a copy of *Horizon* magazine that featured an article on Millbrook entitled "Boo Hoos and Gurus," with a nice picture of me leaning out of the top window of the stone tower on the bridge behind the Gatehouse with my arms out as if I were blessing the multitudes or getting ready to take a swan dive. The greatest practitioner of the political arts I have ever known had once more succeeded in changing the subject by substituting an "upper" for a "downer," perhaps his favorite rhetorical trick in a large and varied repertoire. A week or two after Tim's abrupt departure, the Ashram settled for $25,000. The Neo-American Church got $10,000. There were several reasons why I allowed myself to be shortchanged, not one of which, I can now see, was worth a nickel on the open market.

Otto H. Baron von Albenesius got $1,500. We will meet the inimitable Otto later.

As far as I know, nobody ever found out what Tim got, if anything, for "going over to Tommy's side," whatever that means, if he did.

Chapter 1

CAMELOT

"Camelot—Camelot," said I to myself. "I don't seem to remember hearing of it before. Name of the asylum, likely."

In the fall of 1963, a lead photo in the *New York Times* (or was it the *Herald Tribune*?) with a box story about Tim Leary, Ph.D., Dick Alpert, Ph.D., and Ralph Metzner, Ph.D., moving into the Hitchcock estate in Millbrook showed a corner of the Big House porch. There was a pumpkin in it somewhere, I think. I can't remember who the pictured people were, or even if the story was before or after Jack Kennedy's assassination, although I vividly remember another newspaper picture from around the same time showing Dick walking in the slush with Tim's daughter, Susan, on a Millbrook sidewalk. Susan is looking up admiringly at her tall and handsome, fascinating friend.

Sally, my wife of five years, our three-year-old daughter, Susan, and I were living at the time in the small town of Edwards in the far northwestern corner of the Adirondacks. I was beginning my tenth year of work as a school psychologist and, as usual, I had four school districts to serve. I had also worked as a clinical psychologist in various settings, including three New York State prisons, but I liked school psychology better than anything else available to me, and always returned to it.

Every weekday morning I would drive my Oldsmobile Cutlass

convertible through the misty forests of the northern fall, past sparkling lakes and modest dairy farms, to a "consolidated" school which was always the biggest business and the most interesting place in town. I would give one or two IQ tests in the morning, and in the afternoon give projective tests, advice, and "psychotherapy" to some kid who usually had only one genuine problem: the State Compulsory Education Law, which obliged him or her to attend classes instead of screwing around and/or learning a trade as was consistent with her or his interests, abilities and natural inclinations.

The odd "case" was usually more interesting, sometimes desperate, but surprisingly often not; just a bright teenager who, having recognized me as an adult who didn't click when he walked and play pre-recorded tapes when he talked, had decided to come in and chat. In the past, this class of kids had not only entertained me, but had supported and protected me as well, and I them.

Positive traits are positively correlated.

But the Clinton County kid culture was too primitive and Roman Catholic for informal school psychologists' fan clubs to develop and flourish. Negative traits are also positively correlated. In 1963-64 no sweet nothings or invitations to help myself and the sooner the better were being whispered in my ear by any teenage cuties, which was probably the main reason for my boredom, restlessness, and general sense of dissatisfaction with it all.

Little things can mean a lot, after all.

The combination of sensations I felt on reading those first newspaper stories about Millbrook was new to me, although it was something like falling in love at first sight.

There are ways to explain it. First and foremost, I had taken half a gram of mescaline, a very heavy dose, four years earlier. I didn't know another person, aside from my wife, much less another psychologist, who had any psychedelic experience at all. Attempting to describe the experience and explain why it was important had become so tiresome and unproductive that I had stopped trying. This isolation was probably the main reason I hadn't done it again. The newspaper stories, therefore, had something of the impact that the first sight of Friday's footprint had on Robinson Crusoe. At last! Other creatures like myself were within reach.

There were peripheral factors also, all attractive. I had grown up in Westchester, and was nostalgic for the lush Hudson River Valley ambiance of my childhood. I had read lots of English novels, and watched lots of movies, in which old mansions on large estates were a common setting for the action, but I had never visited anything in this splendid class of human habitation. It would be nice to see something like it in living color and three dimensions after seeing so much of it in my mind's eye and on the silver screen. And it was a plus that all three of these guys had been on the Harvard faculty, tossed out or not. Maybe we wouldn't get along, I thought, maybe they're nuts, but could they be stupid, ignorant, uncouth jerks? It seemed highly unlikely.

David Riesman, whose comments on American society I thought and still think admirable, taught at Harvard, and had recently written me an appreciative letter about my "Neo-Psychopathic Character Test," which had bucked me up considerably.

Yes, *veritas*, with as few reservations as possible. It was just about the only slogan I knew about to which I gave my wholehearted support and always had since as long as I could remember. The truth will make you free. Free of lies, which means free of 99 percent of what's wrong around here.

And everyone in the pictures that accompanied the newspaper stories looked cheerful and healthy-minded and they were described as being that way by the presumably cynical newspaper reporters who wrote the initial stories about Millbrook.

All of the above taken together, however, didn't seem adequate to explain my excitement and enthusiasm. I was absorbed and fascinated to the point of being spellbound. Why should a few newspaper stories make me feel like I had been granted a "new lease on life"?

Somehow, I thought, a mysterious power had been restored to a psychic province long shrouded in darkness.

The trip, as is often remarked upon by experienced Psychedelians, starts before the trip starts. My intuition was working right. Something was up. I sent Tim a copy of the mock "test"

Riesman had liked, and a brief account of my mescaline trip, and hoped fervently that I would get an invitation.

When I promptly got exactly what I wanted from Tim, written on an old picture-postcard of the Big House, I carried it around for weeks in the breast pocket of the gray flannel suits I always wore at work. Between testing kids and meeting with teachers and dictating reports, I gazed at the black and white aerial photograph on the postcard of the Big House in the snow, evidently taken by some scarfed and goggled daredevil early in the century, as if it had magical properties instead of just being an old picture of an old house I had never seen.

Chapter 2
KING ARTHUR'S COURT

Friend, do me a kindness. Do you belong to the asylum, or are you just here on a visit or something like that?

I took my first trip in 1960, on 500 milligrams of mescaline sulfate. A "flying start," one might say. It was a private, ten-hour-long "total visionary." The psychologist who happened to live in the other half of our rented, one-story duplex near the water in Patchogue, Long Island, chickened out at the last minute. His wife, he claimed, had nixed his participation in the project, which the two of us had planned after reading Gordon Wasson's and Aldous Huxley's early accounts of their psychedelic experiences.

My wife, Sally, in contrast, seemed to have no apprehensions whatever about my risking my sanity, if any, and she was on call throughout my trip, which helped. Two weeks later we reversed roles and Sally, without any objections from me but also without much encouragement, casually took the other half of the gram of mescaline sulfate that I had bought by mail from Delta Chemical Company in New York. I was much impressed by this and, although I have learned since that women, in general, seem to be much less chicken about taking large doses of major psychedelics than men are, I'm still impressed. The whole thing? If I was so fortunate as to have 500 milligrams of crystal mescaline sulfate around today, I would nibble at it, and I advise any novice reading this to do the same. You might end up taking it all, but take your time about it. What's the rush? (Synthetic mescaline is virtually unobtainable today and has been for a long time, although a lot of acid has been sold under the name.)

Her trip was more of the emotional-roller-coaster variety than mine had been, with many replays of childhood scenes, but she also saw the same kinds of intricate and colorful displays which occupied almost all of my mescalinized hours.

It probably would have been better to have done it together, with no "ground control" personnel on hand at all, as I now advise most novices to do, but the conventional wisdom of the day was all we had to go by.

After downing the tasteless, colorless, crystalline powder, I decided to take a walk around the block. The reports I had read held that it took about thirty minutes to rev up.

There were no blood-curdling or hair-raising events during this stroll. Every little breeze did not whisper "Louise," or anything like that. But about halfway around, walking along the waterfront, I developed a strange conviction that every tree I passed was alive and moving in the wind.

Back at the ranch house and feeling much more alert than usual, I noticed that a red washcloth was gently winding around like a snake in our light-blue bathtub. After a hasty exit from the bright bathroom to the dim den, I was treated to another active apparition. The yellow flowers in a bowl on our TV set had decided to join the fun at the Democratic nominating convention, then in progress. They were definitely dancing around to the beat of the band and the closer I looked, the more enthusiastic the flowers became in their support of JFK's candidacy.

At this point, on this kind of trip, it is impossible not to ask oneself, what next? What was to stop a monstrous gobbler from outer space from joining me on the couch at any moment?

Nothing. I moved to the bedroom, lay down on the bed, and closed my eyes. Instantly, I found myself watching a three-dimensional color movie on the inside of whatever it is one looks at when there isn't anything there. For openers, aurora borealis-style streaks of colored lights flung themselves from horizon to horizon. Horizons? What horizons?

All night, I alternated between eyes-open apprehension and eyes-closed astonishment. With eyelids shut I saw a succession of elaborate scenes each of which lasted a few seconds before being replaced by the next in line. Extraterrestrial civilizations. Jungles. Animated cartoons. Displays of lights in abstract patterns. Temples and palaces of a decidedly pre-Columbian American type, neither grim nor pretty, but beautifully delineated, textured, colored, and always in perfect perspective.

There was no obvious narrative connection between scenes. I'm indifferent to pre-Columbian art. There was no aesthetic coherence to the whole, although every part seemed flawless.

When I say, as many others have, that some of my visions compared favorably with the best in Western art, I'm being cautious not to overstate the case. I saw little that was Oriental, aside from some Japanese tree and mountain scenes. There were lots of caricatures, some goofy, some classic, some sentimental and old-fashioned, all kinds.

No matter how elaborate the content, there was never any hint of a technical breakdown. If something merely silly was being presented it was always done up with all the slick perfection of a Walt Disney feature, plus all kinds of extra touches Disney could never have afforded. Let's say "despair" was being depicted in the form of the conventional cartoon castaway on a cartoon raft; a two-second throwaway flash. Well, just for kicks and contrast, why not add a transparent ocean, exquisitely tinted in thousands of colors, in which a billion seahorses merrily bob in communal harmony, singing and playing tiny musical instruments?

No problem, Sahib. Coming right up. That was the spirit of the thing. No job too large, no job too small. The difficult we do right away, and the impossible ... we do right away also. (The inconceivable might take a little longer.)

"Despair" was depicted? Yes, so I concluded later. In the first versions of this book I made the error of saying "words" were depicted (imaged) but it's confusing to say that. People tend to think that they think in words but they don't. We think in images, and then communicate, to ourselves or others, our images in words. On a visionary, you eliminate the middle man, so to speak. You may or may not be aware of your images. Some people never are and do not seem to be much the worse for it.

Nabokov, a master word wizard if there ever was one, so envisioned the situation, and so do I. So have many other thoughtful people. (Nabokov also described himself as an "indivisible monist," and even went a bit further, in a glint here and hint there, in his later years. See *Strong Opinions*.)

I turned on our bedside radio, hoping to replace the parade of fantastic pictures with something familiar. Enough is enough, I thought. The radio, in an act of brazen defiance, promptly produced a New York City discussion show, full of trivia and inanities. Instead of stopping or slowing things down, this garbage accelerated and variegated the procession even more.

It was as if every scene produced by the mindless babble on the radio had been the life's work of generations of media technicians on planets given over to the production of such artistic wonders, all for the purpose of this one showing in Art Kleps' one-man screening room.

Adequately describing this kind of thing to those who have no references for it in their own experience is uniquely difficult. It's not only one hell of a literary problem, it's a real doozy of a psychological problem.

How can anyone have an experience of this magnitude and intensity without turning into a paranoid, terrorized blob of quivering jelly? How can anyone stand it, much less enjoy it, if it's as overwhelming and irresistible as we say it is? The reader who has had no major psychedelic experience, however sympathetic he was to start out with, will suspect the author of exaggeration and bravado. As always, I advocate skepticism, but some conditional and provisional suspension of disbelief is necessary if you want to find out what it feels like to be someone else or to get some grasp of an alien practice and philosophy.

I think much of the resistance is based on the natural assumption that the person who took the pill is the same person who has the following experience, which, after all, is an assumption we solipsistic nihilists can't expect not to be made unless we suggest otherwise. The explanation is just as hard to swallow as the facts which make it necessary, but it's true nonetheless: the constancy of the personality is illusory.

I quote David Hume:

> [An individual mind is] a bundle or collection of different perceptions, which succeed each other with an inconceivable rapidity and are in a perpetual flux and movement.
> [The identity which we ascribe to an individual mind is only a] fictitious one since every distinct impression which enters into the composition of the mind is a distinct existence and is different and distinguishable and separable from every other perception, either contemporary or successive.

To some extent, at least, almost all will grant, one becomes what one beholds. Freak-outs, in a way, are caused by a time lag. The truly terrified person is still imagining himself to be the kind of creature to whom such things simply cannot happen, trying to hang on to his former self. It's an error that lies at the root of much simplistic occultist thinking: I "go," if I get this spell right, find the newt's eye that rolled under the sofa, or say my mantra properly, from one world or level to another world or level. No, that is not what happens. There are no "trips," however convenient it may be to use the analogy. There are only transformations, transformations of everything. Does that help?

Visionary experience is always personal and yet almost always fantastic and impressive. One is flooded with it. On a big one there is no way to stop the action to think things over. This is a recipe for fast and sloppy supernaturalist and paranoid ideation, among those who are so inclined.

The pace, the scope, and the contents of the experience are not in contradiction to or in agreement with but are irrelevant to and incommensurable with normative psychology and any "depth" or "structuralist" psychological system I know about, Jung's included.

An experience of this kind will lead some people to conclude that extraterrestrial and/or supernatural beings are expending enormous amounts of energy to "beam messages" to them or something of the sort.

Although there are countless variations on the theme, the ideation which follows will often go something like this:

A. They (the good Higher Powers) have chosen me to be their intermediary and a member of the Company of the Elect because of my unique attainments, or
B. They (the evil Higher Powers) want to drive me crazy because I am the only person on earth with the spiritual power to defy them, or
C. They (the fallacious Higher Powers) erred. This crazy shit was intended for someone else. To hell with it.

Aside from C, which is rare, none of these assumptions work out very well in practice, at least not if the paranoid in question continues to take the stuff. Psychedelic experience refuses to conform to any system involving an external dynamic and will inevitably betray anyone who tries to control either his own or his troop's trips. Indoctrination can confuse or delay the correct interpretation of psychedelic experience, can make doing it much more stressful than it needs to be, can sometimes warp the content somewhat, but cannot determine the content.

I think this fact drives some people, commonly and accurately known as "control freaks," half out of their minds with rage and frustration, but these are the kind of people who would be displeased to discover that their neighbors think a thing of beauty is a joy forever, so not much can be done for them.

Major psychedelic experiences have many highly predictable characteristics, no matter who, where, why, when, what or how the deed is done to, by, for or of. I think that all of these classic characteristics are illustrated somewhere in this narrative.

I didn't take another trip until four years later. Fully aware of my lowly status as a wage slave, I was afraid of making such radical changes in my everyday consciousness that I would become unemployable. These apprehensions were largely groundless but the regular use of major psychedelics and a standard 9-to-5 existence in the United States of America, as presently constituted, don't mix well, and it's useless to pretend otherwise.

My general way of looking at things had already changed a lot.

I found nothing in my visionary experience to encourage me to believe in any occultist or supernaturalist system, which may have been the happy result of taking an "overdose." Instead, dualism of every variety was blown right out the window, never to return.

I was now a monist, but what kind of monist? I did not consider myself "Enlightened," and wasn't sure the term meant anything. But I was sure about some things.

The visions were my images, my ideas, however incompatible that conclusion was with what I had formerly conceived my mind to be "made of." I no longer find it necessary to believe it's made of anything, but that came later.

At one point I seemed to hover over an alien planet, or over a transformed version of this one, upon which were spread various cities made up of grids of multi-colored lights, traversed by thousands of parrot-like creatures. One is tempted to think in terms of Ouspenskian or Tibetan-style grandiose cosmologies but, wait a minute, what's next in line?

The professional liar on the radio is selling a deodorant. Sure enough, out of the Precambrian ooze emerge millions of putrid bubbles; and the noxious effluvia which result, represented by pastel swirls and coruscating vibrations, are as complex and beautiful as what has gone before, but hardly "metaphysical." When people throw up, they often do see "piles of jewels."

Try to imagine all the images in, say, *Locksley Hall,* colored, animated, and in three dimensions, not in sequence, but all at once, and arranged in such a way as to be, if not in actual harmony with one another, at least so well-organized as not to be in any mess or collision. If you can do it, and unless you happen to be on a powerful psychedelic and in a frivolous and tenacious frame of mind, you can't do it, the result will be both hilarious and impressive, which is exactly the character of much of the visionary experience I've had myself and have been told about by other Psychedelians.

It is a combination of qualities not commonly found in the art works of churches and museums (but is not unknown in such precincts, either, if you look for it). The root causes of much psychopathology are as often compounded of absurd misunderstandings as they are of tragic events. The pre-Psychedelian grand theorists, however, and those who have signed up under this or that grand theorist banner, tend to dismiss as inconsequential any insights that people giggle about and treat flippantly. In their view of things, a bunch of people gathered around a nitrous oxide tank, laughing like fools, cannot possibly be having experiences that deserve to be called "profound" or "spiritual." The idea that the comedic spirit and profundity are highly compatible and often go out together and have a wonderful evening offends them deeply. It is an insult to the firmly held beliefs their barbaric ancestors killed and were killed for.

Yes, there is little or no room for the absurd in any of the metaphysical or mythic systems of occultists and supernaturalists. Yet I have never heard one of them say a word during the peak hours of an acid trip about the philosophic hierarchies, organization charts and grim fairy tales that, during normal, repressed consciousness, they say describe everything universal and fundamental. When a person is truly and fully stoned all inculcated ideation about things in general evaporates. Those who are fixated (love and depend) on the crazy ideas they grew up with will usually repress most of what they have learned on their trip or trips in favor of the standard substitutes for the truth with which they are familiar and comfortable. They may renounce psychedelics completely and join the Moonies or, perhaps, declare that only organic psychedelics are any good, not because they are more mild (more manageable) than acid but because of a pantheistic virtue which resides in organicity, a rationalization which will provide them with a new collection of moralistic dogmas to fuss and fret over.

If supernaturalism was not supported by my first trip, neither was scientism (the world is clockwork, however complex). Dualism, in all forms, was undermined.

I don't think that my character and morals were undermined in any way, nor did I abandon the scientific method and empirical reasoning about particular things because my views on things in general had changed. My ideas about the nature of consciousness and the organization of perception changed, not my ideas about the best way to fix a flat tire or educate people with low IQs. There was nothing about my psychedelic experience which made it easier for me to lie, cheat or delude myself. On the contrary, I would say. Dishonesty became more difficult.

During the next three years I thought more about literary, social and political stuff than I did about psychedelics and philosophy. (My literary tastes, perhaps, went up a notch.) As a psychologist, I was probably even more empirical than I had been before the trip. As the memory of the experience receded in time, it seemed more and more like an aberration, similar, in many ways, to my winter in the Alaskan woods after getting out of the army. So, I had done another unusual thing, but how important was it? Was I any happier? No, I couldn't honestly say that I was.

When I discovered that a group of purportedly respectable and learned psychologists were taking dose after dose of LSD and psilocybin and apparently functioning with great practical efficiency at the same time, indeed, having a ball, setting forth on great adventures and taking over mansions in Dutchess County, I concluded that I was just being chicken.

These experts, I assumed, knew all kinds of things I didn't know and had all kinds of contacts I didn't have. Perhaps I could join them once I caught up to their level of specialized knowledge. If I could find a way to live without the income from it, to hell with clinical and school psychology, at least as it was routinely practiced. Plastering over the growing cracks in the public education system was not my idea of the best way to spend most of my waking hours anyway.

Chapter 3

KNIGHTS OF THE TABLE ROUND

There was a fine manliness observable in almost every face; and in some a certain loftiness and sweetness that rebuked your belittling criticisms and stilled them.

Shortly after Christmas of 1963, leaving Sally at her parents' house in Manhasset on Long Island, I made my first trip to Millbrook, up the gentle curves of the lovely Taconic Parkway, through Westchester and past my childhood village of Crestwood, amidst a snowy landscape, in my dark-red convertible, with a bottle of blackberry brandy at my side.

Millbrook was a pretty, bright, white, small town with lots of big trees, the slushy central street of which I hissed through in a matter of seconds. The three-story, stone-walled Gatehouse was about a mile north of town. There was a massive portcullis in its arched entry and a fairy-tale kind of tower at the west end of the building. The whole thing was roofed with curved, light-red, terra cotta tiles. It was lovely. As Tim had instructed, I didn't stop to announce myself at this structure, but entered the grounds by way of an open drive a few dozen yards up the road, drove over a stone bridge, and found myself in Wonderland.

From the moment of my first view of the Gatehouse, my critical faculties rapidly washed away under an overwhelming flood of approval and appreciation.

It all seemed perfect, all the way up to the Big House, potholes and broken branches included: the winding roads, the little lakes and streams, the fields, woods, and mysterious stone structures covered with snow. Everything was exactly as it should have been, beyond critique or analysis, as in a vision or a dream.

I drove through the Big House porte cochère and parked in a courtyard formed by the main building and a wing which contained the kitchen and laundry rooms, and upstairs, the former servants' quarters.

Inside, in the main hall in front of Maynard's mirror, which the plate-throwing Buddha of the Future would rip off five years later, I found teenage Jackie and Susan Leary, Kim Ferguson, and a bunch of younger kids taking off skates, galoshes, coats and mittens. Beautiful children with intelligent faces and happy eyes. I was expected. Tim was upstairs. Why didn't I just go right up and introduce myself?

As I climbed the red-carpeted stairs of the Big House for the first time, I felt a sense of place again, as in a dream.

By the time I found Tim's room I was awash with strange emotions, as well as blackberry brandy, and not in ideal condition to impress my host. Tim was seated at a desk, writing. We exchanged pleasantries, and Tim launched into a description of some recent discoveries in sub-atomic physics which had caught his interest. It was Bronowskian stuff, which is OK in its place. He was trying to play the two-intellectuals-meet game, which normally would have been fine with me, but I wasn't feeling normal at all. I could feel tears forming. This is insane, I thought to myself. It was the first this is insane thought of a long series to come.

"I think you've forgotten how bad it is out there," I said.

Tim looked perplexed and apprehensive. He suggested that I go downstairs and meet the other members of the household and the current visitors. He would see me at dinner.

In the next few hours I met, and without exception instantly approved, in a casting director's sense, everyone then resident in the Big House. I will list and briefly describe them, and the visitors then present as well.

Tim. Without a consort at the time, an unusual circumstance.

I was somewhat surprised to learn that Lisa Bieberman, who was then managing the IFIF (International Federation for Internal Freedom) office in Cambridge, wasn't present and was not expected to become a resident. I was told that during her last visit to Millbrook she had insisted on a right to move in on grounds of her seniority in devotion to the cause, indefatigable diligence, unimpeachable righteousness and so forth, but had left in a highly disillusioned condition. While she was sitting in the kitchen one early morning (musing, perhaps, on the pronounced similarities between her adored Harvard lecturer and J.C.), the Holy One himself appeared, tousled and bleary-eyed, drew a coffee, and inquired of the assembled breakfasters, "Jesus Christ! Do I have to fuck every girl who comes into this place?"

That did it for Lisa. She retreated to Cambridge, where I met her later. As far as I know, she never returned to Millbrook. Soon, IFIF became her baby and hers alone. Millbrook, she often said thereafter, was "a human zoo." Lisa, it turned out later, had been having exclusively "Christian" trips on LSD, or so she interpreted them. In 1971 she had one of the regular kind, and promptly wrote a bulletin to her subscribers in which she renounced acid for Jesus. Lisa, dark of eye and hair, was intense, persistent, and just as impervious to popular opinion as she was to logic. A born slave, she worked her hairy little ass off for whatever she believed in.

Tim had probably been as satisfied as he ever was with his latest free hump, and only said what he said because he wanted Lisa to hear it and abandon any hope of intimidating him into conformance with her middle-class standards of "morality." I have made some pretty outrageous remarks myself over the years, for the same reason, to people of Lisa's type. Why argue? It's much easier, and more fun, to demonstrate that you are a "hopeless case" instead. As Sextus Empiricus would have put it, it's the "philanthropic" way to handle the problem.

Tim's charm, as friend and foe alike admitted, was awesome. As is often the case, I think much of it was due to his voice, which trilled and tinkled, caressing the ear with gentle melodies and punctuations, vulgarizing by comparison every competing instrument. He almost never raised it. Even when angry or malicious, the voice stayed within the limits of its charm. One might hear a hard rain of sleet or the light clash of cymbals, but never squawks, mumbles, whines or any other kind of ugly noise. Furthermore, his voice, as if it had some separate spirit or function of its own, did not, like most voices, simply carry Tim's thoughts like a load in a cart; it often spoofed and laughed at what it was required to support, thereby anticipating and disarming the critical reactions of his audience. Much of Tim's wit relied on these disarming vocal nuances; it does not come through as well in his written words.

Many thought Tim was spoofing when he wasn't, or thought he wasn't when he was. Tim's playfulness had no consistency, no foundation in logical analysis or a stable set of values. It was simply employed to take the edge off, to provide an escape hatch, to disarm. When the natives looked restless, the master musician would shake his jingle bells, perhaps indulge in some goofy histrionics, even take a pratfall. Everyone would smile, and write off their former doubts as "paranoia."

Dick Alpert. Tim's closest associate and co-conspirator, a Ph.D. in psychology like his transformed buddy, but with superior professional and social credentials. Dick had been on the faculty at Harvard, where Tim had been a visiting lecturer, renowned only as the inventor of an ingenious and novel paper-pencil test of personality factors then in use by the California penal system. Dick was the son of a bloated plutocrat who had been the president of the New Haven Railroad while Dick was at Harvard. The tedium of academic life had been greatly relieved, Dick gleefully told me, by his living in a private railroad car with a teenage brother and sister team who provided both service and recreation, day and night. "Art," Dick said, a look of bemused delight suffusing his open and jovial countenance as he reminisced about the wonders of his fortunate life, "I didn't know what to do to whom first."

Dick didn't have an official companion in those days, of either sex. Nor did he ever, during the time I knew him, come to think of it.

Ralph Metzner, Ph.D. A psychologist and biochemist in his late twenties. A neat, dry, scholarly man who made neat, dry, scholarly comments but rarely spoke at length. Ralph had a wife in residence,

Susan. She was a classic, pretty, blonde and busty American Girl who seemed soft and childlike in contrast to Ralph's Germanic seriousness. Somehow, Ralph projected an aura of conventionality and conformity no matter how unconventional, and even illegal, the activities in which he was engaged. He had the makings of a "master criminal" in this respect. Every time I talked to Ralph I was acutely reminded of the dutiful grinds who had made up my circle of chess-playing friends at Concordia, my Lutheran prep school in Bronxville. Cynical to a fault in private, they had all behaved like perfect robots in public and had routinely collected A's in every subject while I flunked, or barely passed, everything in sight.

Jackie and **Susan Leary.** Both cute kids: sixteen and fifteen, or fifteen and fourteen, or somewhere in that happy bracket. They were happy then, and I don't think their father's oddities, our internal community conflicts or their experience with psychedelics made them unhappy in the days to come. To the extent that they did become screwed up later, those who assaulted their religious community and persecuted their father and their way of life should not only be blamed but also tried and punished for crimes against humanity.

Maynard Ferguson. A famous Canadian trumpet player and band leader whose name did not ring a bell with me, which astonished him. Perhaps the sanest guy in the place. Charming wife, **Flo;** extremely super-charming daughter **Kim,** thirteen; **son,** six; **baby,** two.

The visitors were:

An aging, blonde blues singer, said to be even more famous than Maynard, but whose name I didn't recognize and can't remember. She looked sad, wore beautiful clothes, and said little. I think she was even drunker than I was, which was pretty far gone as the evening advanced. Not only was there an open bar (a year later, every bottle would have disappeared in fifteen minutes, to be guzzled at once or hidden in self defense) but I also had my usual pint of brandy stashed in the john under the stairs on the first floor.

Allen Atwell. A professor of art at Cornell. He was preparing for his first "session," as trips were called in those days, to be held in the tower room, the highest room in the house, that very evening. Allen, who looked a lot like Abraham Lincoln after a hard night anyway, appeared particularly resigned at the time.

I went to take a look at the tower room (we will get back to the other visitors) and after many a twist and turn through dark corridors carpeted in worn red plush, I found it at the top of a small spiral staircase. There were windows all around and I could see the lights of Millbrook twinkling in the distance over a landscape of moonlit snow and dark masses of fir and pine. Two fat candles were burning, and some incense, and a cheery fire in a cheery fireplace. Oriental rugs. A low bed. A statuette of Buddha. A statuette of Shiva dancing on Yama, as usual. Trays of candy and nuts and fruit. A copy of the *Tibetan Book of the Dead*. A copy of the *I Ching*. From a speaker in the corner came the drone of a Zen chant, not too loud, and quite pleasant, it seemed to me.

Tim's basic method in those days, I later found out, was to attempt to structure other people's LSD experience in terms of the *Tibetan Book of the Dead*, which is the prime text of the most supernaturalist, deviant and degenerate form of "Buddhism" on earth, namely, Tibetan Lamaism.

It's great stuff for the social control of an ignorant peasantry, and that's about it. A first-class horror show to terrify the kiddies into mindless obedience. An infallible Priest-King. Ruthless taxation to build gigantic edifices for the religious bureaucracy. Institutionalized pederastic, homosexual buggery ("celibacy"). Why go so far afield when we have so much of that so much closer to home, like in Massachusetts?

Many people who never have visionary experience on LSD learn just as much as those who do, if not more. Elaborate embellishments, crazy or not, tend to distract attention from the present and stagnate thought in a morass of enigmatic imagery.

A succession of fantastic spectacles is all well and good, but people must learn to ask the right questions before they can get the right answers. Preposterous stories and garish interior decorations never sent any steamboats up the Ganges.

As decor, I like first-class Oriental art and, as metaphor, it's often instructive also, but you don't need metaphors if you have the thing itself, and the thing itself is psychedelic experience.

Novice trippers were heavily "guided" in those days. Everyone, me included, thought they could be and should be. It sounds right and reasonable in terms of ordinary life, but it just doesn't work that way. Ralph Metzner was to "guide" Allen Atwell.

Jack Spratt. (I can't remember his name.) Jack was a "rich drunk from Syracuse" as Tim put it. My university town. Fat, intelligent, about forty-five, the only person present wearing a tie. He was there to be "cured," and was waiting for his second trip. On his first, he had by no means surrendered his bad habit as a result of meeting the Lord of Death face-to-face. On the contrary, perhaps.

Albert Mole. Can't remember his name either. A large, flabby and fuzzy clinical psychologist from Buffalo, who was my first introduction to the foil or scapegoat archetype usually present in every Psychedelian community. Would that every one of them were as bumbling, foolish, and harmless as Mole. As Ramakrishna said of his nasty cousin, who was always hanging around, when his disciples would ask him why he patiently endured such an obnoxious presence, such characters "thicken the plot," and it is usually a good idea to leave well enough alone. As often as not, the replacement, and a replacement seems to be inevitable, will be twice as bad as the original. Don't put too much pressure on your casting system.

Mole's specialty was snouting out the presumably diseased and clandestine psychological forces at work in the place. I don't think he knew how to do anything else.

When I told him that I was having one of the most fantastic and delightful experiences of my life, although I hadn't taken any drugs, he said that though everyone was certainly "very friendly," he couldn't approve "for example, of the obvious seduction of a teenage boy." He glanced suggestively towards Dick and Jackie who were sprawled out in earnest converse under the soft and twinkling radiance of a magnificent demonstration that a gentle joy can be found in the Gothic and grotesque (a twelve-footer). Mole never relaxed, and finally fled.

If it was difficult for visiting psychologists and psychiatrists to hang on to the detached, inquisitorial role at Millbrook in the early days, it just got harder later. The place was too seductive for that, even during bad times.

Straight newspaper reporters and others bent on "exposing" our hidden agendas were usually disabled for similar reasons. Both cynical and inquisitive, they were fixated on discovering what was "really happening," but no matter how ingenious the questions or ingratiating the style, no cross examination ever revealed anything that satisfactorily explained, within the very narrow and materialistic conception of human nature with which they and their bosses and clientele were familiar, all of the puzzling talk and nuances of feeling and conduct they witnessed. I think this is true of Psychedelian communities in general.

The hardest part to swallow, often as not, for a professional shrink or hired scrivener in the service of the Ministry of Truth, is the general high spirits and good-natured camaraderie which prevail. The jokes, frequently self-deflationary, conflict with his most cherished categorizations of human nature. There is so much honesty and spontaneity that he begins to think the whole thing is a put-on.

I think Mole was deeply offended by Dick's blithe spirits and unabashedness. Why wasn't Dick wracked with resentment over his loss of status in the academic world? Where was all the self-justification and self-analysis one Jewish psychologist had every right to expect from another?

It came out later.

Mole could usually be found in the kitchen, nursing a drink, where he brought up, one after another, every historical and theoretical model and just plain silly notion he could think of in the hope that one of them would be accepted by the rest of us as the way to understand psychedelic experience, so he could then dismiss the whole thing as an imitation, probably shoddy, of something else, or not worth bothering about for some other reason.

He seemed to wither visibly every time someone insisted, as they invariably did, that although there were parallels, the experience was really incapable of being understood or appreciated by the uninitiated. The terrible burden which this truth, combined with demonstrations of non-harmfulness, places on the flattened and homogenized products of America's psychiatrist and psychologist mills cannot be overestimated. I think most of the anti-Psychedelian academic cant, and the slovenly "research" designed to support such cant, is prompted by the terror which grips these wimps at the thought of being expected to take the stuff themselves. Mole, maintaining his defenses against this dreadful possibility, quickly dismissed me as a credulous fool. (Either you are a credulous fool or I am a coward, therefore you must be a credulous fool.) I was left mostly in the company of my natural ally, Jack Spratt, the only other heavy boozer present.

On the late return of Ralph, Susan, Dick, Jackie and Kim, all in a cheery mood with skates slung over their shoulders after a long game of hockey on one of the ponds, Mole shrank once again. "Are they pretending to be normal?" he probably asked himself.

To my expressions of appreciation of the healthy-minded, happy atmosphere which prevailed, Jack Spratt replied, "I've got to admit these people know how to make a person feel at home, but I don't go in for all this Boy Scout stuff. Make my own bed and help with the dishes? I have always been happy to pay for that kind of service." It was clear that Jack regarded me as a fellow patient in a strange and very badly managed psychiatric hospital, so I told him about my mescaline trip.

"I guess I want to see the Clear Light or achieve Enlightenment, or whatever you want to call it," I said, capitalizing those nouns and tossing down another belt.

"I don't go along with all that stuff," Jack replied, and refilled my glass and his own.

Later, Maynard told me that during one of his all-night parties in the large room below the tower, during which it was not unknown for a certain carefree abandon to overtake the participants, who might then, as like as not, disport themselves, whatever their age or sex, in a manner inconsistent with prevailing middle-class American mores, Jack Spratt had briefly appeared at the open door, having descended from the tower, where he was having his first trip.

"He just stood there gaping at us like he couldn't believe his eyes," Maynard chortled. "Then he said, 'Christ, it's crazy enough up there but down here it's completely insane' and went back up to the tower."

Susan Leary showed me to my room, one of eight or nine in the servants' wing over the kitchen and laundry. Everything was neat and clean. I unpacked and took a bath across the hall in a deep, enameled-iron, old-fashioned tub.

Conversation at dinner, which was served at a long table (with legs) with everyone seated on chairs (rather than on the rug), was as animated, natural, amusing and educational as anything in my experience with dinner table conversations. Mole wearily punched away at Tim but, after days of failing to connect, it was pretty clear that he no longer had much heart for it. Tim would laugh at Mole's comments and dryly and slyly make a remark which would not directly answer what Mole had said but instead undercut him somehow, sometimes in two or three different ways, making whatever Mole had said seem ridiculous and unworthy of serious consideration. I was impressed by Tim's display of rhetorical skill, and did not think Mole deserved any better treatment than he got.

Tim was never reluctant to deliver snap judgments, like an undergraduate psychology student, when he thought the occasion and the person seemed to call for it. It was a habit I shared. When not being paid for my professional services, I see no reason to deny myself the same liberty to bandy ideas around which everyone else enjoys. "Judicious" or even "sober" discourse did not prevail. One might shoot the shit with carefree abandon and not be held to account for every minor error or self-contradiction.

Everyone, Mole excepted, was making the standard upper-class assumption about one another's morals and mores: You are an honorable and well-intentioned person until proven otherwise.

As (in the best of times) in the House of Commons, so long

as this assumption is maintained, people may flatly contradict each other as to fact or theory, argue endlessly about what is logical and what isn't, call an opponent's motives, or even his sanity, into question, and even express moral disapproval, in the sense of differing moral interpretation, without anyone's essential dignity being threatened in the slightest. Even one stupid and/or ignorant and/or deranged person in such a group drastically degrades its quality, like a fly in one's soup. Being an intellectual isn't necessary, but being intelligent helps a lot.

I didn't know it but this delightful scene was already doomed, because Tim had decided to play it as a politician rather than as a scientist or philosopher. Charming, modest IFIF was to be abandoned and the grand and mysterious Castalia Foundation erected in its place. Metzner was pushing the books of Herman Hesse, an author not well known in America at the time. Hesse was a talented but virtually humorless fantast whose imagination generally, but with some interesting and pleasant exceptions, ran in the direction of hermetic mysteries, cryptic images and grandiose hierarchical associations. "Meta-political," one might call this model, or "Masonic, sort of." Soon, almost all Psychedelians would be oriented towards appealing to popular tastes, "reaching" the public, "molding" opinion, and changing, or preventing change in, the laws.

Nothing wrong with that, but crucial questions about content and doctrine were being swept under the carpet because of the perceived need for popular support. And, stylistically, I preferred the original light-hearted and frankly elitist spirit of things.

But popular revolutionary movements do not run on refined tastes and high-class social standards. The "troops" demand easy answers and familiar story lines. They have a limited vocabulary. The politics of the Psychedelian revolution, as Tim saw clearly and early, would be like selling beer, not champagne. Support would come from many odd quarters but the objective, as in all revolutions, would be to "capture the hearts and minds" of the only class with hearts and minds as yet uncaptured: the young.

The point of view expressed in my "Neo-Psychopathic Character Test" was something of a novelty then and it may have had some effect on Tim, confirming opinions he already held about the desperate condition of the old culture and the direction in which one ought to look for help.

Allowing visitors to drop in and out at all hours of the day and night was a pain in the ass, but Tim could not, as a good politician, prevent it. Towards the end, he withdrew to the third floor and had a private kitchen installed but the public image he projected was usually one of utter accessibility.

In the beginning, though, it was a high-class show and the memories I retain of Millbrook as it was then, although many satisfactory things happened later, are lit by a special and magical light, like the memories of the Christmases of childhood, or scenes intensely imagined in one's most cherished works of fiction.

Tim, Ralph and I went for a walk late in the evening.

Late in our conversation, which was pretty philosophical, I asked, "Tim, is anything more important than anything else?"

Tim said nothing for a moment and then pointed to a snow-laden branch hanging down in the roadway.

"Look at the way the snow shines in the moonlight. Beautiful, isn't it?"

Evasive, yes, but wrong, no, since whatever is right in front of your nose, so to speak, is always the most important thing. But it wasn't the branch that was occupying my attention at the moment I asked the question. It was Tim, and it was Tim who was the most important thing in my world at the time, and he should have said so.

But that is a hard thing to say to anyone.

I was put in charge of Allen Atwell's music program that night, which amounted to no more than taking records from an approved collection and putting them on the turntable, in a room below the tower. Every now and then Ralph would pop in and ask that something be changed, or to turn the volume up or down. We started off with ragas and Zen chants and such and followed with Beethoven. After an hour or so, Ralph announced Allen didn't want any music at all, so I split for the kitchen.

Musical tastes tend to go through some radical changes as people get higher and higher. Indian music seems to help stabilize a high because it in no way encourages you to notice the passage of time, or better, to notice time has stopped passing and instead is sort of loitering around shooting the shit with space.

As seriality is re-established, taste seems to depend on what kind of trip you're on, and music problems, if any, are usually the result of idiots controlling what is being played, a role often conceded to them by deaf custom.

When some kid puts on the latest rock star, a record he and his friends have been playing repetitiously while inhaling the lesser sacrament, the room will often empty in minutes. Bob Dylan's early songs and almost everything the Beatles produced hold up well (what more can I say?) but rare indeed is the devotee of screaming adolescent anguish who can tolerate his favorites when he is on the Supreme Sacrament, which doesn't mean he won't put them on for everyone else's benefit while he himself departs, perhaps to listen to the music of the spheres and the hooting of owls in a distant pasture or orchard.

Bad music doesn't just cause people to scatter. It is also one of the few things, aside from active malice, which can directly and reliably cause bad trips.

When someone flips, check out the music being played or what has just been played. Often it will be an exhibitionist making millions from his contemporaries by moaning, groaning, and shrieking about how fucked up he is. Under normal circumstances, a performance of this kind may reassure the similarly afflicted that they are not alone, but it will simply encourage bummers on trips. Older people often like sad, romantic songs involving wails from jails by downhearted quails, and the like. Beware. If such stuff is played on a trip, gloom will prevail and many of the participants will remember previous engagements at the nearest saloon.

Haines, who patiently tolerated kid music under ordinary circumstances, smashed quite a few records on trips during the years I knew him. He would point out that the person who put the record on was no longer present, and apparently didn't like the record any more than Haines did, so he felt justified in disposing of it as he pleased. Good point.

Late that night, as I was sitting around the kitchen mulling things over with Spratt, Atwell drifted in like a ghost, his big brown eyes shining and dilated.

"How did it go?" I asked.

"Beautiful, beautiful ..." Allan said, putting some coffee on. "But I seem to have switched sides. My left side is now my right side and my right side is my left side."

We didn't know what to say to that.

"As a matter of fact, I think I left part of myself up in the tower. I have to go back and get it." He drifted out of the room.

I got up and turned off the burner under the coffee pot. Although still determined to do it, I was becoming seriously apprehensive about taking acid. Strange visions were OK, but I'm the kind of guy who likes to know which side is which. And, if at all possible, I like to have all of myself in one place at the same time. I went to bed.

The next day, in the early afternoon sunlight, I took Tim and Susan to town to buy groceries. I put the top down, although it wasn't really warm enough, just for the fun of it.

In town, Tim was greeted by storekeepers and townspeople alike with what seemed to me an affectionate regard. He amused people. They liked his style and so did I. And Tim seemed genuinely happy playing the role of "one of the boys," fellow villager, and good neighbor, with a few easy bantering words for one and all. I was charmed and impressed. Tim, I thought, was definitely my kind of guy. While Tim and Susan filled up their carts, I popped into the liquor store next to the small supermarket. Eddie, the genial owner, with whom I was destined to have a long and mutually satisfying relationship, introduced himself and had me pegged by asking a few questions. A "Dieterich Estate" visitor who might move in? Fine. Fifty bucks or so more a month more for Eddie.

There were ups and downs, but there was very little general animosity towards us from the regular residents of Millbrook until the last months, and even then it was clear that their irritation was not with the us, the established freaks, but with the dregs from New York City who had taken advantage of Tim's blanket invitations to come up and squat.

Not antipathy, but civility, tolerance and much more sophistication than I would ever have predicted were displayed by these folks, many of whom were the products of a high-IQ Italian gene pool of masons and other craftsmen who had built the estate. The Ashram got a line of credit at Marona's grocery store, and even minor transgressions of the law were sometimes covered up for some of us who had been around long enough to be trusted.

Hollywoodized persons who have been brought up to believe that all small towns are inhabited by sinister and depraved morons who live on the take from unwary motorists may think I am blinded by sentiment, but if there was anything psychologically septic about little old Millbrook, town of, I never discovered what it was. Trixie Belden and Norman Rockwell would have felt right at home and so did I. (Nancy Drew might not have felt at home, but Nancy is a wooden dummy written in leaden English, while Trixie has life, as does the clean, workmanlike prose she is mostly written in.)

I bought a case of Hennessy. Tim approved. I gave him $50, which he liked even better, having spent about $300 in the grocery store. We picked up the mail, loads of it, and did a few other errands. When we got back to the house and parked, Dick stuck his head out of one of the windows in the servants' wing and shouted down, "You all look like an advertisement for the American Way of Life," meaning the convertible and the bags of groceries and we three handsome people, I suppose.

With Kim's help, I stashed the groceries in the storeroom behind the kitchen, where I couldn't resist re-enacting the classic scene from the romantic novel in which the mysterious stranger embraces the gorgeous maiden.

The next morning I went to Manhasset to pick up Sally, and returned. What the hell. Nothing ventured, nothing gained. And the whole business seemed saner, somehow, with my better half at my side.

Sally's one and only visit to Millbrook was not a success. She was terrified, not by the presence of acid and marijuana, but by the people and the setting, and she stayed in our room almost all of the day and evening. It was "just too much." Her first words in the car the next morning when we drove away were, "Did you see the dresses on those girls?"

Sally's father, Murray Pease, was Conservator of the Metropolitan Museum of Art, and she was descended on both sides, Peases and Jewetts, from the theocratical oligarchy of colonial New England. In order to eat, we later sold some documents with Paul Revere's and Daniel Webster's signatures on them.

Her parents were part of an exclusive WASP society and cultural world, now much reduced in power and influence by the power of gold but far from dead, which was at that time well represented by the "real" *New Yorker* of old and the *New York Herald Tribune*. Despite her family background, Sally either ignored or was aversive to most distinctions of money, power, intellect and even taste. She liked ordinary things to the point of being virtually ambitionless, an appealing trait in some ways, but exasperating in other ways.

Billy's sister, Peggy, and a friend had come over for drinks and dinner in $10,000 designer evening dresses or whatever and that was "too much." Dick Alpert wandering around the house looking through "psychedelic spectacles," a tiny strobe just then invented (whatever happened to it?) was "too much." Almost everything she saw and heard at Millbrook seemed to be "too much," which was Sally's favorite superlative anyway, and I later managed to decipher what she meant by it. By "too much" she meant too much. This did not bode well.

Susan, our three-year-old, complicated matters also. If we moved in, and I had no paying job, Sally would have to get one, and all kinds of complications would arise.

Tim, Dick and Ralph and I had circled around the subject. Assuming I could find a way to support myself and my family, and started gobbling the stuff the way they did, and if Sally decided that it wasn't "too much" after all, well, it looked like a cinch, sort of.

The most essential requirement, congeniality, was present to an astonishing extent and everyone seemed to recognize it. I just fit in somehow and that was all there was to it. It seemed inevitable that the relationship would persist and deepen. Do not, and should not, birds of a feather flock together? Sure we should, if only to communicate with each other in a language we all can understand and to scare off birds of other feathers who seek to replace our eggs with their own.

"When," it seemed, was the question and I had resigned myself to the possibility that it might be the question for a long time. But, who was to say? Maybe some clinic, hospital or "school" for retardates in the area was looking for a clinical psychologist who would work for a mere pittance. If it allowed me to live at Millbrook, I'd take it.

So, maybe this, maybe that.

We went back to our rented house in the tiny Adirondack community of Star Lake, where we had moved from Edwards, and I immediately started writing a fantastic novel about the adventures of one Christian H. Christian, who visits the headquarters of "The Flower Fiends" and is transported into other realms. I sent a few pages to Millbrook every other day. It was mildly amusing in spots but didn't really make it, and I eventually consigned it to the flames.

Tim, Dick and Ralph's conversion of the *Tibetan Book of the Dead*, a copy of which Tim sent me a month or two later, did not, in my opinion, make it either, but was published by Mystic Arts, a publishing house in Hyde Park, N.Y., very close to Millbrook, and sold quite well. "See, Arthur?" Tim said, holding up a royalty check for $1,600 for my inspection as we were having coffee across from the courthouse in Poughkeepsie during the final days.

I'm sure that what he meant was, "See what I get for publishing horseshit? So why don't you do it, and make me feel better?" but I can't authenticate that interpretation in any way.

According to Tim's letter which accompanied my copy of the book, this bowdlerized "translation" of the Lamaist scripture was to be the first of a series which would include *Alice in Wonderland* and the *Inferno*. The latter concoction, Tim thought, would particularly please me, although why he thought so he didn't say.

The fact is that I had then and have now a low opinion of all of Dante's literary product. As Blake put it, "Dante saw devils where I saw none." Likewise, I'm sure.

This may have been the first instance of Tim projecting his

neuroses on me, a Freudian mechanism which would balloon to gigantic proportions in times to come.

I knew nothing of the "infernal aspects" of psychedelic experience which are so garishly depicted in it but, I thought at the time, since my full-scale visionary productions amounted to a measly fifteen hours or so, a trifle compared to the hours logged by the mighty of Millbrook, I felt that I could only politely question, not assault, as I have since, this stupid, ignorant, crazy and evil book.

On the evidence of my experience and the experience reported to me by a sample I think representative, I can now say that truly menacing visions almost never occur on acid trips, and the unpleasant spectacles which are sometimes seen, the "cartoon freakies" and such, amount to less than two percent of overall viewing time and have less emotional weight than the standard entertainments for children shown every day on television in the great American Insane Asylum.

On the other hand, if you insist on listening to "A Night on Bald Mountain" in a rat-infested cellar with cunning and malevolent acquaintances recently recruited from 42nd Street bistros, all bets are off, and all bets are off if you prepare for your trip by reading "that stupid book of Leary's," as John Lennon called it. Why did Tim go out of his way to evoke these images at the beginning of his Psychedelian career? (Ralph and Dick, I was told by Ralph, had merely "signed off" on it, because Tim said he wanted to maintain an appearance of collegiality, a classic Learian maneuver.)

The more I learned, the more inexplicable, except as a cash cow, Tim's pushing of the *TBD* at the very start of things appeared. It was as if he deliberately and with malice aforethought polluted the Psychedelian cultural stream at its source and gave half the people in Psychedelian society (Lennon being a notable example of a good recovery) a bad set to start out with.

For years afterwards, kids told me they had, as novices, attempted to use the *TBD* as a "guide," and they all reported anxiety attacks and various kinds of craziness leading to eventual frustration and exasperation, for which, at least at first, they had blamed themselves, not Tim or the book. They were not worthy of getting fucked over by class-A Tibetan spooks, or something like that. You had to be a big wheel like Tim, Dick or Ralph to deserve truly ghastly eeriness of this magnitude. To get the Lord of Death on your case maybe you needed a Ph.D., preferably from Harvard.

It's true that Tim, as a good, crucifix-wearing Papist boy, had been brought up to believe in the efficacy of god/human sacrifice by means of prolonged torture and all kinds of related Judeo-psychotic ideation, with the usual consequences, and for a short time early in his Psychedelian career had imagined his "head was melting and running down" over his shoulders (personal communication) so I don't claim he projected darkness when all was sweetness and light within. Even so, why push one's personal nightmares on the public? He never talked that way in private, as far as I know.

Lamaism bears about the same relation to genuine Buddhism that the bloody-sacrifice doctrine of "St. Paul" and the blatantly insane *Book of Revelations* bear to the "Sermon on the Mount" and the *Gospel According to Thomas*, that is to say, almost no relation whatever, aside from contradiction. J.C., like Ramakrishna, was probably born stoned, but picked one hell of a time and place to pop out into, as it were. Given the context, it's amazing that he said anything worth repeating. Thomas Jefferson was right about what should be retained and what discarded from the Christian canon.

I bought a pound of Heavenly Blue morning glory seeds, which were becoming popular because they were legal. Baby Hawaiian woodrose seeds, I learned later, are a better choice because they are much easier to prepare, with about 25 micrograms of lysergic acid per seed compared to one or two mics in Ipomoea seeds, but neither is as good as the New Reliable. (Both are nice plants for the porch.) If you want to try them, remove the shells (soak, dry and peel). As in the case of the humble peanut, it's the seeds inside you're after. The human gut is not designed to digest shells. On seeds one night, I had another visionary trip. In contrast to the mescaline blast, it was "dreamy" in the sense which implies vagueness or abstraction, although I wasn't asleep or sleepy at the time it was happening.

There were three distinct worlds, but I retain only fragmentary memories of them (I remembered more the first few days following and should have made notes): a scene in which, on a beam of light, I entered the kitchen of a sort of tower dormitory in a world-of-the-future to remove a hammer from an ice tray; and a fantastic curtain that fell during what was clearly an intermission, depicting thousands of birds in flight in a sky of brightest blue.

Chapter 4

SIR DINADAN THE HUMORIST

Sir Dinadan was so proud of his exploit that he could not keep from telling over and over again, to weariness, how the immortal idea happened to occur to him; and as is the way with humorists of his breed, he was still laughing at it after everybody else had got through.

When, in the spring of 1964, I had a long weekend free, I made a call, and got an enthusiastic invitation to visit from Lisa Bieberman, and took off for the IFIF office in Cambridge. I had written Lisa, who was the day-to-day manager of IFIF at the time, about my plans for a Psychedelian retreat on an Adirondack lake. I thought I might spend summers at the lodge and find gainful employment elsewhere, maybe at or near Millbrook, in the winter. Lisa thought it was a "great idea."

I found Lisa at the modest IFIF office with two postdoctoral residents of the house in Newton which Dick and Tim had occupied while doing research in a local prison on the effects of acid on the recidivism rate. All three were working at routine office tasks, without pay, getting out the *Psychedelic Review* and a variety of bulletins. Alan Watts was expected momentarily, to contribute something for the forthcoming issue, which was to be a Festschrift for Aldous Huxley, who had recently departed this vale of tears in a most noble and exemplary Psychedelian fashion.

I established myself in the tiny kitchen of the small house on Boylston Street with a quart of Wilson's, a blend I favored at the time. Watts arrived and greeted everyone like long lost buddies. While waiting for the acid head who was to take his dictation to return from an errand, he enthusiastically joined me in attacking the bottle.

Both Watts and I were fascinated by a trashy men's magazine we found on the table, the kind which might depict Japanese nurses attempting to seduce American marines on its cover, with ads for crossbows and mementos of the Third Reich in its back pages. When, somewhat abruptly, but apropos the contents of the magazine we were chortling, cackling and sputtering over, I asked him how he explained the existence of suffering in the world, Watts seemed genuinely shocked.

"You're asking me that question?" he asked.

I guess he thought the answer was in his books. If so, it's in a corner I haven't penetrated. When the IFIFian typist arrived, Alan put down his drink, stood up, walked up and down, and reeled off his panegyric to Huxley as if it were tape-recorded in his head. He paused only once, in search of another example of the kind of thing academic intellectuals and literary sophisticates scorned but which Huxley was willing to discuss, tolerate or even support, and I supplied it: "The myth of the desert island paradise."

It was an amazing performance.

Unfortunately, although my appreciation for Watts as a critic of conventional religion is undimmed, my admiration for his philosophic efforts did not survive my Enlightenment, and even at the time of which I speak, I could not work up much enthusiasm for his point of view. He was, I think, essentially a pacifier, a sort of intellectual male nurse, a calmer of the troubled waters. Nothing wrong with that, of course.

Watts rarely mentioned his Western intellectual ancestors, but he was clearly a Transcendentalist and, in my book, a "Slobovenoid Blobovenoidalist." With an Emersonian disdain for logic and consistency, he assumed the plurality and independence of minds but ignored or evaded the conflict between this and the supposed existence of a benign "Oversoul" (the "Giant Brain"). Although some Giant Brainers are first-rate poets and essayists, they are always lousy philosophers, but Watts was not so low on my personal moral totem pole as those intellectuals who refuse to try the Higher Sacrament. The latter I see as simply frauds in the same class as the mental midgets of Galileo's day who refused to look through his telescope. At least Watts tried.

And Watts, his Slobovenoid Blobovenoidalism aside, was a great conversationalist, a great gossip, a great drinking companion, and a gentleman of the old school. As soon he established that I was literate he warned me he would "steal" anything I said worth "stealing."

I told him to help himself, and we had a happy, bleary, gossipy evening which ended in my meeting the Newton contingent. Good heads to the man, but pale, I thought, in comparison to the Mighty of Millbrook, whom I was beginning to think of as virtual demi-gods occupying a world apart, around some trick corner in a magic mirror of my mind.

Although Alan and I got along well, he didn't approve of my act. He probably saw, better than I did, the philosophic direction in which I was headed and knew what kinds of conflicts would inevitably follow with people of his ilk and Tim's. When I asked him to grace the rosters of the Neo-American Church with his illustrious name, he replied: "I don't like your boo hoo title. It sounds like a crybaby to me."

The stiff upper lip complex at work? I don't know. However frivolous in private, Watts, in the ancient C of E tradition, favored solemn fraudulence in public. It was what the market demanded, after all. He laughed when I suggested that his books were so popular that he could live, if only modestly, on the income from them. His royalties didn't pay for his gin. What did pay off were his cruise ship deals and other more standard forms of lecturing. I would find out for myself in due time. (I have, but I don't think it is absolutely necessary for a person with criminal tendencies to sink so low.)

I appreciate the literary and scholarly virtues of Watts and Aldous Huxley and Joseph Campbell (a very nice and very learned guy who informed me that he had adopted my *Boo Hoo Bible* footnote, "If you think you are getting anywhere, you're on the wrong track" as his "personal motto"), but I do not belong to the doctrinal congregation for which they were outstanding twentieth-century proselytizers, and I think Watts saw this right away.

Although heterodox in minor ways, people of this ilk are essentially Vedantists, Cosmic-Minders, Giant-Brainers or Transcendentalists and thus dualists, although Alan and Aldous and Joe would probably reject and resent the label if they were still hanging around and could read this. Huxley, who dismissed the Zen masters as "unsatisfying," and Campbell were virtually humorless, and, when sober, so was Watts.

When I read the philosophico-religious ruminations of these guys, I see (so to speak) the somber and shuddery shades of such as Swedenborg, Dostoevsky, Kierkegaard, Nietzsche, Sartre, and Camus hovering in the background. Back in the mists a few steps and you are in the jolly company of such as Dante and St. Augustine and the early so-called "fathers of the Church" all the way back to St. Paul, every single one of whom was mad. Only an idiot can have any fun, so the only way anyone who is not an idiot can have any fun is to behave like an idiot. The more one thinks, the less fun one has. "Life Sucks" is the technically correct bumper sticker.

I prefer, and recommend to one and all, the "Playboy Philosophy" of Mr. H. Hefner over this kind of shit any day.

At the beginning of the decade, all kinds of major events seemed to combine to cause a major shift in the general mood of western civilization. In what might be called "metahistorical" terms, LSD and MAD (Mutual Assured Destruction) seemed to balance or complement one another, and the assassination of JFK contributed also, as a demonstration on the American stage (other stages had other demonstrations) of the ephemeral and usually fraudulent nature of most political "progress," and the need to change human nature directly rather than to rest one's hopes in moving the furniture around, changing the cast, and tinkering with the plot.

It seemed to me it was the style and content of everyday life that needed radical revision in the direction of more variety, freedom, truth, spontaneity and wit.

That was what I found so stunning about Millbrook: The names, rules and counters of the ordinary games being played there every day had somehow been changed in a fundamental way. Assumptions which always applied outside meant little or nothing within, and vice versa. Life as it was lived was livelier, more meaningful, funnier, happier. It was an adventure just to hang out, and so it remained, with ups and downs, until the end.

I resolved that anything I produced would be along the same lines. Watts was a smooth talker, but Timothy Leary, I thought, was a magician who seemed to know how to change life as it was lived, and he didn't do it exclusively by flapping his gums. He did it by employing a magic elixir I knew from experience could do things that could not be done by all the King's horses and all the King's men flapping their gums in unison.

Whether or not the magic elixir could put Humpty Dumpty together again remained to be seen.

Chapter 5

AN INSPIRATION

What dream? Why, the dream that I am in Arthur's court—a person who never existed; and that I am talking to you, who are nothing but a work of the imagination.

I waited for Easter vacation with high expectations, and when I entered the Millbrook grounds I was determined to stop treating the place like an amusement park. Instead, I would arrange a "session" right away and be cooperative and act like a "team player" for a change. Humility, that was the ticket. Sobriety. Sanctimoniousness, even. I knew I could do it if I tried.

I walked through the wide-open front door. Not a soul in sight, so took a chair in the library and started editing my latest installment of *Divine Toad Sweat*, the provisional title of my surrealistic novel.

When the house Lolita came in, squealed "Arthur!" and jumped on my lap and stuck her tongue in my ear by way of greeting, my adopted persona was seriously shaken, but I did not respond normally. Instead, I thought of the classic temptations along the same lines resisted by the heroes of the kinds of myths and literary fables I was reading those days, gave her a peck on the cheek, and said, "How'ya doin', kid?" or something similarly idiotic. I don't remember exactly.

This bizarre non-behavior didn't go over very well, as one might expect. I was profoundly shocked myself and, once my vital signs returned to normal, wondered if I had made the right decision. I felt like I had torn up a check for a million dollars. Had I gone totally bananas, or what?

Since the truly extraordinary A+ cupcake was soon replaced, as the focus of any stray erotic impulses, by a standard-brand B-cookie of legal age, secretary to the well-known mad scientist Andre Puharich, who was to function as a thorn in my side during the next forty-eight hours or so, maybe I had. But then again, people have been known to go to jail for a long time for toying with cupcakes, no matter what the provocation, so maybe plain fear explained it better than all that mythic stuff.

Ling-Ling was on close terms with Tim at the time, but disavowed any intent to perpetuate the relationship when I inquired. Her reason for being at Millbrook, aside from screwing around and getting stoned, was to advance the cause of a tiny device, contents unknown, which, when attached to any bone of the head, would unfailingly permit the deaf, even those devoid from birth of any auditory nerve, to hear with perfect clarity. This miracle was said by her to have been invented by Puharich and was in his possession.

First visit: tiny strobe glasses. Second visit: tiny ear box. OK. Hewing faithfully to my credulity, I took Ling-Ling's word for it, and waxed enthusiastic, although I would have been suspicious, if not derisory, under any other circumstances.

She asked me whom I wanted to trip with. I said Tim and any girl or girls who might want to go along for the ride. How about her? She said "maybe" and we went upstairs to talk to Tim, who greeted me with generous praise for *Divine Toad Sweat* and generally made me feel welcome.

Tomorrow night? Sure. He was looking forward to it already. If anyone else wanted to join us we would discuss it. Meanwhile, I should read Hesse's *Siddhartha*, a copy of which he plucked from his bookshelf and handed me. We talked for a while about Hesse, whose *Steppenwolf* I had recently finished reading, it having been recommended by Ralph Metzner on my previous visit.

AN INSPIRATION

Tim showed me around. Changes had been made. Someone had created a "meditation room," by padding a closet off the third-floor hall. Ralph now had an electronic workshop, with a contraption squatting on the table that looked like a prop for a science fiction movie. In a mimeograph room, stacks of circulars announced the replacement of IFIF by the Castalia Foundation of Millbrook, New York.

There was a quote from Hesse's *The Journey to the East* pinned up in Tim's room, in which the protagonist asserted that the major events in the history of Western Civilization were no more than stages in the history of "our League." This caught my attention, as it had when I first read the book. Interesting. Grandiose paranoia on the face of it, but, well, hmmm.

As an allegory for the ancient and various manifestations of Psychedelian religion in human history, "our League" was arguably far more important than the history of war, or any other historical theme for that matter. It was not irrational, or even strange, to say that religion was more important than anything else, and if the use of psychedelics gave rise to the good, the true and the beautiful in religion, as distinguished from all the shit, well, there you were. I had found everything Wasson was saying along these lines to be very persuasive, and I was happy to see that Tim, evidently, did also. Good.

Could I run a mimeograph machine?

"Nope."

I had always been happy to have the taxpayers provide such services.

"What, man, you can't run a mimeograph machine? Don't you realize that mimeograph machines are absolutely essential to every revolution?" Tim laughed.

I said he was right, of course. Should any tedious but necessary services along these lines be required, I would learn, and put my shoulder to the inky wheel like anyone else around.

The whole house had taken on an appearance of contrived bohemianism, with most of the heavy furniture, including the legs of the dining room table, stowed away in the basement and storage rooms, and lots of cushions and mattresses covered with intricate prints substituted.

Tim turned me over to Susan Metzner, who assigned me to a room. She said she hoped I didn't mind sleeping on a mattress on the floor. On a group trip everyone had decided to throw the beds out for "aesthetic reasons."

"Well, considering what you are trying to do around here, anything disorienting is good, I suppose. Like Tim said in that speech in Sweden," I said, trying to be compliant once again.

Susan said I might have the wrong idea about what they were trying to do. She didn't say what it was they were trying to do. Normally, I would have questioned Susan's ability, or anyone else's ability, mine included, to identify with any certainty what a group of people such as this were trying to do, but I was playing the game of taking things at face value, and was therefore appalled, sort of.

"Christ, I hope not," I said. The fact was that "we" was being used very loosely around "Der Alte Haus" (as the original owner had called it). Millbrook was riddled with subterranean rivalries and ideological conflicts but everyone was playing it, as a revolutionary cause encourages one to do in some ways, as if no legitimate differences of opinion about anything important existed or could exist. Axes were being ground all over the place.

Pronouncements about what "we" are doing are most often used not to cement groups but to split them. The class level had gone down a notch. The game of gentlemen and scholars was over and the games of moralist-sinner and doctor-patient and good guys and bad guys had begun. It's a sad thing to see, and perhaps for the best, I didn't see it, at least not clearly ("accept" it) until much later.

After dinner that night, Tim insisted that we all play a "Magic Theater" game. This was to be only a small part of a larger version she and Tim were working on, Ling-Ling informed me. One was asked to write down on a folded slip of paper the first thought one had, on reading the thought of the last person to play, and then to pass the list on with only one's own contribution showing, so a long chain of semi-free associations resulted. This we played on the table top without legs on the rug in the dining room, by the light of candles and the fireplace, while reclining on cushions and pillows and drinking brandy. Living on the floor under such circumstances is an entirely different kettle of fish than doing it in an abandoned house on bare boards and vomit-soaked mattresses surrounded by syphilitic and schizophrenic psychopaths while drinking Sterno and sniffing glue. Poor people need furniture, only the rich can afford to live on the floor.

The objective of the game was, Tim announced, to discover how "all of this" would end.

I forget what Ling-Ling wrote on her fold of the paper, but the image which came to my mind on reading it was of a dock in Amsterdam, lapped by the sullen IJ.

It didn't seem to have anything at all to do with Ling-Ling's contribution.

"Really?" Tim asked, when he read the completed page and came to my image. Nothing else was geographic.

"God made the world, but man made Holland." It doesn't surprise me that this notably empiricist society has learned, by and large, to tolerate Psychedelianism and often to enjoy the sacraments thereof, while more "romantic" nations generally still see the whole thing as some kind of giant bat out of Hell that everyone should throw rocks at.

Wasson and Tim and a number of other amateur anthropologists encouraged legions of kids to identify the psychedelic experience with primitivist escapism. Pueblos and hogans in stark surroundings, complete with charmingly flea-bitten shamans who could be manipulated with the greatest of ease with petty cash, were thought to be "where it was at" for a long time.

I consider this whole mystique to be almost total horseshit.

Psychedelic experience encourages and, in some cases, demands, the recognition of beauty, both natural and fabricated. There isn't anything uncivilized about this, unless one defines "civilized" in a stupid, uncivilized way.

The sacraments will, if you let them, produce a cool and sophisticated perspective, full of nuance and intricate and often ironical allusions and reflections.

I got pretty bombed on grass and booze and went to sleep in the meditation closet.

The next morning, at breakfast, which everyone fixed for themselves and ate at the kitchen table, Ling-Ling told me she and Tim had gone through the entire house, neglecting only the meditation closet, looking for me the night before.

"Why?" I asked.

"Oh, Tim had some bright idea he wanted to tell you about."

"Well, what was it?" I asked.

"It doesn't matter now," said dear little Ling-Ling, girl mystification expert. I never did find out what enthusiasm had animated Tim, since much more important matters were to claim my attention a few hours later.

The trip was set for that night. Ling-Ling "didn't know" if she was going along or not. I decided to erase all such social trivia and devious Oriental machinations from my mind, as best I could, to prepare for the no-doubt earth-shattering revelations to come.

A quiet morning walk in the sparkling woods was what I needed, I decided. I set off past the Bowling Alley which was an enormous chalet, built of huge stones, wherein the former lord of the manor had amused himself and his friends under murals showing famous Hudson Valley horses and horsepersons of the 1800s. The road curved under budding maples and tall stands of spruce which shaded a burbling stream. The stream was captured by a stonework dam and then passed an ironwork gate to a road which led to hundreds of acres of wild country to the north, including the hills later to be named, appropriately, "Lunacy" and "Ecstasy."

The road curved gradually back towards the south. To my right was a gentle rising slope planted in baby spruce, which faced some sunlit hills and fields through a frieze of trees lining the other side of the road.

I had a drink from an old-fashioned water pump which was conveniently situated on the hill and sat down on the grass to think things over. What went through my mind were the same old questions which world literature and the conversation of drunks will indicate are pretty common concerns.

Why am I here? What is all this for? Who am I? Where am I? And other stuff along the same lines.

My one and only big trip had not advanced my progress in finding answers to these fundamental questions, but it had prevented any escape by way of reductionism or displacement. I was unable to think of myself as either an odd product of blind chance, or a deity's dummy, being punished for getting my cords tangled, or having my faith tested, or whatever. Until I had good answers, I was pinned in place.

So, my mood was one of genuine perplexity, which is a rare and sublime mood, as Lao-tzu observed.

On an impulse with no conscious antecedents, I placed my right hand on the earth and crooked my left back toward the sky, and asked, "Where am I?"

Nothing happened, but I maintained my position for fifteen minutes or so, rejecting any ideation which rose to the surface, and hoping something remarkable would occur. No soap. I relaxed. As soon as I relaxed it occurred to me that my assumption that nothing had happened was gratuitous. Why not assume something had happened and be alert to recognize it? I got up, dusted myself off, and walked back to the Big House, determined not to alter my mood, no matter what happened.

Chapter 6
THE ECLIPSE

The mere knowledge of a fact is pale; but when you come to realize your fact, it takes on color.

I don't remember the content of the first synchronistic coupling I noticed, but it was a startling connection between something I was thinking about and a remark made in the kitchen as I passed through. This scrap of conversation, which was not intended, in the usual sense, for me, provided the associational bridge to my next thought, which then became the object of the next synchronistic connection.

I missed a lot at first, mistakenly thinking only some "external" events were synchronistic with my "private" ideas. The tyranny of the fundamental spatial dichotomy me/it was not about to surrender at the first blast of heavy artillery from the forces of synchronicity awareness which had suddenly surrounded it. It had governed for a long time, and resisted being reduced to a mere province of an upstart empire.

I thought cosmicmindedly for a while. Perhaps "the world" was thinking along certain lines, and I was spiraling around, through, into, out of, over and under another, greater progression of ideas, and the synchronicity occurred when I was momentarily "on the button."

This cosmic consciousness crap didn't last long, I'm happy to say. Synchronicity showed me it was false, during the five or ten minutes I spent trying to think of it in a dualistic and spatial way, by providing a flood of images all of which made the same point in different ways: You are that.

There is no way to depart from synchronicity, just as there is no way to have a meaningless dream, although meaninglessness itself may be the subject, or the meaning, of certain highly perverse and frightening dreams, dreams designed to demonstrate how nice it is to have meaning to those who have decided they would rather not have any of that, thanks.

For the first time in my life, I started to put the concept "external world" in mental quotation marks, and was instantly rewarded by a chorus of approving synch: people saying things like "good," "marvelous," "it's about time"; the sun breaking through clouds; domestic problems turning out to have been foolish misunderstandings; triumphant marches and choruses on the stereo; the sudden cessation of a banging in the pipes; and a host of much more subtle and intricate comments which seemed designed to smooth my way and answer every objection, even the objection that the mere existence of objections, of a dialogue, disproves the thesis, which it does not, because any sane person talks to himself all the time.

If one's thesis is that ordinary life is a dream, then anything that can happen in a dream in sleep can happen in waking life also, without disproving the thesis. If you can see that, you can see everything.

(Let's say you lose your marbles in a dream and they all appear to roll under a sofa. Are your marbles under the sofa?)

I was off to the races. I began to re-examine my prejudices, to flip them over, as it were, and I saw lots of nice, shiny faces in mint condition where formerly there had been only a dull array of tarnished tails. Everything was furnished with new and exciting associational trails and everything I heard spoken around me, no matter how trivial the phenomenological context, suddenly became loaded with resonance and the cognitive coherence which had been missing, I thought, on my mescaline trip. I felt, for the first time in my life, an incomparable sensation of being "out from under" which made all other successes in all other games (perhaps excepting release from prison or recovering from a serious illness) seem pale by comparison.

It was as if I had entered another country, and had been given a souped-up language-learning capacity by passing through a trick box at the airport, but the image is far from exact, because some, at least, of the people who were speaking the new "language" didn't know it and since my thoughts were still being formed, most often, in terms of my old awareness, I would recognize them, as it were, twice; the first time the old way and the second time the new way. Since these juxtapositions were often hilarious, I started grinning, which made a bad impression. A worried frown, in contrast, is acceptable almost anywhere.

Almost everyone who isn't enlightened, my former self included, thinks of Enlightenment as an extension of dimensions with which they are familiar, an increase. They expect to become bigger, better, purer, stronger, wiser, holier or whatever.

In fact, there is nothing additive about it. If a structural metaphor must be used, it ought to be subtractive. Enlightenment is the removal of self-imposed delusions which were never justified by evidence or logic (see Hume) in the first place. The experience can be associated with all kinds of glorious imagery or none at all. *Comme décor,* one might say.

While I was going through all this, Zen koans and fables which had formerly struck me as forced conceits intended to disorient the victim took on the objective accuracy of laboratory slides or the common-sense verity of labels on soup cans. (I particularly like "You drop six inches.")

I started drifting around the house picking up books at random, and reading whatever came to hand as a response to whatever question was puzzling me. At one point, I even decided to test it out by not even asking a question but just stabbing a randomly opened book with a blind finger and seeing what it had to offer. As a solipsist, I thought, I was simply asking myself for directions.

The book was in Tim's room and the word was "automobile," so I walked down two flights of stairs and through the hall and the library and out the French doors in the music room, across the porch, under the porte cochère and out to the road, on which a light snow had fallen. Maynard Ferguson, borrowing my automobile without permission, was stuck in a rut. Standing there in his camel hair coat, he looked properly abashed by my sudden appearance.

"Get in and I'll push you, Maynard," I said, before he could say a word.

With only a slight shove, the car came free and Maynard waved jauntily as he slid around the corner. Conclusion: Testing it out instead of using it creatively would produce trivia, embarrassment for others and wasted energy. But why was it an automobile scene rather than something else? Jackie Leary walked past.

"Hey, Jackie," I asked, "what are you thinking about right now?"

"A dream I had last night," Jackie said, not stopping, but producing a typically Millbrookian knowing smile.

Naturally. The language of the unconscious. The car, a vehicle, represented my everyday personality, the means by which I got from point A to point B with maximum efficiency. If I pushed the process too far I would lose control of this valuable convenience. Shouldn't do that.

I then began to wonder about the Psychedelian masterminds by whom I still imagined myself to be surrounded. Surely, they had all caught on to this? How could they avoid it? But, if so, why didn't they talk about synchronicity instead of reproducing supernaturalist trash like the *TBD*? If, for whatever reason, they felt they needed a connection with ancient traditions, why not Confucius or Lao-tzu?

But, not only had I developed great affection for the place and the people, I had also put myself in a position of dependence. My vehicle was gone, in more ways than one.

I had to find excuses for them.

It did not enter my head, at that stage of the game, that people who had given up so much, were risking so much, were working so hard, were so entertaining, so congenial, so intelligent, so literate, so sane, and so right about so many other important matters that most people were so wrong about, and who were taking so much LSD, could possibly be inferior to me in terms of philosophic insight and understanding.

Perhaps, I thought, they all knew the truth but believed they had to put on some kind of spook show for the public to avoid commitment to the nearest booby hatch. Perhaps there was a kind of "secret society" aspect to the whole thing after all. Most people were not aware they were dreaming but a few were? But, if so, why wasn't I getting a warmer welcome?

Perhaps ... perhaps all kinds of weird stuff.

I went into the music room and stretched out on the rug next to a giant goldfish tank, inhabited by two very large goldfish and a snail, to think things over. My faith in the wisdom of Tim, Dick and Ralph had served its purpose. Now it was bending and creaking under a heavy load of fresh facts that didn't fit in and couldn't be dismissed.

Dick came in and suggested a walk, and we headed up the road past the Bowling Alley.

"You've got some people worried," Dick said. "What's going on. You're not on acid are you?"

"Nope. I just suddenly caught on to the fact that I'm living in a dream, that's all."

"The Dream of Brahman ..." Dick suggested.

"Well, I suppose you could call it that. I just see the meaning in everything. No matter what happens, I see it as a message to me, to me personally. It isn't anything grandiose like my mescaline trip. It's friendly and also highly amusing a lot of the time."

"I think I know what you mean," Dick said, "but I don't know if 'messages' is the right word."

"Yeah," I readily agreed. "Since there isn't anything outside myself, how can I get 'messages' from anywhere?"

Dick seemed displeased.

"What about me?" Dick asked. "I have a life of my own, don't I?"

"I haven't figured that out yet," I replied.

We walked in silence for a while.

"Well, you must realize what all of us are hoping," Dick said.

"No, what?"

Dick said it didn't matter.

When we came to the grassy knoll where I had gone through my improvised ritual, I told Dick all about it. He didn't say much.

THE ECLIPSE

Dick was behaving peculiarly, I thought. His "mimic modulation" was off. He wasn't really paying any attention to what I was saying.

It became transparently clear to me later that the well-known "glass wall" had come down, but at the time I thought of Tim, Dick and Ralph as being above such stuff. Closed-minded Millbrookians? It couldn't be.

The term "enlightenment experience" must have escaped my lips at some point, although I can't remember when or to whom.

What (Dick meant) "all" of them were hoping for, or Dick was hoping for, or Dick and his clique were hoping for, or what any or all of the foregoing pretended to themselves and/or others they were hoping for was "the Messiah," naturally.

I didn't get it. Despite having been brought up to think along those lines, I had broken the habit at age fourteen or so.

My vow of credulity had something to do with it. I wasn't thinking of Tim, Dick and Ralph as fallible and frightened human beings. I had idealized them to an absurd extent. It took me years to get over this.

Also, Enlightenment, and simply being stoned also, encourages "absent mindedness" and the first things to become "absent" are the silly ideas the people around you probably have and the silly ideas you formerly had yourself.

The Zen story that illustrates this point is shown in a famous picture: Three old men, engaged in a fascinating conversation, have just crossed a bridge which one of them, a recluse, has vowed never to cross. Realizing what they have done, they are convulsed with laughter. It's a classic experience.

Why couldn't Dick proclaim his "hope" in plain English?

Because he ("we") actually had no such hope. On the contrary, Dick was enormously bothered by my claim of Enlightenment and eager to dismiss whatever I said. He wanted to wear a white robe and be "the Messiah" himself, as became abundantly clear later.

Why wasn't this happening to him? (If it was any good, that is.)

Chapter 7

MERLIN'S TOWER

Of course I was all the talk—all other subjects were dropped; even the king suddenly became a person of minor interest and notoriety.

When Dick and I got back to the house I saw it was about time for the trip, so I went up to Tim's room, where I found Ling-Ling, but no Tim. She told me he had gone to town for cigarettes, and would be back in a half hour or so.

Fine. I relaxed on a pile of cushions. All my fears of acid had evaporated. Ling-Ling went to the bookcase and brought a book over to me.

"Have you seen this?" she asked. "It's Dick's."

I looked at the book as she paged through it. An exotic historical collection of pornographic photographs including several old French shots of mixed shit-ins, or something—six or seven Parisians of mixed age and sex lined up on a multi-hole bench with their pants down and skirts up. In my condition, the standard pictures of people fucking each other seemed too obvious in meaning to deserve much attention. (Ling-Ling wanted to define the situation in terms appropriate to her paramount interests and skills.) But I was fascinated by the group shit-ins. What in

God's name did that mean? I wouldn't let Ling-Ling turn the pages.

"Wait a minute, Ling-Ling," I said, "I have to figure out why these pictures are here."

"Oh, maybe that was the custom in those days," Ling-Ling replied. "Why are you getting so uptight about it?"

"I am not getting uptight about it!" I insisted. Ling-Ling was beginning to piss me off. But she was cute, so I tried to explain.

"I'm interpreting everything. Whatever I see or hear has some direct meaning for me. There are no accidents."

Ling-Ling was uninterested in what I was doing. All she wanted was that I stop thinking my way and start thinking her way. I could see it plainly, and I could see Ling-Ling could see I could see and didn't like it.

When Ling-Ling left the room, the meaning of the co-educational latrine picture seemed clearer to me. The photos represented the condition of Ling-Ling's mind, the current repertoire of her images. One could conclude then, that when she wasn't concerned with sexuality, she was full of shit? And everything she represented was full of shit?

Or perhaps, if that was carrying it too far, I should at least be on my guard with all things feminine and Oriental during the acid trip to come. In any event, the pictures were humorous and no grim or diabolical images were present, so the appropriate attitude, perhaps, would be one of good-natured, old-fashioned, red-blooded, down-home suspiciousness of foreign broads. Easy enough, I thought. Had I not attended many "clap movies" warning me against "so-called nice girls" during basic training at Fort Belvoir, Virginia, in 1946?

While I was musing on these notions, Tim came in, and all the while chatting in a natural and amiable manner about various trifles, started arranging cushions in a circle around a candle and a vase of flowers. When everything in the room was to his satisfaction, he went out and quickly returned with a silver platter, on which rested half a dozen tiny tablets, which he placed in the center of the circle of pillows, next to the candle and flowers.

"Well, here goes," Tim chuckled and reached for the plate.

At that moment, Susan Leary walked into the room and stopped halfway towards us from the door, obviously set to deliver an important message.

"Susan Metzner says he's crazy," Susan announced, in the most baleful manner imaginable. I couldn't believe my ears. Neither could Tim believe his, it seemed. He stared at his daughter in astonishment.

"What?" Tim asked. "Who's crazy?"

Susan pointed at me.

"Him."

Susan left. Tim and I stared at each other.

"What the hell is going on around here?" Tim asked. "Do you know?"

"Nope." I shrugged. It was obvious. The female mind was a bummer. Beware, mankind.

"Well, it's too much for me," Tim said. "Let's put if off. Why don't you just stay here and read *Siddhartha*. Everyone's going to the barns to watch some cattle come in. I'll try to find out what's bothering Susan."

Fine. Supporting my back on a large cushion under the front window, I opened Hesse's book. Although I had a lamp on, the fat candle Tim had lit for the trip, about ten inches high and five inches in diameter, continued to burn not far from my feet. The lightness and sweetness, verging on Bahai-style dopey-mindedness, of *Siddhartha*, in contrast to the dark surrealism of *Steppenwolf*, and the downright paranoid (and tedious) craziness of most of his other stuff, surprised me. It supported the idea that he wasn't smoking edelweiss up in those Austrian Alps. Anyway, I found it possible to make the transition, and was soon lost in the story.

Chapter 8
THE BOSS

To be vested with enormous authority is a fine thing; but to have the onlooking world consent to it is finer.

I had been reading for no more than an hour, and had just come to the riverboat episode, when Tim and Ling-Ling entered the room. "What happened to my candle?" Tim blurted out, looking down at the rug with open-mouthed amazement.

"Did you do that, Arthur?" Ling-Ling asked.

The candle, which should have burned for days, was all splattered out, in droplets and streaks of wax, in a rough circle about four feet in diameter, mostly on the rug but also on my shoes and on the curtain to Tim's sleeping alcove. At the center of this mess, or magical mandala, depending on how janitorial or poetic you want to be about it, the flame still burned, perhaps a quarter of an inch off the floor, on a bit of wax and string.

Weird, very weird, but I hadn't noticed a thing.

"Well, I suppose you could say that," I said in response to Ling-Ling's question. "But I'm as surprised as you are."

"Art, what in God's name are you up to? You're scaring the piss out of everyone around here, and frankly, you're beginning to scare me too," Tim said.

"I don't know why that should be," I replied. Little old me was scaring the piss out of everyone, Timothy Leary included?

In terms of my assumptions about this band of hardy adventurers, and the nature of my current persona (very pacific), this didn't make any sense at all. Sure, Susan Metzner had evidently gotten a paranoid bee in her bonnet about something or other, that could happen to anyone anywhere anytime, but general alarm? Universal urination? What about? I was genuinely upset and puzzled. "All I've been doing is sitting here reading *Siddhartha*. Do you think I put a bomb in the candle or something? As for my interpretation of events, it seems to me it's what Hesse advocates. What do you want me to do, be dishonest?"

Tim sort of danced around, head down, in a kind of ritual shuffle I had seen him adopt before when he wasn't sure what to do or say next.

"I don't think you understand Hesse," he finally said.

"Then what is all this supposed to mean?" I asked, tapping the Hesse quotation on the wall next to his bed.

Tim's response to this question about a statement he had deemed worthy of typing out and putting up where he could see it when he woke up in the morning (there was nothing else of this kind around) was so defensive, reductionist and generally feeble that I could hardly credit the evidence of my ears. It was "just" psychological, a literary device, poetic license, dramatic exaggeration. Stuff like that. Was Tim saying that all the claims he had been making for the importance of the psychedelic experience and the "movement" were phony? It sounded like he thought the whole thing was an illusionist's trick, more impressive than, but not different in kind from pulling a rabbit out of a hat.

"Yeah, sure," I said, and walked out of the room, feeling paranoid.

(I now think that Tim was right about my not understanding Hesse. I had given Hesse, along with everyone else around at that time, credit for more genius than he possessed. Hesse had certain intimations of wisdom, best realized in *Siddhartha* and *Steppenwolf*, and that was about it. Elsewhere, these glimmers are submerged in a Hegelian murk of grandiose moralistic hierarchical fantasies in the worst Germanic tradition, saved, to some extent, by a gloss of irony, but not nearly glossy enough for me.)

Sincerely puzzled by what was happening, Tim suspected a con job of some sort. The trouble with that theory was that I wasn't the type, and he knew it. A "no win" situation for Tim. And what possible good did that do me? What was the point? If there was one, I didn't get it.

I spent the rest of the evening splitting and bringing in firewood for the six or seven fireplaces in the house. Interpreting life as an ongoing dream, I tried to figure out what to make of the soundless explosion of Tim's candle. As far as I could tell, this odd event hadn't improved my credibility or sanity rating. A fine, upstanding young candle had been wasted and a mess created in order to ... intimidate Timothy Leary?

What good did that do?

I couldn't figure it out.

The obvious Freudian interpretation ("castration") seemed silly, or was it?

The river scene in *Siddhartha* had something to do with it, I thought. Crossing rivers has a well-established meaning in all allegorical literature. Death. The other shore. The flow of time. The progression of the generations. A ferry and a ferryman? Charon. The Styx. Relations intermediate between life and death.

Major psychedelic experience, according to Tim at the time, should be interpreted in terms of such conveyance. Perhaps the candle blowing up was a warning not to go any further. If I crossed the "river" to the "land of death," perhaps all kinds of odd and inexplicable things would happen and I would frighten and alienate everyone in sight. Every rug in the house would be soaked with urine. Don't push it too far, Art, or you will isolate yourself.

Take it easy.

Pretty soon, I started grinning like my new self again.

I stayed up late that night in the kitchen to read the Evans-Wentz translation of the *Tibetan Book of the Dead*. Since my own body was as much of an illusion as anything else around, there was no good reason to think of its disappearance as a termination of consciousness. Maybe the book had some useful tips on the topic. So far, I hadn't found any. In fact, the book seemed stupid, ignorant and crazy.

Susan Metzner walked in, fetchingly attired in a little-girl nightgown.

"Thanks a lot for fucking up my trip," I said, smiling. I had smiled almost continuously since I had left the hill, which led me to re-evaluate my position on perpetual grinners of the Ramakrishna variety, whom I had assumed in the past to be suffering from blindness to the ugly facts.

"I'm sorry," Susan said. "Ralph and I have been talking about you and I think I was wrong. Anyway, I didn't expect Susan Leary to repeat what I said to Tim. Susan and Jackie are very protective of their father, you know."

Susan and I talked amiably for a few minutes and, for perhaps the first time in twelve hours, I found myself thinking in a "normal" fashion, without paying any attention to what I had decided to think of, pro tem, as "the second level of meaning."

"Can you explain what's been happening?" Susan asked.

Certainly. Nothing to it. I gave her a detailed rundown on what I had been going through.

"And right now, I'm revising my theories on the subject of death," I concluded matter-of-factly, as if I were describing a project in domestic carpentry. "Since the only book on death available at this moment is this one (I held up the *Tibetan Book of the Dead*) it should be the right one, somehow or other. I'm trying to take things at face value, which is one hell of a change for me, Susan."

Susan looked slightly glassy-eyed. She protested that the Evans-Wentz translation contained all kinds of disgusting and meaningless undertakers' and embalmers' details which Tim had eliminated in his version, so why bother with the nasty old thing?

"Easy," I said. "If I find I am repelled I will stop reading, since it would be contrary to the principle of taking things at face value to continue." Which is exactly what happened.

The tantric left-hand path is full of nauseating methods, not the least of which is to dance around with any convenient corpse until its tongue protrudes, at which point you are supposed to bite it off. The tantric literature and its many spin-offs include a wide range of "drug alternative" methods for achieving "higher states" which have this grim, spooky character, ranging from

Castaneda's relatively mild lizard mutilations to the ritual murders of the Kali-worshiping Thugees and the bloody-minded crusades of such religious leaders as Charlie Manson and the popes.

When our enemies invoke Manson as evidence against LSD, I point out that the statistics are on our side. If the Psychedelian sub-culture has "spawned" one genuine fiend, and there is plenty of reason to believe it was the California prison system, pop occultist novels, and TV horror shows that "spawned" him, he was pretty ineffectual and pathetic compared to such unstoned mass murderers as Adolph Hitler, Dwight Eisenhower, Harry Truman and Lyndon Johnson, who had the drug tastes of the average American housewife, that is, speed and booze.

As for Evans-Wentz, I now think he was a learned fool, a kind of idiot-savant, and in his books, as in almost all the academic studies of the subject which have followed his lead, one will find the same sort of hilarious mixture of trash and wisdom which would result if, say a thousand years from now, a modern Tibetan scholar were to resurrect the ancient, mysterious doctrines of Thoreau and Emerson from the rubble of America and present them all helter-skelter, mixed in without discrimination, with selections from the works of Mary Baker Eddy, Joseph Smith and Billy Graham, as examples of the mysterious "Christian" mysticism of the ancient West.

Evans-Wentz could not think, a failing which seems almost sublime in a person of such scholarly attainment and mental industry and makes one wonder, when faced with an example, if one is missing something. In his case, I don't think so.

Consider the following remarks taken from *Tibetan Yoga and Secret Doctrines* (Oxford University Press, 1958) by W.Y. Evans-Wentz, M.A., D.Lit., D.Sc., Jesus College, Oxford:

1. Were the Heat Yoga to be taught universally in all the schools and to become a world-wide practice, there would be no need for central heating in the dwellings of men, not even in Alaska or Siberia, or throughout the arctic and antarctic regions. [The graduates of these institutions would also] become transcendent over gravitation, there would be no need of motor vehicles and airplanes, nor of bridges and boats.

2. By Mind the Cosmos was shaped. By Mind the Cosmos is sustained in space. By indomitable control of his mind a supreme master of yoga can control all mundane conditionality; he can make, or bring into visible manifestation from the unmanifested, all the things that men can make, without wearisome tools and clamorous and noisome factories.
3. On Earth, as in a University granting many degrees, man shall continue to matriculate at birth and enjoy the long vacations afforded by death, as he passes on from lower to higher degrees of Buddhahood, he quits Earth's Halls of Learning, prepared to perform his duties in the guidance and government of the Cosmic Whole, of which, in virtue of evolutionary growth in Right Knowledge, he has become a spiritually conscious part, an Enlightened One.

No records exist of the learned Oxfordian practicing what he preached. He trudged to the Jesus College mess hall in the rain with all the other Jesusians, resorted to the mundane bridge when rivers had to be crossed, etc.

The Snazzm meaning of the *TBD* being a big deal at Millbrook at that time was, I concluded, cautionary. Don't trust books. Don't trust academic credentials.

Snazzm? At about the same time I excommunicated Tim for cometolatry in 1973, I invented a set of epistemological terms, and explained them in a series of *Divine Toad Sweat*s. These terms discriminate between three orders, or levels, of delusionality and thus help to prevent confusion when thinking about such matters as synchronicity, exploding candles, and the *Tibetan Book of the Dead*. Taken together, they are the "Zmms."

In descending order of delusionality, they are "Snazzm," "Fazzm" and "McPozzm."

Snazzm is ideation founded on the assumption that all experience is (in the nature of) a dream. The externality of relations is denied. The only delusion maintained is that a self exists, within whose dream, and by and for and of whom, all appearances are determined.

This is solipsism and is only one step short of maintaining that nothing whatever exists, which is pure Buddhist Nihilism of the old school, into which solipsism must collapse upon close examination. (See Hume re "inattention.")

Fazzm is ideation which, although often claiming to be monist, maintains the delusion of multiplicity, plural minds, and a space-time continuum with an independent dynamism, however mutable and related to psychic determinants, and however removed, the particulars therein may be from ordinary experience.

Although Fazzm ideation assumes multiplicity and a space-time continuum, those who use it attempt to get over these restraints (transcend them) with word-magic smoke and mirrors. Ordinary, physical things are endowed with psychic and abstract super-natures and psychic and abstract concepts are manipulated as if they were physical objects. "He is trampling out His vintage where the grapes of wrath are stored." Virtually all myth, poetry and non-supernaturalist, but non-enlightened, "cosmic mind" occultist religion is Fazzm. All "metaphysics" is Fazzm.

Straightforward expositions of Fazzm belief systems are rare. Here is an example, an early and unusual quote from America's leading Fazzmaniac, Ralph Waldo Emerson (*Nature*, 1836), in which he actually lays all his cards on the table instead of playing them close to his chest, as became his standard practice later:

> Nature is the symbol of spirit.... The use of natural history is to give us aid in supernatural history: the use of the outer creation to give us language for the beings and changes of the inward creation ... man is conscious of a universal soul within or behind his individual life, wherein, as in a firmament, the natures of Justice, Truth, Love, Freedom arise and shine. This universal soul he calls Reason: it is not mine, or thine, or his, but we are all its; we are its property and men.... That which, intellectually considered, we call Reason, considered in relation to nature, we call Spirit. Spirit is the Creator. Spirit hath life in itself. And man in all ages and countries embodies it in his language, as the FATHER .... There seems to be a necessity in spirit to manifest itself in material forms; and day and night, river and storm, beast and bird, acid and alkali, pre-exist in necessary Ideas in the mind of God, and are what they are by virtue of preceding affections, in the world of spirit. A Fact is the end or last issue of spirit, the visible creation in the terminus of the circumference of the invisible world.

The reader who is reduced to sputtering incoherence in attempting to explain exactly what he has against this kind of stuff (mass-market science fiction is loaded with it) is an anti-obscurantist after my own heart and is in good intellectual company in general. I could try to take the above apart, but dissecting "moonshine," as Herman Melville called it, is no easy task. After all, how do you solve a problem like Maria? How do you hold a moonbeam in your hand? Damned if I know.

Yet much that is good and even great in art and literature is Fazzm. "The sun is the width of a man's foot," said Heraklitus of Ephesus, making one of his many startling-but-true Fazzm observations. The best Fazzm always borders on Snazzm. For a good collection of Fazzm epigrams (the ideal form, beware of lengthy expositions) from noble sources, see Norman O. Brown's *Love's Body*, a remarkable book.

McPozzm ideation assumes the externality of relations. It is based on the delusion of a self which is one of many other similar and dissimilar (but never identical) objects in a space-time continuum with a dynamism independent of one's own or any other person's personality or life. There is an infinite, or almost infinite, number of things (minds, souls, black holes, light quanta, neutrinos, archangels or whatever) contained within this imaginary universe. Mental and/or spiritual entities and operations, whether or not they have any "existence" other than in the abstract relatedness of physical things, are governed by rules different than the rules that apply to physical things, thus producing a dualist totality no matter how they are construed. The operations described by modern physics, common sense and strict empirical reasoning are no more or less McPozzm than anecdotes about an Eastern Mediterranean tribal deity hardening Pharaoh's heart or mooning Moses, a conviction that one is in telepathic contact with flying saucers, or the proceedings of the Council of Trent. All assume a container/contained epistemological situation: There is something out there; I am within it; and I can know something about other beings and things within it, and possibly something about the whole thing, by one means or another.

It's safe to say, McPozzm, that almost everyone thinks in McPozzm terms most of the time.

One may, however, develop a capacity for thinking all three ways, or, more often, two ways. Literary intellectuals, poets, prelates and paranoids often think in both Fazzm and McPozzm terms. "I have become Shiva, destroyer of Worlds," thought Oppenheimer, both a scientist and a poetic soul, upon observing the first model of his contraption do its stuff. This beats "gee whiz," one must admit.

Genuine, systematic, sequential, analytical Snazzm ideation is as rare as Enlightenment itself but Snazzm, good or bad, is almost always the dominant Zmm at the peak of a Big One.

Tim's Kohoutek phase was a good example of bad Fazzm running rampant.

The following quotes are taken from a press conference given at the time, prior to the non-appearance of the widely touted comet, by Joanna Harcourt-Smith Leary, in which she asserted that she and Dr. Leary were "brought back" to the United States to "decode" the "message" of this comet. It was reported, without comment, in the *New Yorker*, of all places (the real *New Yorker*, kids, not the vulgar imposter of the present day):

1. The comet Starseed is to leave the womb planet Earth. The Starseed is a comet of prophesy.
2. Life seeds egg planets throughout the galaxy. When life leaves the womb planet, it attains immortality in the Galactic Star School.
3. When the embryonic nervous system can decipher the genetic code it receives instructions for leaving the earth-womb and contacting higher intelligence.
4. There is no choice. Life must leave the womb planet to survive and evolve.
5. The Starseed transmission was received by Dr. Leary in his cell at Folsom Prison.

Notice the pompous, ex-cathedra tone. The authors of pronouncements of this kind, speaking as they do from Mount Olympus or other famous peaks, would sound even sillier if they qualified anything, and the projection of this omniscient certainty is the actual point of it all. To learn more, one "has no choice" but to "contact" Dr. Leary ... or the viper at his side.

This Kohoutek crap, coming on top of *Neurologic*, was too

much for me. I made major changes in the language and doctrines of the Church. No matter how poetic or metaphoric the intent, I could no longer bring myself to use terms like "God" or "Self." I abandoned all efforts to be ecumenical.

Instead, in a series of *DTS*s of increasing severity, I defined the Zmms, excommunicated Tim, changed the Second Principle, and made the Church doctrinaire, exclusive, hierarchical, monarchical and dynastic. Membership in any other religious organization, including the Masonic Order, Alcoholics Anonymous and the Church of Universal Life, meant automatic excommunication and still does.

I didn't want anyone to make any mistake about it. The horseshit Neo-Americans wanted victory over included the metaphysics of my former guru. Better examples of horseshit are hard to find.

Thus, in Snazzm and Fazzm terms, Kohoutek and Tim's attempt to exploit it, and the comet's failure to show, helped me to clean up my act and to define the doctrine of the Church.

In a Fazzm sense, Psychedelianism underwent a dialectical transformation and occultism got a well-deserved shot in the chops in the time-honored way supernaturalism and occultism get their shots in the chops. Something was supposed to happen but it didn't.

McPozzm? It didn't mean anything. McPozzm doesn't have to mean anything, which is the beauty of it.

Hard to play croquet or write a uniform commercial code without it.

Imputing to Susan much higher intellectual attainments and philosophic sophistication than she probably had or even wanted, I asked her what she thought about the problem of suffering.

She said she thought it was all a matter of karma, the first of many invocations of the term that I was to hear from stoned but unsophisticated people for years to come. Somehow, karma (fate) explains how suffering is distributed, and that takes care of that. It's merely an incantation for getting rid of unpleasant thoughts. Just kid stuff. I didn't know what to say.

A large moth came zooming into the kitchen and rapped me smartly on the forehead.

"That's the kind of coincidence I mean," I said. "That kind of thing has been happening all day." I gestured towards the moth which was fluttering down the hallway to the basement and laundry room.

"What coincidence?" Susan asked.

"The moth hitting me when you mentioned karma," I said.

"I didn't see any moth," Susan said.

I said that it had been a rapid transit and she would have missed it if she had blinked, said I was tired, excused myself, and went to bed.

So Susan hadn't seen the moth.

She should have. I had uttered a fib in the cause of peace and tranquility.

OK, what difference did it make? Since I no longer believed in the externality of relations, the degree to which my perceptions seemed shared by others was not of crucial importance. I poured a drink from the trusty bottle at the side of my low bed, and lit a cigarette. Moonlight was pouring into my room through the open window along with a refreshing night breeze. The Bowling Alley and the stark pines looked like an illustration from a book of fairy tales.

What if only I had seen the exploded candle? If, as it seemed, strange events were somehow required at this stage of the game, better oddities in the ordinary events of the everyday world than bizarre hallucinations or even mescaline-style visions. I had already been through all of that. Let things continue along these lines, by all means!

I put out my cigarette and went to sleep, and slept soundly until awakened in the morning by the cheerful chirping of chickadees outside my window. I was in a good mood. No hangover. My thoughts effortlessly took up where they had left off the night before.

When I walked into the kitchen I found Dick Alpert, Billy Hitchcock and a couple other coffee drinkers having a discussion about national politics. Dick introduced me around.

Billy struck me as a charming person. It hardly registered that, as one of the two owners of the place, he alone qualified among those present as my actual host. Billy had an open, confident and witty conversational style and perfect manners; a sort of Frank Merriweather archetype who had risen from the depths of Old Money bearing a banner with a strange device. In retrospect, I think he reminded me of myself because he was tall and blond, and had psychological qualities similar to mine, difficult for the person who has them to identify precisely, which produced a feeling of almost instant affinity. He was sure as hell the first zillionaire, and the last, who made me feel this way.

Billy asked what I thought of Goldwater's chances in the upcoming elections. I forget what I thought, but I was probably wrong, as I usually am about such things.

A day or two later, Tim played some session tapes for me. Part of his routine at the time was to ask people what question they wanted answered by the psychedelic experience they were about to have. Everyone seemed to want the same kind of stuff: "ego-loss" and a "merge" with the "Oversoul," a better attitude, more love, etc. I don't recall any philosophic questions, good, bad or indifferent.

As a matter of fact, most of these requests were couched in terms that suggested that the requester understood himself and the world around him perfectly.

I was delighted when I put on a tape and heard someone say, in a self-assured tone, "How can I make more money on the stock market?" The voice seemed familiar, but I couldn't place it.

"Now there's a question I like!" I said to Tim, who was scribbling away at his desk. Although the wish expressed was devoid of philosophic curiosity, it was also devoid of hypocrisy and pretentiousness. Tim peered at me over the top of his reading glasses. He was grinning.

Tim almost always responded happily to demonstrations of humor and cynicism on my part. My philosophic utterances, on the other hand, stimulated what might be called a "fight, flee or steal" reaction.

"You do, hmmm?" he said. "Do you know who that is?"

"No."

"Billy Hitchcock." Tim turned back to his writing.

Billy was clearly an uncommon character, but Tim, Dick and Ralph had an established relationship with him, about which I knew almost nothing, and upon which I felt I should not presume to intrude. Also, he lived up the road somewhere in another building called "The Bungalow," which I hadn't seen and didn't expect to ever enter.

I went back to my musings, walks in the woods, and firewood splitting on the porch and later in the day went upstairs to talk to Tim.

"Listen, Tim," I said, "what I want to know is what am I supposed to do next?"

"What do you mean? Are you still on the kick you were on yesterday?"

"Of course," I replied. "I know what everything means. Who I am, where I am, and all of that."

I airily waved my arm in disdainful dismissal of such elementary matters. "What I want to know is why there is so much suffering in the world. I'm willing to do whatever you suggest. Take a thousand mics, go sit under a tree for three weeks, anything."

"You're having a bad trip," Tim said. "Don't worry. You'll come out of it."

I was completely baffled. I left the room without saying a word. Down the hall I found Dick seated at a desk in a small room in the servants' wing, whistling a merry tune and signing a big stack of $100 government bonds.

"Tim says I'm having a bad trip," I said to Dick.

Dick shrugged his shoulders and laughed.

"Listen, Art. I'd like your opinion of this." He handed me a periodical reprint of something he had written on juvenile delinquency. I took it down to the front porch, pulled a rocking chair up to the balustrade so I could put my feet up, and read it.

Terrible stuff. Assuming all kinds of things which probably ought not to be assumed, his comments were reasonable, but his style was lifeless, academic pussy-footing prose all the way. I felt like telling him that when it came to writing, he should stick to signing $100 bonds, but that would have been unkind. When I returned the paper, I told him to try to be more natural. My thoughts were beginning to feel relatively clogged and heavy. I was losing my high. I missed Sally and the kids. Most important of all, did I really want to take a trip with Tim? I was having a "bad trip"?

What?

A flood of synchronicity awareness does not, I have learned since, always cause people to jump for joy. On the contrary, it's often the launching pad for paranoid ideation, delusions and freak-outs. "Messages," already a misleading concept, can be swiftly converted into "orders" if they are misinterpreted in terms of supernaturalist assumptions.

The TV set is telling me to kill my wife, instead of showing me some of the repressed feelings I have about women. Or, because of a remarkable association between some Bible verses I have just read and other events, I have been chosen by God to lead the Israelites out of bondage. So hijack a bomber and nuke Mecca, naturally. And so on.

A list of the different kinds of synchronicity would be a list of all imaginable relations. The best rule is to stay loose.

Synchronicity will teach you how to interpret synchronicity, if you will let it. It is not a foreign language. Anyone who can grasp the principles of cause and effect reasoning in the context of a material universe of space, time and randomness can also grasp the principles of synchronistic relatedness if he is willing to imagine the alternative context of the non-spatial, non-temporal and psychically determined dream. It doesn't require a high IQ to do this; all it requires is an ability to see things in Snazzm terms without freaking out. The *I Ching* is the most refined synchronicity condenser available to those of us who constitute the only class for whom the *I Ching* was intended and for whom it works, that is, superior people. It may be thought of as the actual "magic book" of the myths and fairy tales. It's in a class by itself. If you refuse to see things in Snazzm terms, your hexagrams will urge you, one way or another, to settle for coin flipping, tarot card shuffling, daisy petal pulling, or whatever.

Always use the Bollingen Foundation edition (which was financed by Paul and Mary Mellon).

I won't try to analyze the synchronicity of all the events in this narrative. The reader will see what is meaningful for him, if he's ready for it.

Synchronicity resists retrospective examination. It is OK to talk about one's life and note the synchronicity of various events as they occur, but scanning one's memory for startling and entertaining instances and slapping them down like melds in a game of rummy is ridiculous. It implies there is something unusual or meritorious about synchronicity.

A thin line separates enlightened ideation from paranoid ideation, the crucial difference being that synchronicity is correctly understood in the first case and consistently misinterpreted in the second.

Tim automatically and understandably assumed that anyone talking about "messages" and acting as I was had to be paranoid, in the sense of having a delusional system, grandiose ideas, fears of imaginary enemies, and so on.

As a general rule, this is not a bad general rule, but I had decided to regard people who seemed to be screwing me up, McPozzm, as demonstrating certain principles for my benefit and thereby, so to speak, "warning me," Snazzm, not to get involved in this or that bad trip.

This is also the way to interpret the changing lines of the *I Ching*. They are warnings or encouragements which, if properly understood, can help bring about or prevent or modify the change depicted.

As for grandiosity, I had gone through that phase in five minutes.

Pride in my imaginative accomplishments? How about shame for all the misery and horror in the world?

Emerson's little gem "Brahma" automatically comes to mind. No moral or even "spiritual" superiority is involved. An enlightened person does not move to the head of his class. He is his class. The best attitude towards Enlightenment for those content without it is probably indifference and inattention.

Aside from smiling all the time and exclaiming "of course" and "naturally" over everyday events, there were no dramatic alterations in my character as a consequence of becoming enlightened. My likes and dislikes remained pretty much the same, and so did my favored game routines and styles of expression.

Certain fantasies and lines of thought, however, just dropped right out of the picture, never to return, and gradually, over the next few years, were replaced by suitable alternatives.

Enlightenment itself is sudden. Learning how to play the games and finding a style appropriate to an enlightened intellect is gradual and tricky.

The standard cosmicminder and supernaturalist fantasies, which I had allowed some elbow room in my youth, now walked the plank or were elbowed overboard. They disappeared much as love of the cat does in the life of a woman who has just had a baby, or hobby horses in the life of a boy just given a pony.

There is a superficial resemblance between synchronicity awareness and rank, low-down, beware-of-the-black-cat-style superstition. Whenever I encountered a Millbrook Bread truck, for example, from the day of my Enlightenment onward, I took careful note of what I was thinking and what else was happening at the moment. Moments, in general, become the crucial category of time.

The numbers assigned by post offices and telephone companies fell into clearly meaningful patterns. I liked Box 191, Star Lake, the first address of the Neo-American Church. Nine was big in the early days.

A flat tire caused me to question my intended destination, and still does. Indeed, anything about my vehicle also refers, Snazzm, to the way I'm functioning as a personality.

Physical health is more often related to the condition of one's dwelling, not one's vehicle. Psychologically, the body doesn't move around in the world. The world moves around the body.

I'm not exactly delighted when a black cat crosses my path, but I wouldn't try to avoid a black cat, any more than I would avoid a "bump" sign rather than the bump itself. Supernaturalism leads to futile avoidance of, while solipsism leads to constructive learning from, the black cat.

It's a good way to explain the difference.

As for the synchronicity of names, check out the cast of characters in the Watergate affair. Check out doctors' names against their specialties. Now apply the same rules to writers, artists, philosophers and your circle of friends. Smoke some pot. Free associate.

If one assumes that life is a dream, there is no difficulty in seeing life in these terms. If you assume that it is partly a dream and partly a machine, you're up the Amazon with the alligators, baby.

But, how did it feel, one might ask, to become an Enlightened Being? Vertigo? Groovy vibes? Droopier earlobes? Greater compassion for venomous insects and reptiles? None of the above. In terms of general stonedness, the experience resembled a sinsemilla high lasting about ten hours, or was it two days? It didn't have the wild, speedy, "spacy" quality of an acid trip, the absolutely whacked-out quality that distinguishes the Supreme Sacrament in action, but I was definitely stoned.

I behaved myself for two days, just hung around and lent a hand with this and that, and then went home. Let's not forget I had not, at that time, learned all of the above lessons, or, if I had, learned them well. I was enlightened, all right, but in a half-assed way.

However, because I had "stolen" my Enlightenment, that is, gotten it from someone who didn't have possession himself but had produced the setting that I needed, I had nothing to complain about, and I didn't.

Chapter 9

THE TOURNAMENT

They were always having grand tournaments there at Camelot; and very stirring and picturesque and ridiculous human bull-fights they were, too, but just a little wearisome to the practical mind.

On returning to the North Country and the world of public education, I found I had a new moral problem: I knew about something good, didn't I? Well, unless I was satisfied to play the part of a hack and a hypocrite, I had to do something about it. I had to spread the word.

But, I must admit, for almost a year, I didn't. I had a good family and bad habits to support, so I went about my business as usual. When I had time, I worked on my book.

Tim, Dick and Ralph, down at Millbrook, were not behaving much differently. The professional, scholarly, literary, and scientific ruts to which we were all accustomed continued to be followed, and the words "revolution" and "movement" had imaginary quotation marks around them if they were used at all.

As for religion, well, yes, so far as other people's religions were concerned, and the older, odder, vaguer, more primitive and distant the better, it was now seen, in the light of psychedelic experience, that it was not necessarily all mumbo-jumbo after all.

Personally, however, we were above all that. We were psychologists living in the twentieth century. Scientific research was the name of the game.

But something known as "visionary experience," as distinct from hallucinations, delusions and imaginings, was back in the lexicon, and with a new twist. This was highly disagreeable to many powerful and entrenched interests, some of whom thought they had slaughtered all these animals a long time ago and sent their lifeless trophies to the taxidermists, but they had not defined themselves as combatants as yet and neither had we.

So I finished the school year of '64 without serious trouble. When Sally had thrown her first *I Ching* hexagram at Edwards she had been informed in no uncertain terms that she was pregnant, and she was. Klytie was born on July 14 at the hospital in Star Lake, another small town to which we had moved; prettier than Edwards, with more and better conveniences. Sally, Susan and the baby stayed at Manhasset for the balance of the summer, while I went off on various jaunts. Poker games with old pals and parties with old palettes, in a triangle from Port Jefferson on Long Island to Plattsburgh to Syracuse and back again.

This sporting life, I found, wasn't as much fun as it had been. I was preoccupied with philosophic questions. When I told my old friends about my new interests, the subject was usually quickly changed to the tried and true, although at Syracuse I found that an old pal, Karl Newton, M.D. (a shrink) was very interested, as were some of the other high-IQ people around. I stopped off at Millbrook two or three times for brief visits during that strange summer following the JFK assassination.

Nothing very remarkable happened, but people in general seemed to be in a peculiar frame of mind. Had a cabal of some kind taken over their government? I came to believe this in the years to come, but at the time I was as uncertain and confused about it all as the next guy. Joining the Millbrook community seemed to be an economic impossibility and that was that. At least the place existed. This meant a lot to me, as it did to many other people who had become bored and angry with the materialism and militarism of American life and dazed by the truly bizarre events in Dallas.

The main thing I seemed to be doing was wasting money. Perhaps, unconsciously, I was trying to wreck my 9-to-5 existence. I usually had no summer vacations in those days. As I often put it to people who inquired, if I wasn't "in school," I was "in prison." It never entered my head that it was possible to do anything without, sooner or later, working to pay for it. What was I supposed to do, rob banks?

When the 1964-65 school year started, Sally seemed happier with two kids to look after than one and we had found a better house than usual in Star Lake, a town with the woodsy atmosphere I favored. Even if my novelistic effort seemed labored and derivative to me, with bright spots here and there, the Millbrookians seemed to like it, and after all, it was only the first draft.

Consciously, I didn't want to get fired, but by mid-winter my driver's license was suspended for speeding, and Sally had to bundle up Susan and Klytie every morning and drive me to the schools, often over icy roads in abominable weather. Each of my four violations had been for going ten miles or so over the limit on deserted straightaways cutting through the forest preserve. Was the well-known "unseen hand" at work? Could be.

These ambushes, always by the same cop, may well have been a deliberate shot across my bow, an introduction to harassment by selective enforcement. As I would learn in the years to come, it's the American Way of disposing of dissidents. Virtually every car that passed him was exceeding the speed limit. On the other hand, I was the school psychologist for the area and it was my job to tell people the truth about their kids. My antagonist may have been some local dull-normal kid's mother's brother-in-law, or something, getting even because I had said that it was bad luck with the genetic lottery, rather than bad teaching or moral depravity, that accounted for the kid's low grades. A lot of people, for wildly different reasons, hate to hear this.

The FBI paid us a visit, without a preliminary phone call, one Saturday afternoon. Two young guys in gray flannel suits, very polite, very pleasant. They just wanted to discuss the subject.

Nothing alarming was contemplated, etc. I asked them to sit down, the usual arguments on both sides were trotted out, and they left.

Sally did not appear during this exchange. When the G-men left, I found her crouched at the top of the stairs with my little automatic pistol in hand. I was stunned. The extremely combative inclinations of her illustrious forbearers had apparently risen up, brushed common sense aside, and taken over for a while. I gently removed the weapon from her grasp and spoke a few words of admonishment, not unmixed with awe, and she quickly calmed down.

Events cast their shadows before them, all right. In a way, I guess, Sally saw the battle lines more clearly than I did.

I knew very well that my new and very exotic way of looking at things, and my new interest in psychedelic drugs, would not go over very well with most of the public school principals and superintendents to whom I reported, but I did my best to continue functioning as I had in the past, on the theory that the fellow professionals with whom I associated on my own time, and the kinds of psychological research in which I took an interest, were nobody's business but my own.

I'm sure there were leaks. I had teacher friends, whose views on other matters were similar to my own, in whom I confided.

My attitude became public when the rulers of New York State decided to increase the penalties for the distribution of the Lesser Sacrament. Under the governance of mass-murderer Nelson Rockefeller, these sadistic laws continued to escalate until the suffering imposed on pot smokers equaled or exceeded the punishments for robbery and manslaughter. This witch hunt provoked me to write a "general report," which was a mimeographed paper I occasionally distributed on a subject of general interest, on marijuana.

There wasn't anything in this brief essay that wouldn't be regarded as standard liberal opinion in future years: Don't become alarmed at a little experimentation; cannabis isn't addicting; it may well have medical and psychological usefulness; the facts aren't all in; the laws are much too harsh and ought to be moderated, etc., etc.

What the hell, I thought to myself. If a psychologist with my kind of experience couldn't express a minority opinion on a matter such as this, of what use was the First Amendment to the Constitution?

I was fired the next day.

The school boards of two of the four districts I served voted for me, and two voted against me, but this was enough to terminate my services, according to the rules then in place. The M.D. president of the school board in Star Lake, a Dr. Person, led the attack. No official reasons were provided, which was legal because I didn't have tenure.

Note that two of my school boards stood by me. The public education establishment in those days was not nearly as supine or irrational as it became in the decades that followed, although the first serious capitulations to the forces of unreason were beginning to appear as the parents of low-IQ children organized and pressured the schools to ignore all but the most extreme differences in intelligence and achievement in promotion, grade placement and, eventually, almost everything else including graduation from high school. Educational psychologists were demonic figures to these people. Since discrimination on the basis of race was bad, all discrimination was bad and all integration was good. The fact is that discrimination and segregation for the right reasons are the cornerstones of all good educational systems. But it was early. The dumbing down of American education had just begun. Because Sputnik was still fresh in people's minds, there were countervailing forces at work, now (1994) almost entirely vanquished. Maybe I got out just in time.

Fortunately, I had just borrowed a couple thousand. Instead of buying a new car, I went over to Cranberry Lake, about ten miles from Star Lake, and started asking around for something roomy and isolated off the road and on the shore, 90 percent of which was in the forest preserve and declared "forever wild" by the New York State Constitution.

It was nice, if somewhat anxiety provoking, to be free.

The major insights gained from psychedelic experience are at odds with the myths and fantasies of institutional life in a dualist culture, and it is most often not a matter of choice that "turning on" and "tuning in" are swiftly followed by "dropping out." It isn't impracticality, per se. Psychedelians worry about survival problems as much as anyone else in trouble. It's often a matter of gagging when called upon to pronounce the prevailing incantations, once one no longer believes in them.

The few supposedly turned-on professionals who manage to remain in institutional life doing research and teaching will often be found, on close examination, to be not turned-on at all.

Gwenn Longbotham, former bee hee of Burlington, Vermont, told me about some isolation chamber research she had done with Jean Houston, who had been anointed as an authority on LSD by the mass media and mass publishing. Gwenn asked Jean if she had taken much, and Jean said she had had one 50-microgram trip, period.

"I'm too analytical," Jean explained, with a brazen smirk.

Yeah, sure. That's the problem with all these great-mystery-that-surrounds-the-pyramids kind of people. (See *Mind Games*, Viking, 1972.) They are too "analytical."

As an Aries kind of guy (I regard astrology as just another frame for synchronicity, a convenient typology for the cast of characters, and not a matter of "influences") and a son of a Lutheran minister, it was unlikely that I could have maintained a fraudulent persona for long, but it took years before I fully accepted this fact. True, I was free of many restraints, but I was also free of $500 paychecks every two weeks, which I didn't like at all.

In private, Tim was pretty good at accepting the grimmer consequences. I remember one occasion in particular, when I was bitching to him about the amount of dog, cat and goat shit in and around the Big House during the last few months when the place had disintegrated into a mere comfort station for people and animals living in the woods. Tim, who was very fastidious personally, replied, "Art, that's your problem. You have to learn to love shit."

Never!

Chapter 10

BEGINNINGS OF CIVILIZATION

I was pretty well satisfied with what I had already accomplished.

Morning Glory Lodge (originally named Sunset Lodge) was about a mile south of the public campsites on the eastern shore of Cranberry Lake, and from the real estate agent's description it sounded like what I wanted and also what I could afford. A house, four cabins, and a shack out back containing a generating plant for lights and the water pump. No road in. You either took a boat or walked. $15,000, with $2,000 down on a $100-a-month land contract. No title until paid up.

This was the spring of '65, but it was a pretty sweet deal even then.

The agent gave me a set of keys, and I went to inspect the place with a friend Sally and I called Bucky Beaver, an outrageously misplaced aesthete and snob who was suffering from first-year teacher's culture shock. We walked through the cold spring woods, past small bays and beaches covered with sparkling rotting ice, in the general direction given by the agent. When we stepped out of the woods and into the clearing and saw the buildings spaced out under some tall old-growth deciduous trees, I immediately announced:

"This is the place!"

I don't think I have ever been happier in my life than at that moment. It was love at first sight.

The house had a full-length screened porch, where Bucky and I paused on entering, to survey the view. The dock was about fifty feet long and made of boulders, staked and chained together in an L shape to provide safe mooring in all weather. Decking was stacked on the shore in front of it, along with three overturned wood boats and a canoe. Two old but apparently serviceable outboard motors rested on the porch floor.

The furnishings were better than I had expected. A stone fireplace, complete with a hand-hewn oaken mantel. A slip-covered old couch on one side of the fireplace and two old plush overstuffed chairs on the other. A kerosene heater at the other end of the room. Two large propane refrigerators in the kitchen, which would make Sally's life easier, contrasted with a tiny galvanized metal sink, which would not. A bathroom with an old-fashioned tub, sink and toilet, all in working order. Two bedrooms with double beds in each.

The second story was one long room under the roof, with four bunks in a row and a desk and chair in an alcove projecting out of the roof facing the lake. Great view. The silence was broken only by the occasional brushing of tree against tree and tree against roof. In the sunlight, last year's grass, now turned silver, rippled and flowed like the sea. A chipmunk darted in and out of the stacked decking.

"Hey," Bucky said, "look at this."

Bucky had discovered a stack of *The Saturday Evening Post* and *Harper's Magazine* from the 1930s. Irresistible. On waves of nostalgia, I was carried back to happy childhood summers at Schroon Lake and North Hero Island on Lake Champlain. $700 for a new Plymouth. Cartoonstrip adventures with Eveready batteries. NRA eagles. Christ! What if some other buyer came along before I could finalize the deal, or the owners changed their minds?

All four cabins had water connections and sinks, two had toilets, and one of the toileted cabins sported a bathtub as well.

How opulent can things get?

The shack out back, we discovered, contained a washing

machine as well as the generator. Yards of pipe. Tools. Paint. Oars and oarlocks. A path led us back through the woods to a covered spring in a bed of ferns. Delicious water. I was going berserk with joy. Bucky looked at me with alarm and greeted my ejaculations of delight with sputters of disdain.

"You're not actually going to buy this place are you, Kleps?"

"Of course I'm going to buy it! Why the hell shouldn't I buy it?" I replied, amazed that anyone could fail to fall madly in love with it at first sight, even Bucky.

"Well, there's nothing HERE!" Bucky said, waving his fat arms around. "You're too much, Bucky," was all I could think of to say.

As we walked back through the woods to the campsite road where I had parked the car, my imagination revved up to full speed. Tim would send me people, certainly. Billy Hitchcock might kick in with some money for promotion and repairs, and the Psychedelian religious association (a "church," in the common parlance) that I had been thinking about organizing would now have a headquarters with room for visitors, privacy, and all kinds of dramatic, scenic and romantic associations which ought to charm any red-blooded American boy, as I understood the term, who happened to be an acid head as well, into a state of mind which would virtually guarantee his enthusiastic approval and maybe his name on the dotted line. Maybe we could winterize the house and travel by snowmobile to town! Vroom, vroom, and over the snow to town we go. How much groovier could life in the winter get than that? There was a tiny island with a cabin on it out in the center of the lake right in front of the lodge. Perhaps we could buy that too, and use it for sessions, and so on and so forth. Perhaps this, perhaps that. I didn't stop speeding for days. It was a fantasy come true. (The term "delirious," unfortunately, comes to mind.)

As for members of the opposite sex, well, if they wanted to hang around with real guys they would just have to put up with this kind of shit whether they liked it or not, I thought. And wasn't there something known as an "outdoor girl"? The charm of the place would, I hoped, transform Sally into one of these fabled creatures.

By the end of the week we were all moved in and I had invented the Neo-American Church. I ordered 1,000 peyote buttons from a "peyote rancher" in Texas named Elsie, whose name had been given me by Lisa Bieberman. It was legal. Each new member would get five buttons and a membership card. An old artist friend from my days of drunken debauchery on Long Island designed the card. Mystic Arts book society, which published Tim's conversion of the *TBD*, printed the announcements for me for nothing.

Aside from signed agreement with the three principles of the Church, which consisted entirely of definitions and claims of rights, there would be no rules. This was a silly notion, but consistent with the emergent spirit of the times.

The principles were:

1. Everyone has the right to expand his consciousness and stimulate visionary experience by whatever means he considers desirable and proper without interference from anyone.
2. The psychedelic substances, such as LSD, are the True Host of the Church, not drugs. They are sacramental foods, manifestations of the Grace of God, of the infinite Imagination of the Self, and therefore belong to everyone.
3. We do not encourage the ingestion of psychedelics by those who are unprepared.

I changed Principle 2 in 1973, and filed the change with our incorporation papers in Vermont, to read:

To disseminate the principle that the psychedelic substances, such as LSD, are sacraments, in that they encourage Enlightenment, which is the realization that life is a dream and that the externality of relations is an illusion.

But during the time period covered by this book, the original set of principles stood. I tried to include in the embrace of the Neo-American Church Psychedelians of a supernaturalist disposition through the use of terms like "God" and "Self," which, although they only represented poetic or impressionistic ways of talking about the *antakarana* function of the mind to me, left the door wide open to those who wished to maintain the various traditional externalizations. I chose to be vague instead of clear, always a serious crime for a philosopher and always punished one way or another.

At the time of this writing, the complete set of principles reads:

1. The psychedelic substances, such as cannabis and LSD, are religious sacraments since their ingestion encourages Enlightenment, which is the recognition that life is a dream and the externality of relations an illusion (solipsistic nihilism).
2. The use of the psychedelic sacraments is a basic human right and all interference therewith is an assault on this right.
3. We do not encourage the ingestion of the greater sacraments such as LSD and mescaline by those who are unprepared and we define preparedness as familiarity with the lesser sacraments such as cannabis and nitrous oxide and with solipsist-nihilist epistemological reasoning based on such models as David Hume, Sextus Empiricus and Nagarjuna.

Our clergy would be called boo hoos. "Bee hee," to designate female clergypersons, came later. The name just popped into my head, but there are associations on which I may have drawn. "Boo" is old Negro slang for marijuana; John Jay Chapman, for whom I have a very high regard, was known, during his best years, as "the Goo Goo." "Hoo" is Old English for "house."

There are plenty of other possible associations, including tears, but I don't think "boo hoo" encourages people to make too much of their sorrows. On the contrary.

My conscious motive, if any, was to keep things light. I did not want the Church to appear solemn or Oriental. Nothing like moralistic, ceremonial, ecumenical, consensual "churchianity" would be allowed to take over. Psychedelian religion in general was one thing and the Church, and its doctrines and style and customs and rules, was another thing. We were iconoclasts.

Tim accepted a place on the board and played along in some ways, but did almost nothing to promote the Church in public. He called himself a Hindu in his Texas trial, and when that got

BEGINNINGS OF CIVILIZATION

him nowhere ditched IFIF and started the League for Spiritual Discovery, with pretentious aliases for one and all, secret passwords, robes, and whatever else might appeal to those given to sophomoric fantasies.

Did Tim ever sincerely believe that the psychedelic experience was religious? To answer the question, one must penetrate two misty and treacherous realms, the definition of "religion" and the mind of Timothy Leary. I have gone on both expeditions, and I have returned with a few samples of flora and fauna, some photographs of foggy landscapes and ill defined forms, and a few tape recordings, which are mostly commercial messages aimed at a target audience of half-wits and children.

Turning them over, I have come to the conclusion that all of Tim's attempts to categorize the experience, particularly those concepts he thought most "scientific," such as the "seeding" of "egg planets" by "comets of prophesy," were examples of genuine religious ideation under the first definition given in *Webster's* at that time, which was:

1. belief in a divine or superhuman power or powers to be obeyed and worshiped as the creator(s) and ruler(s) of the universe.

When Tim used "mystical" terminology at Millbrook it's hard to say if his underlying concepts were supernaturalist or not, but during the *Neurologic*/Kohoutek period in the '70s, he regressed all the way back to the old sod to grovel with his ancestors before imaginary "saviors" from Outer Space.

Earlier, however, he called himself a "Hindu" or a "Buddhist" or a "Taoist" as the spirit moved and the wind blew. He was not alone in this. A lot of people in those days who should have known better, tended to treat these distinct ideational systems as virtually interchangeable brand names for a generic Oriental "wisdom" all pumped out of the same hole. The packaging might change, but Slobovenoid Blobovenoidalism was what you got. It's what almost all academic philosophers mean by "monism," since it is the only concept for which they can form any kind of image.

You can be a Hindu and think this way, in fact, you can be a

Hindu and think almost any way you please, or not think at all. Was Tim ever a Buddhist? Not in my opinion.

It did eventually dawn on Tim that genuine Buddhism, leaving Lamaism aside, was alien to his way of thinking, and he said so, at least to me and a couple other guys. I don't know if he ever said it in public or in print.

Hinduism hung on longer, but Tim eventually saw the incompatibility of even that extremely plastic religion with his political objectives, and he became, for a crucial year or two at Millbrook which might be called his charlatanic period, a Machiavellian pragmatist politician with no operational philosophic convictions whatever.

Neurologic is Roman Catholic recidivism, for sure. The names are changed, but the game is the same. Don't think, pray. The Almighty Comet knoweth all.

Am I, and is the Neo-American Church, in the terms currently and generally accepted by scholars of the subject, "religious"?

In an important sense, it doesn't matter and never has. Religion defines religion just as philosophy defines philosophy, which is the main reason both are such a problem for lawyers and politicians.

But, even by conventional scholarly standards, only the most primitive definition of "religion" will exclude us. In terms of doctrine, if Buddhism is included, we are included. In terms of the antiquity of our practices, we have seniority, and at ecumenical revels should take precedence over everyone in sight, except for the surviving native peyote, mushroom and morning glory seed eaters, who should sit at the head of the table and barf in golden spittoons.

We have every reason to look down on the upstart pretensions of the Roman Catholic Church in this respect. It's a synthetic cult, invented to pander to modern tastes.

Webster's second definition at that time:

2. any specific system of belief, worship, conduct, etc., often involving a code of ethics and a philosophy, (the Christian religion, the Buddhist religion, etc.)

was OK, because it included us.

The editors brutally slashed this excellent definition from later editions of *Webster's*, thereby demonstrating the folly of allowing corporate conglomerates to define one's terms. As a nominalist of the old school, I will define my own terms, thanks.

"Religion" ought to be broadly defined. It appears that the ink-stained clerk over at *Webster's* who held down the religion stool in those days was so discerning as to be aware that genuine Buddhism has no idea of God or a "higher power," and wrote his second definition so as to include Buddhism. I hope he got a goose for Christmas, and wasn't fired when his definition was expunged because it might be cited by the likes of us in furtherance of our fiendish schemes.

Check the definition of "religion" before you buy a dictionary, to find out if it is a work of scholarship or propaganda.

I don't think the Mormons or the Scientologists are not religious. I just think they are wrong, that's all.

A name for the generality of Psychedelian religionists is needed. "Psychedelianism," the obvious choice, is OK with me, and I will use it until something better comes along.

"Is this man a Psychedelian or a Presbyterian, sergeant? I can't make out your handwriting."

"Argh, an' ee's a doity Presbyterian fer sure, sor. When oy haprehended the mutha behin' th' latrine, sor, ee was hunk'ring down upon the cald grass, a fuckin' of a duck by the light ub de silv'ry moon, as Gawd is moy witness, sor, as Ee was ub dat 'orrible scene, begorrah. Th' pitifool quackin' ub dat po' boid still rings in m'eers, gor blimey, sor."

Aldous Huxley, Timothy Leary, Charlie Manson, Gordon Wasson, Hunter Thompson and I all are or were Psychedelians, I think, but only one of us is or was a Neo-American as far as I know.

Tim and I corresponded regularly during the spring and early summer of 1965. When he wrote me that he was getting married to Nena von Schlebrugge, a popular Swedish model of the day, and going to Nepal for his honeymoon, I decided to squeeze in one more visit to Millbrook before our rent on the house in Star Lake ran out. Sally didn't want to be left alone at the isolated lodge with the kids and I couldn't blame her.

Chapter 11

THE YANKEE IN SEARCH OF ADVENTURE

There never was such a country for wandering liars; and they were of both sexes.

Tim, never one to diddle around when a trip to Nepal with a Swedish model was in the offing, had already left when I got to Millbrook. Michael Hollingshead, about whom I knew very little, despite his having written me a long and smarmy letter a week or two earlier, was now in some kind of alliance with Dick and Ralph as a coadministrator of the house. Nena's mother and brother were still in town but the baroness never visited the Big House because, Ralph told me, she loathed Hollingshead. I gave Nena's brother, a nice guy, a baron and a sports car enthusiast, a driving lesson. He thought he needed practice with an American car before venturing out on the public roads in one. He was right.

My introduction to Hollingshead was appropriately bizarre and vaguely unpleasant. I was in the kitchen during the first evening of my visit, talking to Ralph and Susan, when a tall man with unreadable features, dressed in slacks, a sport coat and a fedora with a ribbon of photographs around the brim, came twirling into the room, revolving like one of those "waltzing" mice which can't move in a straight line because of a genetic fault. They were pretty popular pets for kids back in the '30s.

As this apparition spun around the table muttering to himself, Ralph's eyes narrowed and Susan took a deep breath and held it. He acted as though he wanted to sit down on one of the empty chairs but couldn't figure out how to do it. I pulled one out for him, which seemed to piss him off. He moved his arms angrily and sputtered. Still twirling, he moved out of the room.

Susan exhaled.

"What the fuck?" I asked.

"Michael Hollingshead," Ralph said, poker faced as usual.

Dick and two young guys with the look of New York hustlers came in. They all seemed very stoned. I was introduced. Ernie and Arnie. They proceeded to mix up some pancake batter while giggling and whispering to each other.

"Listen, Art," Ralph said to me in an undertone, "let's go to the music room. I want to talk to you."

We sat down cross-legged next to the fish tank in the center of the floor. Ralph pulled out a joint, lit it, took a drag and passed it to me. It was pretty good stuff for those pre-sinsemilla times.

"Have you been tripping much?" Ralph asked. I told him about the morning glory seed trip and a small acid trip Sally and I had taken, which had produced some eyes-closed visionary effects and an interesting sequel: I had taken the next day off and while out driving we both had seen Bucky in his car. We waved to him but he ignored us. Later, Bucky swore up and down that he was teaching Latin to future apple knockers at the time and hadn't left the school all day. A hallucination? A mutual hallucination? A mutual hallucination hours after the trip ended?

Hmmm. Well, so, McPozzm, maybe the use of psychedelics produces a hallucination, as distinct from a vision, every now and then. So do all kinds of other things, like sudden withdrawal from amphetamines or fasting. It remains sleazily dishonest and typical of the American Psychiatric Association to insist on labeling psychedelics as "hallucinogens." Hallucinations are not among the usual or desired effects and the filthy swine (whom I can see very clearly) know it very well. I refer the reader who doesn't think these distinctions are important to George Orwell's "Politics and the English Language," which can be found in *Shooting an Elephant and Other Essays*. In fact, in the general interest of encouraging sanity, I refer everyone everywhere to this masterful homily.

I told Ralph I was hoping to take a trip with Tim, but since he wasn't around, well, er, hmm.

"That's what I wanted to talk to you about," Ralph said. "I don't think you should take anything while the house is like this. Things are really crazy around here right now."

"OK," I agreed. I felt a mixture of disappointment and relief. Ralph asked me to drive him to the train station in Poughkeepsie to pick up his sister-in-law. She needed a minor operation and had decided to have it done in a small hospital in Sharon, Connecticut, which wasn't far from Millbrook. When we got into my car Ralph pulled out another joint. It was a very dark night.

On the way to Poughkeepsie, Ralph explained the general situation. This was Thursday night and the last chance for people living in the house to do as they pleased, because visitors would be arriving Friday night and staying through Sunday. *Paying visitors*. Economic necessity had reared its ugly head. The "guests" would be met at the train Friday afternoon and not allowed to speak to each other or anyone else until Saturday morning. Then there were lectures and exercises and whatnot and they went home Sunday. No drugs. They had been doing this for the last three weekends and Ralph thought it was working out reasonably well. I could help if I liked. Ernie and Arnie were to put on a "light show," whatever that was, and Hollingshead was a drug smuggler who had provided Tim with his first acid hits. Aside from those bare facts Ralph seemed reluctant to talk about the new residents. He wanted me to see for myself.

We then entered the dirty, dismal and decaying streets of Poughkeepsie, New York. Ralph ceased to pull out joints. There was no way that either of us would inhale deeply in an atmosphere such as this.

Unattractive as the name may be, I find it hard to believe that "Poughkeepsie" really means "Place of Overflowing Shitholes" in the language of the Iroquois, or that this tribe founded the city and maintained it for centuries as the center of their sadistic "federation," which either destroyed or enslaved all the other tribes in the region. By what means could these savages have cross-bred with a species of giant rodents, now extinct, resulting in the hideous monstrosities who dominate the Dutchess County religious, political and financial establishment to this very day? The answer is blowing in the wind.

One thing is for sure: Poughkeepsie does not appear, under any name, on most maps.

No matter where one goes in the Place of Overflowing Shitholes, there is always something disgusting either right in front of one's nose or right around the corner. The haggard, slack-jawed, vacant-eyed pedestrians who trudge its streets appear to have been stunned since birth into a condition of chronic somnambulism.

All over town, farts of poisonous gasses burst from the cracks in the sidewalks as one treads near or on them. This doesn't seem to bother the inmates at all, perhaps because they know that inhaling these exudations will help to shorten their lives.

The angles and vistas are all wrong. Things do not fit together the way they should. Scabrous, Dickensian tenements and crumbling warehouses, used for the storage of bilge from decommissioned nuclear submarines, entirely block the view of the river.

Any aesthete worthy of the name would be rendered *hors de combat* in the Place of Overflowing Shitholes within a few seconds of exposure, but lawyers and publishers, as one might expect, find the place very much to their tastes and often retire there so they can savor the ambiance in their old age.

It is said that Theodore Roosevelt had a deep, assured and resonant bass voice until, while governor of New York State, he read the report of a secret commission on the true history of Poughkeepsie. He sank down under his desk and remained there, curled up on the rug, in a kind of hysterical coma for a period of twenty-seven days. On recovering, he had retrograde amnesia for the entire incident, but spoke in a shrieking falsetto for the rest of his life. (The other oddities he developed, such as Eskimostuffing, are well known to historians, but too numerous to mention here.)

As soon as he was elected governor, Franklin Delano Roosevelt offered to grant full pardons to several Mafia murderers then awaiting electrocution at Sing-Sing, if the rulers of New Jersey would accept the Place of Overflowing Shitholes as part of their state. The Jersey City gang lords of the day rejected the offer, resolutely stating, "There is some shit we will not eat."

Ralph's sister-in-law was very appreciative of the third and final joint, which Ralph passed around as soon as we were outside the city limits and on our way back to Millbrook.

So was I.

I think I have written the above description of the Place of Overflowing Shitholes in the spirit in which Henry Miller wrote his description of the planet Saturn in *The Colossus of Maroussi*. He called it an "emotional photograph." Right. There are some subjects which cry out for this kind of treatment.

The comforting darkness and Ralph's generous helpings of hemp greatly moderated the ordeal of this particular visit. Unfortunately, this balm was not always to be available on future visits.

Driving while stoned on the lesser sacrament is safer under any and all circumstances than driving while drunk, and may well be safer, for experienced users in general, than driving straight.

Stoned drivers rarely, if ever, get on angry, competitive, high-speed kicks, so any errors we make are likely to be trivial. We tend to be methodical, thoughtful, cautious, defensive drivers. It might be a good idea to pass out free Alice B. Toklas brownies at rest stops on New Year's eve, along with the coffee. Then there would be more of a there there for many people for sure.

Awareness, after all, is what being stoned is all about and it figures that the more aware one is of one's surroundings, the better a driver or pilot or operating engineer one will be. I think this thesis is supported by the strange absence of any (publicized) research on the subject.

The theory could easily be checked out in a triple-blind study of bus drivers, using real and fake Alice B. Toklas brownies. I bet the moderately stoned drivers would prove to be better drivers in every way.

LSD-taking that evening was concentrated in the Bowling Alley, where Dick, Hollingshead, Ernie, Arnie, and a rich girl from New York, famous for maintaining dozens of indigent heads in her town house, were camping out, without running water or electricity, for the night in front of the fireplace. I dropped in for a few minutes just to say hello. Hollingshead was still twirling and Ernie, while fondling and kissing Dick's hand, was still mumbling about going up the Amazon to interact with alligators. I exchanged a few pleasantries with the inmates, returned to the Big House and went to bed early.

Going to sleep, I resolved to stick with Ralph for the duration of my visit. Hollingshead, Ernie and Arnie were neither scholars nor gentlemen. Life at Millbrook had taken a turn for the worse, with creeps in high places. It was a good thing I had the lodge to return to. If not, I might find myself up the Amazon with the alligators.

The next day passed without excitement. I went to a nearby state school, picked up three young retardates to help clean the Big House, supervised their work, and brought them back. High-grade morons. They enjoyed the experience enormously, particularly the opportunity to ogle so many pretty girls.

The Fergusons now occupied the Gatehouse. But even with Millbrook's cutest absent from the Big House most of the time, the place was still loaded for bear, so to speak. Psychedelian communities almost always are. Gotama wouldn't let an unattached female "within a hundred miles" of his ashram, Haines would say, every now and then, a somewhat hyperbolic way of putting it. But this attitude, to put it mildly, did not apply at Millbrook. Positive traits being positively correlated, there were "super-girls" all over the place, from start to finish.

If that's a curse, it's one I am willing to up with put.

The visitors arrived late in the afternoon and quietly trooped up to their rooms in the servants' wing, most of which, I had noticed, had been decorated in a gaudy, spooky style with cracked mirror fragments glued to one wall, swirls of clashing colors on another, magazine photo collages on a ceiling and so forth. Ernie and Arnie at work. I didn't like it. I didn't like the light show that was shown later in the evening either. What was so "psychedelic" about colored blobs floating around?

Some very prosaic imaginations were at work, that was for sure.

Dinner with the silent guests, however, was hilarious. About twenty of them, mostly conservatively dressed and middle-aged, had come in the front door, smiling grimly but with fear in their eyes, to follow a silent but beaming Dick up the stairs. When they came down a couple hours later, after we had cooked dinner and set it out on low tables around the dining room, a place card in front of every cushion, I could hardly believe the evidence of my senses. The "guests" were all wearing white robes made out of bed sheets. I came close to choking trying to get back to the kitchen without laughing out loud.

In the kitchen, Pat McNeill, Susan Leary and Susan Metzner were having a major giggling fit, in which I immediately joined.

The robes, they explained, were intended to obliterate social distinctions, but they cracked up over it anyway. A giggling fit, when you are stoned on grass, as we all were, is, one might say, no laughing matter. Susan Metzner, between sobs and gasps, asked me to read some kind of paper, authored by Hollingshead, to the Ku Klux Klan in the next room.

"Very simple ... gasp ... you just hit the gong ... tee hee hee ... and read this bullshit ... ha, ha, ha ... until it says GONG ... sob ... when you hit it again ..." she dissolved into tears. Susan Leary had her head down on the table and was shuddering all over, and Pat was not in much better shape.

I peeked out at the dining room through the pantry door. Dick, Ralph and Hollingshead were solemnly seated with the guests. They were being silent but not wearing bed sheets. Back in the kitchen, I tried to read the paper to myself, but my hand was shaking so badly from suppressed bursts of merriment that I could hardly make it out ... *with the next mouthful of food contemplate on the wonders of the body; where the food goes, how it is digested.*

What the fuck? Mouthful? Where it goes? How it is digested? At a very early age, I had been firmly instructed that the dinner table was not the place to bring up clinical topics such as these. One might discuss them in the doctor's office or the classroom, or maybe on the front porch, but not while people were trying to eat.

I made some kind of strangled effort to express my dismay, which merely caused Susan Metzner to collapse next to Susan Leary at the table. In this respect, I was fairly certain, Susan, Susan and Pat had been brought up as I had. Well, I would just have to get a grip on myself.

I went out into the dining room and tried not to look at the solemn congregation. Where the fuck was the damn gong? I didn't see any gong. Oh yeah, there was a big gong, at least three feet in diameter, hanging in a frame next to the front door. I went out in the hall and brought it in ... heavy bastard. There was a big beater with it. I heaved the frame up onto a serving table next to the pantry door and gripped the hammer with my right hand while I held the paper with my left. Everyone was looking at me with utmost gravity. I was afraid that I would burst into loon-like shrieks at any moment, but my apprehension struck me as hilariously funny, also.

I hit the gong a good whack, with the usual consequences (GONNNNNNNG) and started reading, pretending all the while that I was somewhere else and that some mechanical dummy was reading the paper. Somehow, I got to the last sentence without incident.

When you hear the sound of the gong ...
(GONNNNNNNG)
Were those screams I could hear coming from the kitchen?
... observe its structured wonders, skin, hair, tissue, blood, vein, bone, muscle, net of nerve. Observe its message. (For one awful moment, I considered going on with *appendix, colon, ... memories of a misspent youth*, but I suppressed the urge.)
Om Shanti, Shanti, Shanti.
(GONNNNNNNG)

I fled to the kitchen. No member of my audience had so much as chuckled during the recitation, but the girls in the kitchen had reached the stage of final exhaustion. They were just sitting there, limply, like rag dolls, with tears streaming down their cheeks.

"Arthur," Susan Metzner said, a tremor or two passing over her face, "you weren't supposed to use the big gong. There was a tiny one right next to you the whole time."

I went out and took the first vacant place I could find, forgetting about the place names entirely. "Hi," I said to the people at the table. At the same time, I noticed that I was Dr. Morris Tannenbaum, M.D., and the guy across from me was trying to tell me something in sign language. I closed my eyes ... *all you have to do is behave normally,* I told myself. I opened my eyes and turned to the white-robed lady at my side. "Hi," I said in a perfectly normal voice, "I'm Art Kleps, not Dr. Tannenbaum. Where is Dr. Tannenbaum?" The three other people at my table looked at me with consternation and dismay. The guy making the sign language pointed first at his place card and then at his mouth. He was making motions as if to first zip and then sew his lips together. Christ! I had violated the rule of silence. I got up and left, and stayed away from the visitors for the rest of the evening, except to look in on the light show for a couple of minutes. I wondered once again why some people thought floating blobs were "psychedelic." I went back to my book.

Late that night, after all the visitors had been put to bed, everyone got together in Tim's room for a critique of the day and plans for the morrow. A hash pipe was passed but the whole scene bored me stiff. It sounded like a PTA meeting. Fortunately, I was sitting on the edge of Tim's bed, which was in an alcove, next to the rich girl from New York. She didn't mind at all being pulled back on the bed for some routine sophomoric behavior. But the reclining position and the long, full day and the brandy and the hash were too much for me. In five minutes I was out cold.

Chapter 12

SLOW TORTURE

About the third or fourth or fifth time that we swung out into the glare—it was along there somewhere, a couple of hours or so after sun-up—it wasn't as pleasant as it had been.

When I woke up, my head was clear as a child's and there wasn't a soul stirring. It looked to be about 6 o'clock of a fine, bright morning. I sat up on the edge of the bed, in the same place I had occupied during the Psychedelian PTA meeting the night before, which was also the site of the candle mystery of my previous visit. I looked around for traces of wax and spotted an aperitif glass at my feet with what looked like brandy in it. Well, I thought, the cute rich girl from New York, fully conversant with every known form of human degeneracy, had probably left it there to steady my nerves in the morning. Very considerate of her. Good thing I hadn't kicked it over, although I didn't really need it badly because I hadn't put away more than half my usual intake the day before.

Heavy drinkers will sometimes become moderate drinkers if there is plenty of cannabis around. One just forgets about booze, or getting up and finding the next one seems like too much trouble.

Hmmm, perhaps it was bad form for me to have passed out on Tim's bed. It might be considered "a sacred shrine area" or something. This idea caused some minor anxiety so I tossed down the brandy and went to the bathroom to brush my teeth. It wasn't so easy. I felt slightly dizzy. Things looked a little strange. I headed back towards the bed. The first rays of the sun were coming through the big window on my left, and I turned to get a full view of it.

I was knocked to the floor, as all normal sensation and motor control left my body. The sun, roaring like an avalanche, was headed straight for me, expanding like a bomb and filling my consciousness in less time than it takes to describe it. It swirled, clockwise, and made two-and-one-half turns before I lost all normal sense of place and passed out, right there on the floor of Tim's room. The next day, Susan Metzner told me she had heard a thump, perhaps the sound of my body hitting the floor, and had crossed the hall and looked in to see me prostrate and apparently unconscious.

"I wasn't stoned in any way," Susan emphasized. No reason why she should have been, at 6 in the morning. "You turned every color of the rainbow and then you disappeared right in front of my eyes!"

I don't remember that. The next thing I do remember is rolling around on the floor in Dick's room, which was across the hall from Tim's, adjoining Ralph and Susan's.

Although I didn't see myself disappear, there is nothing in my philosophy which would make such an occurrence impossible. You can't see sight, as Buddha often remarked. And Susan was the last person in the house whom I had any reason to think would encourage me to believe anything magical or extraordinary had happened. So I believe her report, but only, I am convinced, because I have a conceptual context in which to place it. I think there are many people who have forgotten equally bizarre occurrences within a matter of hours. The memory of events that don't "make sense" just fades away.

On the floor of Dick's room I had what I later found out was called in the East the Kundalini ("serpent power") experience, a kind of mirror image of the vision of the exploding sun. I seemed to be inside a whirlwind of electrical plasma which also made two-and-one-half gigantic turns, this time counter-clockwise.

Ralph, Susan and some other people I couldn't identify were in the room trying to get tablets of thorazine, which I couldn't swallow, down my throat.

All I could do was roll around and pronounce a few phonemes, such as "ah," "oh," "duh" and so forth. It wasn't that I couldn't think. The trouble was I couldn't think any single thing. It seemed as though all the thoughts which had entered the minds of men and beasts in the last million years were going through my mind at the same time and with the same intensity and velocity, resulting in a kind of violent white hum. I felt a needle in my ass. Ralph had hit me with some thorazine in a way I couldn't refuse. "I'm not ready for this," I found myself saying, much to my surprise.

"That's why we gave you a thousand mics," Ralph said.

A foolish, arrogant and evasive answer. I think they gave me a thousand mics hoping it would turn me into a cosmic-minder like themselves. The thorazine, if it had any effect at all, didn't have the effect of bringing me down. When I closed my eyes in Dick's room, I found myself in Tim's room when I opened them and vice-versa. I switched back and forth a half a dozen times before I settled in Tim's room, seated in the lotus position, which I almost never adopt unless extremely stoned, on the bed.

For a while I sat on the bed with no thoughts in my mind, no sense of personal identity, no feelings about anything one way or another, while the program for the visitors presumably continued downstairs. Since my sense of elapsed time was one of the first things to go, I can't say if this condition lasted for hours or minutes. The third floor was deserted.

Then people appeared, clustered around the record player, which was connected to speakers in the visitors' rooms. I heard someone say, "Listen, who does that look like over there?" Someone else said, "Yeah, you're right." Various people, some of whom seemed familiar and some of whom didn't, sat down next to the bed and asked me silly questions. I tried to talk to them but, in most cases, they disappeared in front of my eyes. I remember grabbing Hollingshead by the arm and asking him if he was "really" there. He said he was and then disappeared. At some point in the midst of these absurdities, I made a decision:

I did not want to live without the appearance of continuity or cause and effect rationality, at least not yet. I lapsed back into the no-thought world. I would wait it out. Sweat poured from my forehead, but the rest of my body was dry.

Months later, while loitering around the library of the University of Miami waiting for a junkie friend of Ed Rosenfeld's to show up, I found myself at eye level with a large volume called *The Serpent Power*, written by Arthur Avalon, pen name of a high English high official who had made, in the old and admirable English tradition of the scholarly amateur, a serious and sympathetic study of Indian religions in general and yoga in particular. I was astonished and delighted, when I flipped the book open, to find my two-and-one-half turns and sweating forehead ("the rain of jewels," I think it was called) described as the salient features of the classic experience. The garish meta-anatomical diagrams of chakras and ectoplasmic plumbing I had seen at Millbrook and elsewhere bore no relation to this classic description or to my experience.

The scholar dealing with ancient religious texts can rarely be certain if he is reading the productions of a fantast, a con man or the genuine article. By the time these works are lodged in closed stacks or museums, they are jumbled together in putative value, although the authors may have contradicted and despised one another while they lived. The smallest LSD trip is a more reliable source of information about supernormal consciousness than any book.

When I came out of it and started moving around (drink, cigarette, bath) I was still stoned in terms of perceptual enhancement but, compared to what I had just been through, this condition seemed unexceptional. So all the walls and carpets were rippling and glowing with arcane life. What else was new? I was glad to be back in the humdrum everyday world. Ralph stopped me as I was coming out of a bathroom.

"How are you doing?" he asked. Knowing smile.

"Fine." I shrugged.

"Listen, we would appreciate it if you would stay away from the visitors until you're completely down, OK?"

No problem. The last thing I wanted to do was talk to someone who was straight. I went to the library and reclined on a couch. Beautiful room. I contentedly looked around admiring the way the lamplight gleamed on a gilt binding or contrasted with a soft nest of dusk under a table. Ernie came in and sat down. He was wearing a Robin Hood hat.

"How are you doing?"

"Oh, just getting used to it," I said. "Beautiful in here, isn't it?"

"Getting used to what?"

"Being God, or whatever you want to call it," I said.

"Yeah, man!" Ernie seemed delighted with my explanation. "I'm a magician, you know. A few days ago I decided to try it out, you know? See if it really worked? So I got this .45 and shot myself right in the head."

"What happened?" I asked.

"Nothing, man. Absolutely nothing."

"What about your relatives?" I asked Ernie.

Ernie seemed upset and frightened at the question. With a hurried "I gotta go, man," he left the room.

Some people insist on testing out the theory, which Tim and Evans-Wentz preached, that one could do "anything" if one's "head was right." Later, Tim altered this pitch somewhat to "you can be anyone, this time around," and published a recording on this theme, which has the advantage of being vague and impossible to corroborate or disprove.

Dick, at the time of this visit, was hobbling around with a cast on one foot. He had jumped out of a window, intending to flit about like Mary Poppins, and broken his ankle. Susan Leary's favorite was to take off in her Daddy's car without a registration, license or money.

It's usually a matter of taking wild chances with the police as a demonstration of one's magical or spiritual "powers." This delusion seems to have lost popularity, for which happy development I give some credit to Tim's series of carelessness-caused busts and his subsequent series of imprisonments, all highly publicized. Kesey's busts probably helped too. If such notable super-magicians couldn't fend off the cops, what hope did junior magicians have of doing it? I can therefore find it in my heart to entertain the notion that Tim's and Kesey's busts did a lot of good although saying that they "deserved" them would be going too far.

In Snazzm terms, I think I went through the same kind of shit for the same kinds of reasons. For years, I encouraged people to think in terms of magical powers and supernaturalism, the original Principle 2 and my Senate testimony being the best examples of this shameful compromise with supernaturalist ideation. It's easy to say, "Why not let it go at that? Some Psychedelians will never understand solipsistic nihilism, so why deny them their comforting superstitions?"

I no longer worry about it. Those who require comforting superstitions will keep them, no matter what. My incarceration rate, I'm happy to say, moderated considerably after I tightened Church doctrine. McPozzm, I was now a nut case. Wish I had done it earlier. Oh, well. Live and learn.

I had asked the question which caused Ernie to flee out of genuine curiosity. Did this troll-like creature have a philosophy or was he just a mischief maker? If he had a philosophy, what was it? Did he believe his punctured corpse and grieving, or celebrating, relatives were to be found in some other dimension, plane, level, bardo, or "multi-verse"? I wanted to ask him what he thought would have happened if, instead of shooting himself in private, he had chosen to blow himself to pieces with dynamite in Yankee Stadium with thousands of witnesses present.

I wonder, could Ernie's story have prompted Dick to jump out of the window? If this were fiction, I would write it that way.

In a dream, phenomenological order can be preserved by forgetting everything which, if remembered, would make an unpleasant event necessary, and substituting a history of impressions which do not make that event necessary, all without disturbing the "laws" of "physical" causality. It's typical of such transitions that one knows nothing of them, but many people can recall certain discontinuities in their lives, highly improbable escapes from impending disaster, "near death" experiences, and so on, which may be thought of, Fazzm, as transitional.

In general, I agree with the classical Greek Skeptics of the West, from Pyrrho of Elis to Sextus Empiricus (about a 500-year stretch there, which produced all kinds of terminological oddities, like the idea of cultivating "apathy" in order to reach a state of "ataraxy") and modern Western philosophers of the empiricist congregation, such as David Hume. The Mysterious East has parallel doctrines, but the semantic murk is even thicker, as one might expect. Nagarjuna, for example, denied that he was an "x," with "x" being the then current label for philosophers of a certain school in his part of the world, now routinely translated as "nihilists" in English. Yet Nagarjuna denied that anything existed. What are we to make of this? In my opinion, not much. It all depends on what you mean by "nihilist," just as it all depends on what you mean by "apathy" and "ataraxy." All words are merely marks and sounds, and have no meaning other than the sensations and images to which they relate.

The *antakarana* of Samkara, although sometimes a useful term when talking about the Snazzm organization of intra-psychic events which appear to be external, is bad Fazzm if a cosmic *saksin* is implied, a doctrine which leads to a plurality of "selves" in a container-contained dualism.

Berkeley's "Mind of God" solution to the (perceived) epistemological "problem" is a fallacy because it is an unnecessary multiplication of entities. There is no problem. Remember Occam's razor. Cut out the Middleman. Poof! Gone. Good riddance to bad rubbish.

Assume a plurality of selves only in a phenomenological sense, analogous to ordinary dream content. The *yogacara* doctrine of *vijnanadvaita* and the *atamadvaita* of Samkara, which postulates a sort of "absolute" or "cosmic" *vijnana* series, should both be rejected. I see no use for this metaphysical junk or any other kind of space junk or space junkies.

I reject *sankya* yoga with extreme prejudice, as merely a dualistic substitute for the original Psychedelian soma practices which were suppressed by the Brahmanist priests who, unable to control the stuff and too cowardly to take it, abolished its use by political means (fire and sword). A thousand curses on the filthy, flea-bitten bastards.

There is no "subtle body" (*linga-sarira*). The phenomenological body is always imaginary. Aloofness from *prakrti*, *kaivalya*, or whatever you want to call it, is impossible since distance and the space-time continuum itself are *prakrti*, and there is no distance between abstracts, at least not where I come from. The monist Vedanta of Badarayana and his ilk is less objectionable than the Vedanta of Samkara or Ramanuja, but much ado about nothing in any case.

All phenomenology is flux (*samtana*) and an aggregate lacking self (*samghata*), as Hume, in effect, says. Instantaneous "manifestation" of capacity instantaneously "obliterated," so to speak. Not only is there no objective "reality" whatever (*sunya-vada*), there is no subjective "reality" whatever. The term "reality" is meaningless. Nabokov, a solipsistic nihilist, was right. It is the only word in the English language that should be placed, routinely, between quotation marks (to emphasize its mere idiomatic utility).

All the effort and the "self-discipline" serve to prevent Enlightenment, not to "find" it. This can be overcome by taking large doses of LSD, making the truth irresistible, at least for a few minutes.

Snazzm, there is no past, present, or future, only the categorization of images so as to maintain the illusions of seriality and continuity.

"That time which we improve, or which is improvable," as Thoreau said, "is neither past, present nor future."

Virtually all philosophic difficulties with these concepts may be solved by recalling that life is (is in the nature of) a dream. If you have some event in mind which you think might argue against the solipsist hypothesis, ask yourself if it is possible to dream of this happening. It always is.

Read the *Mulamadhyamakakarika* of Nagarjuna, David Hume's *A Treatise of Human Nature,* and *Outlines of Pyrrhonism* by Sextus Empiricus. The epigrams of the Zen masters can also help. Abandon all spatio-temporal "metaphysical" metaphors, including (it's all done with mirrors) holography. Use the *I Ching*.

Testing it out by jumping out of a window or shooting yourself in the head may lead to your miraculous survival as a basket case or a "human vegetable." There's nothing wrong with suicide, per se, but do not "test it out."

I assert the convertibility of phenomenological order, not the characterlessness of fate.

All reasoning from cause to effect and effect to cause is founded on "custom and belief," as Hume put it, on a "harmony" with a "nature" entirely composed of impressions and ideas which cannot be demonstrated to refer, accurately or inaccurately, to any objects or relations in an external world. Hume, unfortunately, chose to call this a "problem."

There is no problem here at all for solipsistic nihilists, and this fact ought to be mentioned by the academicians who make so much of this supposedly intractable philosophic difficulty when they "do Hume" in the classroom. It may be a serious psychological problem for them but if it is, it's their own fault. If they would only get stoned out of their gourds and deny the externality of relations for a change, they would have some "real" problems to deal with, like keeping their jobs and staying out of jail.

The "principle of association of ideas" which the young Hume excitedly promised and for mysterious reasons never delivered, is the principle of solipsistic synchronicity as shown in dreams.

Hume had nothing to say about dreams. I think he saw the connection, but backed off when he realized how mad such talk would seem to his learned contemporaries who were, with one or two notable exceptions, as obtuse about all this as are most of the academic philosophers of the present day who delude themselves, out of desperation, into thinking that various specious inKantations "answer" Hume.

Nothing "answers" Hume. Hume's epistemological conclusions do not require "answers," and, as far as I know, aside from declaring that solipsism is "insane," nobody who thinks so has ever explained why they should, or why they are "insane."

What Hume's insights require is further development, and I am satisfied to see my formulations as contributions to this noble cause.

I renounce any claim to be heard founded on the foolish thesis that persons who find candles exploding in their vicinity, or who momentarily disappear from their own or others' fields of vision, are necessarily wise or good or even remarkable. The reader who is put off is a man after my own heart.

Take a thousand micrograms yourself sometime, and then look at the rising sun.

These strange and impressive experiences have no bearing whatever on the credibility of philosophic or religious assertions made by those who have them or witness them. Likewise, there is no more good reason for modern folks to believe in the philosophic ideas they might get from impressive beings from outer space than there was good reason for the Amerindians to believe that the institutionalized insanity brought to them from across the ocean by Columbus and Cortez was any better than the institutionalized insanity they had cooked up for themselves.

Technological advancement is no guarantee of wisdom or virtue, as has been amply demonstrated by the history of this century.

Nor are the opinions of an Enlightened person on this or that ethical rule, political party or economic theory necessarily any better than those of Joe Shmoe from Kokomo. Such things are McPozzm and are derived from this, that and the other thing. Enlightenment is Snazzm and concerns the true nature of all things. The Zmms are incommensurable.

When I went to bed, a big book appeared, suspended in space, about three feet in front of me.

Fine. A little light reading before falling asleep. The pages turned automatically when I finished reading the bottom lines. It was a mixture of Dylan Thomas-style poetry and prose. Unfortunately, I can't remember the content any better than I can remember Dylan Thomas' poetry, but at the time it was all as clear and definite as anything I might have looked up in the *Oxford English Dictionary*.

Every letter was illuminated in gold and the pages themselves were sky blue. A Disney-style production, very common in the second bardo.

When I got tired, I told the book to go away, which it instantly did, and I went to sleep as quickly and easily as a baby.

If all visionary experience were so obedient, agreeable and modest, there wouldn't be any problems with it. It may be that avoiding threatening and spooky experience is a matter of avoiding fear itself, which is easier for some people than it is for others.

Folklore has it that dogs attack only if one is afraid of them. Something similar operates in determining the visionary content of trips. If one is afraid, the emotion may be expressed in appropriate archetypal images. When one learns nothing horrific is involved in death/rebirth experiences (what else is new?) anxiety decreases, and visionary experience calms down and becomes part of the background, like vivid wallpaper or a dramatic sunset.

But good "control," as such, doesn't impress me as being evidence of anything except good control. Ramakrishna, far from having good control, had to have people around to prop him up and point him in the right direction, as he staggered around making profound statements and giving the Boy Scout salute. If one concentrates, as Ramakrishna did, on the most whacked-out aspects of experience, and virtually ignores everything else, there won't be much in the way of control. Good old crazy Ramakrishna, my favorite "avatar." Since he lived in the nineteenth century, there are lots of primary-source stories and even photographs, showing his life in details highly discordant with the standard myths. His most frequent demand of his disciples was that they "pass the pipe," and his diapers were always falling down.

Perhaps his wisest saying was, "When the choice is between up and down, go down." Don't push it, in other words.

The next day, Ralph asked me if I had "learned anything." I told him that all my suspicions had been confirmed. Ralph said nothing, but did not seemed pleased with my reply.

Ernie came over to where I was sitting at the kitchen table and broke an egg over my head. I backed him into a corner, where he squealed and giggled and begged for mercy. To hell with it, I decided. Anyone who would suggest to someone coming down from a big trip that shooting oneself in the head with a .45 was a harmless diversion was too crazy to be beaten on by me. Let his peer group do it. I washed the egg out of my hair and went home.

Chapter 13

FREEMEN!

Here was another illustration of the childlike improvidence of this age and people.

Back in the mountains, Sally and I moved all our belongings from Star Lake to the lodge. The physical activity required to get everything organized was exhilarating. Dealing with the hardness of material things rather than the softness and mutability of human relationships is one of the best reasons for living in the woods as far as I am concerned. It's very nice to be able to stand back from a job and say, "Well, that's not going anywhere," and know that, barring disasters, it won't.

I repaired the dock, bolted down the decking, connected the water system, repaired the old water pump under the front porch, which drew through a stop valve from the lake, fiberglassed and painted our biggest boat, a fourteen-footer, cleaned and repaired the outboard motors and, with considerable help from a seventy-five-year-old handyman who had spent his life on the lake and was full of fascinating historical anecdotes, got the generator out back in working order.

I made a trip to town once a day, landing at a floating dock behind the general store and proceeding immediately to the tiny one-room post office across the road to see if enough memberships had come in so we could make it through another day or two. The weekly average was usually enough for daily expenses: milk, cigarettes, beer, wine, kerosene, whiskey, gasoline, gin and food. The mortgage payments had to come from visitors' contributions.

If I had it to do over again, I don't think I would include a generator in a scene like Morning Glory Lodge, but depend on kerosene lamps, and a small gasoline motor for pumping water. It was nice to have music, however, and I included Susan's favorite, "Linus the Lionhearted," in every evening's entertainment, usually right after Bobby Dylan, whom I had come to appreciate after great initial resistance caused by his phony accent. "Linus" also provided an opportunity to point out to visitors the philosophic and psychological lessons one might learn from a kid's record interpreted in terms of solipsism and synchronicity. I can't cover all the visitors here but I will mention those who turned out to be important later.

They almost always showed up at night. Johnnie Merchant's big boat would appear off the end of the dock, pitching and wallowing; people waving, horn tooting. I would throw a switch which activated the generator and turned on a floodlight lashed to a tree overlooking the dock, and we would run out and take the mooring lines. We would then pull some city slickers up on the dock. They were usually stoned on grass and fortified with drinks they had just downed at Johnnie's father's motel-bar, the only such place in town. A merchant named Merchant. Having played the visitor role at Millbrook, I could fully sympathize with our visitors' mixed feelings and apprehensions, as well as with their technique for solving the problem.

When Lisa Bieberman and a chemist friend from Boston, Tord Svenson, showed up, however, there was none of the usual nonsense. Lisa and Tord were old hands at the game. Good, I thought. Now is the time to have some fun with the stuff; take maybe 50 micrograms and enjoy the lake.

Tord, who had written some flowery letters, proved to be a delightful character. A weight lifter and motorcyclist as well as a "real" chemist, he looked like he had stepped out of a movie about the Vikings of old. His interests were as broad as his chest and he was always up to date on the latest psychological, sociological and political topics and loved to talk about them. His disposition was invariably sweet and almost childlike. When we were settled in around the fireplace with beers, Tord pulled a little bottle from his pocket and proudly announced that it contained the psychedelic bufotenin, normally found in the glands of the common Australian cane toad.

He had synthesized only one dose, so he planned to take it himself before they left. Would it be OK if he and Lisa tripped on acid tomorrow? Did we want to join them? Sally had to look after the kids, but I said I would be delighted.

Lisa filled us in on the latest developments in the Psychedelian world. The *Psychedelic Review* was alive and well, as was her own mimeographed bulletin, for which she charged practically nothing. She had carried an announcement of the formation of the Church in this bulletin and was herself bee hee of Cambridge. Since Tord had bufotenin in his possession, I suggested that he take the title of "Keeper of the Divine Toad," which he accepted with glee. This post, ever since, has been reserved for "real" chemists.

Let's not forget LSD was legal, more or less, at the time. There were no federal laws and few states had anything more threatening than vague, unenforced and unenforceable laws about "dangerous drugs" in general. Upstairs in the lodge, hundreds of peyote buttons, sliced in half laterally, were drying on the floor, yet I had nothing to fear. People who joined the Church had nothing to fear. As a result, although all of us worried about the laws which we feared might come, a spirit of enthusiasm and wonderment prevailed: Was it possible life could be so fascinating and enjoyable, so free, so full of promise?

I didn't know anyone in the movement at the time who wasn't basically happy. What "paranoia" existed resulted from possession of the lesser sacrament. I told those visitors who had any to bury it back in the woods and recover and smoke it one joint at a time.

This was the harbinger of evil times to come. The oligarchy's mass media machine routinely ignores the psychological and social damage which the longest "war" in American history has done to us, while going on forever about the horrible consequences of the persecution of other minority populations, even if those persecutions have become ancient history.

If the drug laws frighten us as intended, and they certainly do, why don't we give up the criminalized practices?

The unstoned are astonished that seemingly rational people continue, under such circumstances, to insist on doing something that isn't profitable and isn't addicting.

If the sacraments are merely "recreational" drugs that produce interesting hallucinations, this is indeed puzzling.

But even a light marijuana high is much more than a recreational experience. It is a liberating and uplifting experience which tends to bring out the best in people. ("The best" in some people may not seem like much to other people.)

At the other end of the spectrum, a death/rebirth trip on LSD generates the religious emotion in its most elemental form, so pure and elemental that few know what to call it, even when they have it, not having been introduced to any pure and elemental things since infancy. Named or not named, it's hard to trivialize it, but they keep trying.

The typical liberal, but unstoned, observer cannot see any of this because religion, to the non-religious, is almost always seen as a wish system of fairy tales or mere institutionalized opinion, like political ideology. I ought to know. That's exactly what I thought from about age fourteen to thirty-six.

In the terms acceptable to the pampered house niggers of the oligarchy, who are well paid to saturate the airwaves with the official line, thereby controlling the mental lives of the field niggers, the fact that many field niggers and almost all of us swamp niggers are willing to hazard life, liberty and property for certain drugs must be some kind of mass psychopathological aberration caused directly by the drugs themselves. I think most of these people are honestly unaware of any other way to explain it. (You must first con yourself to be a truly reliable and trustworthy house nigger.)

In former times, the conflict between Sado-Judeo-Paulinians and Psychedelians would have been seen clearly for what it is, an attack by the established power of religious orthodoxy on religious novelty. Nothing new about that.

But we live in a police state in which mass deception is the chief technique of domination. Almost nothing political is what it seems to be or claims to be. Spreading sociological and psychological horseshit around in the mass media is cheap, and the public will always react with gratitude and applause if it is the kind of crap they like to hear.

The con artists and swindlers with the gold, the guns and the TV sets at their command can hide the truth from the public and, to some extent, from themselves, behind a smokescreen of benign concern for the "mental health" of their victims and the protection, not of certain institutions they control, but of the "social fabric" or some such seeming universal good.

Whose social fabric, yours or mine? That's the real question.

If no laws banning LSD had been passed and cannabis had been legalized in the early years covered by this book, the quality of American life would have undergone a radical and pervasive revolutionary change for the better. Large areas where *nacht und nebel* now prevail would be governed instead by sweetness and light, as some places are in fact so governed in the European Union today.

For the oligarchy and the established churches and the military-industrial complex, the drug laws have worked very well, not only in fending off the dreaded specter of European welfare statism (or "socialism" or "social democracy," or whatever you want to call it) but in virtually abolishing the Bill of Rights and constitutional government in general, and dethroning rationality itself as the guiding principle in public life in the United States.

The fundamental beliefs of Psychedelians have changed very little since the days I am describing, in the sense that the answers to a questionnaire about attitudes towards drugs would be much different now than then, but the prevailing spirit and the everyday expectations, fears, wishes and attitudes that make up that spirit have been radically perverted because of the unrelenting persecutions to which we have been subjected.

Having been brought up in a professional religious household in which the history of religion was table talk, I expected something like this from the start, while hoping that I was wrong, but most Psychedelians at that time thought of the government as a benign but temporarily mistaken parent. All we had to do was "be nice," cite all the objective evidence and ancient precedents, appeal to the First Amendment, and all would be well. Lisa was a classic example of that frame of mind.

The following morning dawned warm and blue as usual with just enough of a breeze to make the lake scintillate the way a good lake should. After we had all swallowed our pills, Lisa plunked herself down on the living room floor and indicated that she expected Tord and me to join her.

"Lisa," Tord said, "it's beautiful out there. Come on, you don't really want to spend the whole trip indoors, do you?"

Despite his efforts to get Lisa to move, Tord didn't seem very surprised by her assumption that we would all be delighted to spend the day squatting on the floor. I could hardly believe it. I wasn't going to stay inside, no matter what Tord and Lisa did.

"But I believe in staying in one place during a trip," Lisa said.

"That's in Cambridge," Tord answered. "You don't have to worry about other people here. We're out in the woods."

"Well, OK," Lisa said, getting up. "This will be a new experience for me."

"I'm jealous," Sally said from the kitchen where Klytie was getting cereal spooned into her mouth. "I promise I'll watch the kids next time," I said.

Although I pretended insouciance, I felt apprehensive. If another colossal visionary trip was coming up, I might be better off on the floor, but it seemed to me that if I was ever to enjoy acid the way I enjoyed grass and hash, I would have to change set and setting the way Learian doctrine indicated.

I was glad I did, because it worked. For the first time I had the kind of trip described in Huxley's *The Doors of Perception*. No visions, just an incredible heightening of awareness. Tim, when in this condition, developed a variety of ploys for avoiding unwelcome visitors. One of his favorites, which never failed to amuse the rest of us, was to say, "Sorry, I can't talk to you now; I'm a cloud of energy." That's exactly how I felt as I took Tord and Lisa on a tour of the lake, although I didn't need to use it as a reason not to communicate because the only other people around were Tord and Lisa, who were just as stoned as I was.

Lisa, once she was out in the open air, fell right into the spirit of things and wandered around freely at our various stops along the shore, exclaiming over this or that natural wonder one would pass by routinely in a normal, stupid, blind and constipated state of consciousness. Our last stop was Birch Island, directly across from Morning Glory Lodge. There was a log cabin on it, surrounded by trees. The owner, a mysterious figure with, I had been told, a heavy Russian accent, never visited during the months we lived on the lake. I hoped to buy it, or find a fellow Psychedelian who would buy it. I told Tord about my plans:

"What we'll do is prepare visitors for their first trip at the lodge," I said. "Then, when we think they're ready, we'll have a boat waiting at the dock early in the morning with a mysterious, hooded figure at the oars. The boat will be painted black and have poles fore and aft with weird banners and flags and black gauze billowing out all over. We'll have someone on the island ring a bell or beat a gong during the ride over, starting when the rising sun first touches the island."

"Yeah, and just before the boat leaves a marijuana goddess will come running down to the boat and pass around a crystal goblet of champagne with acid in it. They all take a sip, and then the boat leaves for the Dawn of Nothing."

Tord, a great giggler despite his bulk, giggled appreciatively.

"What kind of a scene will you have over here?" he asked, as we tied up the boat.

"I'm not sure. Maybe we should say there are several people on the island who will assist them but actually leave the place deserted. Let them make up their own people. No, too paranoia inducing. I suppose we could just take turns. Everyone who lives here would take shifts on the island to look after people taking their first trips."

While Tord and I discussed such plans for the development of the scene, all of which required money we didn't have, Lisa wandered off and then called us down to a mass of shelving rock on the north side of the island which served as a natural dock. She was sitting next to a puddle in the stone, peering into it intently.

"What's that?" she asked, pointing to something in the puddle. Tord and I got down to nose level and looked. Some kind of tiny creature was swimming around frantically in the puddle. An immature tadpole, probably. It was hard to make out any distinguishing features.

Lisa was fascinated. She didn't want to leave.

I rose to my feet and, adopting a mock-dramatic manner, asked, "Ah, you know what this means, Lisa, do you not?"

She didn't.

Gesturing grandly towards the puddle, Lisa, the rocks and the lake, I gave Lisa the benefit of my interpretation: "This tiny creature, trapped here in its puddle and separated from the great waters beyond by these masses of rock, is your personality!"

Lisa seemed a bit stunned but, sweeping metaphors being her bread and butter, so to speak, she seemed willing to entertain the notion. She nodded her head.

"Yeah, that's right Lisa," Tord said. "Do you want me to catch this little fella in my hands and put him in the lake? It won't hurt him."

Lisa gave the idea a lot of thought, but decided against it. The little fella liked it right where he was, she concluded. It is best not to interfere with the mysterious workings of Mother Nature, and all of that. We went back to the lodge.

The tadpole incident was the peak of the trip for Lisa. Mine came when, during lunch, I tried to play the usual baby-style games with Klytie, who was burbling away in her high chair in her characteristically happy fashion. Klytie took after Sally who, leaving aside her hang-ups, was a warm-hearted, good-natured, spontaneous person, while Susan was more like her father, intent on figuring out what was going on instead of simply making the most of it.

Playing with Klytie turned out to be more than I had bargained for. I was astounded at the complexity and virtuosity of the wordless games she played. It seemed that Klytie understood, in some weird way, all the implications of what was taking place, and was delighted to stage-manage the whole affair. I felt like I was talking to some fantastically brilliant creature from another planet, rather than a human baby. She was also hilariously funny. It finally got to be too much for me. I began to suspect that I might spend the rest of my life sitting around having conversations with babies, as St. Francis did with his birds, so I suggested that we all go swimming, which we did.

Tord's bufotenin trip, a couple days later, was unspectacular, at least from the viewpoint of his audience. He went out to the end of the dock, meditated for an hour or so, and then drank the contents of his vial. To collect bufotenin, I understand, one subjects the Australian cane toad, *Bufo marinus,* to a weak electrical current, and the resultant very dangerous exudation, which is a cocktail of poisonous compounds and must be greatly diluted and imbibed in experimental sips, drips into a dish. (If you try this, wear safety glasses.) Tord had the pure stuff. He stayed where he was for about four hours. I interrupted him once, about halfway through.

"How's it going, Tord?" I asked.

"Well, it's interesting. I'm convinced there is nothing on the other side of those hills over there."

I congratulated Tord. A profound half-truth, in my opinion.

That was it. The trip lasted four hours and seemed, as interpreted by Tord, to be standard Yogacara Buddhism, which is the eau de parfum of the best doctrine, but about the most you can expect from most people. Even this after-shave lotion was too alarming for Tord, however, as we shall see. Many are called but few are chosen.

The "Void," or any one of the many other terms meaning the same thing, is rarely mentioned in casual Psychedelian converse, although it is the central concept of the best classical teachings. People tend to shrink back in fear and trembling from the idea of utter nothingness.

Tord, a sweet guy in a desperate search for love and warmth, simply couldn't take it. Before he and Lisa left, Tord told a story about one of his experiments with acid that seemed to sum it all up.

He took about a thousand micrograms of Sandoz one Saturday night and then went to a neighborhood Irish bar in Boston on his motorcycle to experience social interaction while manifesting a play opportunity situation, or something. Once there, he announced he could drink every man in the place under the table.

Tord, who was not a heavy drinker, then proceeded to prove his point to the dozen or so Irishmen who eagerly accepted his challenge and his free drinks.

"I must have put away a quart at least, Art," Tord said, chortling merrily at the recollection. "The last thing I remember was seeing all these guys crowded into a corner while I was advancing on them. One of them kept yelling, 'Throw him Ernie! Throw him Ernie!' The next thing I remember is waking up on the kitchen floor out back the next morning with the bartender and the cook stepping over me. I didn't have a hangover and there wasn't a mark on me. Never found out if they threw me Ernie either."

Tord wanted "involvement," at almost any price.

I hated to see Tord and Lisa leave, but they both had jobs.

When it was Sally's turn to trip a week or two later, two visitors having arrived whom we mistakenly considered to be our type, we learned that being at the lodge was no insurance against having spooky or frightening experiences.

The visitors were Ed Rosenfeld, at that time boo hoo of the West Side, and his girlfriend. They hadn't been in the house fifteen minutes before Ed pulled out a vial of tablets and asked if it was OK if they dropped. It was around two in the afternoon, but I didn't know then that the middle of the day is a chancy time to start a trip, because you come down in the middle of the night. It's best to start late in the evening, so your return to the world of ordinary game routines coincides with the rising of the sun, or in the early morning, so you are well down by your ordinary bedtime.

Aside from the shock produced by hearing the crazy laugh of a loon flying over the lake early in the trip (thereafter, I warned visitors to expect unearthly shrieks as the shades of night were falling), Ed and girl had no particular difficulty, but Sally, who was unusually quiet for the first few hours, went through a classic death-rebirth in our bedroom as soon as it was dark. As long as she was agitated, the phenomenal world continued to exist for her. As soon as she relaxed, it disappeared. We all sat on the bed holding on to her and saying the usual reassuring words. After half an hour of flipping back and forth, she came out of it and the rest of the trip proceeded along normal lines in the living room, but Sally remained shaken for hours.

When everyone was down, Sally and I drove Ed and girl to Saranac Lake to catch a bus. The talk was almost entirely about death. Ed described several DMT trips he had taken in New York and the effects sounded similar to my peak experiences and, to Sally, a lot like what she had been through the night before, but so fleeting in duration as to be in a different class altogether.

Perceptually, Sally was in great shape. The world, she said, looked brighter, sharper, and generally more delightful than it had in a long time.

The question was the usual one: Is it "real"? Sally and I had talked about this before, but it's one thing to indulge in philosophic speculation while smoking a joint or two and it's another thing altogether to consider certain fundamental questions after having just died and been reborn on 500 micrograms of the Supreme Sacrament. The images summoned up have a certain immediacy and familiarity unknown to most philosophers. A veritable clamor is heard in the forefront of one's mind that these issues be given prompt attention, as if they were long overdue bills or a toothache.

Many virtually illiterate but natively intelligent lads and lassies rush to the library after their first death-rebirth experiences as if their lives depended on it. Similarly, literate people long sunk in naive realism will suddenly awaken to the fact that "naive" is actually the right word for it, and they will reexamine their prejudices.

In the early days of the movement this aspect of things was generally recognized, even in the mass media. Writers, painters, musicians, scientists and even mathematicians testified to the stimulating effect of psychedelic experience on their creative work. It was taken for granted that intelligent people who took LSD would develop a serious interest in philosophic thought. Tastes in literature and art would move up a notch or two also.

Does one "really" die on a death/rebirth trip?

The reason people doubt that they have "really" died is that afterwards they "come back" and people tell them they were never absent for a moment. Furthermore, they witness other people, who later say they died, being right there, breathing, the whole time. Supporting the above arguments, however, is the unspoken assumption of the externality of relations. One's life or death is thought of as something within another, greater continuum of space and time. Reincarnation, as it is ordinarily thought of, is but a special case of this. The entity, whatever its relative power, still exists within a continuum with an independent dynamism.

If the externality of relations is denied, on the other hand, there is no reason, Snazzm, to consider a death-rebirth experience as more delusional than anything else around.

I have as yet to hear anyone on a death-rebirth trip express a wish to come back as a cherub in a world of pink clouds or anything like it. Every now and then, on or off trips, people will drop dead and stay dead, requiring the disposal of the corpse, but what of it? If people didn't come and go in dreams, things would become unbearably crowded and crazy, and so it is in "real" life. A dream jammed with people who never go away is as good a vision of Hell as I can imagine. A sort of Bangladesh of the mind, but Bangladesh is the Bangladesh of the mind.

These "problems" about death remind me of Dick Alpert's question on our walk at Millbrook, shortly after my Enlightenment, "Well, I do have a life of my own, don't I?"

Why ask me?

All I know about Dick, or anyone or anything else, in waking or sleeping life, is what my sense impressions tell me. And I'm content to have Dick, or anyone else, think about me the same way.

I wish they would. Peace on Earth might be the result.

When things become extraordinarily non-dualistic or "magical" and the usual guideposts to what is (to be presumed as) external and what is (to be presumed as) internal vanish, some people will freeze, freak out, become paranoid, and so forth, particularly if they recall no previous experience with the state. That kind of stuff cannot be called a reduction of suffering, per se, but the experience of being in this condition and surviving can demonstrate that one is a lot tougher, mentally, than one thought one was, and that can lead to a great reduction in suffering.

The Slobovenoid Blobovenoidal variety of monism is no better than conventional supernaturalism for handling this kind of stress and answering these kinds of questions. Just as God may be drunk or insane, so your "Higher Self" may be drunk or insane. There's lots of evidence to support either diagnosis.

If He is, and you believe you are merely His creature or holographic fragment or appendage or outpost or whatever, you are not in an enviable position. If one is a solipsist, however, the miserable history of mankind need not oppress, for all of that may have been one's last and final nightmare. How does one know hell has not frozen over? Why assume otherwise? Is there any good reason why one's *antakarana* functions should continue to be drunk or insane?

Perhaps, if one switches from booze to the psychedelic sacraments, the whole world, which is one's dream, will become stoned also, which would be an improvement over its history as recorded in both supernaturalist and secular literature. Perhaps, if one, as a personality, tries to be more honest and kind, the world in general, in the long run, will become more honest and kind also.

Give it time. So long as one insists on the illusion of externality with a McPozzm world and everything it entails, there will be ups and downs, *antakarana* function or no *antakarana* function.

Sally's psychedelic experience did not overcome her imprints and conditioning and since I hadn't yet invented the Zmms, I didn't have the terminology to make the most important distinctions clear to her and, even if I had, living with me at that time required radical changes which Sally was not young enough, or free enough, or rich enough, or brave enough, or crazy enough, or stoned enough, to make. Oh, well.

The rest of the summer passed in a succession of neat episodes. Visitors would arrive at our dock, one kind of drama or another would develop, and then they would leave from the same dock, usually happier and perhaps, so some claimed, wiser.

A couple of good old transcendentalist boys showed up: a wino professor of English literature from Canton and Walter Houston Clark, at that time a full professor of theology at Andover

Newton Theological School, which had been founded by Calvinists to combat the Unitarian heresy of Harvard Divinity. Clark looked and talked like Dr. Spock, and his buddy reminded me of Jack Spratt, but of a somewhat older vintage. All they wanted to do was shoot the breeze, look the place over, and perform their sacred function as general gadabouts and learned gossips of Psychedelia. Fine with me.

They had met a few months earlier, they told me, as enthusiastic recruits to what I thought was an extremely interesting experiment. Who conducted it, I can't remember. Some quasi-academic association, I think, of which there were several at the time, and I'm happy to report that one of them did something useful. The subjects, all mature and well-educated adults, took increasingly large doses of LSD every day for several days until they "maxed out." The big surprise at the time was that after three days or so no dose, no matter how large, had any effect whatever on anyone. It's a "trigger drug" all right, as this and many other trials have shown, and so it seems are all major psychedelics. The actual sacraments are in the brain, awaiting activation.

According to his buddy, with whom I had one or two private conversations as the day wore on, Clark was a "millionaire" (why is this term routinely applied to both those who have the capital and those who have the income?), but also a skinflint of the old school. "You'll never get a dime out of him," said the Blake expert, "so save your breath."

Unabashed selfishness is in the grand old Transcendentalist tradition. Since "everyone" is an "aspect" (or something) of the Giant Blob, everyone must be, somehow, getting what he deserves, Blobwise, sort of. Neither justice nor charity (nor truth, in my opinion) is an important idea among Oversoulians.

"Do not tell me, as a good man did today, of my obligation to put all poor men in a good situation. Are they my poor? I tell thee, thou foolish philanthropist, that I grudge the dollar, the dime, the cent, I give to such men as do not belong to me and to whom I do not belong," wrote Emerson.

No wonder Ralph Waldo, like Tim, did so well on the lecture

circuit. He made people "feel good about themselves." If you tell people (who can afford the price of tickets) what they want to hear, they will come out for it.

I did get more than a dime out of Clark, however. Along with other notables on Lisa Bieberman's hit list, he put up a couple hundred towards my bail when I was busted in Florida. I didn't pay him back right away and he neglected to mention the Neo-American Church in the *Encyclopedia Britannica* article he wrote on psychedelic drugs and religion shortly thereafter. The Church of the Awakening, of which Clark was a director, and which hoisted the white flag around '70 or '71 after losing some feeble administrative law skirmishes for tax exemption, was mentioned. In the years to come, Clark requested a few dozen small favors of me and I obliged him at no cost, which I figured made us come out about even, pretty much.

I think I irritated Clark for the same reasons I irritated Lisa and other academical refugees from the classic New England seance circuit. I wasn't playing by the rules. I wasn't trying to find common ground. I ignored the canon. I showed little or no interest in the various "psychedelic" groups then around which derived from the traditions of the Higher Learning in America and were mostly composed of college teachers and always led by them. Based largely on personal experience, I had developed a very Veblenish view of the professorate and of scholarly traditions and customs in the U.S. of A. in general.

However high-minded and sincere the individuals involved, I was convinced that these associations would dissolve on receipt of the first stern memo from the Dean or the Provost or the President or the Chancellor or maybe even the janitor, and so they did. (I was very pleasantly surprised when these people actually put up a fight over Vietnam.)

But it was pleasant to associate with book-reading gentlemen for a change, summer soldiers and sunshine patriots though they may have been. Emerson, so long as no donations were requested, was a reliable cheerer-upper in any kind of weather and among all classes and conditions of mankind, and Clark and pal were most amiable also.

Shortly before their visit, Sally and I had been ripped off by a mating pair of Jewish heroin addicts from the old-style druggie world, whom we foolishly trusted, simply because they talked like Psychedelians, to deliver her coin collection to a dealer in New York. People of this kind had a field day for a while. Pickings had been slim, and then an enormous flock of starry-eyed lambs had appeared in their midst, ready to be fleeced. But most of the people we met that summer were, like ourselves, harmless unless tormented.

Sally and the kids left for Manhasset early in August. Her father had died shortly after we bought Morning Glory Lodge, only a few days after he had retired from the museum to his version of the great American dream, a charming Cape Cod which descended in three levels to front on a small beach on Gardiner's Bay near Southold, Long Island, complete with red sails in the sunset, etc. He died of a fast stroke, standing in the watery morning sunshine, while on the phone with the movers.

Her mother was selling the new house and moving to Florida. Sally's help was needed. Perhaps we would move to Florida for the winter also. Since there was no money available to winterize the lodge, and Sally was opposed to staying anyway, it didn't seem to me I had much choice, but I was damned if I was going to leave before things got too chilly for comfort.

September is often the best month in the North Country. Most of the tourists are gone, the foliage becomes so magnificent as to verge on ostentation, and the weather is delightful. It's usually warm enough to swim during the day, but clear and cool enough at night so the stars appear in overpowering numbers when one steps out to take a piss or goes down to the water's edge to think something over.

After Sally's departure, with a boatload of lesbians from New York City, who had enjoyed freaking freely in the woods like the Amazons of old, I had a few days to myself.

Then Kimberly Harrison and Stove ("Ah is all stoved in, man.") arrived, followed by Steve Newell and then Mike and Gai Duncan. It was an entertaining group.

Stove and Kimberly had a strange story to tell. They were both from Miami, where Kimberly, a classic blonde beauty, plied her trade as a Miami Beach hooker. She had met Stove after he had freaked out on the most colossal and one of the weirdest bummers I had heard about up to that time. It involved hordes of fleas appearing in his house on some crazy but exact schedule, not being able to take a shower because the water wouldn't touch his skin, and aimless wanderings during which he was pursued by flocks of blackbirds and was picked up on the road by kindly spades driving white cars who knew all about him even though he had never seen any of them before in his life.

Kimberly, who had heard about the lodge from a friend of Ed Rosenfeld, had driven Stove up to be cooled out, paying all the bills along the way, in the ancient and honorable tradition of the whore with a heart of gold. She loved every variety of psychedelic drug, and never had anything but splendid and happy experiences while stoned.

Steve Newell was something else, also. An alcoholic with a large private income and a family he frequently deserted to go on month-long binges in Mexican whorehouses and amnesic tours of the USA in his big, black Thunderbird, Steve had discovered peyote about a year prior to his visit and, as he put it, had "forgotten to drink."

His kick was magic, pure and simple. He used Renard's *Grimoire* to summon up demons, travel around in his "astral body," and so on. He tripped alone in every one of the cabins and reported that each one had a different set of entities, rather ungeheimlich in the North, but decent sorts in the South, which, I noted, correlated with the quality of the plumbing.

Mike and Gai Duncan, not yet married, whom I found sleeping in the grass in front of one of the cabins one morning (not having noticed the arrival of the boat the night before on account of being stupefied), were what I would later come to recognize as classic "heads." They were ragged and appeared to be poor but, it turned out, were well-off, having incomes from trust funds adequate to do pretty much as they liked.

Mike displayed, in high relief, every characteristic of the head, or "freak" or "kid" subculture. "Hippy?" The media and media mongers like Tim used the term constantly but the Psychedelians I knew in the '60s almost never used it to refer to themselves. For good or for ill, whatever this population was doing Mike and

Gai did also. And they could be counted on to do it early, not being simply imitative, and to do it in a big way.

It's hard to name any enthusiasm which enjoyed a transitory popularity in the kid culture in which Mike and Gai did not, at one time or another, participate. For several years, they zoomed around the country in a crazy-quilt pattern, trying every psychedelic drug available and visiting every guru they heard about. The earthly perfection which they sought was always just over the horizon. They wanted someone to tell them exactly what they wanted to hear and to transfer something to them. They didn't know what this was but they knew what it wasn't. They expected, upon hearing The Message and/or getting whatever It was, to be elevated beyond all mundane cares. Their conversation was almost exclusively about drugs and gurus. They were pursuing happiness with the zeal with which the English country gentry is said to pursue foxes.

I approved of this, sort of, but found it almost impossible to talk to Mike without losing my temper. He would ask me exactly those questions which I wanted to hear, and I would answer them with a feeling that I was accomplishing something important. Mike would listen attentively and respond in such a way that I was sure he had grasped my meaning perfectly. Then, often as not, a few minutes later he would quote with approval some moronic, supernaturalistic tripe he had picked up from a trashy pamphlet somewhere, thereby demonstrating that my efforts had been a waste of breath.

Michael and the class he represented so accurately likewise, lacked the primary requirement for all successful prospectors for gold: the ability to recognize it when you have it in hand. They had read too many dumb books and listened to too many shithouse rumors describing the stuff as, perhaps, heavenly blue in color, at least when Venus was in Aquarius, and as having a powerful odor of sanctity and cant about it at all times. And if the current claimant didn't fit those specs, something was wrong somewhere.

Sages are not generally honored in their own country, because their countrymen are so full of self-doubt they cannot believe anyone who speaks their language and lives the way they live can be worth much, and so it was with Michael. Whatever glittered at the bottom of his pan had to be fool's gold, while anything he couldn't see, but was told, or had read, existed in some exotic place, was most likely the genuine article, or at least he thought so until he got there and whatever it was became familiar rather than exotic and therefore not good enough for him, more or less by definition.

But, despite my irritation, or perhaps partly because of it, I did better than the average guru with both Mike and Gai, and I must also mention that Mike's most characteristic remark was, "Well, since we're already this stoned, why not have one more and get really stoned?" This is an attitude which compensates in my system of bookkeeping for a multitude of sins.

I spent a lot of time talking to Stove, whose crazy adventures fascinated me. In former years, I would have regarded him as a "well-defended" paranoid and let it go at that. He would have been considered "well-defended" because he did not, most of the time, do anything particularly bizarre or fail to handle the routines of ordinary life in an acceptable manner. Stove's sense of humor, for example, was intact. He had classic Capricornian saturnine features and a deep, rich voice to match, and his favorite gag was to reply to any blithe or optimistic statement made in his vicinity with a drawn out "Oh, yea-a-a-a-a-ah?" which expressed his earnest conviction that all those who saw the future of Psychedelianism in a positive way were doomed to disillusionment.

"Listen, Stove," I said at one point, "why don't we build you a tree house out back? Then, when visitors come we can tell them we have this hermit who will answer one and only one question for each group of visitors. They should take their time and work out some question that's really complex and covers everything. Then they have to prostrate themselves under your tree and go through some kind of mumbo-jumbo to get you to come out on your porch or limb or whatever. You don't say anything. Just listen gravely as the question is read out. Then you say, 'Oh, yea-a-a-a-a-ah?' and go back in your house."

Stove thought this was a good idea, but he didn't want to be separated from Kimberly, even though he had been impotent since his strange adventures began.

One quiet afternoon, while Stove was on the porch reading, Kimberly came upstairs and knelt on the floor next to my chair, where I had been alternately writing and looking out over the lake. She had a problem. It wasn't that Stove was "uptight," she explained. Far from it. Night after night she would apply every devise of titillation known to a class-A Miami Beach hooker, but Stove would merely gaze at her fondly and compassionately from a million miles away. Resting her lovely head on my knee, Kimberly drawled in her soft Texan accents (her father, she said, was a big shipper in Port Arthur), "Ah jus' don understan' it, Ahthur. Ahm known on the beach for mah haid jobs. Wah, nobody can resist a good haid job!"

Although this was clearly an invitation, Kimberly delivered it as casually as if she had been offering me a stick of chewing gum.

"Well, I can resist it if the young lady in question has a boyfriend who is likely to walk up the stairs at any moment, Kimberly," I said. "As far as Stove is concerned, he thinks you're an angel or something. If he allowed himself to have dirty ideas about you, it would break the spell."

This analysis went over well, probably because it was correct.

I had a private trip with Kimberly a couple nights later, or at least she had a trip and I just smoked a lot of hashish while she told me the story of her life, which hadn't been all that bad, really. When the sun came up, we went down to the dock where, in a matter of two or three seconds, a fish jumped out of the water at our feet, two ducks landed a little further out, and a big tree fell, with a long, rending crash, in the woods right behind the lodge.

This was but one of the many times I did not take LSD at Morning Glory Lodge and elsewhere.

Stove came down from one of the cabins right after the tree crashed, and reclaimed his prize. Her honor had not been stained in any way. Poor Kim, whom I liked enormously, probably thought she was losing her touch, but the fact was I thought she was pretty inhuman myself, and therefore invulnerable, and therefore not a natural object of masculine desire, or something. That's a pretty vague "fact," I've got to admit.

Stove, more often than he wanted, was still having visions with eyes closed and occasionally with eyes open, such as movie-style Indians running through the woods and similar unenlightening absurdities. I told him about the "winkle buttons" I had been seeing, off and on, ever since my Kundalini experience.

These were colored, illuminated discs and sometimes sharp glaiks of bright light which appeared for one heartbeat or so from three to ten feet away from me in space. I still get them, although not as frequently as I did in those days. They seem to function as exclamation points or question marks to what I'm thinking or hearing or reading. Most often they are blue, contain many parallel horizontal lines, and are about two inches in diameter, although once, just before coming upon a bear in the road during a night drive from Cranberry to Star Lake, I saw one as big as a dinner plate over the hood of the car, which made me slow down, thereby averting minor or major damage not only to me and my car but to the bear as well.

Stove was delighted to hear about these apparitions, since they were evidence a few pseudo-hallucinations here and there were not necessarily fatal, and he listened to my discourse on the subject of synchronicity with intense attention. He had interpreted all the synchronicity he had experienced in terms of vast and impersonal occult forces contending for possession of his soul, in the worst Judaic tradition. Monstrous forces were at work, guiding the historical process and playing with men as if they were toys. I showed him how these events could be interpreted in an entirely different way. I was talking about Snazzm, as opposed to Fazzm, although I hadn't invented the terms yet.

It's important, when talking to someone in this kind of fix, to never question the genuineness of the events themselves. I don't think there is much difference between ordinary, down-home paranoids with cheek of tan and people on paranoid trips. Almost all delusional paranoids were labeled "paranoid schizophrenic" in the days when I worked as a psychologist, but most of them were not schizophrenic at all. It has become pretty clear that schizophrenia is a biochemical brain disease. Paranoia, on the other hand, is often entirely "functional" in origin. No disease process need be involved.

Paranoids are most often just ordinary people who have noticed the synchronistic aspect of events in their lives, and made the worst of it, frequently as a consequence of supernaturalist ideation instilled in childhood. They can be talked out of it simply through the use of reason.

If you're in the business and dealing with institutionalized paranoids who have "acted out," try getting three or four of them together around a table. Have them read sentences in succession from the pages of books picked at random to show how coincidences will, up to a point, fit almost any system, if you're looking out for them. This kind of demonstration can snap some paranoids out of it in one easy lesson.

Steve Newell was an entirely different kind of guy. He liked it in the dark and spooky woodlands of Weir, and his "magic" was unusual and, in a way, admirable because his attitude towards it was completely lacking in the pseudo-scientific double-talk and fantastic ontological categorical speculations which pass for philosophy among most occultists. Steve arrived, naturally, on a pitch-dark, windy, rainy night. After he had settled in he let us all know his idea of a good time was to walk through walls and talk to the dead, or at least to beings that did not conform to the usual restrictions of time and space. Could we buy that? Did we think it was crazy?

I responded with my standard "life is a dream" pitch. "You can go on any kind of trip you like. I don't think you will learn much by doing that kind of stuff, but maybe that's what you have to learn," I concluded.

Steve was relieved at my response. That was how he saw it too. About once a week on average, Steve did the things one reads about in occultist literature, the kinds of things most of the authors of such works have no first-hand experience with at all, but only dabble with and babble about, pretending all the while to be "objective" and "scientific" although very few of them even know the meaning of the words.

All occultist-supernaturalist philosophy is based on the fear of death and a wish for personal immortality. In my experience, the difference between people like Steve who practice "magic" and the standard occultists who only talk about it is that the former concede, based on their experience, what the latter frantically deny, based on their ignorance: that the whole thing is mental. The genuine practitioner will admit that walking through a wall and walking down to the corner to buy a six-pack are both illusions, thereby making ordinary life more strange and "astral" life more ordinary.

People like Steve have grasped the basic principle of Enlightenment but are having serious trouble with the application. Supernaturalists, on the other hand, attempt to preserve "reality" as an ontological base, and therefore imagine themselves pulled out of shape somehow, or their memories transferred from one box to another, as it were, within a mechanical universe. All they actually save are vague images of moving, labeled blobs, or, to use the term many of them prefer, "souls."

As adventure and entertainment, rather than philosophy, a spook show every now and then has its place. And, given the moons and the loons and everything, an isolated lodge in the Adirondacks, in which a heterogeneous group of people, until recently strangers to one another, are gathered together after nightfall for the avowed purpose of undergoing strange changes, is not the kind of place in which to turn on fluorescent lights and listen to the radio, rather than discuss, and perhaps even practice, some of the spookier diversions which such a setting suggests to the imagination.

If communicating with the elves is your trip, well, give my regards to the King of the Elves! But in the morning, let's go fishing.

An astrologer who had named himself "Yossarian" after the hero of *Catch-22*, and Anna (I never learned her last name), his newly acquired and extraordinarily voluptuous mistress, showed up and stayed for about a week. They tripped on morning glory seeds, properly prepared, and had a good one, by both reports, mostly private, but partly public, down by a campfire near the shore. Yossarian, however, like most astrologers I have known, showed various paranoid inclinations then and more later, on those infrequent occasions when I ran into him here and there. He didn't think he could hold on to Anna, and, as it turned out, he was right.

At the Ashram in Arizona, after Millbrook broke up, Anna switched to Ted Druck, who came to Millbrook with the Ashram in 1966. Fed up with abuse from Haines in Arizona, Ted and Anna moved to Tucson, where they were a big help to me during one of the lowest periods of my life. Hearts of gold in both cases, and good examples of why LSD should not be restricted to the intellectual elite. It can be of enormous service to regular folks also, who have as much right to practice their religions as anyone else.

I usually stopped in at Merchant's bar in the morning after picking up mail and groceries, which I stowed in the boat. (Another nice thing about the North Country in those days was that you didn't have to worry much about petty theft.) After I had taken the first sip of my usual Michelob draft, Charlie Merchant, who looked like an old Chinese warlord, minus the pigtail, told me there had been a call for me from Millbrook. I was supposed to call back.

When I was connected with the Big House, where a pay phone had been installed at the foot of the stairs, Tim got on the line. He and Billy Hitchcock would be flying up in Billy's plane that afternoon. Could I meet them at the Tupper Lake field?

Certainly!

Even Charlie Merchant got excited. He was old enough to remember newspaper stories about Billy's father, the polo-playing champ of the '30s. Dr. Leary, the Mephisto of the modern world, would also be worth looking over. I promised to stop in before we went over to MGL.

I boated to the lodge and picked up Mike Duncan, and we drove to Tupper Lake, but not before I bought a bottle of Wilson's from Charlie.

Tim and Billy arrived on schedule, but so did a vast bank of black clouds, apparently fulfilling an assignment from Olympus to fuck up my most important visit of the summer. By the time we got back to Charlie's bar it was raining cats and dogs. Spears of water were dancing all over the shrouded lake. Mike and I were already smashed on whiskey and stoned on grass. Tim seemed preoccupied and neither smoked nor drank. Billy, since he was flying, wisely refrained. When we got in the boat, Tim crawled under the small covered area in front but even Tim was soaked by the time we came bounding and sliding into the dock. In rough weather it was no joke to land on a lee shore.

Aside from one hell of a roaring blaze in the fireplace, practically nothing notable occurred during Tim and Billy's short, wet sojourn at the cabin. The whole thing reminded me of the God-awful ministerial visits to members of the congregation I had to sit through as a child. Here we were, a collection of screwballs such as the world seldom witnessed, and the conversation was downright forced. I found out later that Tim was in the process of losing his fair-haired beauty to a bald-headed, fake-Tantric specialist in coitus reservatus. Billy, unstoned, was worrying about the weather. Mike and I were just plain drunk. I think everyone else was overawed.

The professional in the religion racket will not be surprised to learn that Mike and Gai, whom I treated bluntly, to put it mildly, out-contributed Billy Hitchcock, whom I treated with kid gloves, by about 20-to-1 in the years that followed. I hope they became Enlightened Beings with auras at least six feet in diameter (very convenient for stunning mosquitoes) and nice beach houses in Hawaii for every member of the family.

Indeed, Mike and Gai became my salvation, which is one of the reasons I have never given up entirely on fake Indians and the occultist multitudes, although, any day now, I intend to discard all hopes of big bucks from the filthy rich.

After closing up Morning Glory Lodge for the winter, all visitors having departed (Kimberly had to sell the air conditioner and the radio out of her car to make it back to Miami with Stove), I set out for Southold in the hope that Mary Francis could be persuaded not to move to Florida. The new house was big enough for all of us and, it seemed to me, might make a great setting for a groovy-guru-type Psychedelian psychologist during the winter. Nothing I had heard about Florida sounded attractive to me, whereas the "Far East," Long Island variety, was still a wild and romantic place in many ways, with the kind of population mix that suited my inclinations and ambitions besides.

I stopped at Millbrook on the way down.

The place was loaded with visitors. Starting from the Big House, cars were lined up along the road halfway to the Gatehouse.

Tim gave me a copy of his *Psychedelic Prayers,* which had just come out. He inscribed it to "Art Kleps, a laughing man with a bad reputation," one of the types listed as "trustworthy" in the back of the book. I liked both the inscription and the "prayers" themselves, which Tim claimed were "based" on the *Tao Te Ching.* I have doubts about that, but this book was a step up from the *Tibetan Book of the Dead.*

Tim wanted to hear everything I could tell him about Kimberly, who had stopped at Millbrook for a few days after leaving the lodge and had made a big hit with him. He also wanted reports on some more or less routine cases, usually couples, whom he had sent up to take their first trips away from the Millbrook maelstrom during the summer.

When I told him acid seemed to function more as an aphrodisiac than a key to the Mysteries for some of them, he was enormously pleased. Millbrook was definitely on a sex kick, and it was, one might say, an official sex kick, as if Hugh Hefner had taken over. Dick Alpert, who seemed to be enjoying himself enormously, was specializing in producing a sort of Reichian transcendence of "body-armor" and Tim, never content with ordinary objectives, was talking in terms of 1,000,000 "orgasms" a second. His *Playboy* interview is worth reading, as are many other *Playboy* interviews from the era. They convey the spirit of the times better than any of the "social histories" published since.

Personally, and all of my remarks on this subject are based on my own experience and the testimony of friends, I have found acid to be as sexually distracting as it is intensifying, but the lesser sacrament almost always seems to encourage people to screw like mink if they are so inclined to begin with.

Although one should keep in mind that grass highs often have more of a "mini trip" quality for people who have had major LSD experiences, as contrasted with those who have not had such experience, and all kinds of other class and individual variations abound, cannabis, in general, takes second place only to nitrous oxide as an aphrodisiac. Motels owners should provide both substances, as an alternative to overindulgence in booze, and thus do well while doing good, and make life more pleasant for their housekeepers also.

Acid intensifies immediate experience like crazy, but is much harder to control. One is directed not only to certain preselected charms, but to all and any charms around, and charms not normally around at all. Under such circumstances, getting laid may seem like something you might as well put off for a while.

If you insist, however, it's true that the experience is in a class by itself, especially on a visionary level. Enough variety to satisfy the most jaded palate, one might say. It's like taking on central casting. But, in my experience, those who routinely and exclusively use acid this way are tamasic characters in almost every case, devoid of higher aspirations or interests beyond the satisfaction of their immediate personal impulses and untrustworthy on that account. If you want to get ripped off, or betrayed, just associate with couples who spend all their time on trips screwing.

On to Southold. Mary Francis and Sally thought I should take a train to Miami, where my brother Leonard lived, to look things over and return with a report. This I did.

My report was unfavorable. As far as I could see, the place was some kind of giant glob. My-am-I. Possession is identity. The sky was too low. General somnambulism seemed to prevail, even among the heads, several of whom arrived to pay their respects soon after I arrived. My kid brother's middle-class style of life depressed me. Miami struck me as a purgatory world, in which nothing of consequence would ever happen, at least not to me. On the other hand, it would just be for the winter. Sally's mother wanted to go. She had the money. We went.

That winter passed like an alcoholic fantasy or coma, or both. We rented a modest house and held meetings once a week. I met some interesting people and got local TV and radio coverage, but the sensation of suspended animation persisted. So I stayed half smashed most of the time, and fooled around with a Tuesday Weld-type University of Miami student, Jean Valier, who deserved better of me, as did Sally, to dispel the general miasmic boredom which seemed to seep out of the ground itself. I couldn't face a full-scale acid trip in Florida. I was sure I would bolt.

Sally, aside from the apprehensions engendered by having sacramental sugar cubes in the refrigerator, loved the place. During meetings, she would take the kids over to the uninteresting house her mother had bought. The meetings were fairly sedate affairs, involving, if anything, tiny doses of the Supreme Sacrament. We would have multiple readings, watch TV with the sound off while listening to a radio program to pick up the synch, and discuss the usual Psychedelian philosophic questions.

I couldn't allow full-scale group sessions in the house because we were surrounded on all sides by conventional burghers, who never gave us any trouble although they knew what was going on, but who would surely have called the cops if naked freaks claiming to be pelicans had appeared on their doorsteps asking for directions to grandmother's house, or something similar, as would have happened if everyone had been routinely stoned on large hits whenever we had a meeting. The freedom and honesty I had enjoyed so much at MGL and Millbrook had been replaced by all kinds of restraints and compromises. I felt trapped, so I drank a lot.

News of Tim's bust in Laredo, Texas, didn't improve my mood. After crossing the border, the Leary family had been turned back on the Mexican side because Tim was on a *persona non grata* list in Mexico, and they were then stopped and strip-searched by the border guards on the American side. Sure enough, Susan had what was left of the family stash, a very small quantity, in her panties. Her father, as most honorable fathers would in similar circumstances, took responsibility. He refused to cop a plea, and was convicted and sentenced to thirty years in a federal prison, but was released on bail pending his appeal, which he based on a claim that he was a "Hindu," which, if true, he thought, meant that his possession of cannabis was protected under the First Amendment.

These events, as reported on TV and in the Miami paper, were almost too crazy and pathetic to bear thinking about but very suitable to drink about.

Jack Kerouac called up and then showed up one evening, smashed on wine, and entertained us with great wit, verve, and erudition until the wee hours. We added a little acid to the wine. As luck would have it, I had just finished reading his latest romance and was feeling pretty Kerouacish myself in consequence.

Jack was a true monologist of the old school if there ever was one. When smashed, he would go for days without sleep with his friends working in shifts to look after him. His greatest performance when in this condition, according to a story Watts told me, was an appearance before an exclusive group of literary and academic figures at Harvard shortly after *On the Road* was published. He staggered to the lectern and said, "Well, this is a fine-looking collection of cocksuckers." Then he threw up. His audience, but not, I suspect, the janitor, rose as one man and applauded, with genuine appreciation and respect, according to Watts, this masterful performance.

Ah, where is that glorious spirit of yesteryear which once prevailed? Be gone ye dour faced demons!

"A Christian could and should be gay, but the devil shits on him!" (Martin Luther)

Although Jack and I hit it off very well, I forgot to ask him to sign up, or to invite him to visit MGL or even to get his phone number, which is as good an illustration as any of my characterological inability to imitate Tim in the mass-media-mongering way of life, much less compete with him. Tim would probably have appeared arm-in-arm with Jack in front of a TV camera within a few hours of meeting him. I'm convinced, based on my record, that I'm not only not very good at that kind of stuff, I'm downright subnormal.

We did manage to enlist some useful members in Miami, although only a few lasted very long. I was greatly surprised when a Jewish psychiatrist from New York, Joe Gross, signed up after attending a meeting. Almost all of the psychiatrists I had met in my career had struck me as being so far beyond redemption that only shock treatments or lobotomies could shake their rigid orthodoxies. Accordingly, Joe's adherence to the cause lifted my spirits considerably. If a psychiatrist could defy his trade association, so could almost anyone, no matter how depraved. I stopped drinking for about twenty-four hours to celebrate.

However, the most fateful event which occurred that winter in Miami was also the most disgusting first trip I had ever witnessed.

Steve Newell showed up one evening with a friend, a lawyer named Frank Green, whom Steve had convinced to try acid as a possible cure for his psychopathological disorders. Throughout his trip Frank blubbered about his ex-wife. She had recently divorced him, getting custody of their only child and denying Frank any visiting rights. He rolled around on the floor in front of the couch on which Sally was sitting, moaning and groaning and occasionally addressing Sally by his first wife's name.

Sally, he asserted, was the spitting image of this unfortunate woman. When he went to the toilet, which was frequently, it took two of us to get him past the gas heater in the hall, which he thought was "a passageway." It had been placed there to suck wife beaters down to their just rewards in the infernal regions. When he left, after Steve apologized profusely for his friend's behavior, I thought no more of the matter. Little did I realize that this monumental creep would be the proximate cause of much suffering for me in the future.

In Miami, I also learned that there are people who seem to be constitutionally incapable of tripping, no matter how much LSD they take, and that individual reactions to identical doses may vary widely. Light and infrequent users may have fantastic and glorious experiences on a few tokes of the Lesser Sacrament. And others, who take what would normally be staggering amounts of LSD, may experience only minor changes in perception and learn comparatively little from it. These are the extremes of a distribution which seems to be normal (bell-shaped), so the reactions of most people are about what one would expect, but the reactions of any particular person, chosen at random, can't be predicted with certainty.

A prosperous, middle-aged couple from Coconut Grove, who showed up at about the same time a drunken reporter and a photographer from *Life* magazine were hanging around, demonstrated both extremes of the distribution. The wife was so eager to try the stuff she almost drooled when she talked about it. For years, she had devoted her spare time to checking out the standard swamis and such and, much to her credit, had rejected them all.

Then she had read about Tim, IFIF, the aborted Zihuatenejo experiment, the Castalia Foundation, and the rest of it. This was it! She dragged her husband, a good-natured and open-minded person, hundreds of miles to hear Tim speak, and contributed generously to the cause, but somehow could never lay her hands on any acid. My appearance in Miami, therefore, struck her as a godsend.

I made arrangements to turn her on at her house one morning, when everyone would be away. They had two college-age sons living at home. Since I had just put a gram of new crystal in vodka in portions of 250 micrograms per drop, I gave it to her right on the tongue, after signing her up. With rare exceptions, I didn't turn anyone on who hadn't joined the Church. An hour later, nothing had happened. I gave her another drop. She seemed to become slightly nervous.

So did I.

I took her over to my house, half convinced by this time that there was something seriously wrong with the acid, if it was acid at all. I gave her a sugar cube from a former gram. Nothing! I was dumbfounded. By evening, she had taken 2,000 micrograms from both the new gram of supposed crystal LSD and the previous gram, which I knew from personal experience was as good as it gets, with no observable or reported effects whatever.

When her husband came over I had twenty or thirty Necco wafers, with a drop from the new batch on each, drying out on the coffee table in front of me but I wasn't sure what I ought to do with them. I wanted to nibble some myself but I still believed in the "ground control" idea, and for all I knew, the 2,000-microgram woman, still an utter novice, would suddenly start tripping like crazy at 3 a.m. and need my assistance.

"I guess I'll just hand them out free to some of our most

experienced people but I will have to warn them," I said. "The fact is that I don't really know what this stuff is."

"Why don't I try one?" her husband suggested. I handed him a slimy pink disc, thinking he would take it later, but he popped it down without a second's hesitation. Off they went in their Cadillac. I lit up a joint, poured a drink and turned on the stereo.

The phone rang. It was the 2,000-microgram woman, still straight. "Everything" was "fine" but she thought I ought to come over to their house. Whew. When I walked in I found her husband, wearing a bathrobe, seated in an easy chair, surrounded by his adoring family and beaming away like a lighthouse.

"Ask me anything!" he announced, making a lordly gesture. He was on one of the most beautiful, well-balanced, dignified, humorous, kind, loving, optimistic and altogether glorious trips I have ever witnessed. The man was brimming over with good cheer and happy news for one and all. His sons both had good trips in the days that followed, but their poor mother never got an inch off the ground, although she tried several times.

When *Life*'s hired scrivener asked for the name of someone to interview, I arranged a meeting for him with my favorite new Psychedelian family. His article, entitled "A Midwestern Businessman's Trip," appeared on the first page of *Life*'s spread on LSD. The Neo-American Church wasn't mentioned, so I put a curse on *Life* and it has since become a mere shadow of its former self.

Miami was educational and I had some fun, but it was largely a big drag. I could hardly wait to get back to MGL. When, in the merry month of May, I heard that the ice was melting in God's country, I packed up the car and told Sally, who was unwilling to leave so early, to follow with the kids by plane as soon as she could. Things were not going well domestically but it seemed to me that once we escaped from Florida this would change. We had enough money to pay the bills. An enjoyable spring, summer and fall at the lodge stretched before us. Surely Sally would see how lucky we were to have escaped the dreary lockstep of the typical American family. Right? Wrong.

Unfortunately, I decided to drink my way back north. No

doubt certain anxieties were gnawing away at the back of my mind, despite the pleasant prospect at the forefront.

Most heavy drinkers have an alternate personality which takes over when they are drunk, and I was no exception.

Arch Kleps, whom I might as well call this character, was generally nonviolent, but extroverted, boisterous and reckless. Drunken consciousness can have a delightfully dramatic and magical quality, and it's no accident that the best poets are so often lushes as well. Used just right, alcohol (and barbiturates, which are much more dangerous, also) can produce a state in which there is no difference between thought and talk; it all just reels out effortlessly, without any sense of alienation or self-doubt and, assuming one has interesting ideas (Watts comes to mind), the results can be worth the cost and risk, both of which are high.

Unfortunately, just a couple drinks beyond this happy state, in which everything appears clear as a bell, lies the land of the stupid, drunken slob, in which there is no tomorrow and no yesterday, a world which will vanish when the hangover starts. I see it all in terms of split personality. Arch would have been better suited to former times, when life was generally nasty, brutal and short and the only way to live was to forget about personal safety and try to generate as good a show as possible with whatever was at hand before the inevitable happened. It was a matter of style, as if Arch were an actor on a stage. Drama was what he was after, and what he fled was boredom, futility and routine.

I guess it was some such consideration for keeping the script lively that moved me to offer a gas station attendant in central Florida, who seemed disgruntled, a sugar cube. Here, pal, try one of these sometime. It will cure what ails you. Middle of the night. Black as ink. I had no idea where I was. Ten minutes later I pulled up in front of a closed grocery store and went to sleep in the front seat. I awoke to find a cop shining his flashlight directly in the plastic bucket of foil-wrapped sugar cubes at my feet.

"Whatcha got there, buddy?" he asked.

"I have nothing to say," I replied, as all students of ACLU pamphlets are taught to respond under such circumstances.

I felt no anxiety. The meaning of the word "anxiety" was as unknown to Arch Kleps as it was to Superman, Batman or Captain Marvel. How can you have an adventure unless it looks like the villains may win? At the same time, Batman, or his author, knows in his heart it is all a farce and he just can't lose.

At the police station I was locked in a featureless holding cell painted a sickly yellow, while my captor called his captain. During the hour or so while I waited for his arrival, I actually dozed off for a few minutes, although I was thinking with perfect clarity and was by no means "stupefied" or in any similar state of mental inefficiency.

When I was ushered before the captain, he asked, "Do you care to tell me what this is, Mr. Kleps? We can have it analyzed, you know."

The correct words seemed to come out of my mouth as if the whole exchange had been scripted and I had it on tape. "No, I can't tell you exactly what it is but it is the sacrament of my Church." A brief summary of the practices of the Native American Church and our belief that our organization has the same legal rights under the constitution reeled out of my mouth. Click.

"Exactly what does it do to you?" A brief summary of the mystical tradition in Western and Oriental literature, brilliantly and modestly expressed, reeled out. Click.

The captain sat back in his chair and fingered his chin. Maybe he had a personal interest in my cubes. Maybe this, maybe that.

"Captain," I said, "I don't blame your man for picking me up, and I understand that you have to hold on to what you have confiscated. If you like I will give you a release for it. But all I am interested in right now is being on my way. I have an appointment with a writer who is doing an interview with me for *Pageant* magazine up north and I don't want to be late for it. All I can tell you is that if you arrest me your county is going to have one hell of an expensive case on its hands." Click.

What I had said about the *Pageant* article was true. Bob Eddy, an old college friend who had become a Unitarian minister in Michigan, had asked me to fly over from New York to his place to do an interview as soon as I got there.

"OK," the captain said. "You can go. But I have to hold this stuff."

It was a mixed blessing to be introduced to the anti-Psychedelian cold war this way. It encouraged me to entertain the foolish notion that I might be invulnerable to such inconveniences as being arrested and incarcerated for my religious practices, although it was routine for less noble mortals. Did I have a metaphysical "get out of jail free" card? Why not? Offhand, I couldn't think of anyone more deserving of the honor.

Without a worry in the world, Arch went on to Gainesville and dropped in on the local bee hee for some well-deserved rest and recreation, but Art woke up with the hangover, and all kinds of worries.

The usual. Pregnancy? Clap? Divorce? Where is my wallet? And, holy shit, the unusual but distinct possibility some junior G-man was busy analyzing my sugar cubes soaked in LSD at that very moment.

Once this virtual certainty became a clear image in my mind, the entire affair didn't appear at all to be the amusing adventure Arch had described to the fascinated and wide-eyed young scholar the previous night. In a matter of minutes I was out of the house and into my car and I didn't stop except for gas, until I was out of the state of Florida.

The only real stop I made all the way back to New York was in Pennsylvania, to visit a couple old friends, Jean Lewis and Brad Jones, who had married and were living in Bethlehem.

In the '50s, Brad had looked a lot like Warren Beatty, but taller, and with soft brown eyes, instead of that ethereal blue, the looking into of which became so tiresome to Queen Victoria. To continue evading descriptive details by means of what might be called the Hollywood shortcut, Brad behaved, even more than I did in those days, like Errol Flynn, an inclination he did nothing to hide from Jeannie, who merely frowned like Natalie Wood would, and perhaps tapped a little brown loafer, when neglected because of such diversions. It didn't seem to annoy Jeannie much more than poker nights. "Boys will be boys," one could almost hear her thinking. Or perhaps, "Men are like putty in the hands of these sluts. What can one do?"

I had shared an apartment in Syracuse with Brad one summer, and Jeannie and I had known each other since she was fifteen and I was twenty-one, back in Utica in 1949.

In many ways, pretty but deliberately unflashy Jeannie and handsome, charming Brad embodied the essence of '50s coolitude, as I had known it. Jeannie had long, light-brown hair, a red MG roadster, into the passenger's seat of which I could fit only by jamming my knees against the dashboard, and a seemingly unlimited supply of plaid, pleated skirts and muted, matching sweaters. She belonged to Alpha Chi Omega, the "best" (richest) sorority adorning the University at the time. Brad, also faultlessly attired in the collegiate styles of the day, drove a big Buick convertible, seemed to know everyone and something about everything, at least glancingly, had a hollow leg and, naturally, was a member of DKE.

The three of us got along fine. I can't remember exchanging as much as a cross word with either Brad or Jeannie. I met Sally while sharing the apartment with Brad. After reviewing the psychological profiles of the four of us, I'm pretty sure most good psychologists would have advised us to switch partners immediately, for the greatest good of the greatest number.

Yet, improbably, Jeannie and I had always been "just friends," and we stayed that way. Whenever our paths crossed, the party of the second part was involved in an entangling alliance with a party of the third part which the party of the first part could not but respect.

On arrival, I was happy to see that J&B had acquired a cute house and produced two cute kids but it swiftly became apparent that all was not well. Jeannie gamely tried to catch up with my intake all afternoon as we talked about old times. It seemed strange to be on such intimate terms with an unstoned person.

"Shouldn't have wasted those cubes," I said to myself as I turned back onto the interstate, and also, "I have got to sober up," which I did.

The last ice of winter was still on the lake when I arrived at Cranberry Lake, although the air was balmy. The wind was from the west. Fountains of sparkling ice crystals spun up in the sunlight where the last long, wide, thin sheets crashed against the shore. To fully appreciate this display of aesthetic whimsicality on the part of Mother Nature (a wonderful, tinkling music is part of the show), I stayed with the rocks and boulders and cobbles and stones and pebbles and little sandy beaches along the shore as much as I could, all the way to the house, which was unchanged. It didn't even seem weathered, much less, as I had feared, vandalized.

There is no joy like being exactly where you want to be.

I flew to Michigan to do the interview. It's in the *Boo Hoo Bible*, just as *Pageant* magazine printed it, complete with the god-awful "With LSD, I Saw God" title they slapped on it. This stupid concept haunted me for years but I came to regard this as just punishment for the sloppy language I used in those days, long before I learned that if you give the bastards an inch they will take a mile or more.

On my return, I spent a happy week with various tools in hand, getting everything in order, and not thinking about slithery semantics in the slightest.

Since I had to walk to town before the ice went out and I could use a boat, I had plenty of time to notice how the state campsite road was being extended in loops and tentacles down the shore and towards MGL. Land in the forest preserve in New York State is protected, not by ordinary law, but by an amendment to the state constitution which declares that it shall be "forever wild," an amendment which the Conservation Department has attempted to overturn, unsuccessfully, several times. The amendment is also peculiar in allowing any citizen of the state to bring a suit against the state for violations. What the Conservation Department was doing was clearly illegal. I wrote and threatened suit if the road went any further. They wrote back and said they had no such plans and the road they had put in was for "fire control" purposes only. Provisions for campers were "incidental."

Sheer horseshit, no doubt. But such facilities are better than a lot of garish motels in the towns. I let it drop. So did the other owners in the region.

The principle is clear. When, in the United States, a government agency breaks the law because the law fails to take everything into account and gets in the way of genuine and pressing human needs, the individuals whose rights are violated thereby are expected to adopt a liberal attitude and let it pass, and usually do. The "Golden Rule" comes first, in other words. When, however, a mere citizen of this republic violates the law, an entirely different ethic, based on what might be called "the spirit killeth, but the letter giveth life" rule, derived from the tribal customs of an insane and murderous mideastern cult, and perhaps imposing thirty years in a dungeon for anyone whose daughter has the wrong kind of flowers in her panties, applies with unforgiving wrath.

Chapter 14

"DEFEND THEE, LORD!"

I would have considered this a doubtful errand, myself.

I was talking the matter over with Charlie at the bar one morning when a call came for me. It was Carl Perian, who worked for Senator Dodd's (the elder, kids) Juvenile Delinquency Subcommittee. Senator Dodd was under heavy attack at that time for accepting bribes, and did not seem to figure at all, as planner or participant, in the scenario Perian painted. He and other members of the subcommittee staff had formed a favorable impression of me when they read an article in Walter Bowart's *The East Village Other* magazine which quoted, in full, my letter to the Food and Drug Administration demanding that our Church be exempted, as the Native American Church had been, from the peyote prohibition of the Drug Abuse Control Amendments of 1965.

They wanted me to testify at one of the hearings the subcommittee was about to hold. Tim had already testified, before a different committee, but, in Perian's opinion, had badly let down the home team. The religious case for psychedelics deserved to be made, Perian thought, but Timothy Leary had not made it. Tim hadn't even bothered to prepare a written statement but had aimlessly rambled, Perian said, making quite an ass of himself in the process. Based on the "great job" I had done in my FDA letters, Perian hoped I might make up for some of the damage Tim had done to our cause. My expenses would be paid in full. They would mail me a ticket and a check to cover my hotel bill. Would I fly down as soon as possible so they could help me prepare my statement?

I certainly would. Holy shit, it was like something in a Frank Capra movie. Could it be that I had become overly cynical about the powers that were? I instantly forgot about the state campsites, MGL, family problems and the nature of the universe. National publicity! My name and doctrines, very possibly, broadcast far and wide! An opportunity to make my case directly to the highest powers in the land! Feelings which, with some difficulty, I identified as being patriotic, or at least semi-patriotic, crept into my cranium, which I had thought fully inoculated against any such invasions. For a very brief period, there was some excuse for such idiotic emotions. At least at the federal level, a number of people who actually knew what they were talking about on the subject of psychedelics were granted an opportunity to protest the laws against us which were already in place and the new repressive measures being contemplated to extend the "tyranny" over "the mind of man" which Thomas Jefferson swore "eternal hostility" against "every form of." Me too.

It's the "eternal" and the "every" that make this such a great line.

Never again has there been anything resembling fair and open public hearings on the subject of psychedelic drugs and religion at the federal level. Instead, we have the "drug war," and as is oft observed, the first casualty in any war (or "war") is truth. Flat-out lies are the standard weapons for daily use but much of the deception is more sophisticated and harder to spot. The established power defines its enemies through control of the media. Revolutionary movements have always had this problem. For years, during a period of enormous growth of the socialist movement throughout Europe, the name of Karl Marx was never mentioned in the popular press.

Jonathan Swift had it right: "Should a man of genius appear among you, you may know him by this infallible sign; all the dunces will conspire against him." No doubt about that, but the dunces will often conspire against each other, also, thus confusing matters considerably. Modern technology has made this old scam easier for its practitioners in some ways and more difficult in others. One sub-trick that's now easier is to expose parts of an opposition player in the mass media while leaving out other parts, thus putting some very hideous (or, worse, pitiful) freaks on the field. On the other hand, it is much harder now than it was a hundred years ago to totally suppress anything. Does it all "balance out"? Damned if I know. I decided to drive to Millbrook and take the train from Poughkeepsie to Washington. When I got to the turnoff for Millbrook, however, I pulled over at a rest stop, opened a beer and thought it over.

Tim's Laredo bust and the extremely high probability that his appeal would fail greatly confused matters for me. Would it help or hurt to talk to Tim in his present condition? Hurt, probably, I decided. Tim's defense against the Laredo bust had pretty much rested on his declaration that he was a "Hindu." ("Hindu" is not a good term, but its usage is so well established that there isn't much sense in fighting it.)

Although many Hindus smoke cannabis, and little is thought of it one way or the other by Hindus who don't, there is no Brahmanical Vedantist sect I know about that religiously obliges or even officially encourages the practice. To try to overturn the marijuana laws of the United States with such flummery seemed senseless, if not suicidal.

Why hadn't he copped a plea? And if there was any hope at all for a religious defense in a pot case at that time (I don't think there was), why didn't he just say he was an Emersonian or "a William James kind of guy," a transcendentalist, or something else an American judge and jury might feel they ought to respect?

All of this was crazy and hazy then and it's crazy and hazy now. Those of us who admired him thought of Tim's latest moves and pronouncements, including his declaration of a "moratorium" on the use of psychedelics and the persecution of Psychedelians, as the aberrations of a mind unsettled by desperation and the Kafkaesque quality of a thirty-year prison sentence for entering the United States, when he hadn't really left it, with a daughter who had a few shreds of a common plant on her person. How rational would I be if I suddenly found myself looking at thirty years, even if I deserved it?

One thing was sure. I didn't want to hear anything from Tim, or anyone else, about a "moratorium" on my constitutional right to the free exercise of religion. To hell with it. Advice from Tim, in his present condition, would be a distraction. I would go directly to Washington and stop at Millbrook on my way back. I tossed my empty Budweiser can into a trash receptacle provided by the State of New York, took a piss in a state urinal, and passed Millbrook by.

On the train, I reviewed my correspondence with the FDA, as printed in the *East Village Other*:

NEO-AMERICAN CHURCH GIVES 'EM HELL
by Walter Bowart

Kleps told EVO of a letter received from Carlton Sharp of the Food and Drug Administration's Division of Industry Advice, Bureau of Education and Voluntary Compliance, stating that the Neo-American Church would not be allowed to administer psychedelic substances but that "based on the centuries of traditional use of peyote by Indian members of the Native American Church and the intent of the Congress as evidenced by the legislative history, the Commissioner of the Food and Drug Administration has exempted this church and this church only from the registration and record-keeping requirements of the Act for peyote use for bona fide religious ceremonies." The letter said that peyote was not exempted from the requirements of the Act under any other circumstances. "We do not know of any similar justification for exempting LSD from the requirements of the law," said Mr. Sharp.

In answer to Mr. Sharp, Kleps posed the question of exactly what constitutional amendment it was that gives to Congress the right to establish a religion on the basis of longevity. "As I read the First Amendment, it says Congress shall make no law respecting the establishing of a religion or prohibiting the free exercise thereof.

"If you seriously maintain you can make a legal distinction between one church and another on the idiotic basis that one is older than the other you are propounding a doctrine that would give Catholicism a higher standing than Protestantism, and

Judaism a higher standing than Catholicism and Animism a higher standing than Judaism.

"If you maintain that religion has nothing to do with it, and your favoritism is merely a recognition of a cultural difference, then I would like to point out that I am an intellectual person with an interest in mysticism, and that for thousands of years, members of my sub-culture have experimented with consciousness expanding substances for religious purposes; or is the distinction you make strictly racial?

"The fact of the matter is that you would not have made this exception if the Indian use was merely social, no matter how ancient the custom, and that you have made it because of court decisions favoring the Native American Church based on the First Amendment.

"You also establish a religion in exempting what you refer to as 'ceremonial' use, while presumably not exempting the use of peyote by, say, some heretical Indian who prefers to take his peyote alone on a mountain top as an aid to meditation, who, indeed may be obliged to do so because he is not permitted in the Church, on account of his heretical opinions on theological matters."

Kleps asked, "Exactly what do you intend to do about splinter groups from the Native American Church?

"I suppose the non-orthodox will be put in prison?

"If our church adopts the use of peyote instead of LSD, will we be granted an exception? What about mescaline? These distinctions, as you know, are all superficial; the effects are pretty much the same except that peyote makes many people sick.

"In the event that a clergyman of our non-established church is sent to prison for distributing the sacraments to his congregation, and he recants and embraces the doctrines of the established church and is accepted into the established communion, may his membership in the established church be made retroactive, thereby legalizing what was formerly a crime, on account of his heresy?"

Boo Hoo Kleps continued: "If these substances have nothing specially holy about them, then the state may prohibit them. But if they do have something specially holy about them, then the state may neither prohibit nor control them, nor even encourage nor discourage their use, for they are entirely outside the province of government and are under the protection of religion and conscience alone.

"It is not the business of legislatures to define what is holy and what is not, although the courts may rightfully inquire into the sincerity of religious assertions, if those assertions lead to a proper question of law.

"The discovery of LSD may be taken as the intervention of God in human history; if the government says this is not possible, then the government has in effect made a law respecting an establishment of religion, disallowing all that is present and future and permitting only what is past.

"To define these divine bio-chemicals as 'drugs' in statutes is to do nothing but render an opinion, very possibly wrong, and no one is obliged to act accordingly, for, in the same manner the wine of the Christian communion might be called an intoxicant and narcotic given to minors and the Jewish circumcision termed an assault on infants. If sane and orderly men say that a thing is religious, and the thing is no murder or robbery, then it is their natural right to have it, no matter what multitudes of believers in the holiness of other things, or even in the holiness of nothing, may be arrayed against them.

"We do not believe these substances may be taken from us by whatever means, under any circumstances, no matter what the courts may decide, for free men have a natural right to the exercise of their religion which transcends all ordinary laws should conflict arise, so long as the matter in dispute is integral and essential to the practice of the religion and involves no direct injury to the person or property of non-participants.

"This is the official position of the Neo-American Church on the question of government control and/or prohibition. It is not binding on the clergy or membership of the Church, but I intend to steer by this course, and those who disagree should make their views known, so there will be a minimum of confusion."

Kleps took issue with Dr. Timothy Leary stating that he specifically rejects a "moratorium" on the use of LSD until its legal status is cleared up, or any acquiescence to government controls of any kind, however mild. Kleps expounded: "No court exists with such jurisdiction."

Kleps encouraged all Church leaders, called Boo Hoos, to defy the law and continue to celebrate holy communion as they have in the past, but said that "Timothy Leary continues to be the single most respected spiritual guide of the Church, and we will do all in our power to save him from persecution and the torture of imprisonment."

Good stuff, I thought. It had been written at night with pen and pad at the lodge by the light of three kerosene lanterns. Nice shadow effects. Cozy, also, with a cheery fire going. Synchronistic with the Age-of-Enlightenment, eighteenth-century, Rights-of-Man tone of the thing.

If I could maintain the "grand manner" in my statement to the subcommittee, I thought, I might be wafted to the Elysian heights of national media coverage. The dreary landscape of industrial New Jersey arrived and departed in segments through the train window. I wasn't drinking. Don't fuck this one up, Kleps, I kept telling myself. I thought of the train trips I used to take between Crestwood and Scarsdale or Bronxville during the war, to go to the movies when I was a kid, and how I fantasized I was an important adult on some great expedition. Well, here I was. To get smashed would be to betray my youthful image of myself as an adult. Fuck this one up and I won't have anything more to do with you, I told myself.

In D.C., I quickly found a nice room at a reasonable rate in a small, old-fashioned hotel near Union Station. The weather was ideal. I strolled up to the Old Senate Office Building. There was a small town atmosphere about it all? No guard checked me out as I entered. I walked right in and got on an elevator with Ted Kennedy, who gave me a big but appealingly shy grin as we elevated.

Déjà vu feelings washed over me. My emotions were similar to those I had felt on first entering the grounds at Millbrook. What in God's name was happening to me? I felt at home in this sinkhole of corruption amidst this gang of blackmailers, extortionists and serial mass murders? To this day that feeling remains in my memory as one of the weirdest I have ever experienced.

This down-home feeling increased when I introduced myself at the subcommittee offices. I instantly liked everyone I met. Their motivations and attitudes seemed clear and reasonable; they wanted to put on a good show, and if any truth emerged in the process, so much the better.

Carl Perian explained the situation to me. Senator Dodd's Juvenile Delinquency Subcommittee, of which Carl was the administrator, had been holding hearings on drugs for some time, but Senator Bobby Kennedy, scenting publicity, had decided to muscle in on the act, and was now ringmaster of a Shrinks & Cops Show before a different subcommittee.

Tim had appeared on 13 May but, according to Carl, hadn't made much of an impression. We got right to work. Carl showed me to a desk and offered me a pad and pencil with which to write my statement and said one of the three secretaries in the office would type it up for me. Bernie Tannenbaum, one of Carl's two assistants, would help me editorially, if need be.

Far out, cool and groovy. I settled down behind the desk and started writing. Nothing to it. Not only did the words roll out effortlessly, but the synchronicity in the newspapers was ideal. A lady in California had just been ordered sterilized because some marijuana was found in a room in which she was present. I included that information in my presentation. Senator Murphy of California had testified about a friend of his children who had been bombed by some acid-spiked punch at a party? Good for him. I worked that in, too.

Carl and Bernie were delighted with the pages I handed them. Visions of blanking out Bobby started dancing in their heads, no doubt. His next hearing was to be held at exactly the same time as ours. A spirit of enthusiasm prevailed. At closing time, I went out and bought a new shirt and tie, had dinner, and went to bed, cold sober. This, I thought, is the way to live. There's no business like show business.

The next day, as I sat at my desk, surrounded by displays of machine guns and other lethal weapons left over from former subcommittee hearings on gun controls, I could see I wasn't the only one who liked show business of the Senatorial sort. A parade of dark-suited and frowning professional thugs came and went. Most of them were lobbyist hirelings of the AMA, according to Bernie. They were there to beseech Carl for an opportunity to speak, lest the Psychedelianisticalonian power fall into the hands of the likes of me. On the way out, they favored me with dirty looks.

One minion, more courageous than the rest, came over and introduced himself. Doctor so and so. Had met Tim and did not share the usual view that he belonged in a snake pit. Just an irresponsible visionary. He went into a song and dance about the necessity for "medical control," and the great loss to the healing arts that would occur if the police were allowed to have their way and ban all psychedelics. Having had a few small doses himself, he knew what I meant about the "religious aspect," but other people would never understand that. One must consider what "other people" would think, etc., etc. I was getting bored.

"What other people?" I asked.

His mouth fell open, just as in the movies. He got up from his chair.

"My God, are you going to talk like that tomorrow? You're confusing levels! You can't confuse levels, Art!"

"What levels?" I asked. He had a point, but I just wanted to get back to work. Lamentably, I did not intend to "talk like that" in there, partly because I did not yet have a satisfactory vocabulary to do it with, but mostly because I was suffering from the delusion that my role in the Psychedelian world was political, not philosophical. I intended to deliver high-class smarm like a loyal Learyite.

He lifted his arms, looking heavenward, and left.

Sandy, a cute secretary from another office, who had been hanging around, came over and firmly nudged the back of my neck with her left tit as she looked over my shoulder at what I was writing. "Mmmm, good stuff, Chief!" Did I want to come with her? She had to go out and buy the morning papers.

Aha! Fun and games in the places of the mighty! Walking over to the store, she pointed out the building where Bobby Baker's club used to operate. "Boy, we used to have some high old times in there!" she said. In the store I got a few more nudges and bumps amidst the stacks of papers and mags, and she showed me the announcement for the hearings in the *Washington Post*. Sure enough, there I was, listed along with a Dr. Baird, a Dr. Berger, and Sergeant Bellinger, a narcotics cop from Miami whom I had met on a TV show the previous winter, before there were any possession laws banning the Supreme Sacrament. They were all scheduled to speak before I did. Good.

"Why don't we have a couple drinks after work today?" I asked her, as we walked back to the office. Sure. Bernie and one of the other girls would probably like to go, too. Fine.

By 7 p.m., my statement was finished and mimeographed. Carl was delighted with it. He asked a lot of intelligent questions and confessed to a great urge to try some acid himself. "God knows I wouldn't have any supply problems," he said, laughing and opening a drawer in his desk to reveal a truly impressive collection of psychoactive drugs. There was enough potential "energy" in that drawer to lift Washington (heavy hydraulic metaphor) six inches off the ground. Bernie and the two secretaries also seemed to take a lively and personal interest in Carl's collection. How would I like to be the guest of honor at a party on the following evening? Sure. Well, here we go again, I thought. That night, in Sandy's apartment, I asked her if she had had much contact with Senator Dodd, whom I hadn't seen once since arriving, although his name was often invoked.

"Yes," she said, "all the time. He's a nice old man, and I really feel sorry for him. He's so sick and unhappy and can hardly do anything anymore."

"Well, he sort of deserves it, doesn't he?" I asked.

Sandy didn't think so. He didn't do anything the rest of them didn't do. No, they were out to get him for other reasons. The "gun people" were behind it all.

"You know what?" she asked.

"No, what?"

"His arms are covered with tracks. I saw them myself."

Well, could be this, could be that, I thought to myself. I had better things to think about than Senator Dodd's drug use.

I have found lots of heavy synchronicity associated with the damsels who have appeared and disappeared in my life. There is no such thing, Snazzm, as a chance encounter and no matter how casual and transitory the relationship, the person you are with will tell you a great deal about yourself as of that moment. I know you guys who hang out exclusively with stupid, ignorant, crazy sluts don't want to hear this, but so it is.

In this case, I'm sorry to say, the girl I was with did better in public than she did in private. She even apologized. Lying flat on her back, closing her eyes and, perhaps, gritting her teeth, was the best she could do. Up-tight Southern Baptist upbringing, she said. I told her not to worry about it. She might be in for one hell of a pleasant surprise in twenty-four hours or so, if the party we had planned took place.

Chapter 15

SANDY'S TALE

The truth is, Alisande, these archaics are a little too simple: the vocabulary is too limited, and so, by consequence, descriptions suffer in the matter of variety; they run too much to level Saharas of fact, and not enough to picturesque detail, this throws about them a certain air of the monotonous; in fact the fights are all alike: a couple of people come together with great random—random is a good word, and so is exegesis, for that matter, and so is holocaust, and defalcation, and usufruct and a hundred others, but land! a body ought to discriminate—they come together with great random, and a spear is brast, and one party brake his shield and the other one goes down, horse and man, over his horse-tail and brake his neck, and then the next candidate comes randoming in, and brast his spear, and the other man brast his shield, and down he goes, horse and man, over his horse-tail, and brake his neck, and then there's another elected, and another and another and still another, till the material is all used up; and when you come to figure up results, you can't tell one fight from another, nor who whipped; and as a picture, of living, raging, roaring battle, sho! why, it's pale and noiseless—just ghosts scuffling in a fog.

The next morning, an hour before the hearings were scheduled, I went for a long walk around the Capitol area in an attempt to become a little physically tired. I hate giving speeches and lectures, except perhaps to small groups of high-IQ, college-age kids and, even then, only when I'm well prepared and stoned out of my gourd. Reducing physical tension reduces emotional tension, and I was tense. I had one double vodka and 7-Up, not more, no more, Kleps.

The scene at the subcommittee office reminded me of the hustle and bustle backstage just before a church service. In a group, we took an elevator and walked down a long hallway. I was getting tenser by the moment. Lockjaw or a complete mental vacuum seemed to me a definite possibility. Suddenly, however, I was stoned. I felt like I was walking on air. There wasn't a trace of anxiety in my body. I looked forward to the whole scene with buoyant anticipation. I felt like the corrupt pope who remarked, "God having seen fit to give Us the Papacy, let Us enjoy it." I started talking animatedly to Bellinger, who had been saying something to Carl a moment before that I could hardly hear, such had been my concern for my internal condition.

In the hearing room, Baird, Berger and I were seated directly behind Bellinger, who was shown to a table in front of us adorned with several microphones. Senators Javits and Burdick and a couple others I didn't recognize were seated behind a long, high, curved, paneled bench facing us. Behind them were secretaries and assistants. Sandy gave me a big wink. She was behind Javits. To my left were two television cameras, which started humming, but soon stopped, as first Bellinger, then Baird and then Berger, delivered their statements.

Bellinger's statement was standard copovenoid logic, not unreasonable if you granted certain utterly undemonstrable copovenoid assumptions, but Baird's statement was so crazy and incoherent I must have reacted with a look of astonished disbelief that such horseshit should be tolerated without derisory comment. Here are some selections:

> DR. BAIRD: A minority of the college professors have been spewing this poor propaganda upon the college campuses that there is nothing wrong with marijuana and LSD. It was just recently we had a professor from Adelphi University who stated that marijuana does not necessarily lead to addiction. It is this type of propaganda when foisted upon the children at our colleges and high schools which is causing more and more of a problem of drug addiction. And he came out with another remark. I would like to know which Senators they are. He said,

"Many Senators, doctors, ministers, and theology students and thousands of others use LSD for their betterment." I would like to know the doctors and Senators who use the LSD for their own improvement.

Also, he came out with another remark.

SENATOR JAVITS: I can assure you, Dr. Baird, that I have not seen any evidences of hallucination of Senators.

Baird continued:

I plead with you that this problem of drug addiction a narcotics addiction is spreading rapidly more and more every day.

Now we are concerned with the increased consumption of LSD, which to me does not mean just lysergic acid. It stands for a nasty little word, "Let's sell decadency or let's start degeneration."

The individuals that I have seen on this have been chaps that, No. 1, are very hedonistic with a marked gratification complex; two, extremely insecure people. One, they are psychologically unaware of their own mental inadequacies. No. 2, they are extremely hypercritical of their own physical shortcomings and project their hostilities sometimes overtly, and these are generally people who have many of these things in common.

Now I know we all wear glasses, but some of these people suffer from severe strabismus; they are extremely thin, very asthenic type, have receding jaw, large pugnacious nose, or they might be short, but their own physical defects bother them.

Then you have latent homosexual or overt homosexual conflict.

Then you have a group of the young college intellect or the self-taught pseudo-intellect, and these are mostly students who are being trained for the arts, music, and literature who will take LSD.

Then you have the college marijuana graduate. He is the chap who goes to college and thinks there is nothing wrong with marijuana, and then after having been on this hallucinogenic marijuana wants to increase his consciousness and then he starts to take LSD.

And then the last group you have are escapists from the stark world of reality of education, economics, and social business.

I would like to just give you a few sad stories of this LSD, this great drug which I think can be great if it is used under very careful limitations by physicians and only by physicians...

Bernie came over behind my chair and whispered in my ear. "Don't lose your cool, Art," he said, "but cut out the contemptuous smile. You gotta play it solemn in here."

I nodded, and adopted what I hoped was an appearance of stoical unconcern.

Baird went on and on, as monomaniacal paranoids tend to do. Finally, one of the Senators cut him off. Berger gave a brief, fairly liberal and rational statement, granting his undemonstrable assumptions, which were pretty much those of Bellinger, except that medicos, not cops, should control by force everything and anything people ingested that was not commonly sold in grocery stores. It was my turn. Here's how it went:

> SENATOR JAVITS: The chairman wishes me to announce that Mr. Kleps was called as the director of the Neo-American Church located at Morning Glory Lodge, Cranberry Lake, N.Y.
>
> Mr. Kleps is essentially a psychologist with a bachelor's degree from Utica College in New York, and a master's degree from Syracuse University in school psychology.
>
> The purpose in calling Mr. Kleps is that he represents another discipline which has experimented with or used LSD without medical supervision, apposite to the testimony we heard from Dr. Leary, representing the largest group of users in the country on a scientific basis, and as some allege, a pseudoscientific basis.
>
> Mr. Kleps represents a religious approach to the use of these drugs, and hence the possibility that his testimony may be of use to us in determining what legislation shall be passed.
>
> Mr. Kleps, again may I ask you to confine your statement if you can to ten minutes, and it will be received without objection and printed in full.
>
> MR. KLEPS: Yes, sir, my statement is fairly brief. It's an honor to be here. I want to thank you very much for the opportunity to present my views.
>
> SENATOR BURDICK: Mr. Kleps, would you mind telling me if you are really called Chief Boo Hoo?
>
> MR. KLEPS: I am afraid so. It is difficult to explain this. That is always the first question that comes up. The reason we do it is

to distinguish between the church and the religion. We think it is very important not to take ourselves too seriously in terms of social structure, in terms of organizational life. We tend to view organizational life as sort of a game that people play.

SENATOR BURDICK: So is the appellation a spoof?

MR. KLEPS: It is sort of a spoof.

SENATOR BURDICK: Sort of a spoof.

MR. KLEPS: It is so people will not get beyond themselves too much.

SENATOR BURDICK: Please proceed.

MR. KLEPS: It is a help to me to have a title like that because I do have to explain it as I am doing now.

Listening to the testimony before your subcommittee on Monday, I was, of course, struck by Dr. Goddard's characterization of what we call consciousness expansion as 'bunk,' and I would like to reply to the reasons he gave for making such a judgment when Senator Dodd questioned him further.

Dr. Goddard said that consciousness expansion did not occur with LSD because the results of objective tests of intelligence and so on given during the session showed negative results; a drop in performance. His argument contains the unspoken assumption that consciousness expansion is necessarily associated with a rise of measured IQ during the psychedelic session. I do not know of any psychedelic person who would agree that that is the case.

If I were to give you an IQ test and during the administration one of the walls of the room opened up giving you a vision of the blazing glories of the central galactic suns, and at the same time your childhood began to unreel before your inner eye like a three-dimensional color movie, you would not do well on the intelligence test.

LSD puts you in the mind of God, and God has little interest in our IQ tests. We might say that God has no IQ. God is not a verbal being as we are to such a large extent.

Now this assumption that consciousness is somehow equated to, or is an aggregate of, those mental faculties which are measurable by objective tests is representative of an entire approach to the subject of psychedelics which is superficially plausible and yet is fundamentally erroneous. It is the only approach which finds favor in the eyes of those administering research grants. It is based on the assumption that if you cannot measure something, it does not exist. In psychology it is rooted in a kind of professional, if not personal, atheism. It produces the horror stories we read about in the field of animal vivisection experimentation resulting from a narrow-minded fixation on trivia, an almost trancelike inability to see the forest for the trees. It results in thousands of people each year earning advanced degrees because they have proved, in effect, that when you put 13 rats in one end of a box, lo and behold, 13 rats come out of the other end of the box in some combination or other.

Senator, I spent ten years working with young people in the public schools and in my career as a psychedelic activist, since then I have come to know the younger generation very well. They do not buy the kind of pseudoscience I have described. They are looking for the truth, they are trying to find out "what life is all about." Their cynicism about the conventional answers, the conventional routines, the conventional games is so profound as to pass beyond cynicism into a kind of entirely praiseworthy honesty and bravery of the highest type. Their eyes are open in the midst of all the death and heartlessness around them.

It is difficult for us to imagine what it is like to have been born in 1948, but it is very much like being born into an insane asylum. I will not repeat what Dr. Leary told you; I am referring to his concern with the lack of communication between the generations; but I will draw your attention to this week's issue of *Life* magazine which contains two articles very apropos of LSD and the gap in communication between the generations.

The first article is about Allen Ginsberg, the poet, who is also a member of our Church. In your generation or in mine, this man, who is the living antithesis of all that is officially pronounced admirable, would have made, at best, some small stir in Greenwich Village. Today, he is a folk hero. The article does a beautiful job of explaining why that is so.

It is because he is a man who has always disregarded the conventions when they have interfered with his personal quest for beauty and truth. Today's young people insist on direct experience; they are suspicious of all secondhand reportage; what they admire above all else is honesty and personal commitment. I think we can see this in the civil rights movement.

The second article concerns the latest style in discotheque interiors, which may sound trivial, but is actually very revealing.

The synchronization of light patterns and sounds, the cryptic flashing pictures, the constant random flow of colors; these are all well-developed techniques for approximating that inner world which is the common experience of all of us; a world both exquisitely private and yet wholly universal. To those of us who have had the experience, it is very obvious that all of this is the result of LSD, right down to the fact that little alcohol is consumed in these places. The people who go there do not need to get drunk, they have found something better. These are the style setters, not people in some cultural eddy or backwash.

Now before I get into the religious aspects of this, I would like to say that the incident Senator Murphy described as occurring near his home, Senator, in which some LSD was surreptitiously introduced into the punch at a party, is not the kind of thing I advocate, nor does anyone I know advocate it. It is a very silly and cruel, or at least thoughtless, kind of thing to do. If you pass laws against such sneak attacks with LSD, none of us will object. But we are surrounded by all kinds of potentially dangerous materials, machines, and chemicals. Book matches, for example, or automobiles. How many children are killed each year from drinking cleaning fluid? If safety were the only goal of life, we would have to prohibit everything, and not even that would work, because as far as I know, life itself is invariably fatal.

It is our belief that the sacred biochemicals such as peyote, mescaline, LSD, and cannabis are the true host of God and not drugs at all as that term is commonly understood. We do not feel that the Government has the right to interfere in our religious practice, and that the present persecution of our coreligionists is not only constitutionally illegal but a crude and savage repression of our basic and inalienable rights as human beings.

The leader of the psychedelic religious movement in the United States is Dr. Timothy Leary. We regard him with the same special love and respect as was reserved by the early Christians for Jesus, by the Moslems for Mohammed, or the Buddhists for Gotama. I am merely the head of one of several psychedelic churches.

The psychedelic churches exist to promote and defend the psychedelic religion, a religion which sees in the transcendental experience produced by the sacred substances the key to understanding life and improving the condition of man on earth.

We have been in existence a year; I am speaking of the Church; and have 500 members. Perhaps if the growth of the peyote religion and the Native American Church is any guide, we will have 500,000 members in a few years. Perhaps the psychedelic people will find some other church more to their liking. It is not important. What is important is that the religion, as distinguished from the Church, is spreading at a fantastic rate, and the Government, in the case of Dr. Leary, and the repression in general, has put itself in the position of attempting to destroy by force a genuine indigenous religious movement. I see no moral difference whatever between putting our religious leader in prison for thirty years and the incarceration of a rabbi in a concentration camp by the Gestapo of Nazi Germany. Perhaps Hitler was less hypocritical. If he operated the way our religious enemies operate in this country, he would not have mentioned Judaism at all in the laws designed to oppress the Jews; instead, he would have (a) made ceremonial wine illegal on the grounds that it was a narcotic intoxicant given to minors; and (b) made the nonpayment of so-called wine tax result in enormous confiscatory fines and thirty years in Buchenwald or Treblinka.

The history of Treblinka, by the way, constitutes a perfect example of how the psychedelic people of the United States will not respond to persecution and imprisonment. The Jews, in that instance, cooperated completely in their own destruction. We have no intentions of cooperating.

On the day the prison doors close behind Tim Leary; if these ill-considered laws of religious suppression are upheld by the courts, this country will face religious civil war. Any restraint we have shown heretofore in the dissemination of psychedelics will be ended. We can, without difficulty, render most of the prisons in the United States inoperative, if it comes to open conflict. Open conflict will most certainly result if the courts uphold these laws against us, if our men are imprisoned, our wives sterilized, our children consigned to unloving institutions and so-called reformatories; and I would most certainly advise my people to use LSD to fight back, to make life impossible for the prison administrators, rather than resort to actual violence. But I will never ask them to passively submit to such outrages. The police of the United States, ordered by their superiors to function as terrorists, as destroyers of happy and decent families who only ask to be left alone to practice their religion as they see fit, will have to make a moral choice, just as did the police of Germany when Hitler took over. Those who remain would do well to regard themselves as a military rather than a civil force. If I seem to exaggerate I direct your attention to a story in yesterday morning's paper about a woman who was ordered sterilized because a quantity of marijuana was found in a room when she was present. This was in California I believe. I personally will never forget sitting in on the assignment board at Sing Sing and watching a parade of armed robbers and grand larcenists go by with three- or four-year sentences, only to be followed by a poor weak little Puerto Rican with an IQ of 85 or so who had been sentenced to seventeen years because three or four sticks of marijuana had been found in his possession. At the time I was under the common illusion that marijuana was a dangerous drug, but I was still shocked. Now I know marijuana is a mild psychedelic and I am no longer shocked, I am numb. I have seen so much cruel injustice it seems commonplace.

The Food and Drug Administration has seen fit to attempt to establish one psychedelic church as legal, the Native American Church of the Indians, on the grounds of historical longevity, leaving the rest of us open to the kind of punishment visited on Dr. Leary. This is a constitutional outrage, of course, and I would like to submit my full reply to the FDA letter announcing this attempt at the unique establishment of a religion in the United States for the committee's study. However, I see in this exemption, unconstitutional though it may be, some grounds for hope that the people responsible may come to their senses. Apparently those in control of the instrumentalities of coercive power in the United States have no difficulty in recognizing that a psychedelic religion is a psychedelic religion when that religion is safely encapsulated in a racial minority group living outside the mainstream of American life. All that is required then is that we should follow the Indian example and make ourselves as peculiar as possible. Perhaps the Government would allow us to live unmolested on reservations. We would be willing to discuss this, if it would prevent open conflict. Possibly the Government would negotiate a treaty with some foreign power which would grant us religious sanctuary in return for receiving to its shores the large numbers of scientists, technicians, teachers, doctors, and intellectuals of all kinds who constitute a large proportion of our members. Most of us love this country dearly. It would break my heart to think of never seeing the Adirondack Mountains again. But we must think of our children, and we could always hope that some day the Government of our beloved country would return to that fierce defense of human rights, to that spirit of freedom and tolerance under which it was founded, and we could come back.

But there will either be some kind of accommodation or there will be conflict. We are not drug addicts. We are not criminals. We are free men and will react to persecution the way free men have always reacted to persecution.

There is no reason why anyone need be surprised by all this. To understand our emotions and our attitudes it is only necessary to imagine how you would react if we were in the majority and passed laws making the practice of your religion a criminal offense.

SENATOR BURDICK: Thank you, Mr. Kleps. I have a few questions here that I would like to ask you.

MR. KLEPS: Yes, sir.

SENATOR BURDICK: Would you care to tell us something more about your Church? How does one become a member?

MR. KLEPS: It requires agreement with three principles, the principle that the psychedelic substances are not drugs but actually sacred substances, that they are a sacrament.

It requires agreement to the principle that people are not to be given these substances unless they are prepared for them, and agreement to the principle that everyone has a right to free access to the sacred substances, since they are a gift of God. If one agrees to this, we make him a member of the Church. We do not make distinctions on the basis of intellect, education or anything of that sort. I feel, by the way, that this is the difference between a church and a cult. We are frequently called a cult, but cults do make these distinctions. They are small groups. They want to be small groups. We are a church. We will take anybody. We take people at face value.

SENATOR BURDICK: Do you contend that the substances, whatever they are, do not have harmful effects?

MR. KLEPS: Not entirely. In very rare cases, particularly when they are improperly administered, if they are taken by people who are unsuspecting of the results, have not done any reading on the subject, have not discussed it with anyone who knows, they can have bad effects. I have seen some bad effects myself.

But there are many, many, many other substances in this world that are much more harmful, much more dangerous.

SENATOR BURDICK: Does your order appeal more to the young people than to old people, or of all ages?

MR. KLEPS: Mostly to young people. I would say at least 50 percent are college students, perhaps more.

SENATOR BURDICK: How many churches are there like this in the country?

MR. KLEPS: We have twenty boo hoos, approximately twenty. We are getting new people all the time. We have a fairly large group in Miami, fairly large groups in New York State, California. There are about 500-plus members at the present time, but we have only been in existence a year. I hope for better things to come.

SENATOR BURDICK: You have 500 members in your Church?

MR. KLEPS: There are 500 members in all of the organization.

SENATOR BURDICK: All of the churches?

MR. KLEPS: In the whole country.

SENATOR BURDICK: Well now, you have told me something about membership. What about the tenets, the precepts of the Church?

MR. KLEPS: We mainly we feel that these psychedelic substances give you a vision, an entry, a ticket, a trip ticket in a sense, to a higher level of awareness, of an expanded consciousness. It is almost impossible to describe in words if not in fact impossible to describe in words what this is. Words fail. As I said, God is not like us. He does not have an IQ. He is not a talker. When you are in the mind of God you are beyond everything that you ordinarily experience. Everything that you ordinarily consider to be real. There are higher levels of reality than this one, and I believe it is very important for people to see this. It gives them an entirely new outlook on everything, a better outlook, a much better outlook.

SENATOR BURDICK: Is it correct to say that your Church does not have any creed?

MR. KLEPS: No, we do not.

SENATOR BURDICK: Or any tenets or anything like that.

MR. KLEPS: Tim Leary is generally accepted by most of us as the equivalent of Christ for the Christians and so on, not in any foolish way. I think Tim makes mistakes and so on, but we look upon him as a great religious teacher, the books he has written, the papers and so on constitute the creed of our Church, if there is any creed. But we do not have a dogma in the usual sense. You might say that it is more like the Society of Friends in that regard. We do not insist on any specific definition of these things.

SENATOR BURDICK: Do I understand you correctly to say that in view of your establishment of twenty churches, in view of your membership, that you believe this organization will grow?

MR. KLEPS: I believe it will, sir. I believe it will.

SENATOR BURDICK: In what proportion in your opinion?

MR. KLEPS: I honestly believe that we will have a million members in ten years.

SENATOR BURDICK: Are these churches located near college campuses for the most part?

MR. KLEPS: Many of them are. The older members of the Church and the many, many people who are associated with our Church but who do not join are the older and the more respectable people, the people with something to lose. We are being persecuted, and the people who fight persecution most effectively are those who can take some chances, who do not have families to worry about, who do not have to worry about their jobs and so on. The older people are very hesitant to join up because they are afraid to stick their heads above the ramparts. They are afraid to be known in public, but they are there. They are there in very large numbers.

SENATOR BURDICK: How frequently do you have church services, if that is the correct word.

MR. KLEPS: Usually there are meetings once a week. There are some of the local groups that just function as information centers. Lisa Bieberman of Boston runs information centers, a newsletter. People come and discuss problems. She does not hold any regular meetings. I understand she is planning on setting up a seminar this summer. It all depends on the individual. Now as we grow, I am sure that we will develop more structure. There will be an accumulation of hallowed patterns, traditions, and so forth. This is the way these things always grow. But at the present time it is all pretty loose and free and we like it that way.

SENATOR BURDICK: You mentioned the American Church of the Indians.

MR. KLEPS: The Native American Church.

SENATOR BURDICK: The Native American Church, that is right. Is this patterned much after that church?

MR. KLEPS: I cannot say that it is except that we also use a psychedelic as they do. From what I understand, they do have a very definite ritual that they follow, and they do not deviate from it very much. We do not have any rituals. I am not saying that we do not develop them. There are some things that are already in the process of development. The use of the techniques I described in the case of the discotheques, the light machines, certain kinds of music, this kind of thing can be used to heighten your experience, and even to produce it in some cases without the use of psychedelic substances."

SENATOR BURDICK: You said not infrequently but it does have a harmful effect. Being on the Indian Committee;

MR. KLEPS: Yes, sir.

SENATOR BURDICK (continuing): I have learned that this peyote does have an ill-producing effect. It causes vomiting.

MR. KLEPS: I know. I have tried it, and I have had the same experience.

SENATOR BURDICK: Does this drug which your Church uses have the same effect?

MR. KLEPS: No. Very, very rarely people will suffer some discomfort during the early stages of an LSD experience, but that is a psychological conversion of anxiety in the physical form. Peyote does, however, routinely produce intestinal upset and this is a very negative way of going into the experience, throwing up. I do not know how the Indians manage to do it. Somehow they have overcome the nausea.

SENATOR BURDICK: You think that the experiences that the members have makes them compatible with society, makes them eligible for pursuits that the nonmembers follow?

MR. KLEPS: Sometimes yes and sometimes no. We have members in almost every walk of life. We have people who are successfully pursuing almost any career you can name.

On the other hand, some people who are of religious temperament perhaps to begin with, there are degrees of true religiosity in our Church just as there are in other churches. I would say Tim is more religious than I am perhaps. These people, the people who are extremely religious, may want to withdraw from ordinary life for a period of time. I personally see nothing wrong with that. It is accepted in other traditions, the monasteries and so on. Why not in this?

SENATOR BURDICK: If you will permit a personal question,

do you participate yourself in these ceremonies, the use of this drug?

MR. KLEPS: Yes, sir.

SENATOR BURDICK: And part of your answer is based upon your own personal experience.

MR. KLEPS: Yes, sir.

SENATOR BURDICK: I have heard that these drugs produce a "color television effect."

MR. KLEPS: It can do that. It depends on the individual. There are a lot of people who have had many psychedelic experiences and have never really had that kind of a vision. They come back with the same messages when they are all through. This is very strange. Other people will have extremely colorful and brilliant detailed three dimensional movie kind of things. I have had both. I have been in both situations.

SENATOR BURDICK: I wonder if you would also tell us whether this practice is indulged in every time there is a Church meeting.

MR. KLEPS: No. The Church actually is more in the tradition of the mystery religions of ancient Greece. The key experience is not the weekly meeting as it is in the Christian tradition. The key experience is the big transcendental experience that comes to you maybe once or twice in a lifetime. But we center around this. The meetings are secondary. Now at the meetings perhaps a very tiny amount of LSD, 5 or 10 micrograms, will be distributed, just to increase the feeling of communion, to produce some of the effects. Or marijuana may be smoked for that matter. None of this is laid down in our regulations. It is up to the individuals.

SENATOR BURDICK: When this substance is distributed you say to the members, who pays for it? How is it acquired?

MR. KLEPS: Well, it is easily available. That is all I can really say. To discuss the details of the economics of the matter probably would not be proper for me.

SENATOR BURDICK: Does it operate like a farm cooperative, which I am acquainted with?

MR. KLEPS: Well, I would say this. That it is not at all like the heroin world. The people in the psychedelic world are kind and loving people. It is almost like automatic affection. Oh, of course there are exceptions, but it is not this sick, greedy, vicious world of the addicts. Nothing could be more dissimilar.

SENATOR BURDICK: The committee knows that it is

acquired. We do not know how it is acquired but it is paid for, is that right?

MR. KLEPS: That is right, sir.

SENATOR BURDICK: And you cannot enlighten us any further.

MR. KLEPS: I really cannot.

SENATOR BURDICK: But whether it is given to these members of the Church or whether they buy it for themselves, they do participate as a group in this.

MR. KLEPS: Yes, sir.

SENATOR BURDICK: You mentioned marijuana. Is that brought into religious services, too?

MR. KLEPS: Occasionally. We regard marijuana as being a very mild psychedelic. It is very similar to a very tiny, tiny amount of LSD. The effects are almost identical. One of the best things about marijuana is that it is very easy to control the amount ingested because you are smoking it. If you take something orally, you are leaving it more to chance. When you are smoking, there is very good control. I consider marijuana to be a completely benign substance.

SENATOR BURDICK: You see no harmful effects.

MR. KLEPS: None at all.

SENATOR BURDICK: Have you read or heard the testimony given before this committee?

MR. KLEPS: I have.

SENATOR BURDICK: And you dispute that?

MR. KLEPS: Completely.

SENATOR BURDICK: The results and findings?

MR. KLEPS: Yes, sir.

SENATOR BURDICK: Is it your intention to continue to personally experiment with and to advocate the use of LSD by the others?

MR. KLEPS: Yes, sir.

SENATOR BURDICK: Would your answer be the same in regard to marijuana?

MR. KLEPS: Yes, sir.

SENATOR BURDICK: Or similar drugs?

MR. KLEPS: Any drug; I do not even like to call them drugs.

SENATOR BURDICK: Substance."

MR. KLEPS: Any of these substances that are psychedelic that are not narcotic I believe to be sacramental. I believe that they come under the protection of religious freedom, the right to practice one's religion as one sees fit, and I do not believe that there is any evidence to the contrary, no real evidence to the contrary.

SENATOR BURDICK: You think there is no evidence to indicate that marijuana is habit forming or a narcotic?

MR. KLEPS: There is no evidence to indicate that marijuana is a narcotic. In fact even our most severe critics admit that. To say that the substance is habit forming is really to say nothing, because Rice Krispies are habit forming in the sense that if you like something you do it again. This is true with a lot of things.

SENATOR BURDICK: You should not equate marijuana with Rice Krispies.

MR. KLEPS: It is even better.

SENATOR BURDICK: What was your answer?

MR. KLEPS: I would, sir: I would say that marijuana is a very good thing. I believe in it very strongly. It is certainly better than alcohol.

SENATOR BURDICK: Just for the record, are you aware of the testimony before this committee which indicates that the uncontrolled, unsuspected use of LSD can result in panic reactions, psychotic episodes, suicidal tendencies, and other bizarre reactions requiring hospitalization?

MR. KLEPS: Yes, sir: and I do not dispute these things have happened, but it must be understood in the context of the broader picture. There are hundreds of thousands of people who are having these experiences and out of this tremendous number there are going to be a few misfortunes. It is inevitable. If these people were taking LSD under religious circumstances, if they were allowed to, if they were given accurate information, if they were warned of the dangers, if they were asked to read the literature on the subject, they probably would not go through these things.

SENATOR BURDICK: Have any of these effects that I have related to you here visited upon any of your Church members?

MR. KLEPS: Not that I know of. I would like to say in this connection too that much is made of people being hospitalized after LSD, but this hospitalization in most cases is just a simple matter of someone having a panic reaction because they do not understand what is happening, and there is no one present who does, being taken to a hospital, given a shot of a tranquilizer, spending the night in the hospital and going home the next day. Sometimes they are kept for longer periods, but this is because the psychiatrist in charge says that the man is sick. And then if you ask him are these people sick, he will say, "Yes, they have been hospitalized so they must be sick."

SENATOR BURDICK: In view of this conflict in testimony that has developed in this committee, would you agree that we should establish control over private and unsupervised use of LSD until we can make a scientific determination both of the potential harmful and useful properties of this drug or substance as you call it, either way?

MR. KLEPS: No, sir; I do not believe that you should.

SENATOR BURDICK: Do you not think it would be safer for the community to find out scientifically what the effects are?

MR. KLEPS: I do not believe that there is any scientific relevance in this area. Science is not competent to deal with this. This is religion. It is philosophy. It is a philosophy that goes beyond the narrow confines of the kind of science that we accept in our society. Science will never accept the psychedelics. It may pretend to, but it will not.

One must understand how terribly threatening this kind of experience is to the average scientist, physician, psychiatrist, psychologist. Just to hear about it is an insult to his whole notion of the world and of what is real and what is not real and so on. So they go into it with a tremendous desire to destroy it, to bring about its downfall.

SENATOR BURDICK: We referred to the fact that most of your members are young people, college students, and that most of your churches are located near college campuses.

MR. KLEPS: Yes, sir.

SENATOR BURDICK: I wonder if you could generalize and tell me in what area of the country are your churches most prevalent?

MR. KLEPS: In the Northeast and Florida.

SENATOR BURDICK: The Northeast only?

MR. KLEPS: Northeast—Massachusetts, Connecticut, New York State, and in the State of Florida. This may not be the eventual pattern. We have just started. It has only been in existence a year.

SENATOR BURDICK: Do you think that this committee should recommend any legislation regarding the sale, distribution, or possession of LSD?

MR. KLEPS: I would have no objections at all, and perhaps it would be advisable to prohibit the giving of LSD to people unsuspectingly, a sneak attack of LSD.

SENATOR BURDICK: The punchbowl type.

MR. KLEPS: Right, this is very cruel, very dangerous, I think.

SENATOR BURDICK: Should any criminal charges be imposed on administering LSD to an unsuspecting person?

MR. KLEPS: No. Oh, well, perhaps so. I am not an expert in law enforcement. I do not know what would be the most effective thing. I am against this kind of practice. I think it is socially destructive. I would not recommend any penalty going further than that.

SENATOR BURDICK: I do not think in your statement you gave me your personal educational background.

MR. KLEPS: I have a master's degree from Syracuse University. I was a school psychologist in New York State for ten years. I also worked as a clinical psychologist in a prison, Sing Sing, Dannemora, on a summer per diem basis.

SENATOR BURDICK: Did you have any particular major?

MR. KLEPS: Psychology. I was a psychologist for ten years.

SENATOR BURDICK: And it is your purpose to dedicate your life to this church work rather than to follow the scientific areas.

MR. KLEPS: Yes, sir.

SENATOR BURDICK: Why?

MR. KLEPS: I feel it is more important. I think the profession of psychology is going around in circles.

SENATOR BURDICK: First of all I ask you if your statement contains this language: you threatened civil war by saying you would make the prison system inoperative. In a previous letter to this committee you stated you would contaminate the entire Nation's water supply. Did you make a statement like that?

MR. KLEPS: No, sir. I did; what I said was that in the event that our religion is persecuted, if our wives are sterilized as in this hideous example in California, people are imprisoned for a term of thirty years as in the case of Dr. Leary, a sentence anyway, if these laws are upheld by the courts, if our basic human rights are violated, then there is going to be some kind of conflict, and I would much rather, if the conflict does occur, I would much rather do it nonviolently, turning on prisons, to use the vernacular, which would do less harm than shooting people.

SENATOR BURDICK: But you at no time threatened any uprising.

MR. KLEPS: I have not threatened; no, sir.

SENATOR BURDICK: Violence.

MR. KLEPS: No.

SENATOR BURDICK: Not having law and order.

MR. KLEPS: No, sir. I am speculating about a possible future which I would hate to see come about.

SENATOR BURDICK: Apparently the basis of my question is as follows from your statement: "I would most certainly advise my people to use LSD to fight back to flood the prisons with LSD and make life impossible for the prison administrators rather than resort to actual violence."

MR. KLEPS: Yes, sir. If that was the choice, I would rather see the prison system made inoperative, and it would be if enormous amounts of LSD, in terms of LSD; an enormous amount is an ounce, for example; could just be delivered into a prison and distributed among the inmates, it would be impossible to locate it. The entire place would fall apart as a functioning operation very quickly. I know how absurd this sounds.

SENATOR BURDICK: What would your mechanics be? How would you intend to flood the prisons?

MR. KLEPS: I do not intend to flood the prisons, sir. I am talking about a possible future. It could be done in hundreds, in thousands of ways. Smuggling things into prisons has always been very easy. The places are designed to keep people inside, not to prevent things from coming in from the outside. You could shoot it over the wall in a slingshot, with a slingshot.

SENATOR BURDICK: Do you not consider this a breach of law?

MR. KLEPS: We would have to regard these places as concentration camps; if our people are being imprisoned because they are practicing religion, then it is a concentration camp. It is not a prison anymore. It is outside the framework of decent law. We would have to think about it the same way the Jews in Hitler's Germany thought about it.

SENATOR BURDICK: But this is a product of one of our institutions, a product of our country, the laws of our country.

MR. KLEPS: Well, we would maintain that it would be unconstitutional. That to persecute us would be a violation of the first amendment.

SENATOR BURDICK: And to that extent you would take the law into your own hands?

MR. KLEPS: Rather than submit to the violation of my basic human rights, I would if I had to, I would resort to violence. I think free men have always done this. This is the way this country started.

SENATOR BURDICK: But a free country does not maintain itself without law and order.

MR. KLEPS: I believe in law and order, but I also believe in basic human rights. Basic human rights I believe come first. This is the most important thing.

SENATOR BURDICK: Is there anything further?

(No response.)

SENATOR BURDICK: Well, I must say that your testimony has been forthright and most unusual.

MR. KLEPS: Thank you, sir.

SENATOR BURDICK: I cannot agree with your conclusions, but it will all be considered with the rest of the testimony.

MR. KLEPS: Thank you very much.

(Whereupon, at 12:40 P.M., the committee was recessed, to reconvene subject to the call of the Chair.)

The TV cameras had covered the other guys very briefly, but had remained live throughout my testimony and the questioning which followed. When the show was over, the reporters concentrated on me while Baird and Bellinger, ignored, sulked in a corner. Berger vanished.

Back at the office, everyone was in a gleeful mood, but there was a fly in the ointment. Carl had just put in a call to someone he knew in Bobby Kennedy's office. It was already clear, from local coverage, that we had deprived JFK's kid brother of the space-time he expected to get, more or less as a divine right. It was obvious, Carl said, that we would get all the national coverage too.

"He's foaming at the mouth, Art," Carl said. "My friend says you had better get out of town fast. I guess the party is off. I wouldn't put it past him to have you picked up. If you play against Bobby Kennedy and win you've made an enemy for life."

Delightful prospect. Ironic, also. Compared to most politicians, I liked the Kennedys. I had actually gone to the trouble of voting for Jack. "What about you?" I asked.

Carl grinned. "Oh, I'm not worried."

So I packed my bags and took the next train. On the way up the Hudson on a local, I sat in the back of a car and read all about myself in the *New York Daily News*. Not only was the story in the front of the paper, I rated a photograph, which represented me as looking pretty much the way I hoped I looked.

A dozen or so of my fellow commuters were reading the same paper. One girl turned around and looked at me intently for a couple seconds. When I grinned, she looked away. The sensations engendered by knowing that millions of people were having my ideas, second-rate and imperfectly expressed though they were, implanted in their craniums was not at all disagreeable.

At the time, I liked it, although it didn't seem all that amazing and wonderful to me that a good sermon would attract a crowd. Tell people stuff they like to hear, and they will come out for it, etc. My father had done it for as long as I could remember, very often twice a Sunday, once in English and once in German.

But where was the collection plate? For that matter, where were the church, the steeple, and all those furiously wiggling peeple? Now, I thought, is the time to get busy. I would, I resolved, concentrate on writing and trying to set up lecture appearances.

"Enough of this penny-ante shit, Kleps," I instructed myself in no uncertain terms. "Strike while the iron is hot, and all that sort of rot. Grasp the day, for many a rose is born to blush unseen and waste its fragrance on the desert air," and so forth. A little of this stuff goes a long way. Being hectored by myself is worse, in some ways, than listening to someone else do it.

"Ah, the conquering hero!" Tim said, when he saw me.

As it turned out, the benefits I anticipated from my penetration of the frequency spectrum turned out to be far from spectacular. I just wasn't ready to exploit that kind of publicity. I didn't have anything to sell. No book. No magazine. No regular public appearances. NO MONEY.

On the other hand, much later, Carl would tell me he thought my testimony that week did more to hold up the passage of federal possession laws, for about two years, than any other single factor. (The laws already passed only covered distribution.) I had convinced a few key Senators, Carl said, that belief in the religious nature of psychedelic experience could be passionately felt by a person who appeared otherwise rational.

Could be, I guess, but how much difference did it make? Most of the heat came at us at the state level anyway, in laws passed by Republicrat punishment freaks to satisfy the needs of their brainwashed and sadistic constituents. Nelson Rockefeller showed no sign of having been impressed by my testimony, nor did any of his counterparts and imitators in other statehouses around the country.

Snazzmly speaking, I didn't deserve better results because, imitating Tim like some kind of god-damned wooden dummy, I had resorted to the "Mind of God" image and invoked other cosmic crap as well, although I knew it was public-relations smarm designed to suit the mentality of my audience and not the pure and highest doctrine. The laws would not have been delayed if I had preached the pure and highest doctrine, and there probably would have been less coverage, but it would have cleared the air, and distinguished Neo-American doctrine from the general media mulch then being spread around by all and sundry of a Psychedelian persuasion. So, shame on me.

Millbrook, I found, was practically deserted. Dick, Ralph, Maynard, Hollingshead; all gone. Tim showed me a "shrine table," with flowers and incense on it, standing next to the front door. The centerpiece was a nicely framed photograph of a dark-haired young woman with large and lustrous, if somewhat vacant-looking, brown eyes. This was Rosemary. Not my type, but very good-looking by the usual standards. Tim seemed sincerely smitten, and assured me that I, also, would revere this woman as a virtually celestial being, as did all who knew her, when I beheld the whole works going in all four dimensions, although I don't recall that those were his exact words.

Rosemary, and good for her, was confined to the Dutchess County jail for refusal to testify at a grand jury hearing about Tim. There had been a major assault ("Liddy's Raid," April '66) at a time when the Big House happened to have an unusually high number of straight visitors on hand, including reporters and photographers, who had never before been treated like enemy aliens. Once released, these people saw to it that Liddy and his thugs did not enjoy anything resembling a public relations triumph, but they could do little more. I had managed to miss it.

Blatant civil rights violations all over the place or not, grand jury hearings were being held in the Place of Overflowing Shitholes, and Liddy was not the target, as he should have been.

Tim introduced me to a tall, saturnine new recruit named Bob Ross. According to Tim, Ross, who seemed to want to turn the place into a cabbage patch with himself as chief manure spreader, was one of the leading lights of the Psychedelian world. It was my first contact with a true acid-head primitivist, and I wasn't impressed. Ross's motto, I learned later, was "Don't think!" But Tim and three or four other newcomers appeared to be following Bob's lead. The house looked like a deserted cattle barn, everyone was dressed in dirty, colorless clothes, and grunts and terse comments about the weather seemed to be the general order of conversation during the day. Once the sun had set, however, and we gathered in the kitchen to drink red wine and exchange gossip, I got the feeling that perhaps things at Millbrook hadn't changed so much after all.

I asked Tim about the old crew. Where were Dick and Ralph and, whatshisname, Hollowhead? Hollingshead?

Well, Dick was here, Ralph was there (I really don't remember) but the subject of Michael Hollingshead seemed to interest Tim a great deal more than the locations and activities of his former close associates and he proceeded to acquaint me with some of the facts of Hollingshead's gyrations which he later wrote about in *High Priest*.

"I keep getting reports on him that are hard to believe, Arthur. He's in England now and I hear he is doing all kinds of really diabolical things."

"Like what?" I asked.

"Like turning people on to LSD and then turning them in to the police."

"Jesus H. Christ," I said, and then mentioned that it had been Hollingshead who had bombed my morning brandy during my visit when Tim had been away in India, although I remembered a comment of Ralph's which strongly suggested that he had at least known about it in advance also.

Now it was Tim's turn to be astonished; nobody had ever said anything to him about it. I told him the whole story and it immediately became clear to me that it was to be a case like the exploded candle all over again. He didn't want to believe it and didn't want to hear about it, so I changed the subject.

Later, when Tim wrote a review of the *Boo Hoo Bible*, it dawned on me that Tim's reason for refusing to believe that I had been bombed, despite the presence in the house at the time of someone whom he knew to have the character and inclination to do it, was the classic quality of the trip I reported. I had to be lying about that, according to his scheme of things, so I probably was lying about everything else also. I had once pretended to have an "Enlightenment" experience, hadn't I, complete with some kind of trick candle explosion? Well, I had probably looked up the Kundalini experience in a book and faked that also. Such things were not supposed to happen to Art Kleps, who was filed in Tim's highly compartmentalized cerebrum under "comedian, alcoholic, paranoid inclinations." I was not worthy of the honor. Such things were supposed to happen to Timothy Leary and, I imagine, when they didn't happen to him, he decided they were a crock of shit anyway, and gave up the Tantric kick he had been on and returned to his first loves: gigantic entities from outer space, science fiction and mob politics.

"An Irishman's imagination never lets him alone, never convinces him, never satisfies him ..." says George Bernard Shaw. I think Tim and Shaw had a lot in common: faddishness, Mephistophelean conceits, philosophic barbarisms (Shaw's "Life Force" and Tim's Genetic Code God) and great talent largely wasted on the ingenious seduction of fashionable simpletons.

Tim also, as H.G.W. said of G.B.S., was a "philanderer with facts," which can be highly amusing unless you, yourself, happen to be the fact being philandered with.

Once loosened up, Tim wanted to know every detail of my adventures in Washington, and he seemed particularly impressed by the good treatment accorded me by the Juvenile Delinquency Subcommittee staff. When he had appeared, he hadn't bothered to prepare a statement, and he admitted to being disappointed with his own performance on that occasion. To make matters worse, Ted Kennedy, who was a member of the Dodd subcommittee, although he usually didn't show up for hearings, had walked in after things were underway, and barraged Tim with a series of hostile questions.

"I tried to be conciliatory," Tim said. "I can see now that I shouldn't have done that."

The fat little volume of the *Congressional Record* which contains the transcripts of these hearings makes fascinating reading. Every Psychedelian activist of the day, with the odd exception of Ken Kesey, seems to be represented, including Walter Bowart and Allen Ginsberg.

Tim had been conciliatory all right, as the following examples of his testimony demonstrate:

> ... As, for example, in Mr. Tannenbaum's testimony, you notice that the LSD users are very eager to talk about their experiences. They weren't like junkies. They didn't feel like criminals. They wanted to have this committee and have Mr. Tannenbaum know why they were using these drugs.
> SENATOR KENNEDY OF MASSACHUSETTS: Mr. Leary.
> DR. LEARY: Yes.
> SENATOR KENNEDY: Mr. Chairman, I am trying to follow the best I possibly can some themes that must be coming out of your testimony here this morning, and I am completely unable to do so. You talked in the beginning about the communications problem which exists between different generations, and then you indicate and describe why that exists. Then we hear a description and analysis, as valuable as that might be, about the different reactions to different drugs. You talk about the statistics which are going to be larger next year. Then you say you are not alarmed by them because if they are in training, people have them, and there is a careful distribution, then this isn't really a problem. And then I hope we are going to have at least a discussion on who those trained people might be and what the regulations might be.
> I am completely unable to follow anything other than just sort of a general hyperbole of discussion here. Since your testimony isn't written, and this is a matter with which we are deeply concerned, I hope at least for those of us who are not inimitably as familiar as apparently you are with LSD, that you will try and see if you can analyze this somewhat more precisely. At least I would find that helpful. As I say, I haven't had the background or experience in this area as I am sure the other members of the

committee have, but I think it would be extremely valuable to the members of the committee if you could at least outline to some extent what you are going to try and demonstrate here today, and then if you could somewhat more precisely and exactly come to those points.

DR. LEARY: I was, Senator Kennedy, just about to do that. I am pointing out the differences that exist among drugs, and I am going to suggest that special types of legislation are needed.

SENATOR KENNEDY: Are you going to talk about the lack of communication between the generations before that or after that?

DR. LEARY: I finished doing that. I hope that that is clearly on the record. I feel that constructive legislation is obviously and badly needed, and I recommend respectfully to this committee that you consider legislation which will license responsible adults to use these drugs for serious purposes, such as spiritual growth, pursuit of knowledge, or in their own personal development. To obtain such a license, the applicant, I think, should have to meet physical, intellectual, and emotional criteria.

I believe that the criteria for marijuana, which is the mildest of the psychedelic drugs, should be about those which we now use to license people to drive automobiles, whereas the criteria for the licensing of LSD, a much more powerful act, should be much more strict, perhaps the criteria now used for airplane pilots would be appropriate.

SENATOR KENNEDY: So we are going to train high school students? Are we going to have high school courses as well?

DR. LEARY: I would let research, scientific research answer the question as to at what age the nervous system is ready to use these new instruments.

SENATOR KENNEDY: Then what are we going to do now for the boys that, say, go into the Army prior to the time they get to that age? Are we going to have the Army give training courses too on how to use it?

DR. LEARY: I should think that in the Army of the future, we all hope there won't be, but in the Army of the future LSD will be used to expand consciousness so that these men can do their duties more effectively.

SENATOR KENNEDY: That is very responsive. Now you feel that anybody who distributes this ought to be carefully trained, is that correct?

DR. LEARY: Yes, sir.

SENATOR KENNEDY: And you admit that it can leave an individual so that he does not know the difference between right and wrong in the socially acceptable terms, is that right?

DR. LEARY: Yes, sir.

SENATOR KENNEDY: So that he is relatively unaccountable for his actions?

DR. LEARY: Well, I don't think anyone.

SENATOR KENNEDY: Does he know the difference between right and wrong?

DR. LEARY: You are talking about hypothetical persons.

SENATOR KENNEDY: I am not talking about hypotheticals.

DR. LEARY: What are we talking about, sir?

Good question. Of course, Tim went on to say that he was against criminal penalties for use, even for unauthorized use by non-holders of "pilot's licenses," but he had given Kennedy all the opening he needed to make Tim sound like a nincompoop:

SENATOR KENNEDY: I could not agree with you more, that he mentioned in there about when it was used, particularly for terminal cases, administration in the case of intractable pain, mostly in patients with terminal cancer, we do not question that.

We do not have any dispute about that, Mr. Leary. But I think what you have testified to is indiscriminate possession of this, as well as use, that it is dangerous, and I think the question now is for legislators to determine whether it can be controlled by legislation or whether it cannot be.

I think that you have testified as well that you want to see the control over its being brought into the United States, its production, and you have also testified that you think the indiscriminate use of this is dangerous, and I think you have pointed out what you feel personally are some of the advantages of it. You feel as well that it is a matter which cannot be legislated over. I think that is a question for the Congress.

But is seems to me that your testimony has been extremely convincing about the dangers of this drug, as well as its opportunities. And I think for someone who has been associated as long as you have been, have been intimately involved in it as long as you have been, I think that is extremely weighty evidence which you have given to this committee this morning, and we want to thank you.

DR. LEARY: I cannot agree with that summary, respectfully. I must disagree, Senator Kennedy, with your statement.

SENATOR KENNEDY: Let's take the various aspects of it. You feel that there ought to be control over at least importation?

DR. LEARY: The sale, manufacture or distribution, yes.

SENATOR KENNEDY: The sale and manufacturing?

DR. LEARY: Yes, sir.

SENATOR KENNEDY: Why do you think that this should be?

DR. LEARY: Because these are matters of commerce and manufacture.

SENATOR KENNEDY: And that is the only reason you think this because it is a matter of interstate and foreign commerce? Is that the only reason? I mean, we have things which are produced, textiles in Massachusetts, furniture in Massachusetts that are not restricted, Dr. Leary. You have testified. Now why do you think they should be?

DR. LEARY: I feel that activity, particularly commercial activities involving the manufacture, sale, and distribution of these substances definitely should be controlled because you do not know about quality, you do not know about safety, you do not know what you are buying. Obviously you have to have laws, just as you have laws about the amphetamines. I want the amphetamines and the barbiturates controlled.

SENATOR KENNEDY: Let's go back.

DR. LEARY: I do not want people who use these, who have a handful, put in jail.

SENATOR KENNEDY: You said you do not know about the quality. What is it about the quality that you are frightened about?

DR. LEARY: We do not want amateur or black-market sale or distribution of LSD.

SENATOR KENNEDY: Why not?

DR. LEARY: Or barbiturates or liquor. When you buy a bottle of liquor ...

SENATOR KENNEDY: Why do you not want the indiscriminate manufacture and distribution? Why not? Is it because it is dangerous?

DR. LEARY: Because you do not know what you are getting.

SENATOR KENNEDY: Is it because it is dangerous? Are you interested only in the consumer and whether, like truth in packaging, whether there are too many strawberries or not enough strawberries in the pie, or is it something more dangerous than that, Dr. Leary?

DR. LEARY: No, sir; I think LSD is much less dangerous than the amphetamines and barbiturates.

SENATOR KENNEDY: I am not asking that. The reason, as I would gather it, is because this is a dangerous drug; is that right?

DR. LEARY: No, sir; LSD is not a dangerous drug.

SENATOR KENNEDY: Why have you admitted then, why you have latched that onto the other questions of the control and distribution and manufacturing of drugs?

DR. LEARY: I feel the same as I do with alcohol, you want to know what you are getting. It has to be supervised by Government FDA standards of health and packaging.

SENATOR KENNEDY: Do you not agree that alcohol can be dangerous?

DR. LEARY: I think that alcohol is probably the most dangerous drug around.

SENATOR KENNEDY: All right, it can be dangerous, can it not?

DR. LEARY: Yes, sir; if it is used improperly.

I will draw the curtain at this point. The exchange between Tim and Teddy became even more incoherent thereafter, although restricting the use of LSD to people who qualified for "pilot licenses" was probably the craziest idea of all. The most astonishing thing about Tim's testimony was what he didn't say. The religious nature of the experience, and the First Amendment rights that therefore applied, were never alluded to in any way by the creator and leader of the Castalia Foundation, chief instigator of and participant in the Marsh Chapel "Good Friday Experiment," and all of that.

For a person in Tim's position, facing thirty years in some hellhole, and determined to defend himself with the First Amendment's "free exercise" clause, this seems like self-destructive madness. Was he trying to make some kind of a deal? (OK, so it isn't religious. I was just kidding. Let's be scientific about this. Drop the charges and put me on The Dope Commission.) There doesn't seem to be any other explanation.

Had I known about this testimony before I made my statement, I could not have defended Tim as our religious leader. Instead, I might have attacked him as an insidious menace to the religious spirit and to human freedom in general. But that would just have solidified Tim's position. As it was, he dropped his pilot's license horseshit soon after and came over to my side, maintaining that the psychedelic experience was religious and therefore no laws could interfere.

Exactly what kind of lunatic bureaucracy would have arisen if Tim's proposals had been taken seriously and the government had attempted to regulate Psychedelian religious practices is difficult to imagine. I suppose supervised trips would be part of it. Imagine coming down from a big one in a happy state, only to be confronted by Meat Hook Baird, M.D. with a tape measure, ready to determine if your nose has become more prominent and pugnacious, or your chin more recessive, or whatever.

Trying to control other people's choice of mental states by force has nothing to do with what I mean by elitism. I mean meritocracy. Tim's pilot's license nonsense was just standard We Are the Masters of the Universe and Everyone Will Think and Act the Way We Do, or Else absolutism. Old as the hills. The villain with a thousand faces.

Well, we all have our "off" days, and Tim deserves credit for admitting his error and reversing his course as he did.

Residents of the United States are assigned, by who knows whom, a kind of bureaucratic pope of an established meta-church, which rules over all associations claiming to be religious by granting or denying them tax-exempt status on the basis of who knows what. During the late '70s this tyrant was known as "E.D. Coleman" and his title was Chief, Exempt Organizations, Technical Branch, Internal Revenue Service, Department of the Treasury. If you doubt this, just initiate a Freedom of Information Act correspondence with the IRS and demand to know under what laws and rules of evidence and procedure a mysterious bureaucrat is allowed to promote the welfare of the Church of Satan and the Native American Church of South Dakota and the Church of Scientology, but deny equal treatment to the Original Kleptonian Neo-American Church.

If you get anything back from the IRS resembling a straight answer, let me know.

Tim looked tired. Not only was he pulling weeds and milking goats, he was also speaking at any college that would have him and working on his next book. He was explicit about his strategy: we had to take our lead from the kids from now on. If we had them with us, it didn't matter what the government did.

Could be. Thereafter, whatever Tim said in public was almost entirely determined by what he thought "the troops" wanted to hear. The whole idea was to keep abreast. If they wanted to pretend to be simple peasants, fine. If they wanted to dress up in robes on Saturday night and pretend they were weird monks, who cared? Black pajamas and Molotov cocktails? Why not. Tim had made a fundamental decision about himself.

This frame of mind left me cold. Never in a million years could I act that way. Yet, as head of the Church, wasn't I the one who ought to be doing that kind of thing, while Tim, our spiritual leader, spoke the truth without fear or favor? After all, I had just seen a demonstration in Washington of what the political game was all about: a mad scramble for media space-time. Tim was better suited, despite his poor showing in D.C., for playing that game than I was. Another identity crisis? Not on your life. When you have had one identity crisis, you have had them all. Let everyone do his own thing. I would go my way and Tim would go his and we would see how everything turned out in the end.

What I would like to see is the substitution of "instruments of torture or images thereof" and "forced circumcision of an infant" for the names of the currently prohibited drugs and the substitution of "negative" for "positive" and vice versa, in all statutes governing urine testing. All property held by the punishment freaks should be transferred to their victims. That would only be fair, and would invigorate the American economy with "fresh blood," so to speak.

Chapter 16
MORGAN LE FAY

If knights errant were to be believed, not all castles were desirable places to seek hospitality in.

Back at Cranberry Lake, Charlie Merchant greeted me with great excitement. All hell had broken loose. I had been on the national morning and evening news. The Watertown paper had put out a special edition with a full page devoted to the North Country's latest tourist attraction, me. Some guy had driven over to sell it at the Star Lake high school and had been thrown off the property by Person in person. The name of Art Kleps adorned every lip. Charlie was delighted. Any publicity for Cranberry Lake was good publicity as far as he was concerned.

I called Sally a day or two later and told her to get on the first plane she could manage. Things were looking up. With all the publicity we earned from the Senate hearings, it would be duck soup to fill MGL all summer with paying visitors. There would be a ready market for anything I wrote. Suddenly, the mailbox was loaded with membership applications for the Church every morning. All we had to do now was attend to business and in a short time our troubles would be over. There would be enough money by fall to winterize the lodge, or we could rent a house in Syracuse. Every prospect pleased. Good scenes coming up.

Sally, it turned out, wasn't exactly seeing things in these terms.

She liked Miami. She wasn't even sure she would come up during the summer. It wasn't that she had given up chemicals. Far from it. She was hanging around with the college kid speed freaks and paregoric heads whom I had tried to convert to finer things while I had been there. She described a fight she had witnessed between one of our boo hoos and a junkie who had burned him in an acid deal. She was helping her mother look for a house in Sarasota. Good old Frank Green, the wife beater, who lived there with his mother, had suggested the area.

Jesus Christ!

Ramakrishna, whenever he was informed that a nice, "spiritually inclined" young man he had just met was married, characteristically responded as if he had been told the man had a bad case of tuberculosis and wasn't expected to live. If it turned out the guy had children, Ramakrishna would, as oft as not, burst into tears. In terms of social control, it is no accident or trivial matter that the state almost always gives all the property and custody of the children to the mother.

This simple threat has probably nipped more potential revolutionaries in the bud than all the armed might in Sado-Judeo-Paulendom. Social deviance is no less common in women than in men, but the form it takes is rarely a threat to established institutions, since it's usually mere escapism or misbehavior like hanging out with the "wrong" crowd. No matter how radical her opinions or how intelligent and elevated her tastes and ideas, a woman with children will almost always behave according to tamasic values. The state can depend on her, as long as she has food and a roof over her head, not to give too much trouble. I have not seen many exceptions to this rule, I don't expect to see many and, because kids need protection first and foremost, I don't really think there ought to be many.

At a time when all flags flying seemed to signal fair weather, I was holed below the waterline by a torpedo from left field. With all the assurance in the world that the law was on her side and there wasn't a thing I could do about it, Sally was telling me I would either do things her way or I could forget about my kids. My mental condition went directly from euphoria to black depression. I couldn't write. I did nothing to encourage visitors.

Cranberry Lake, glittering in the early summer sun, might as well have been a gigantic cesspool for all I cared. I started drinking quite a bit more than was good for me.

I'm not interested in contributing another account of emotional misery to the already swollen collection. When one is caught in one of these situations the best thing to do is fight like a cornered beast to rectify matters and, if that proves to be impossible, crawl into a hole somewhere and pray for a speedy recovery, but I don't have any respect for the condition itself and I didn't then. This bummer lasted from the time of which I am speaking, early summer of '66, to January of '67, when I moved into the Big House at Millbrook, divested of everything except the clothes on my back and my indomitable will, etc. I'm going to give a sort of telegraphic account of the high and low points just to keep the record straight, and resume a more discursive style when I'm on the train headed back to Millbrook from Birmingham.

A teenage boy and girl, who had joined the Church in Miami, came up to visit, flat broke. I let them use a cabin but told them to forget any delusions they might have formed about my willingness to feed the poor while in the same condition myself. Dorothy, the marijuana goddess, was a hot little number, in a scrawny kind of way, but I couldn't have cared less. They were classic Miami-style nitwit street druggies. They didn't even try to find jobs. I went to visit Bob Eddy for a few days. When I returned, I found my best boat half under water on the town beach. Fortunately, I had preserved enough common sense to stow my outboard motor, a charming little Mercury, in the trunk of the car before I took off, along with my charming little semi-automatic Browning rifle chambered for .22 shorts, the prettiest and most fun firearm ever manufactured, in my opinion, and cheap to use also. Back at the lodge, I discovered that most of my library was gone, including all my letters from Tim.

Sally flew up for a three-day visit in a supposed attempt to "adjust." It was as if I were asking her to move into a tenement in Harlem for the summer. She returned to Miami. She flew up again. Money for which there were much better uses was being wasted.

The whole family was back together, but "only for a month." It was a demonstration of the ancient truism that you can lead a horse to water but you can't make him wash his armpits. We had some interesting visitors who didn't steal anything; we went swimming and fishing and such almost every day; but there was no genuine enthusiasm or satisfaction, because we both knew there would be no happy ending. Sally intended to return to Miami. I didn't know what I would do, but whatever it was, I knew I wouldn't like it. Sally's mother sent her tickets. The next day she and the kids left with Yossarian and Anna, who gave them a ride to the airport in Albany.

My Life in the Woods adventure had been converted into a stupid soap opera. Because of the kids, I just couldn't say to hell with it and find another girl. I went to Syracuse a couple times and screwed around, but didn't enjoy it much. I returned after one such excursion around 3 a.m., drunk and stoned on hash. In the boat, when I wrongly thought myself about halfway home, an elaborate and gigantic image in neon blue, which resembled a Sanskrit letter or a Chinese ideogram, appeared in the pitch darkness in front of me. I cut the motor. The vision vanished. As my eyes refocused, I saw that I had taken a false bearing and had been seconds away from piling up on some rocks which were a well-known hazard in the north-central section of the lake.

The emotional effect was close to zero. To the question "sink or swim" I would have answered "as you like it." This state of mind, at that point, represented progress. It didn't bother me at all to sell the outboard and the rifle for half of what I had paid for them.

My car having been confiscated by one of my creditors, I hitchhiked and then took busses from Saranac Lake to Millbrook. J.D. Kuch, bee hee of Washington, D.C., and husband had agreed to pick me up at Millbrook in a few days and then drive me to Steve Newell's place in New Jersey. Steve had good connections. Perhaps he could get me a job for the winter.

Chapter 17

A ROYAL BANQUET

I will say this much for the nobility: that, tyrannical, murderous, rapacious, and morally rotten as they were, they were deeply and enthusiastically religious.

I arrived one evening in a well-lubricated condition. The place was virtually overflowing with attractive young ladies of frivolous, lascivious and tolerant dispositions. Most were wearing "ecstatic clothes." I knew only two or three, but the rest seemed to know me by reputation, and to have liked what they had heard.

Tim and his inner circle of the moment were away on a lecture and light-show date somewhere, but the partial resurrection of the furniture and the spirit and attire of the home guard made it clear that another ideological corner had been turned. I had no trouble finding drinking companions. I should have concentrated on Betsy Ross, Bob's sweet, sensible and sexy sister, but when I woke up in the morning I was all tangled up on a mattress on the floor with a true air-head Learyite named Karen Detweiler, who, although far from repellent, wasn't my type. A typical alcoholic misunderstanding. Oh well, any port in a storm and, as it turned out, this port had interesting connections.

Karen, in a way, wasn't a troop after all. She was just visiting, on what might be called a vibe-gathering expedition, from a yoga ashram across the Hudson.

A complicated story unfolded. Karen's ashram, Ananda, at Monroe, N.Y., had been started by a Dr. Rammurti Mishra from India, who was a psychiatrist, a yogi and, in Karen's opinion, a "beautiful person." Until the advent of the Psychedelian age, the place had potted quietly along supported by a gaggle of middle-class, middle-aged fogies in search of the kind of cheap miracle the less opulent sought at Madame Igapoo's corner seance. When the acid hit the fan, however, the demographics altered radically. All kinds of young people showed up who could not be turned away, because they were willing, if not eager, outwardly anyway, to follow all the rules for full-time devotees. The older generation, known collectively as "householders," basically treated the place as a weekend retreat.

Now, Karen told me, all "the kids," such as herself, plus their new and groovy guru, a certain William Haines, were about to be evicted for general stonedness.

By the time the older crowd, who had firm control of the place administratively, discovered that all the kids were zonked and intended to remain that way, the kids had bombed Haines, who was about a year older than me and had been functioning for some time as Mishra's right-hand man, or vicar or straw boss, or something.

Panic! The Devil was within the gates! As things stood, Karen told me, all the young people and Haines had been given thirty days to leave. The householders had hired an armed guard who was patrolling the property.

Mishra had refused to take sides. On one occasion, however, when asked his opinion of the drug movement by an older resident, he had replied, "Drugs? I love drugs!" so the kids had some hope, but less and less as time went by, that he might change his mind and save the day. Did I want to visit? I would love Bill Haines. He was just my type, Karen asserted, a jovial Sagittarian gorilla with a checkered past.

Of course I did.

At the Ashram, which turned out to be much more splendid than I had expected, with a small lake at the center and several pleasant wood-frame buildings, I was introduced to Haines, who was holding court in a small room jammed with Oriental objets d'art, and people crammed into every chair and corner. In the center of the floor a small person with a shaved head, whose sex I could not determine, was squirming around and giggling every time anyone said anything. Aside from this creature, I really liked the looks of the kids. They were happy, open-faced types. The girls were all pretty, with one or two knockouts.

I immediately liked Haines, just as Karen had predicted. He had spent nine years in India and was telling outrageous and hilarious stories about the private lives of the leading lights of modern yoga and Hinduism, although he himself, and most of the kids, were dressed in the proper robes, beads and sandals and were surrounded by authentic signs and symbols of the ancient Eastern traditions. A picture of Mishra, seated in the lotus on a rug near the lake, was on the wall, with fresh flowers under it. He looked dark, stern and well-barbered.

After a pleasant hour or two during which I heard, for the first time since Watts, someone who knew what he was talking about discuss the religions of the East, the speaker, none other than Bill, a.k.a. "Sri Sankara," Haines invited me to join in the evening "meditation" and tell everyone all about the Neo-American Church, which sounded "perfectly reasonable" to him, he said.

On the way over to Mishra's residence where the meeting was to be held, Karen told me it was obvious to her I had already made a big hit with Haines, because he was "the kind of guy who puts everything down, no matter what." It was unheard of for him to say anything good about a visitor's trip. Instead, he told everyone who showed up at the place how full of shit they were, right off the bat.

I could well believe it, and I could well understand it, and I have generally followed this policy myself, with the result that I am usually one step away from the poorhouse but rarely obliged to endure obnoxious company unless locked up with it.

After my presentation, which was well-received by one and all, Karen took me to her room in a dormitory close to the lake, where several Ashramites joined us in practicing, by inhalation, what I had just been preaching.

Haines, the kids said, didn't smoke grass, but ever since his bombardment at a big weekend religious festival, he had been taking large doses of acid at least once a week. I signed up boo hoos and bee hees right and left, and met a couple of older Ashramites: Tambimutto, a relic of the old Greenwich Village literary scene, who conned me out of a six-pack; and a guy who was recovering from several years in a Buddhist monastery, using that well-known tranquilizer, lysergic acid diethylamide, to make a smooth adjustment to the outside world. I also met my future wife, Wendy Williams. She flitted in and out, but didn't make much of an impression on me at the time.

The next morning, hearing that I needed a bottle, Narad, the "man of iron," offered to drive me to town. Narad was famous as the young lover of a well-known female teacher of hatha yoga described in a fairly popular book of the day by Jess Stearn called *Yoga, Youth, and Reincarnation.*

Narad, Karen had informed me, was "quite a character." According to her, he spent much of his spare time rolling huge stones around the property and welding furniture out of steel parts so heavy that a coffee table, for example, might require six men to move it from one room to another. He was also incredibly horny but none of the girls would have anything to do with him. His basic technique was to cast horoscopes which invariably demonstrated that the young lady in question must either submit to his embrace or, in consequence of her failure to obey the stars, miss out on her only crack at Nirvana.

"I used to live next door to him," Karen said, "and he drove me crazy. You'll see."

Haines told me later he had once heard Karen, who claimed to have distinct memories of prior lives, including one tour as Queen of the Nile, or something similar, slam a door behind her in the middle of the night and flee the building screaming, "No, never! I didn't love you in the sixteenth century and I don't love you now!"

Narad lived up to his reputation. During the trip to town and back he didn't stop talking for a minute. This kid, if there was any truth in what he said, should have been ruling the universe with an iron fist and steely nerves since he knew exactly how it was screwed together down to the last etheric nut and metaphysical bolt. Oddly enough, for someone who could tell you in exactly what "vibration zone" anything was located, Narad apparently had a lousy memory. He made three wrong turns in the short trip to town and back.

One should not be too hasty in ejecting irritating but harmless paranoid characters like Narad from Psychedelian communities. It's probably better to have one severe case who will serve as a bad example than six mild cases who will hide or disguise their delusional systems. Enlightenment is impossible for anyone caught up in "metaphysical" ideation. Give me a naive realist or an old-fashioned supernaturalist any day.

It was clear to me that Bill Haines had to meet Timothy Leary. I got on the phone, after Bill said he would be delighted, and set it up. We were all invited to the Big House for dinner. All the Ashramites were excited about it.

Sarasvati, the girl who was rolling around on the floor the night before, had to be locked in her room lest she throw herself in front of Haines' car as she had on a prior occasion when he left the property without her. Sarasvati, so called by her own election, had first appeared a few weeks earlier at a wedding Haines had attended at a fashionable synagogue in New York City. She was a junkie, a hooker, and obviously stoned on acid. In full view of the crowd on the sidewalk after the service, she had thrown herself at Bill's feet, calling him "guruji" and begging to be accepted as an Ashramite. She would do anything he said, she said. Haines had accepted her, sort of, but had made several attempts to dump her after she appeared in Monroe.

One fairly serious attempt to do so, after she had been found taking a bath in Mishra's apartment, which was sacred territory, had resulted in her cutting all her hair off. Haines seemed resigned to his fate. Although he grumbled and growled at Sarasvati constantly, he had acquired an industrious housekeeper at the cost of her room and board.

I later discovered that Sarasvati took "the teachings" very seriously, which explained much of her mirth about lesser matters, her own fixation on Haines included.

Sarasvati was always asking good questions like, "Is this for real or am I going crazy?" or, "Who's doing it, that's what I want to know?" or, "If I'm God, how come you all aren't scared out of your wits?" and then giggling uncontrollably until Bill told her to go mop a floor or do some laundry.

Everyone dressed up, some of us took a little acid and Haines took a lot, and we drove over to Millbrook in two cars and a VW van. High drama, I thought, as we crossed the Hudson River in the fading light.

At the Big House, which was all lit up and looked like a gigantic and fantastic ornament set in the unbroken darkness of the trees, Haines immediately demonstrated his ability to hang on to his sense of humor while elevated on the Supreme Sacrament. When a scrawny Ashramite named Jean-Pierre emerged from the van wearing a bed sheet, Haines, who had also alighted, boomed out, "Ah, Jean-Pierre! You look like Jesus Christ after a hard night!"

I wish someone had taken a group photograph at the first meeting of the Ashram and the League. Everyone except me seemed to be dressed to kill in the best beads and batik money could buy. Flowers, candles and incense galore. The meeting was held in the dining room, which the Leaguers had arranged and decorated for the purpose. Tim's people sat on one side of the low table, Bill's on the other.

Bill and Tim bowed to each other with fingertips together at the forehead, as was then the fashion. Everyone sat down and several lit up and passed joints. Bill puffed on his pipe. Pleasantries were exchanged. Finally, Bill opened the serious part of the proceedings by announcing, "I often think, Dr. Leary, that if we could only get rid of the Holy Mothers we would solve all our problems, ho, ho, ho."

Tim refused to bite. Instead, he readily agreed to Bill's thesis. Meetings between established teachers are, in the ancient traditions of Oriental gurumanship, highly stylized performances put on, presumably, for the benefit of the audience. There is supposed to be an argument which continues until one party admits he is wrong or drops from exhaustion. On later occasions, as we shall see, Bill and Tim had no difficulty finding things to argue about, but on their first meeting, everything was sweetness and light, even though Tim's group included three or four women who probably regarded themselves as "Holy Mothers," one of whom, Bhavani, had actually consulted primary sources and seemed to know what she was talking about.

Tim, immediately aware of Bill's condition, asked some questions about how Bill reconciled yoga with the use of LSD and Bill responded for fifteen minutes or so with an earnest and sensible account of his feelings and attitudes on the subject. He stressed the idea that the whole purpose of yoga was to reach Enlightenment and that this could only be done through intense personal experience of the kind the psychedelic drugs provided.

Good show. Tim seemed satisfied he was dealing with a fellow maniac, and suggested that everyone just do as they pleased and we would all have dinner together in a couple of hours. Bali Ram led some women from both groups into the kitchen, where, he said, he would show them how to prepare a vegetarian feast worthy of the King of Nepal. The boys started milling around checking out the girls and the girls started milling around checking out the boys.

Dinner was delightful, as Bali had promised. Later, I found Bill in the library, staring moodily at the fire, and took a seat near him. "Did I make an ass of myself, Kleps?" Bill asked, in a childlike way. Among his other attractive characteristics, Bill became emotionally vulnerable on trips. So did Billy Hitchcock. Tim, in contrast, became cold, brilliant and decisive. I think I'm somewhere in the middle, but such things are for others to judge.

"Hell, no, Bill," I said. "You did beautifully. It was just right for the occasion."

"Well, it's hard to tell when you're on this stuff," Bill said. "Did the kids tell you how they bombed me the first time? The place was jammed with straight Ashram members from New York, all the Holy Mothers, and all kinds of visitors and it was up to me to organize everything and there I was on my first trip, and it was no baby dose either, let me tell you. I had only two thoughts: Who is high and who isn't, and who did it? ... because I'm going to kill the son of a bitch!"

Bill laughed ruefully and shook his head, "What really got me was that these dumb little buggers had been doing it for years, some of them, and the whole time I was trying to tell them where it was at. Why did they listen to me?"

"Just because they take a lot of acid doesn't mean they have learned much from it, Bill," I said. "That was a mistake I made for a long time. I'm not sure I'm enlightened either. I'm sure I am sometimes, but then at other times I seem to forget, or at least I don't live up to it. I guess I'm enlightened in a half-assed way."

"You're enlightened, Kleps," Bill said. He seemed a little embarrassed at having made this pronouncement. "Well, I guess I had better go find the Mad Scientist, swallow my pride, and beg for sanctuary. You really think I did all right, huh?"

"You've got just the style that's needed around here," I said.

Bill went off to find Tim.

A couple days later, J.D. and her husband, whom she would shed shortly, dropped me off at Steve Newell's house, a few miles from Princeton and Humphry Osmond's New Jersey Neuro-Psychiatric Institute.

Before we take our leave of J.D., whose name appears to be forever enshrined in American legal reference books as a representative of the Neo-American Church (*United States of America v. Judith H. Kuch,* Criminal No. 1473-67), I must mention that this ignorant, wealthy, creepy little occultist, who in appearance so much resembled a moldy dumpling, had a character to match. She attracted creeps and creeps attracted her. Along with her closest associates such as Donald Mead and Kevin Malone, all she actually represented was an occultist-creep network extending from Boston to Washington, D.C., which degraded the image of the Neo-American Church in many places in the early years of the movement. I didn't know. If I had, I would not have been asking for or accepting favors from her. It was appropriate that it was J.D. who delivered me to a place where I was to suffer the worst blow of my Psychedelian career up to that time.

Steve's setting was in perfect keeping with his mental set: an isolated old house in the country with a crumbling graveyard behind it and an old stone barn next door inhabited by an incommunicative "mad" inventor whose large and incomprehensible constructions Steve had only glimpsed through briefly opened doors.

Steve seemed to be in fine fettle, and thought it likely he could find me a job for the winter. He introduced me to his boss and lover, who struck me as a nice, sensible woman who didn't have the slightest idea of what acid was all about. She was one of the few members of the research staff of the hospital who had never tripped. I filled out a questionnaire and was interviewed by a staff sociologist. I met Humphry Osmond. Instant feelings of affiliation.

Sure enough, two days later I had a job at another nuthouse right up the road from Osmond's place. I noticed, however, as we drove back and forth, that flocks of blackbirds constantly appeared on our left. A sign of impending murder, according to the Thugee superstitions of India.

Did this apply in New Jersey, and if so, to whom?

Chapter 18

IN THE QUEEN'S DUNGEONS

No, confound her, her intellect was good, she had brains enough, but her training made her an ass—that is, from a many-centuries-later point of view.

It didn't take long to find out. When I called Sally to tell her the good news and ask if she wanted a house on the hospital grounds or off, the answer was neither. She wasn't coming up and I shouldn't come down. Good advice, in more ways than one.

Frank, the wife-beater, had found the key to her heart. I had the exquisite pleasure of envisioning my two daughters being brought up by one of the biggest assholes I had ever met. The first thing Steve did, when he got home and heard the news, was to mutter "that miserable bastard" and then hide his beautiful S&W .38 Special revolver which, although I hadn't mentioned it, was the only thing in the house in which I was interested.

I took a bus from Princeton to Miami and called up Karl Newton in Syracuse from my brother's house. Karl had visited MGL a couple times and loved it. $2,000 for my equity? Fine. The money came by Western Union. I bought an old panel truck for $600 and went to collect Sally and the kids. It was night. I was smashed. A cop started following me. There was every probability a warrant was out for me in Florida because of the old seizure of the sugar cubes. Delightful. I stepped on the gas and careened around Miami's chessboard of look-alike blocks until I lost the cop, then abandoned the truck. The next day we all took a plane for Syracuse.

Airplane fares, incidentals, and a month's rent and a month's security on an apartment in Syracuse near Sally's old sorority house quickly disposed of the two grand. Broke again. I remembered that a visitor to MGL had claimed to have seen marijuana growing next to the highway between Star Lake and Cranberry while hitchhiking home. My Syracuse boo hoo and I went up to check it out. Sure enough. To celebrate, we got drunk, got picked up for P.I., and spent the night in jail. But we returned with the goods. Sally wasn't pleased with these developments. The next day, when I returned from shopping, she and the kids were gone. Two days later, divorce papers arrived. There was no way I could return to Florida without going to jail. I had sold Morning Glory Lodge for nothing.

Karl gave me his old Volkswagen convertible and I drove down to Millbrook. Tim wanted to know what I wanted to do. I told him I seemed to have two choices. I could either stay at Millbrook or go to Alabama. An admirer from Birmingham had offered cash for the trip, but the letters he had written were almost illiterate, so I had grave doubts about the wisdom of accepting his offer, although he had also said he owned land in the region, some of which he might give to the Church, he said.

"Listen, Art," Tim said, "you're no more fucked up than I have been several times in the past, and don't think I haven't considered committing myself. I may yet, if it's the only way to avoid prison. But I have decided that if I do, I will pick some nice quiet VA hospital in the South. I can't stand this place in the winter. I think you ought to go down there and let this character pay your bills while you work on *Divine Toad Sweat*."

Yeah, well, I don't know, maybe so. My only genuine interest at that point was making sure I had enough whiskey on hand. During a slide show in a darkened room that evening, Billy Hitchcock appeared and asked me what I was up to. I told him.

"My wife left me, I lost the lodge, and I'm a complete fucking drunken mess."

"There's no room in the house," Tim said, from the other side of the projector, which was producing the usual squiggly forms on the wall.

"Well, what about the Gray Buildings out back?" asked charming Billy, and may the heavenly hosts forever praise his name, for that one, anyway.

"I think we could fix up a room," Billy said.

The "Gray Buildings" were a farmhouse, garage, stables, carriage-house combination into which the Ashram would move in '67. One of the farm hands, Hurdle, and his family lived in the house section but there was plenty of empty space at the other end which I could have fixed up.

"No," said Tim, flatly, from behind a cloud of cigarette smoke in the gloom. "I think Art ought to go down to Alabama for the winter."

I looked at Billy, rolled my bloodshot eyes, and waived with a wave. Billy slouched down in his chair a bit and started nibbling a fingernail.

Chapter 19

KNIGHT-ERRANTRY AS A TRADE

And, moreover, when you come right down to the bedrock, knight-errantry is worse than pork; for whatever happens, the pork's left, and so somebody's benefited, anyway; but when the market breaks, in the knight-errantry whirl, and every knight in the pool passes in his checks, what have you got for assets?

On the way to my parents' retirement house in Booneville, up in the Adirondack foothills north of Utica, where I intended to dry out, I was picked up for having an expired registration (one day over) and spent the night in jail. For the first time, my withdrawal symptoms included the delirium tremens hallucinations I had often heard and read about but never before experienced. The visionary content differed little, if at all, from what I had experienced on mescaline, acid and morning glory seeds. I have learned since, from extremely primary sources, that the bugs and snakes of the fabled DTs are rare.

With complete disregard for everything the pop culture and learned opinion has depicted, most alcoholics going through withdrawal see the same beautiful and elaborate spectacles witnessed by peyote eaters and acid heads.

With my eyes open, I seemed to be inside a tiny cathedral. The spaces between the bars became stained-glass windows.

With my eyes closed, I seemed to be somewhere in Southeast Asia under an enormous multi-chambered tent in which old men with long white beards, seated on elaborately figured cushions and rugs with hookahs and objets d'art at their sides, were silently meditating. The only hint of anything repellent in these visions was a tarantula, which seemed to be a pet of one of the old men, but there was nothing at all menacing about it. Everything I saw was stable, well defined and serene.

But I wasn't, at least not on the "physical plane." I was shaking all over and convinced I would hemorrhage any moment from the continuous retching. I didn't. The visions faded after a few hours and so did the shakes.

My father drove down and paid the fine, and I dried out in the guest bedroom. My parents, as usual, were kind, but not understanding.

Kind is good enough, usually.

Chapter 20

THE OGRE'S CASTLE

This was not the sort of experience for a statesman to encounter who was planning out a peaceful revolution in his mind.

I now found myself dependent, at least for the roof over my head, on the charity of a bootlegger, or rather, a rentier to bootleggers. Jim was much too disorganized to manage anything as complicated as a white-lightning run. His spacious brick home, in one of the wealthiest sections of Birmingham, was a mess within, strewn with cheap occultist literature and all kinds of trash and garbage of a less abstract variety.

In the basement, carefully tended by two "good old country boys," an enormous, galvanized tank poured out a steady stream of that substance with which I was least competent to cope, at the turn of a tap. A short walk down the cellar stairs and I was in the presence of a fountain of forgetfulness. In a way, one might say, my "prayers" had been answered, damn it.

The country place, which I had all to myself, wasn't so bad, but my depression was so deep I couldn't write a word or do much of anything, except walk around in the dreary woods. Legal problems Jim had neglected to mention in his letters prevented him from giving the Church any property. He was the black sheep of a "good" family, and everything he had was tied up in trusts.

Brandye Maske, a southern peach who had joined the Church in Miami, and who was then bee hee of Birmingham, where she attended an exclusive school for girls, drove up with the best intentions in the world. It was useless. I had the libido of a jelly donut. A big trip probably would have brought me to my senses (wise idiom), but those who need a trip the most are the least likely to want one, and I was no exception.

Should Brandye have bombed me? Yes, I now declare with great confidence. If all the other ducks are in order (they were), a good friend of a Psychedelian who is clearly depressed should at least throw a Ching about it. But those were the early days. Almost everyone was uncertain about such interventions and it was against the prevailing doctrine.

Through a private detective friend of Jim, I found that there was, no surprise, a warrant out for me in Florida, and I got Sally's address in Sarasota. One more try, I told myself.

I took the bus. Sally wouldn't budge an inch. She was staying in Florida and the kids were staying with her. If I wanted to visit, I would have to take my chances with the police. Waiting in the train station in Sarasota to return to Alabama, I had one belt too many of Jim's 190-proof product. White lightning is also known, for good reason, as "sneaky Pete." I passed out on a bench and woke up in the city jail. The next morning I was transferred to the county jail. The old warrant had turned up.

The Sarasota County jail must have been a real dungeon even during the off season, but this was January 2, 1967, so it was also overbooked. No daylight. Twelve men, on average, in a tank with six beds, so late arrivals, me included, slept on the floor on flat and filthy mattresses.

The dominant inmate was a deranged gorilla, ordinarily good-natured but given to sudden bursts of mindless violence. He had been in this dismal hole for nine months for lack of bail. Two seventeen-year-old boys, who had passed some bad checks, had been there for six months for the same reason. The gorilla usually picked on them. When he got overactive, the custom was to smile, and attempt to treat it all as playful roughhousing. When he approached me during one of these outbursts, I said, meanwhile breaking out in a cold sweat, "George, if you lay a finger on me, I'll bang a ballpoint pen through your ear with a shoe in the middle of the night." I meant it. George treated me with utmost politeness thereafter.

After a week or so of this shit, I was transferred to a newly built slammer in Ocala and bail of $1,000 was set on a charge of possession of a dangerous drug. It took Lisa Bieberman a couple weeks to raise the bail from various Psychedelians around the country. The first thing I did after being released was buy an orange from a nearby open-air stand. Citrus fruits, which grew all around, were never served in the two jails I had been in.

Spending some time behind bars became fairly common among white, middle-class American kids in those days and, in a way, it was a good thing it did. In this area, there's no substitute for personal experience. Few people who have fallen victim to it fail to notice that the American criminal justice system is organized to protect the rich and to rob and demoralize the poor. What justice is available is sold, virtually as a commodity, to those who can pay for it. As Defoe put it, "Knowledge of things would teach them every hour that law is but a heathen word for power." All governments are fascist at heart and are restrained, if at all, only by fear of French or Russian Revolution replays, one of which has been overdue around here for a long time.

For solipsistic nihilists, however, there is another side to it. One must also wonder why, Snazzm, one has brought this kind of nightmare on oneself. I do not say this to excuse in any way the cruelty of the punishment freaks who have created and who operate the barbaric American system. If you are attacked by a monster in a nightmare, and have a shotgun handy, let the creature have it with both barrels. But nightmares cannot be conquered or ameliorated or avoided merely by deploring them. Honest analysis is called for.

Trite as it is, it will often turn out that one's errors are due to bad habits and hanging out with the wrong crowd. Frivolity with money doesn't help either. No agitator, revolutionary or professional criminal should expect to escape unscathed forever. John Jay Chapman is very good on this topic. Resolutions made in jails may hold up better than those made in less stark surroundings. In any case, if one is stuck with a dangerous line of work, one ought to give serious thought to how best to protect oneself while doing it and get advice from seasoned professionals.

Back in Alabama I found Jim's place deserted. Checks for several hundred dollars which I had been expecting in the mail were nowhere to be found. The still was gone, and there wasn't a drop of anything alcoholic, legal or illegal, in the house. The phone rang. It was Jim. The distillers had gotten word of a raid only a few minutes before it was scheduled to take place, and had fled at once, leaving the evidence in place. Jim had taken my checks to a bank and tried to cash them, but the teller had gotten suspicious, so he had stepped outside and thrown them down a sewer. He was now in Florida, hiding out at a girlfriend's house. No, I had better not sell his furniture. The boys suspected me of being the rat. I had better get out of town before I got killed. Delightful, first Bobby Kennedy and now this.

I called Millbrook and Bill Haines answered. Tim was in California. The Ashram had moved into the Big House and Bill was in charge. They were broke, but he would try to scrape up $75 to get me back to civilization. The next day, the money was at the Western Union office. Bali Ram had come up with the cash. He had had a vision that I would pull them out of their difficulties. You're as good a man as I am, Bali Ram. Well, that was that. As I write, "The Prisoners' Chorus" from *Fidelio* is on the stereo, and my mood on the train going north was on the same track. Even the industrial wastelands of New Jersey looked good, but the snow-covered landscape of the Hudson Valley looked like fairyland. My depression was lifting: I could distinguish between good places and bad places. Compared to my days at MGL, I was still in sad shape, but I could now see how fortunate, in many ways, I was in my condition and my prospects. I had friends and I had a place where I could go. Only suffering and loss will show many of us, born in luxury relative to the mass of mankind, how lucky we are, and how important those simple requirements are to a happy life.

I took a cab from the Place of Overflowing Shitholes. The driver got a lot of kidding from his dispatcher when he reported his destination over the radio.

There were two changes in the outward appearance of the Big

House. A giant face, called the Universal Man, had been painted on the facade and a formidable metal monstrosity of vaguely telescopic appearance squatted on the roof of the porch. It had been built by Narad, the Man of Iron, who had left without explaining what it was for. Someone eventually disassembled it.

The Universal Man was not much admired. He looked more like a leering gigolo than a hero or philosopher, but the visiting artist who had painted him had known well what he was about. He had left his Mark upon us, and there was no way to stash it in the storage room with all the other bizarre productions left behind by less audacious artists. I think most of us, although nobody ever said so, became sort of fond of the old boy.

Chapter 21

THE PILGRIMS

It was a pleasant, friendly, sociable herd; pious, happy, merry, and full of unconscious coarseness and innocent indecencies.

Bill Haines was nominally in charge of the whole works but the house, I swiftly discovered, was split between Ashramites and Leaguers. There had been some crossovers, largely the result of love being blind, or something. Although the house was not as jammed as it had been during my last visit, when there had usually been some visitors sleeping on the floors in the dining and music rooms, almost every space that might be called private was now taken, including the wine cellar, where Otto slept, and the attic, where Jean-Pierre and one or two others had made cubicles for themselves.

I will list all inmates, and try to describe them in terms of place and role and outstanding characteristics, although, as we shall see, nothing remained stable for long.

Bill Haines had taken a small but beautiful, parquet-floored, bay-windowed room center front, second floor, opening on the landing and also, by way of a sliding door, onto a large room with a fireplace that served as the Ashram's common and meeting room. Bill's captains cabin contained all his Oriental bric-a-brac and had two framed photographs on the wall over his desk, one of Tim Leary and the other of W.C. Fields looking crafty over a hand of cards. Haines refused to discuss his pre-yoga past, but hints would drop here and there. As near as I can figure, it went something like this:

Well-to-do parents in New York. Strict upbringing. Joined the Army at seventeen at the end of WWII, about a year before I did, just in time to be present as the concentration camps in Germany were discovered. Stationed at Berchtesgaden, of all places. Struck an officer, and spent two years in stockades. Theological school? The Sado-Judeo-Paulinian (Dutch Reformed) ministry? Nine years in India (that's definite). Back to the United States as some kind of show business impresario. Every now and then, the Ashram showed a film in which Bill introduced Bali's performance at a U.N. gala. The Ananda Ashram at Monroe, New York. Bombed.

Haines, it must be said, never advanced himself as a model personality for others to imitate or anything like that, nor even pretended to play with a full deck at all times. Once, in Arizona, exasperated by some characteristic act of folly, I said, "You know, Bill, sometimes I think you really do have a screw loose somewhere."

"Never said I didn't," he cheerfully replied.

He didn't double bind himself over his own failings, which gave his abrasive traits and occasional outbursts of blatant irrationality an open and frivolous air that seemed to me, most of the time, reason enough to excuse them in favor of the appreciation, which was general, of his wisdom, humor, candor and vitality.

Sarasvati. Already described. She and her little daughter, the offspring of a union with a Chinese cook who visited occasionally bringing presents, had a small room in the back of the house. Sarasvati spent as much time as she could manage in Bill's presence. If banished, she hung out with Susan Shoenfeld and Bhavani. She was banished regularly. One morning, noting that Bill seemed to be in a particularly black humor, I asked him what was wrong. Sarasvati was slumped in a corner, head down. It was impossible, as usual, to tell if she was giggling or crying or both. Bill pointed an accusing finger at her. "She smiled at me!" he growled. That serious error got her three days in outer darkness.

Tambimutto. Tambi had the room next to Bill's on the side opposite the common room. Through the wall, Bill could hear Tambi chanting and retching during his bouts with the bottle. "I am not a pot-head. I am an alcoholic!" Tambi had announced with imperious Anglo-Indian dignity when the officials of the Monroe Ashram descended on the place with their armed thugs. True. Tambi, at this point, was edging away from Bill and identifying with Tim, who had flattered him outrageously because of his supposed excellent connections in the literary world. Tambi was graying and toothless and looked at least slightly angry and/or malicious at all times, even when he was unconscious.

Later that winter, Tambi's hostility towards Bill became deep and "metaphysical." During one long period when Sarasvati was banished, Bill maintained he could hear the two of them through the wall plotting his destruction, with Tambi egging Sarasvati on to take "decisive action" against the "evil one." When, at last, she did, her assault was dramatic but ineffectual: She put her fist through a stained-glass window between Bill's room and the landing.

As was usual at Millbrook, the whole drama thereupon mysteriously vanished into thin air, and Sarasvati was once again permitted to clean up Bill's room and to be present during discussions so long as she kept her mouth shut. Tambi stayed with Tim when the Ashram moved out of the Big House but did not remain in Tim's orbit after the general collapse.

Howie Druck and **Betsy Ross.** Betsy was a crossover from the League. They had a room in back, on the second floor, on a corridor off the landing. Because of Thorin, Betsy's son by a former alliance, whom Bill loved dearly, and because Betsy's family was well-off and, I hope, because Betsy was an OK person, Haines was not at all displeased to see one of his most devoted followers given this subsidiary domestication. Betsy had successfully run a jewelry shop in Greenwich Village before coming to Millbrook to join her goat-loving brother, and Haines hoped that the Ashram, once it had some capital, could at least partially support itself with a similar operation, but this scheme never came to anything.

Howie was at that time in charge of the Ashram's finances.

As is traditional for those who play this role in spiritual communities, he was regarded with suspicion and envy by the rest of the boys, including his brother. He did little useful work but always seemed to have money and was rarely subjected to the kind of verbal abuse meted out daily by Haines to the rest of his followers. Perhaps Howie reminded Haines of the sick and starving prisoners he had helped to liberate in Germany. No matter what his actual condition, Howie seemed to project emotional vulnerability and a need for support. These traits, combined with Howie being a likable guy, deterred me from making a play for Betsy, who flirted with me whenever an opportunity arose and turned me on in a big way.

Jean-Pierre. A wispy, cheerful man who dressed in a vaguely Levantine manner, with absurdist touches all his own. One evening Wendy and I met him at the railroad station in the Place of Overflowing Shitholes and he stepped down from the crowded commuter train wearing a fancy lamp shade on his head. Jean-Pierre was in the background category, at least as far as I was concerned. It was said that he had a famous father, of whom I had never heard, a French Dadaist poet or something of the sort, from Tambi's old circle. Looking back, I'm fairly sure Jean-Pierre, who left at the time of the great split, rather than choose sides, was waiting for "something to happen" of a general and spectacular nature, such as mass levitations or balls of fire from outer space.

He wasn't the only one. I heard it all the time during the counter-revolutionary "drug-alternative" period of the '70s, when the establishment hacks, media moguls and academic frauds of the United States discovered nadirs of blithering idiocy unplumbed in human memory, in an effort to smother what had gone before in smarm. People would say, "But nothing happened. In those days we all expected something would happen."

Well, it all depends on how you look at it. I happened, and from my point of view, that makes mass levitations and balls of fire pale by comparison.

Marshall and **Pat McNeill.** Leaguers to the bitter end. Marshall was a sturdy yeoman type, big, good-natured and earnest, who always looked somewhat dazed by all the lunacy going on around him, while his wife, Pat, was the image of the cute Irish tomboy type one could almost always find in the '50s at the corner bar on Saturday night, swapping dirty stories with the boys. They had two very young daughters and lived on the second floor, in two rooms off the main corridor, across from Tambimutto.

John and **Vinnie.** Ashramite couple. A pair of clean-cut American kids who never seemed to think of anything except how best to enjoy themselves. Vinnie was one of the sexiest little nitwits I have ever encountered, an opinion universally shared. When she discovered I had literary inclinations, she suggested that I collaborate with her on the story of her life. It would be "very pornographic," she assured me. Wouldn't John mind? Why should he? Despite my libidinal lassitude, there was something about this concept that appealed to me, but John, it turned out, did mind. He thought we should sell her as a *Playboy* centerfold instead, he said. John and the Druck brothers had visited Israel together, before their Ashram lives began.

Wendy Williams. Ashramite. Wendy had a room in the servants' wing. Pretty in an unremarkable kind of way, clever but not a serious reader; the child of a wealthy but not opulent New York Jewish family. According to Bali, who was usually right about such things, Wendy was "really" interested in "only one thing," because she wasn't really much interested in it at all, a common syndrome among females with inherently low to moderate sex drives, which has been the foundation of many fortunes in the late twentieth century, when it first became popular dogma that this normal variation, like normal genetic variations in intelligence, could and should be "cured," by various lotions, potions and incantations.

Lou Friedlander. Ashramite. Lou, who was about my age, seemed seriously troubled by chronic internal conflicts and philosophic questions so dark and ominous as to not bear utterance. Although he had a room to himself in the servants' wing, and was one of Wendy's admirers, he also spent a lot of time in the meditation closet, where he was given his meals on a tray. We hardly ever spoke. When the snow melted, Lou departed.

Michael Green. League. A commercial artist of almost arcane facility, Michael, who created the church seal and the cover for the *Boo Hoo Bible,* had abandoned Mad Ave at the age of twenty-three to devote himself to getting stoned, painting elaborate mandalas and such, and learning how to go barefoot at all times, even in the snow. He had a room in the servants' wing and a tiny studio, converted from a bathroom, off the music room. A nice boy with a good sense of humor despite it all, he was Wendy's latest at the time I arrived.

Prints of Michael's posters were popular head shop items for years afterwards. One shows a series of Jesus Christs jetting out of a central maelstrom of forms, and another is Timothy Leary's face composed of hundreds of tiny figures and designs. Oh well.

Ted Druck. Howie's older brother. Ashram. An ex-teacher of Hebrew recently divorced, Ted was tall, gaunt, sad-eyed, and unimaginative but a very warm-hearted and good-natured person. Ted slept in the common room in those days.

Fred Blacker. Ashram. A dealer, petty thief, and small-time con man, Fred slept in the common room but later moved to the Bowling Alley with his girl,

Alexandra, a super-cutie who sometimes dressed like a Hollywood harem dancer, even going so far, if in a particularly decorative mood, as to leave the bra off. Years later, Alexandra told me that Fred, who seemed harmless enough in public, was often crazy and violent in private, beat her up, and so forth. I guess darling, romantic Alexandra, who could have done much better without half trying, it says here, thought she could and should reform Fred. How oft it is.

Susan Shoenfeld. Susan, a tough-minded but amused and amusing bi of about thirty, was one of Bill's hopes for a big bundle in the future, since her family was seriously rich and Susan was scheduled to collect a full and fruity trust fund in a year or two. Servants' wing. Originally Ashramite, her true allegiance, if any, was a mystery to me.

Bhavani. League. Nobody ever called her by her outside name and I don't know what it was. About my age or a little older, Bhavani looked like everyone's ideal of serene American motherhood. According to Bill, she was the only Leaguer who could discuss philosophic and religious subjects with any degree of knowledgeability or rationality. Lesbian. She occupied Tim's room during his absence, and was in charge of the Supreme Sacrament supply. Any resident could knock on her door, and name a quantity (within reason), and Bhavani would supply it. It's probably the best arrangement for Psychedelian communities in the U.S. One person should be responsible for what might be called "the central stash," and be prepared to flush it or burn it fast if the community is attacked by the mind police.

Bob and **Carol Ross.** Bob has already been introduced. Both were decidedly, almost ferociously, League. Carol, a tall, gray-eyed blonde, swept around in diaphanous, pastel gowns, put up admonitory signs in the kitchen addressed to "Loved Ones" and otherwise generally behaved like the headmistress of a school for juvenile delinquents. Her admonitions, although always derided, were usually deserved. They occupied the tower room where guided "sessions" had been held in the early days.

Bob was the leader of the anti-Haines forces. From his perch above, he controlled the music heard from those speakers in the house which had not been disconnected, and surveyed the progress being made by his filthy goats in covering the sacred environs with a sprinkling of turds.

Susie Blue. An African-American teenager who had been a maid during the early days and was now just one of the kids. Beset by weird superstitions and paranoid fears, she had retreated to the animism of her ancestors and was said to worship various trees and rocks in the woods.

Arthur Frelinghausen. Probably more similar in outlook to Susie than anyone suspected. Arthur had been instructed by Tim to produce a newsletter for the League. Instead of news, his productions consisted mainly of mini-sermons declaring that we were all unenlightened searchers in the maze, bewitched, bothered and bewildered, and so forth. This didn't go over very well with Tim, and Haines and I informed Arthur that he could leave us out of this generalization also. His journal didn't last long, and neither did Arthur, who left a few weeks after I arrived.

At the Millbrook Diner, where I happened to run into him while he waited for his bus out, Arthur responded to my astonishment at his abrupt departure by telling me the one and only horrific bad-trip story I ever heard at Millbrook. He then informed me, with great emphasis, that he was "a seed-bearing young male," Tim's favorite euphemism for horny young guys in those days. Although this undisputed fact struck me as highly irrelevant, given the opportunities for sowing wild oats herein described, it seemed to be the crux of the matter as far as Arthur was concerned. I wished him luck and left the diner for the snowy street, none the wiser, but a little the worse for wear.

The only genuine newsletter produced at the time was a mimeographed sheet cranked out irregularly by the McCready boys called *The Daily Blah*. It was read avidly by everyone in the house as soon as it appeared, and frequently contained highly embarrassing quotes of comments people made when they thought they were speaking privately to their respective cliques. The kids also kept track of the game of musical beds and, as far as I know, they were never wrong.

Arthur lived in a room on the third floor with

Jill Henry, which may explain his problem with his nuts. Jill, a transfer from Vassar, so to speak, was said by all to be recovering from a love affair with her ex-roommate. Jill was a cool, delicate, intelligent, dark-haired beauty. Old-fashioned, sort of. Glossy, even. League, but not fanatical and well liked by one and all. I took her to dinner at Noel Tepper's house once, shortly after the other Arthur left, and we fooled around a little, but we were not really each others' types. I think we felt sorry for each other. She gave me a gold, three-eyed-toad pendant which I thereafter wore, almost at all times, during the years covered by this history.

Jill later married Nicky Sands, a nice guy and a West Coast underground chemist and co-conspirator with Billy in the Orange Sunshine acid manufacturing deal, for which, along with Tim Scully, a real prick, he took a fall while Billy walked. How much did they collect for doing Billy's time? Who knows.

Jean McCready. League. Recently divorced, in her early thirties, with two small boys, Jean was the archetypal Learyite. Her selfless devotion was demonstrated by her doing Tim's typing and filing although Rosemary was the broad in his bed. Bill, who treated Bob and Carol with derision, was wryly respectful to Jean. She was a lady, and her goody-goodyness had no hidden malice behind it. She seemed serenely oblivious to most of the conflicts around her, however much they occupied the attention of her fellow residents.

Jean's most recent ex-husband, not the father of the children, **Walter Schneider,** a Navy pilot, showed up every now and then during the winter to visit, and eventually took a trip, quit the Navy and joined the League in the woods, where he became a kind of super flower child. After the place broke up, Walt became one of the founders of "The Brotherhood of Eternal Love" in California and, occasionally, Billy Hitchcock's co-pilot. He also wrote an interminable blank verse epic about our struggle with the Dutchess County Sado-Judeo-Paulinians called "Millbrook Thanksgiving," which eventually appeared in print in a condensed version. I unreservedly recommend this work to those historians who may feel that I have not adequately conveyed in these pages the full aromatic force of the flower-power mystique.

Allan Marlow. Already introduced with a wild look in his eyes. Allan lived with his consort,

Diane Di Prima, in the Bowling Alley, along with two of Diane's daughters by former alliances, a nine-year-old, and a little brown charmer, the child, reputedly, of some well-known spade literary figure. One time I ran across this doll in the hall early in the morning and asked her if she had had good dreams the night before. She thought about it for a moment and then replied, "They're not on my diet." Haines made a point of sneaking candy to Diane's kids whenever he could. League. Allan and Diane were constant thorns in Haines' side but had brought with them treasures which Haines coveted and later acquired: complete letterpress and photo-offset systems and all the necessary equipment to go with them. Diane had some reputation as a writer in certain circles, but her poetry struck me as being lifeless, trivial and uneasy, just like her husband.

After Allan and Diane moved out in the spring to find more congenial pasturage,

Allen Atwell and his new girlfriend,

Susan Firestone, who looked like his twin sister, took over Allan and Diane's old quarters in the Bowling Alley, and stayed until mid-summer, spending most of their time with the League. Atwell once prostrated himself on the road to town from the

Gatehouse when he saw me coming, which resulted in a modesty contest of extravagant pantomime gestures, which amused our companions and maybe passing motorists as well. We were both members of the first graduating class of the place, so to speak. I liked Allen, but I did not appreciate his "psychedelic" paintings, which mostly looked like interlaced guts to me, and I couldn't pretend otherwise. One critic, writing in *Horizon,* declared Allen's paintings to be "one of the high points of the psychedelic art movement," and employed the phrase "a hot, molten fantasia" to describe one example of the period pieces of which I speak. Well, to each his own is what I always say.

After Allen Atwell left, we half expected Alan Watts or Allen Ginsberg to show up to claim the "AL Ranch," as it might well have been called, but then Alexandra and Fred moved in.

Far out. What did it mean? I haven't the foggiest, except to say that massive frivolity was heavily involved all around.

Len and **Teresa Howard.** A couple of noncommunicative Leaguers from Las Vegas, who seemed to me to be just passing through, they were so impassive, but stayed for a long time. I guess they were just born loyalists, as some people are, both to each other and to Tim. Len, a former dealer, always seemed like a man with difficult business problems on his mind, while Teresa, a former showgirl, appeared absorbed by an intense consciousness of her body, which richly deserved the attention she paid to it. One time I patted her on the ass (she was standing on a chair, putting away dishes) while passing through the pantry and got slapped for this sincere expression of aesthetic appreciation, a rare example of hideous brutality blotting our noble, peaceful record.

Aside from Fred Blacker's private conduct, I can think of only two other examples. Clum once hit Jackie for moving a log Clum had placed across the road to block traffic, and once I had a small scuffle with an uninvited and hostile visitor who wouldn't leave. An astonishing record, considering. No deaths, either. No serious fires. No serious illnesses.

Otto H. Baron von Albenesius. Otto lived in a small wine cellar under the kitchen with his German shepherd, Winnie. I hesitate to attempt much of a capsule description of Otto. He will be introduced gradually as the story unfolds. Too much Otto at one time might cause the reader to wonder if I might not be exaggerating things for effect. I'm not.

Allegiance? Hmmm.

Bill Sheatsley. Sheatsley was the rugged, hardworking, sandy-haired son of the superintendent of a midwestern Protestant private school system. He had been Haines' roommate during the Ananda ("bliss") period. "Sheats," as he was known to most of us, was having difficulty adjusting to the elevation of his filthy-mouthed, drug-soaked former buddy to the status of guru. He was the only member of the Ashram who never took psychedelics, major or minor. The kids had bombed him once at Ananda, Wendy said, and he had fought it all the way.

Sheats worked about sixteen hours a day, half of them in the Place of Overflowing Shitholes' morgue, doing his conscientious objector time, and half back at the ranch, usually building things or repairing them or maintaining them or making scale drawings of them or reading about them or figuring out how they worked or why they didn't. Sheats seemed to have the generalized aptitude for such stuff that Teutons are thought, possibly correctly, to be born with more of than is generally handed out in the genetic crap shoot. "Karma yoga," we would almost always say, with a smile, when his way of life was remarked on by visitors.

Sheats, like Haines, was celibate, although later, at the Arizona Ashram, after throwing up a few ingeniously designed buildings almost single-handedly, he took up with a local "hot tamale," as Haines called her. Then he left to form an ashram of his own composed of people who shared his belief that the Devil finds work for idle hands. (There is a lot to this, I would say.) He had a room, suitably furnished with Spartan simplicity, in the servants' wing.

Ed Kalujuak. Ed, a very large, red-headed, slope-shouldered Canadian, usually hung around with Marshall. He never said much and was perpetually mild and good-natured. I have no idea where he slept. Perhaps in a hollow log. League.

Howie Klein. Howie was the second banana of the Ashram. He was a classic funny Jewish boy from Brooklyn, with a big nose and an enormous bush of red hair. He couldn't say "shit" without getting a laugh. Servants' wing. Although his nose was large, he was of normal height. Chin did not recede. No overt or covert homosexual conflicts that I ever noticed. 20/20 vision.

Zen. League, but not really. Zen, a tiny, bearded man with a rural Southern style of speech, who rarely appeared on the scene, even for lunch, lived in the cavernous depths of the Bowling Alley where he reputedly absorbed 1,000 mics every three days. Well liked.

Paul Faggot. League, he said. Paul, a mournful little Jewish swish, was always attired in a dirty brown velvet robe, with hood, and possibly slept in the Bowling Alley. Whenever Haines spotted him gliding around a corner somewhere (he seemed to appear from and disappear into the woodwork like a rat) he would yell, "Would somebody please tell me who let that faggot in here?" As far as I know, this question was never answered. Later, we put Paul to work typing the *Neo-American Church Catechism and Handbook,* which task he performed with the greatest reluctance.

Charlie Hitchings. Charlie was just an ordinary American kid and never pretended to be anything else. Ashram. Slept in the common room most of the time.

Victor. A Puerto Rican boy in his early twenties, Victor was a good carpenter and highly thought of by Haines on that account. He was also a nice, open, unpretentious person, but seemed always to be suffering from the pangs of unrequited love. He later became paranoid on trips and thought Haines was out to kill him, or something.

Bali Ram. A former boy dancer in the court of the King of Nepal, Bali was a true child of the East and, rumor had it, Bill's ex-boyfriend. He carried around a bundle of traditional, crazy superstitions, many of which seemed to work, sort of, and was devoid of the routine Sado-Judeo-Paulinian hang-ups associated with his sexual orientation. Bali was proud of his promiscuous sexual conduct, which, Haines informed me, had caused many "close calls" of "morals" charges, since Bali did not discriminate based on age, religion, allegiance or condition of servitude, only gender, and scorned all precautions and disguises.

As almost anyone would have predicted, Bali and Sarasvati didn't get along very well. Their spats usually began with a disagreement over what Bill had said or not said about something or other or, if an orthodox text might be said to exist, exactly what Bill had meant by it. The more trivial the issue, it seemed, the more prolonged and bitter the ensuing exchange of insults would become.

Those of us fortunate enough to be present when one of these scenes erupted would invariably be highly amused. The idioms employed were often drawn from the New York City underworld of the 1950s, on the one hand, or the Katmandu bazaar on the other, and although vividly picturesque, were even more incomprehensible and surreal to Bali and Sarasvati than they were to rest of us. "What in hell is that supposed to mean?" the two combatants would often ask of each other, to no avail. Since most people have a hard time staying angry if mirth and hilarity prevail all around them, Sarasvati would usually crack up at some point, start giggling, and throw in the towel.

Bali, with rare exceptions, remained stern and unforgiving to the bitter end, no matter what. He had not been brought up to throw in the towel, I guess. ("Throw the towel? I do not throw the towel. I wash and dry the towel. I leave it to you sluts to throw the towel. And what is that supposed to mean, anyway?")

Bali had Maynard's former large room at the west end of the second floor where he could practice his dancing free of distractions. Nobody who had seen him in action begrudged him the space.

Charles Ashmore. Charlie didn't show up until April or May, but then he stayed with the Ashram for the move to Arizona, after which he disappeared into the University of Arizona fringe world in Tucson. Homo black, with the temperament of a pussycat. Nothing ever bothered Charlie, who seemed to grin and giggle from morning to night. For a while, Tim made a point of taking Charlie along on his lectures to function, as Haines put it, as his "stage nigger." I think Tim stopped this practice because Charlie, when asked about it, showed either no interest in the race issue at all or such a lackadaisical interest that it offended the black militants in the audience who had been anointed by the establishment media by this time as their kind of folks, as it were. And I'm sure they were, for the same reasons Tim was.

Rudy and **Jackie.** This (heterosexual) couple were subjects of the Queen of England, on loan, so to speak. Former devotees of Tim, they had become disillusioned for reasons which remained obscure no matter how much they talked about it, which was a lot. They had come in to put on "light shows" for Tim's "Psychedelic Celebrations" in New York. Young, uptight and in limbo so far as group identification went, they lived in a room next to Howie and Betsy.

Karen Detweiler had disappeared during my absence, but later returned. Along with a few other people who were absent too often to be called "residents," exactly, but too familiar to be called "visitors," exactly, Karen tended to "sleep around" and to resist group identification. Since my libido had dimmed down to pilot-light status, I hardly noticed her absence, and Karen, demonstrating some common sense for a change when she did show up, had clearly concluded that I wasn't her type anyway.

During my first two or three weeks with the Ashram at Millbrook, I was content to do housework and hang around the common room, where I slept on a couch, swapping stories with the boys. My imagination was firmly set on idle, to match the pilot lights in my balls.

My fellow inmates seemed to be behind the justly famous psychological "glass wall," but they were so engaging a breakthrough was inevitable.

Chapter 22

THE HOLY FOUNTAIN

The pilgrims were human beings.

It was almost unheard of at Millbrook in those days for anything of consequence to happen in a routine and predictable way. When visitors asked what was "happening," a question we got pretty tired of hearing, the standard reply was, "I haven't the slightest idea. If you ever find out, please let me know."

This was a somewhat evasive response to a question for which there never was a simple answer. Anyone who had been there for a while could have gone on for hours about what he thought was happening. One could have gone on indefinitely, telling only the truth as one saw it, with the general picture probably seeming more and more obscure, if not totally crazy, to the listener as fact was added to fact.

Describing observable behavior would not have been all that difficult. But what were we all thinking about and why? What were we trying to do? What was the point of it all? What were our motives? Why this and why that and why the other thing? In these terms, a coherent overview was very hard to come by.

At any particular time, a reasonably accurate psychological, social and political atlas of the place would have shown lots of hidden corners, culs-de-sac, secret passages, trapdoors, brave highways leading nowhere, evanescent establishments, established evanescences, sanctified misunderstandings, whims of iron and resolutions of sand, as well as the usual stuff, and plenty of it.

There were ironic kickers to almost everything, which Psychedelian life tends to promote. The stylistic aspects of the Neo-American Church that are the most incomprehensible to outsiders derive partly from this. It's an acquired taste, to be sure, and lousy politics, at least in the short run.

But, however irregular or just plain twisted, everyday life in the Big House in those days was, in general, a continuous source of instruction and amusement. I've lived in standard ways and in peculiar ways, and I think life in Psychedelian communities is best, if there is no great anxiety about money for basics, no great fear of the mind police, and room enough so factions can maintain a reasonable distance from one another. Three big ifs.

Routine housework, for one thing, had some fun in it most of the time. Kitchen duty was shared on a rotating schedule. Swabbing up after a dinner for thirty people, which was about average, is no pleasure in itself, and every night two of us had to spend about four hours washing up and mopping the floor. But we were usually well-entertained while doing so, since the spacious kitchen, complete with a walk-in refrigerator and an enormous table, was the forum of the community, and it was there that the issue of the day was often defined, although rarely resolved.

There was always an "issue of the day," besides all the ordinary gossip and routine quarrels. Should people be permitted to have private stashes? Should so and so, a visitor, be allowed to move in? Should we switch to vegetarianism? Although Art Kleps was certainly a prince among men and a handsome devil besides, did he have the right to close off the music room so he and Wendy Williams and Michael Green could work on his book, wonderful beyond description though it was? Was Meher Baba full of shit? And so forth.

It was an oral group. People smoked one or two substances, drank three or four beverages, and cried, laughed, complained, bragged and told funny stories from morning to night. It was a rare night when, even at 3 a.m., one could not find an intense conversation going on somewhere in the house.

Although depressed during my first weeks in the Big House during the winter of the Haines interregnum, I was never bored, and I frequently found myself, to my astonishment, laughing out loud, such was the quality of the comedy. Much time was spent telling each other about our trips. One of the most popular was Howie Klein's account of his latest big trip that winter, which I asked him to retell, and recorded, as he was going up on some STP in Arizona:

> HOWIE: This is good music. Well let's see. I don't know, don't know if I can do this. OK, when I was on this trip, let's see I was, well I wanted to walk in the woods to see if I was afraid and I knew I was going to be. So I started walking and all the trees looked really weird ungngngngngnggggggggg all the branches were just out!
>
> KLEPS: You wanted to know why you were afraid?
>
> HOWIE: No, I just wanted to see how I'd do it. How I'd get into these things. So I started walking, I said this is very weird, very weird, very weird. (Chuckle) I said go out a little further: you can always turn back. So I kept walking and I said why don't you walk in the other direction and you'll still be walking home! (Laughter) So I started walking and I said, don't get into a thing where you'll never get back to the house, you'll fall in the snow here and you'll be laying in the snow here, and all that. So I started to run and I got about fifty steps and I said SHSHSHSHSHSH look, you did it! So I was still pretty screwed up: so I thought I'd go and see Zen at the Bowling Alley; and I'd sit down; and he was getting high. He didn't know I was on a trip, so I sat down and, Oh, I don't know, Ahhhhh, I don't know. I always get into this thing! (Laughter)
>
> Then I got pissed off: you know, "What do I do this for?" So he says, he said, something that really turned me on, you know, "It's all God, or something like that." So I said, yah, I was reading this book that said when you ride on the train you carry all these suitcases and you really don't carry them cause the train will carry them. (Chuckle) So that sounded good, you know, so I said, yah, I don't have to carry them, give them all up. So then I felt good. So I felt I made a discovery, so I went to the Big House and told Victor, and I said, I came to the conclusion that everything is God.

So Victor said that God wasn't found in a conclusion. (Laughter) So I didn't really get too screwed up, but I started to think about it, so I went up to see Charlie, who was in the bathroom in Bill's room, and I said, Victor said God isn't found in a conclusion but since everything is God it has to be a conclusion too. So we drew a conclusion and it came like two cones coming together and it continued. And so from then I discovered it continued. So then I saw Lou cleaning the bathroom and I said, I discovered God, I found God. So he says now that you've found him don't let him out of your sight. (Laughter)

Despite Bill's extremely Buddhist orientation, "finding God, or something like that" was considered synonymous with "finding Enlightenment" for most of the kids in the Ashram and Howie was definitely a "kid." It is difficult to extirpate the term if one has been brought up with it, no matter how abstract, or even meaningless, it becomes, as my own history shows.

If the reader had been present as an invisible man in a variety of these scenes, and heard A telling B something, he would have heard B respond with laughter, perhaps 7.6 times out of 10.

The transparent reader might not have laughed at any given story and perhaps not at any of them. Tastes differ, as does how much trust or distrust one has for one's inherited terminology and the received wisdom, which is often the crux of the comedy. Stoned people often say things with great solemnity and then laugh at what they have just said, along with everyone else present. Lisa Bieberman, had she been forced by some cruel twist of fate to live among us in our "human zoo," would definitely have been in the 2.4 minority, as would almost all of those who found life at Millbrook so dissonant with their ideas about the way things ought to be that they could not enjoy it the way it was.

Almost all who remained, however much they differed in opinion, had the same general outlook on things. As Goethe put it, "Men are divided by their opinions but unified by their outlooks." Nor, although it looked pretty heavenly to me, was Millbrook to everyone's taste in architecture and landscaping. The scale and style of things did not suggest heavenly realms to everyone but, to many, only illustrations and backgrounds from

Tales of Terror comic books and Dracula movies. There were oddities all around: cavernous root cellars under the road between the Big House and the Bungalow; an abandoned kennel which seemed to stretch on forever; beautiful and ingeniously constructed wooden round barns scattered through the woods; the remnant foliage of ruined gardens creeping up and over the walls that had once contained them; and the great stone barns elsewhere described.

Although, in general, everyone who stayed fell in love with the place, Tim and Bill disparaged the architecture whenever the subject arose and so did most of the troops. Only Otto, Billy and I seemed satisfied with Old Man Dieterich's contribution to the Andrew Jackson Downing Hudson River School of Picturesque Architecture, broadly defined. Variety is the spice of life. Most people professed to more rarefied tastes, or something.

Perhaps one reason Tim would rusticate the League in the hills in the summer of '67 was the grotesque and grandiose character of the Big House and its surroundings. The image was inconsistent with his public relations objectives. It didn't fit in with the ascetic simplicity then fashionable. It wasn't egalitarian, it wasn't primitive and it wasn't "nice" (harmless seeming).

After the League moved out to the woods, Otto stayed in the basement of the Big House, which he loved, although he spent most of his waking time at the Ashram.

"I wasn't brought up to live in the woods like a bunny rabbit," he said.

Me neither.

Although Wendy and I sometimes visited what came to be called "League Country," which comprised about 2,000 acres of fields and woodland on the northern half of the estate, I never felt any urge to camp out. If a lake had been among the attractions, with shack, it might have been a case of one hermit coming up.

There were two major hills. Lunacy had a magnificent sweeping view of the Hudson Valley and most of the League clustered there in their tents. Ecstasy was further back by a mile or two. In good weather, Tim and Rosemary lived there in a tent with a view of a sequestered bosky dell full of tall grass and wildflowers.

Almost any place where one has good trips becomes sanctified and glorified thereby, I would say. I recall the surprise I felt when, on my visit to Cambridge and IFIF, Lisa showed me her tiny, ordinary upstairs den in a frame building on Boylston Street and asked me if it wasn't the most beautiful room I had ever seen. For her, I now know, it seemed full of the presence of her ghostly Lord. I forget what I replied but, whatever it was, it probably made Lisa wonder if I was a dullard, as her question made me wonder if she was mad.

There was a tendency among true Millbrook lovers to assume that everyone saw the place as we did, that is, as an almost miraculously perfect enclave in which to lead a stoned life, free of the daily grind, parking meters, etc. Haines, in particular, at first assumed that everyone who visited automatically conceived a secret passion to move in and, it seemed to me, was overly defensive because of this frequently mistaken view.

However, when I brought up the subject one day, maintaining that as many people were frightened, repelled, or just plain bored by the place as were attracted to it, he thought it over, agreed with me and even called a meeting of the Ashram to discuss the matter.

Powerful psychological forces kept many people attached to their cities and suburbs, and the imprints caused by death/rebirth trips taken in such familiar surroundings reinforced those forces. Our peculiar, semi-rural, neo-medieval enclosure appeared to many as an irrelevant and "counter-revolutionary" oddity in which no normal person would want to live any more than he would want to be locked up in the Egyptian Rooms of the Metropolitan Museum.

On the other hand, whether one wanted to move in or not, it didn't take long before the invocation of the name "Millbrook," which had previously sounded no more exciting than "Maple Street" or "Riverdale," began to ring in the ears of seriously stoned people as "Mecca" or "Jerusalem" or "Lhassa" did in the ears of followers of the religions associated with those places. When those of us who lived there happened to be somewhere else, I noticed a flicker of reverence frequently accompanied the pronunciation of the two syllables. A kind of ideal image had been invoked.

The obvious associations are appropriate and attractive; the effortless flow of the river does the work of the world, the jolly miller cannot be faulted in any way for the work he does or the way he does it, and the pond behind his mossy dam is a nice place to fish and swim. Art and industry, nature and civilization, all combine nicely in this pretty Fazzm picture.

In some ways, it does seem incredible that the William and Thomas Mellon Hitchcock Center for the Distribution of Illegal Drugs at Millbrook, N.Y., wasn't swamped with customers right from the beginning. Its existence was known to acid heads all over the world and it wasn't hard to get in, get some, and get out, if one put one's mind to it.

Our official policy was always no admittance without an invitation. Later, as Keeper of the Gate, I would tell almost everyone who showed up without an invitation that the place was not open to the public but, unless they were obviously uncouth, I would give them the Big House pay phone number and the Ashram number and tell them they could call if they liked and try to get an invitation.

Many, however, would simply climb over the wall or go around through a side gate rather than engage in any such disagreeable concessions to the standard canons of polite conduct. They would appear in the midst of a League or Ashram scene without saying anything at all to anyone about who they were, what they wanted or where they came from.

Things would then go something like this: Envision the Ashram going about its business. Pots are being made by potters. Two or three people are working in the press room. Two or three are preparing lunch in the kitchen. Sarasvati is mopping floors. A favored few are sitting out front on the patio shooting the shit with Haines. A pair of bearded, long-haired characters with glowing eyes appear on the outskirts of the group and sit down on rocks bordering the flower garden. They say nothing, except possibly "Hi," to whomever is nearest them. If asked, they give their first names. "I'm Jerry, this is Flash."

Consider the disagreeable task confronting Haines under these circumstances. Asking them what they wanted wouldn't get him anywhere. Almost invariably, they would reply with, "Oh, just looking around," or something equally meaningless, and volunteer no information whatever.

Haines usually reacted in one of two ways. If stoned, he would patiently ask questions until he was satisfied that the visitors were harmless, and then tell them they could stay for dinner but not overnight.

If he wasn't stoned, he would say, with rising emphasis and amplification, "Oh, just looking around, huh? Well, this isn't a zoo! You are on private property, and unless you have been invited here by someone who lives here, I'm afraid you will have to leave!"

They would leave, but then they would go to the Big House, where someone would direct them to the woods, where the same scene would be repeated, except the signals would be more scrambled and susceptible to misinterpretation.

Some would try to ignore all of this and hang around until they realized that they would not be accepted because of their sublime vibrations. Then, with one or two outstanding exceptions, they would go. In the final months, when Tim, in effect, declared the place to be a public park, all of this changed. Even the chicken coops filled up.

Many of these uninvited guests, who crept in like lizards, were anti-Psychedelian activists. They were Jesus Freaks, Scientologists, Meher Babaists, Macrobioticoids, Transcendental Meditators, Hare Krishnas and so forth, who intended to show us the True Path. One would suddenly awaken to the knowledge that, over there in the corner of the room was a weirdo who just didn't fit in and who was staring fixedly at someone; most likely Tim, Bill or me. That stare seemed to be a universal weapon of choice for all of these fantasts. Stare the victim in the eye, and he will recognize the flame within, or something.

When Bill realized what was going on, he would ask, "Who let this fruitcake in here, anyway? Didn't your mother teach you it was impolite to stare at people, young man? What group of con artists do you represent, anyway?" and other queries of the same type, few of which were answered.

No Millbrookian was ever converted, as far as I know.

These groups were and are competing for a slice of a potential market of born hypnotic subjects which comprises about 20 percent of the human race, minus those members of this core group who have been successfully inoculated against any shift in allegiance by massive and repeated indoctrinations during childhood in a standard-brand form of supernaturalism, and mindless reverence for the priesthood thereof, with plenty of booster shots thereafter. (Even such as these will sometimes crack, if your timing happens to be right, because gullibility is a hard thing to control.)

To gather together a core crew of zombies of this kind, all one needs is a forceful manner, balls of brass, and the conscience of a worm, which may help explain why this trade has always been so popular in India and the United States. Being somewhat crazy helps, if it is the right type of craziness; namely, a "well-guarded" form of grandiose paranoia. Out of a captive audience of 100, if you have mastered the right line of patter, twenty people will see whatever they are told to see and feel whatever they are told to feel. How long it will stick is another question.

All professional magician-hypnotists know this. There are simple tests which will identify the good subjects before the show starts. The more public the proceedings, the brighter the lights and the louder the voices, the easier it is.

Once you have a cadre, all you have to do is teach them, or some of them, how to do the same thing to others, and encourage everyone to believe every example of synchronicity they encounter is a demonstration of the power of Swami Igapoo or whomever, always floating overhead, pulling strings.

It also helps to create guilt by making impossible demands, such as always having "pure thoughts," in order to prevent rebellion in the ranks.

Nothing to it, if you don't mind being surrounded at all times by a bunch of zombies. I recommend this racket to anyone who feels he is cut out for it, since both the public in general and the victims in general are in the least danger when there is the most competition. When one horde manages to overcome all the others, the results, as all history attests, are usually unfortunate in the extreme. The Neo-American Church is not in this market at all. How could we be? It is a market composed of people afraid to get stoned, and afraid to have anyone around them get stoned, because getting stoned is anti-hypnotic.

Those visitors who approached us in an honest and polite way were treated in an honest and polite way. At the least, they got a free meal and a chance to talk to people experienced in psychedelic drug use.

Thanks in large part to the underground press, a rigid moral doctrine based on egalitarian assumptions had swept over the kid culture, but even the "Third World" and "Group Image" communists ("Tepee Town" back in the woods and the round barn near the duck pond), according to Tord, eventually rejected most of the people who wandered into their scenes expecting a free place to flop, although those already entrenched became embarrassed and upset over the necessity for doing so.

Life at Millbrook didn't have much to do with social ideals, good, bad or indifferent. Psychedelic experience was the point of it all, and that was it. Everything else, one might say, was logistics. If one accepted Millbrook for what it was, a great place to get stoned, it produced instructive stories, fantastic scenes, good screws and beautiful images in abundance.

If one did not accept this obvious fact, well ...

As an example of the kind of pressure Millbrook put on outsiders' preconceptions, I particularly liked one of Tim's "hasty retreat" stories (he had several) about an uninvited visitor who screamed in terror and fled the grounds when he laid eyes on Tim and Rosemary. This seems highly unlikely until one considers the known and probable facts.

The kid almost certainly took LSD shortly before or after he crawled over the wall, and it may well have been his first trip. It was a glorious spring morning in Pan's garden. (Too many birds and flowers can be as unnerving for some people as too many commuters with briefcases can be to others.) He came upon the posh Bungalow bathed in the rays of the rising sun, and walked right in through the front door, probably thinking he was entering a museum or a temple, or something.

Tim and Rosemary, just back after an all-night drive from a lecture date, were still wearing their "ecstatic clothes." About to put their slides and film back in order, they were posed in unfamiliar attitudes there in the sun-shot living room, rewinding a Hitchcock family home movie at the time the kid stepped in, so the tennis players, dancers and swimmers depicted were moving backwards on the screen.

Even so, a scream seems excessive, although hasty retreats were not unusual for novice trippers in strange places then, nor are they now.

Chapter 23

RESTORATION OF THE FOUNTAIN

They had pack-mules along, and had brought everything I needed—tools, pump, lead pipe, Greek fire, sheaves of big rockets, Roman candles, colored-fire sprays, electric apparatus, and a lot of sundries—everything necessary for the stateliest kind of a miracle.

My first community service project that winter was to pen up Bob Ross's goats.

In the *I Ching*, these beasts represent hardness without and weakness within. They spent most of their time on the front porch, which had in consequence become slippery with shit. Ross, it seemed, thought these animals gave the place the proper rustic atmosphere. Not only did I sharply disagree with this concept in general, I was infuriated to note that the goats were picking on a sheep which had been placed among them, and had ripped several patches of wool and skin from it, leaving bleeding wounds, an outrage which Ross, who looked like a goat himself, seemed to regard with callous indifference.

After hearing Haines complain about the situation for the second or third time, I went out, took another look at the unhappy sheep, and returned to announce that, given materials and tools, I would personally build a pen and beat off Ross with a pole, if necessary, to protect it. Ross had already announced his opposition to any confinement of his favorite animals. Since the Ashram was non-violent in principle, they were at a collective disadvantage in such disagreements with other members of the community. Otto, who was sitting in the common room when I made this announcement, lit up with a big grin immediately and volunteered to help.

"It's about time someone showed that miserable swine where to get off," Otto growled through clenched teeth, sounding like Peter Lorre announcing an intention to kidnap Shirley Temple. "I'll go down to the wine cellar and get my banana knife." He left the room, followed by his faithful Winnie.

"What the fuck?" I asked. "Is he serious?"

"You just made a friend for life, Kleps," Haines said.

"Ross can't stand Otto," Ted Druck volunteered. "Well, who can, but the rest of us like Otto anyway. Ross really hates him."

That didn't make much sense. I asked more questions and everyone told Otto stories, all of them incredible. A coherent picture did not emerge.

Otto looked like the degenerate offspring of a long line of degenerates. He was of medium height and build. Oily, dark hair hung down in disorderly ringlets over a perpetually creased forehead. His face twitched most of the time, and was usually twisted into a sneer, a leer or a snarl. He was always dressed in dirty, black clothes, and wore black boots with black tassels on them. "Love beads" provided the only touch of color. Often, his favorite "banana knife" hung at his side. Just the kind of person who would cut your throat in a dark alley?

Wrong. That was what was so incredible about Otto. In appearance, conversation and preoccupations, he seemed to be a dangerous paranoid character, but in spirit he was as gentle, trusting, and helpless as a child. A lamb in wolf's clothing. Yet there was nothing fraudulent or contrived about his persona, either. When Otto called someone a "miserable swine" he was expressing emotions sincerely felt; but they were weightless. Nothing about Otto had any gravity, yet everything about him had all the outward characteristics of solid lead. The whole production was therefore somehow miraculous and unbelievable and left people who didn't know him dazed and uneasy after their first exposure.

It took me a while to get used to Otto. While we worked together building the pen, I wondered how I could detach myself from him without hurting his feelings, and I also tried to figure out, without much success, exactly what it was about Otto that made me so reluctant to hurt his feelings.

The custom at Millbrook in those days was to have someone in the tennis house, or Meditation House, as it had been renamed early in the game, at all times. One went there in the evening and either dropped at once or slept and dropped in the morning.

Every evening a big bell on the Big House porch was rung at the changing of the guard. A list of "meditators" for the week ahead was kept on the wall inside the front door. One could sign up any time for any night that was free. After so many weeks of unstoned woe, I was looking forward to breaking my set, which no longer suited my setting. I decided on a day trip. Feeling sociable, I had mentioned that I wouldn't mind if two or three people joined me at sunrise to share the wealth. Otto wanted to be one of them. Over my dead body, I thought to myself. I put off setting a date until I could figure out a way of keeping Otto out of it.

The Meditation House was a charming, one-room building made of stone and carved beams, with paneled walls and diamond-paned, Gothic windows. No matter how wintery the weather outside, it could be kept comfortable with only a small fire in the fireplace. There was a covered mattress on the floor and a low, cushioned, closet bench extended along the wall under the windows facing the front lawn and the fountain. The Big House could not be seen from inside because fir trees were clustered so deeply around. From the covered entrance a steep, stone staircase conveniently descended to the sunken gardens. Crossed, wrought-iron tennis rackets adorned the peak of the Meditation House roof, a healthy, happy symbol which I would like to see on the *klep* of every Neo-American structure used for a similar purpose.

(There was almost no yoga exercise or "Buddhist" meditation at Millbrook, as typically understood. These terms, and others like them, were used as covers for getting stoned. They really meant "let's sell decadency" or "let's start degeneration," to us hedonistic, chinless, homosexual midgets with our pugnacious noses and marked gratification complexes.)

Turn off the stupid chatter of your everyday mind, says the average, dime-a-dozen, street-corner "meditator." Good advice, if all you have is stupid chatter. If, on the other hand, you enjoy a grand and breezy procession of thoughts of infinite variety, the formation of which is both an art and a sport, you might be satisfied to take a nap every now and then. To start such a parade of happy ideas, all that is often necessary is a puff of pot. To add golden elephants, giant balloons, exotic dancing girls, and the higher nobility in golden carriages, add a little acid.

What the hell, add a lot.

Bill Haines and I had visited Tim early one frosty morning in the Meditation House, after I had introduced them in 1966, and before I left with J.D. for my trip to Steve Newell's place. I think it may have been the only time in the history of Millbrook the three of us got together privately. It was a pleasant meeting, unmarred by squabbles. Tim, who had just come down from a big one, said his vision of the eventual destiny of the place was a loose confederation of various spiritual communities devoted to different "paths."

Since that was all Haines wanted and all I wanted, we left the meeting pleased with Tim and ourselves. Only later did we discover the wisdom of Lao-tzu's cynical observation, "It is useless to confer with those of a different way," as it applied to us.

Chapter 24

A RIVAL MAGICIAN

These people had seen me do the very showiest bit of magic in history, and the only one within their memory that had a positive value, and yet here they were, ready to take up with an adventurer who could offer no evidence of his powers but his mere unproven word.

The Neo-American Church, by this time, had at least a thousand active members. Most of the residents of the Big House, both League and Ashram, had signed up although we had nothing to offer in those days except sporadic bulletins and a membership card and I rarely asked anyone to join. But the image was right. They volunteered, in the most strict sense of the term, and almost always first heard of the Church by word of mouth.

No doubt the absence of a philosophic doctrine and an exclusionary rule had a lot to do with it. All one accomplished by signing the application form in those days was to go on record as believing that the psychedelic experience was religious. What was meant by "religious" was pretty much left up in the air. Even so, I think the fact that so many and such various people (Allen Ginsberg and William Mellon Hitchcock?) joined so early showed that the general, frivolous spirit of the thing was politically correct. I wasn't the only Psychedelian around who thought it important to insist that one could be religious without conforming, in any way, to what the vast majority of our fellow citizens thought was meant by the term. So, we had a "fellowship," even if it was a loose one. I had invented an institutional form that seemed right for the times. "Good for you, Kleps," I thought to myself whenever a new proof of this came in. "Maybe you're not so crazy after all." But I knew that being right for the times is not what religion is about, and this awareness blunted my satisfaction considerably.

Strange things were happening on the West Coast, however. After Otto and I finished the goat-pen project, I found I had enough psychological elbow room to think about the future of the Church again. At Cranberry Lake, I had decided that since I couldn't afford a phone, much less tours of inspection, it would probably be a good idea to appoint a "Patriarch of the West," who would look after things west of the Mississippi and issue membership cards and ordain boo hoos on his own, although I would continue to keep the central records and send out the literature.

While our first Patriarch of the West was functioning everything went well, but Jim Boudreau resigned after a bust largely brought on by an invasion of his farm in Oregon by egalitarian-primitivist hordes of the same parasitic variety we resisted, somewhat longer, at Millbrook. I then appointed a dentist named William Shyne to the position, and all communication promptly ceased. Shyne simply took my stuff, edited out whatever displeased him, replaced my name and address with his own, and kept all the records, initiation fees ($5 at the time) and donations to himself. Thousands of kids on the West Coast joined under those circumstances, and got a distorted picture of the Church, to put it mildly.

Later, Mike Duncan told me that he had met Shyne and that he was a raving, paranoid, speed freak who traveled with a submachine gun under the front seat of his car and by no means limited his dealing activities to the psychedelic sacraments. But I didn't suspect any of this at the time, having grown up with an image of dentists incongruous with such conduct. I wrote Shyne two or three letters requesting records, but got no answers.

"What should I do about this son of a bitch?" I asked Haines, after telling him the whole story.

"We have a mimeograph machine here, Kleps. Write a *Divine Toad Sweat* and excommunicate the bastard."

"I'm flat broke, Bill," I said. This was true, and one of the reasons it was true was that I hadn't put out a *Divine Toad Sweat* bulletin, *DTS* for short, which always drew new members, in a long time.

"I pay for it," said Bali Ram, who had been listening to the conversation.

Well, good for Bali once again. Had he stolen a ruby out of an idol's forehead before he left Nepal? I thanked Bali, resolved to write the *DTS* after my trip, and immediately went downstairs and signed up for meditation duty.

Ross blustered but offered no real resistance to our penning of his goats. It was too popular a move. With a shed to sleep under, they looked contented and comfortable, although ruthlessness and treachery still lurked in the depths of their marble eyes. Someone cleaned up the porch, and a heavy snow fell which covered up the evidence of their former dominion. We took the sheep to the vet, who found a home for it, he said.

Just before my trip was due, Ross invited me up to the tower. The great goat controversy was apparently to be forgotten. He and Carol were now concerned for the salvation of my soul, or something.

"Listen, Art," Bob said, "Carol and I would be happy to take a trip with you. I have had a lot of experience as a guide."

Bob went on to describe his career. Never lost a patient, etc. They both seemed to take for granted, and to take for granted that I took for granted, the idea that tripping, like surgery or cosmetology, was an activity divorced from ordinary human relationships. It was all a matter of expertise, which derived in some bean-counting way from how many trips you took and how many you "guided." This view has some value for desperate novices who don't have anything better to go by, but I was no novice, and the whole idea of "guidance" was fading away at Millbrook among experienced users by the time I returned. I could have taken umbrage, but I was feeling tolerant, as most people do both before and after they trip, so I was polite and said I would think it over.

My reward was a load of Brooks Brothers duds Bob no longer wore because he had decided they were out of style. Since we happened to wear clothes of almost exactly the same hard-to-find and expensive sizes, and I sure as hell needed replacements for almost everything and had no more concern for what was in or out of style than for who was the president of Ecuador, I was sincerely grateful for this act of charity, although I got a lot of kidding from the boys in the Ashram about it.

Before I went down to the Meditation House in the evening, I told Bill and Marshall McNeill that I would be delighted to have them join me in the morning. I told Otto that I would prefer it if we tripped together some other time. Otto looked wounded, and I felt like a heartless monster. Better heartless than headless, I thought to myself.

The Meditation House had two books in it: an *I Ching* and a large, bound, blank book, in which previous meditators had written their hexagrams and whatever comments they thought appropriate to the occasion. Contrary to what one might expect, this journal made boring reading, since almost every comment was of the "we are all one" variety, which has always seemed to me to be a generalization in the "war is hell" category.

"We?" It's not easy to say anything about anything without using this term, and philosophers of all classes constantly employ it without ever trying to define it. All human beings? As of when? What about the brain-dead? There is no stable referent. It's a vague particular, not a universal. And the same thing goes for "everyone" and "everybody."

As for "one," well, one what?

But the Meditation House wasn't a lecture room. As a slogan or as impressionistic Fazzm, "we are all one" is OK. It conveys the spirit of the thing and, like sex, encourages camaraderie. Let's not be too picky, at least not while under the mystic symbol of the crossed rackets.

The next morning, Haines and Marshall showed up and we had a degenerates' breakfast, washing the pills past our receding jaws with some white wine which Haines had thoughtfully provided. A few minutes later, Otto appeared and cheerfully sat down, having already dropped his acid, which seemed like the most inevitable thing in the world, as did everything else that happened. Several eons seemed to pass while I made my way down to the ruined gardens, took a piss, and returned to the Meditation House. Fifteen or twenty combatively nosed, hedonistic and androgynous shrimps, all sporting marked gratification complexes, jammed the little room, along with trays of food, bottles of wine, pipes loaded with hashish, more firewood, dogs and cats. I kicked out the dogs and all but one cat. A spirit of hilarity prevailed among all of us cross-eyed and undernourished faggot midgets, covert and overt alike. I had brought the Ashram and the League together and made them One, as it were. One party of asthenic degenerates with heavy spectacles squashed down over our cavernous nostrils.

The local, cross-eyed gratification freaks came and went all day but Otto just stayed right there telling me all about his adventures at Numerich Arms' submachine gun factory across the river, where he had worked as a mechanical genius for two years, and then further back into the dim past of Otto's life, but no, not dim, no, vivid. It was amazing. I could see the world the way Otto saw it and yet remain capable of ratiocination!

Even so, I could not help exclaiming with astonishment over certain inherently incredible elements. There was a distinct tendency to overdevelop certain themes, but what the hell, whatever the McPozzm correctness of it all, I was talking to an archetype with a long and distinguished career behind it for screwing up the world. It would be interesting to see the effect that getting stoned was having on this archetype, or what was left of it.

As Otto told it, he had grown up as an only child on the Jersey shore in a Gothic mansion presided over by his father, a Nazi spy, and his alcoholic mother. His father, the spy, Otto thought, signaled to German submarines during WWII. Otto was descended from the Teutonic Knights of the Holy Roman Empire in a general kind of way and from Otto the Great in particular. His father was presently engaged in robbing him of a sizable trust fund, all that remained of a fortune founded in the days of the

Hohenstaufen emperors, so it was necessary for Otto to get into the "love bead racket" as soon as possible or he would be "out picking shit with the crows on Route 44."

The above is merely an outline. The story went on and on.

It was the idioms that got to you, after a while, what cracked people up about Otto when he was in top form. His jovial and homely figures of speech belied the paranoid character of his constructions of events, almost all of which, I assumed, were misconstructions.

As an archetype, and if Otto wasn't one, what was?, it seemed to me that Otto supported the thesis that the militaristic spirit didn't have much of a future in a stoned world. It would be difficult to dragoon obedient slave armies of efficient, disciplined mass murderers from a Psychedelian population. If one could get them into the field at all, they would all be goof-offs and fuck-ups, no matter how closely they fit, as Otto might have, the ideal profile for an officer's candidate on a multiple choice test. A personal interview would have been a different matter.

Perhaps, had I not had this trip with Otto, I would have devoted less time and trouble to the Psychedelian cause in years to come, and more to agitation against the holocaust in Vietnam. This would have been a waste, because the conventional forms of agitation are all ephemera compared to changing the drug preferences of an entire generation in a direction incompatible with military discipline.

Otto, in his own strange way, was as important to my education at that time as were Tim and Billy and Bill in their strange ways.

What might be call the "social inventiveness" of LSD can be as important and as odd as the visionary effects.

Beyond a certain point, there is no use complaining about the kind of company you get on a trip or about anything else, for that matter. If the time has come for certain changes and revelations, you will get them, one way or another, no matter what.

Making oneself hard to find may even result in an increase in what might be called "the entity count" of visionary experience. If one won't accept regular folks with social security numbers and pugnacious noses, etc., one will get the demons and angels and neon parrots from Mars.

If one denies the externality of relations, thinking along these extremely Snazzm lines is not irrational superstition, although most people who notice such changes are not enlightened, and only interpret the observation as support for their favored form of occultist paranoia.

Neither the concept of randomness nor the concept of physical causality explains why, in a dream, one apple falls and another does not. There is no actual "force of gravity" in a dream, merely the appearance of it, no actual mechanical necessity of any kind, no statistical probability, no chance. The empirical, McPozzm fact that the house has a 1.2 percent advantage over the shooter in craps has nothing to do with the meaning of a big dream loss, or a big dream win, in such a dream game in a dream Las Vegas.

To understand things in Snazzm terms, one must search for repressed wishes and fears and other associations which have nothing at all to do with the laws of probability. The laws of chance are "in" the dream as a kind of prop, like the dice, the people and the city. The author of the dream is the dreamer. But it's hell to be alone. One must be nothing or several. Thus, multiplicity. Thus, groups. Thus, variations. Thus, statistics. Thus, probability. Thus, bad news for all of the people some of the time, and for some of the people all of the time.

One of Otto's favorite occupations at Millbrook was searching for "the Kaiser's gold." There was a story at Millbrook that the last Kaiser had visited the original owner, Charles F. Dieterich, and hidden a treasure somewhere on the property. Otto drilled exploratory holes in the labyrinthian cellar floors looking for it, and also discussed the subject with the shade of Dieterich, whose presence he felt most strongly when he wandered about the house and grounds in the dead of night, stoned on acid, grass, ether, or "I.P." (India Pale Ale), which Otto claimed was the strongest of all. In a way, I guess it was, since he usually drank the stuff after sampling everything else on hand.

Despite all of Otto's prowlings, however, he never found the rumored secret tunnel between the Big House and the Bowling Alley. It made sense to think that a man who had spent so much money on other oddities would have built one, and the cats supported the theory, several cat watchers attested, by somehow getting from one building to the other without leaving tracks in the snow.

When I typed up my new *DTS*, subtitled "Dilated House Organ of the Church," I announced Otto's appointment as director general of SPIN. I also condemned the "prominent display of goats" around any property as being "a sure sign that the inhabitants are diseased, depraved and given over entirely to all kinds of hideous lusts and perversions." The response to the new bulletin was gratifying. The difference between $5 or $10 a day and nothing a day is a highly meaningful difference. It liberates the imagination, particularly if you are a heavy smoker. I could, just barely, envision a happy future without Morning Glory Lodge or my former family.

Such are the mysterious ways of the experience which all established powers unite in condemning as "too dangerous." They're right. It is extraordinarily dangerous to the interests of all of them, because it loosens bonds of which they are the holders. Exactly where you move, once you are free to move, is up to you, but you really are free to move. It isn't merely a transfer to a different place of confinement, as is true of most things that claim this.

In Otto's case, I envision a long, black, heavy chain winding up through the centuries from the dark beginnings of organized barbarism, with the terminal link here in the present corroded into a mere strand of bent coat hanger by LSD. Nothing else could have done it, not even I.P.

His Zeitgeist, if not his entire Weltanschauung, survived only as a charming farce in a wine cellar at Millbrook, reduced to a few empty symbols without the power to injure or to degrade anyone. A collection of old history books, some old medals and rusted weapons, and the last man in the chain, here in a new and Psychedelian world, wearing love beads and talking about flower power.

Chapter 25

A COMPETITIVE EXAMINATION

Verily, in the all-wise and unknowable providence of God, who moveth in mysterious ways His wonders to perform, have I never heard the fellow to this question for confusion of the mind and congestion of the ducts of thought.

It wasn't long after my trip with Otto that I got a room of my own: Rudy and Jackie's.

During one of Bill's telephone conversations with Tim on the Coast, Tim had surprised Bill and everyone else by announcing that he wanted to return. Since he had made a deal with the Dutchess County authorities to leave, and never to darken their doorsteps again, if all the charges stemming from Liddy's raid, the one that had cost Rosemary thirty days in jail for refusal to testify, were dropped, his decision was greeted with mixed emotions in the Big House. Leaving aside his inspirational and entertainment value, Tim's lecture fees would come in handy for paying fuel bills and such, but on the other hand, it seemed likely that the ruling rodents of the Place of Overflowing Shitholes would lust for his blood and we all might suffer as a result.

In any event, Tim wanted Rudy and Jackie out of the house before he entered it. Their presence, he said, was obnoxious to him. Rudy and Jackie maintained that Bill had accepted them into the Ashram and therefore it didn't matter what Tim said.

Bill maintained a brooding silence on the subject. Bob Ross was infuriated. The house seethed with accusations, rumors and intrigue.

Ross called a house meeting, and everyone gathered in the music room after dinner, including Rudy and Jackie. After two or three people had made the usual pretty speeches to say that they would not take sides because karma would take care of everything, someone accused Rudy of having a private stash of marijuana in the woods. This person had followed Rudy and observed him digging around the base of a rock. It was then revealed that this person, I think it was Tambimutto, had been followed by Otto, who had hoped Tambi was looking for a stashed bottle of booze. This revelation was greeted with hilarity, but Ross interrupted and launched on a general exposition of his view of the situation.

He, Ross, took what was happening in the house seriously even if some people were only there for a place to flop. He had a private income and could live anywhere he pleased. Rudy and Jackie, as far as he was concerned, were "viruses" that had entered his home. He didn't see why he shouldn't eliminate viruses from his sinus cavity.

At the conclusion of this tirade, during which Ross became extremely agitated and looked like he was about to hemorrhage internally, Rudy defended himself and Jackie by saying he had no idea why Tim "hated" them. They had done nothing against him. Anyway, they considered themselves members of the Ashram. If Bill said they had to go they would, but not under any other circumstances.

None of this struck me as constructive, so I spoke up. Was this meeting supposed to be a trial? If so, who were the judges, what were the accusations, and what were the rules of procedure and evidence? More basic even than that, were we an organized group? If so, where was our constitution, or bylaws, or whatever? As far as I knew, the Hitchcocks owned the place and had put Tim in charge of it. If someone who had invited you into his house decided he didn't want you there, then you left. I had nothing against Rudy and Jackie, but it didn't seem to me Tim's reasons for not wanting them there were any of my business. If, when Tim returned, he asked me to leave, which was a possibility, I would go. I wouldn't hang around and argue about it.

My comments were received in dead silence, but they broke up the meeting, which, in my experience, is what usually happens at such affairs if you tell the truth instead of allowing vague fantasies to prevail. Not even Tim's greatest admirers, such as Ross, wanted to admit they were there on his sufferance, but if they weren't, what were the rules?

Nobody could answer that question. I have been to many meetings, straight and head, and they all seem to proceed along the same lines unless everything important is defined ahead of time. Few people ever follow an argument to its logical conclusions, either in public or in private. Their "arguments" therefore, ought to be taken as mere expressions of feeling like "ouch" or "yum yum" rather than as attempts to define or reason. Professional politicians take this for granted and do not make everyone uncomfortable by treating what they say as if they really meant it. "Feelings rule mankind," Disraeli said. Right.

As absolute ruler of a doctrinaire and monarchical Church, I now define the terms at every meeting over which I preside. I find that this privilege, along with the freedom to excommunicate heretical and unruly persons, greatly relieves the burdens of office.

Chapter 26

THE FIRST NEWSPAPER

It was good Arkansas journalism, but this was not Arkansas.

Haines' first reaction to Rudy and Jackie's claim to membership in the Ashram had been, in contrast to his usual straightforward style, guarded and ambiguous. Although the Drucks reported that Bill had told them that Rudy and Jackie's application for membership in the Ashram had been accepted, he evaded the question when I asked. "Rudy and Jackie will have to figure it out for themselves," he said. Finding themselves without support, they left, and I moved into their room, which was across the landing from Bill's and next to Howie and Betsy's room. Once again, I had the best view of a bowling alley in the United States, if not the entire world.

Shortly after this major elevation in comfort, privacy and aesthetics, an event occurred which I thought was a sign of great progress in my upward flotation from the inky depths of depression. I managed to write something imaginative. The bulletin I had written and mailed out with Bali's help didn't count, according to my standards, because it was just factional journalism, and pretty low-class factional journalism at that, but the little essay I wrote in my new room had a certain something, in my opinion.

THE BOMBARDMENT AND ANNIHILATION OF THE PLANET SATURN

Since all competent bullshitters specializing in astrological matters are agreed on the singularly gruesome and wretched nature of the planet Saturn, competence being determined, of course, by agreement with this very definition, since any just or rational judgment is bound to fail, due to the influence of the planet Saturn, it is apparent that the only solution is to blow the big fat greasy sonofabitch to smithereens.

This is the ultimate objective of the Neo-American Church: nothing less than the bombardment and annihilation of the planet Saturn. Upon the successful completion of the task, with the dispersal of the malefic energy of this gloomy orb into the cosmos (which, if too seriously affected, will be our next objective), the Millennium, or golden age of mankind, will commence without further ado, and it will be possible to dismantle not only the apparatus of the Church but all the instrumentalities of The Divine Will; to permit Peter Rabbit free access to the garden of Farmer Brown.

The entire technical resources of the planet Earth must be marshaled in the service of The Holy War; enormous rockets designed, built and placed in orbit; fusion bombs of hitherto undreamed of power prepared; a special corps of dedicated men and women recruited and trained, all Capricornians identified and watched by a secret service, and all those born with Saturn rising rounded up and interned (in opulent luxury on tropic isles, of course) for the duration.

It may be asked (by certain mealy-mouthed phonies), "Won't this upset the delicate balance of the forces in The Mysterium Tremendum with all sorts of dire results, such as trains not running on time, fucked-up calendars, etc.?" Or, by certain poetic souls of delicate sensibility, "How can such crude means effect good ends?; rather, let us pray unceasingly for deliverance from this dreadful visitation, which we must nevertheless richly deserve for some unknown reason." Our reply to all such crappy nit-picking, hair-splitting, insecure and neurotic rubbish must be polemical; even sloganeering. When grave issues are at stake, a political approach is necessary, and the engagement of the most powerful emotions capable of elicitation, however grotesque.

Nevertheless, we may outline here the major arguments and rebuttals favorable to our doctrine (although refusing to admit for an instant that any argument is necessary; our proposition being self-evident to anyone of good will and sound mind):

(1) Time is the prison of mankind; the spell that binds us.

As men manage space to confine each other, so do the gods use time. To proclaim that one lives in eternity under these circumstances is a waste of breath, merely true, only a scientific observation. Our spatial coordinates (our spatial projections) serve and define us, delight us, take out the garbage. Time is too hard; it concedes now only to a few magicians, all others are enslaved. We must storm the Bastille.

(2) The destruction of Saturn will not eliminate time (it says here), but merely drop it down a few notches to a manageable level, at least I certainly hope so. As for things getting even worse, let's not think about it. To do so would be to fall under the influence of the Planet Saturn.

(3) Taking LSD is no substitute for blowing up planets. I am morally certain that Dr. Hoffman never, in his wildest dream, envisioned anyone putting his discovery to such a chicken use as employing it as a substitute for blowing up planets. If God wanted us to have synthetics he would have invented them.

(4) There are many trivial secondary benefits inherent in the project, such as the unification of mankind and what not, and God knows what serendipitous benefits. With the advent of the psychedelic age, many heavy people and machines will be left unemployed, for example, and the project will keep them busy; provide them, indeed, with a rationale. The great symbolical benefits engendered by shooting enormous steel projectiles loaded with explosives into a big mushy egg up in the sky are so obvious as to need no explanation, especially for Catholics.

(5) Novices require a teleology related to history. Although our actual objectives are the improvement of that time which, in the words of Thoreau, "is neither past, present nor future," it is certainly convenient to have an "ultimate objective" ready-made, so to speak. One may envision the boo hoo, often merely a con man, temporarily satisfying the questions of the novice, or at least obtaining his conditional allegiance, by enlisting his energies in The Holy War; then, should this "answer" prove inadequate upon further soul searching or study, the guru (who might be janitor of the lodge, or the novice's eleven-year-old kid brother), coming up with the Great Mystical Equations at the right moment. In any event, by having something understandable to offer right off the bat, we are at least in a position to deal the joker to the poor fish when he is off balance on our side of the court, without resorting to dirty pool.

In reference to the actual proven nature of the planet Saturn, I refer the reader to an excellent rundown in Henry Miller's *The Colossus of Maroussi*; New Direction Paperback, pages 104-106.

Peculiar stuff, and somewhat slapdash, but not the work of a depressed person. I had astonished myself, which is what most artists like best to do. Haines loved it and seemed to understand exactly what I was getting at. He read it to anyone who would listen.

The Ashram kids, who, although we kidded around a lot, had been basically respectful towards me, became even more so. The Leaguers did too, but more in the way that people respect any show of force, rather than out of appreciation or approval. Almost everyone in the house believed in astrology in a standard, cause-and-effect way. My attitude, which combined a grasp of the subject and a kind of acceptance of it, along with a flippant dismissal of the whole business as just another metaphorical construct to be kicked around at will, was a little over their heads. It was clear to all that I had literary talent, however, and everyone knew the Psychedelian cause needed as much of that as it could get.

The Ashramites, in consequence of being constantly reminded of it by Haines, understood, if only superficially, that the external world was to be regarded as an illusion. It was part of "the teachings," in which they believed, or at least tried to believe. Despite the moderate intelligence and barbaric, supernaturalist heritage of most of them, they got the general idea: The answer to the question who? was one's own self, not "God," or the "Cosmic Mind," or even, and this is where they failed when they failed, "we." They understood, more or less, that the answer to the question where? was "in one's own mind," and not "in the universe" or on any particular planet or solar system or "level" or "vibrational frequency" or "alternative reality."

They knew, sort of, that the answer to the question what? was "Nothing." Off and on, they were aware that the answer to the question why? was "attachment" and the answer to the question when? was "now or never," but they didn't know any of this with much assurance or certainty, which was why they were students and followers rather than leaders and gurus. Some of them all of the time, and all of them some of the time, knew these things, in the same sense that so-called "Christians" know they have been instructed by their Lord to turn the other cheek, hand over their cloaks, etc., but much prefer to cry "Lord, Lord" all the time, which St. Paul, all the Popes, Martin Luther and a bunch of other guys told them was even better, and is a hell of a lot easier.

Since I still harbored the delusion that Tim was an enlightened teacher, I ascribed the occultist tendencies of his followers to his present absence rather than to his former presence. I was wrong. Tim really was a cosmic-mind "Hindu" (or Brahmanist, or Roman Catholic turned inside out) just as he had said in his trial in Texas. What prevented me from recognizing this obvious fact was his ability, wit, grace and specious maladaptations of the truisms of genuine monist philosophy to the subtly perverted usages of opportunistic revolutionary politics, which in those days I regarded as mere froth.

Froth today, scum tomorrow.

Tim and I had the classic virtues and vices associated with our houses of birth, Libra and Aries respectively, which are opposite each other in the zodiac. Tim excelled in sensing what it was his audience wanted to hear and giving them so much more of it than they expected that they didn't know whether to shit or go blind, while my talents lay in the direction of figuring out what was wrong with the bastards and then telling them exactly what they didn't want to hear the most. Tim, a truly other-directed personality, and a master of disguise, appeared and disappeared all over the place as he adjusted his image to the varying demands of the kid culture, while I bored ahead like a ram, even when brick walls intervened or nobody was paying any attention and my target had gone home to enjoy a leisurely lunch.

Astrology can help define, Fazzm, what games are being played and something about the style of the players, but little or nothing about the outcome of any particular game or the fate of any particular player. It does seem appropriate, however, that the Libra in an Aries/Libra conflict/alliance should be rewarded with popularity and the Aries with priority. Since my relationship with Tim had started with my false assumption that he was enlightened, I had thrown the "who's first" game before it had even started, and supposing that being first was the only game in town, I saw no reason for further competition. In comparison to the satisfaction of first, what else mattered?

By granting Tim that honor I had peeled off my astrological

label and had managed to see things in a way that was alien to my character. I made excuses for his failings, which was also uncharacteristic, and it wasn't until Tim produced his *Starseed Transmissions* and *Neurologic* that the last vestiges of my delusions about him evaporated, and I added yet another ironical twist to my collection. I had come in first largely because I thought I didn't have a chance.

Easy, early successes often screw and glue early errors in place forever. The history of the religion racket is plastered with examples. It was a good thing I thought of myself as a relatively minor hod carrier for so long because it gave me the freedom to think things out. By the time I got going, I understood the intellectual minefield I had entered pretty well, and had acquired the Zmms and other strange devices to light my path.

Haines, who did not believe he owed anything at all to Tim, had none of my hang-ups, and one of the reasons Haines distrusted me was that I did not, in his judgment, sufficiently distrust Tim. Bill thought Tim was a "mad scientist" and that was that. Tim's philosophic ideas were on the same level with those of Narad, the Man of Iron, if not lower. Haines was right.

The article advocating the bombardment of the offending planet, which was reprinted here and there in the underground press, added to the effect of the first *Divine Toad Sweat* from Millbrook, brought the Church back to life. Five-dollar bills began to appear in P.O. Box 694, Millbrook, N.Y., with such regularity that I was able to buy cigarettes, replace worn socks, and quaff an occasional pint of wine with carefree abandon. I offered a share of my cash flow to the Ashram but Bill refused it.

"Don't even tell anyone how much you get," Bill advised. "We have enough rich pricks to tap around here without taking money from economic basket cases like you and me."

Serious historians can get as many copies of the *Divine Toad Sweat* of old as they want. The doctrine and the style of the Church have changed since those days, and so has my choice of literary flavors, but I believe in keeping an accurate historical record of things, even if the contemplation of some of it makes my flesh crawl, blood freeze, hair stand on end, etc.

Chapter 27

THE YANKEE AND THE KING TRAVEL INCOGNITO

If you have ever seen an active, heedless, enterprising child going diligently out of one mischief and into another all day long, and an anxious mother at its heels all the while, and just saving it by a hair from drowning itself or breaking its neck with each new experiment, you've seen the king and me.

Haines had a large repertoire of Tim stories, almost all of which were guaranteed to crack up his audience, drawn from the period when I had been consorting with criminals of the old school in Alabama and Florida. Those months had evidently been a silly season for Tim, who for one period of three or four days, had made a practice of lying around the house on the floor, arms outstretched, as if he were being crucified. One morning the mood struck him at the foot of the stairs in the entrance hall, and down he went, although a couple carloads of visitors were due to arrive at any moment.

"I just ignored him," Haines said. "When I showed the visitors around the house, I just stepped over the body and said, 'and this is Dr. Leary,' and they all nodded solemnly and sort of tiptoed over him one by one and followed me up the stairs. Nobody ever asked me for an explanation. Maybe I should have asked one of them to explain it to me."

After the crucifixion mania passed, Haines and all his followers had been invited to attend a kind of ecumenical LSD session with the League in Tim's room on the third floor. Everyone sat in a circle, with Tim at one end and Bill at the other, and this time the implication was that Bill and/or the Ashram in general desperately required some kind of spiritual tranquilization. Tim kept droning "find your calm center, find your calm center" every few seconds and Carol Ross, who was seated next to him, chanted when he didn't.

"I can still hear it," Haines said. "It was unbelievable."

He widened his eyes, made his mouth into an "o," fluttered his hands and assumed a falsetto voice:

"Skies of blooooooo, skies of blooooooooo. She just kept saying that, over and over. If it wasn't 'find your calm center' it was 'skies of blooooooo, skies of blooooooo.' I mean, I don't think I freak out easily, Art, but five minutes more of that and I might have gone out of the window."

"How long did it last?" I asked.

"I don't know. I guess I took it for about fifteen minutes and then I just stood up, excused myself, and walked out the door."

All the other Ashramites, also having failed to find any calm centers under those circumstances, had followed Bill out. Tim left Millbrook shortly thereafter for California, but not before he said, to League and Ashram alike, that Bill would be in charge during his absence. Bill was surprised, but not, like the Leaguers, astounded or confused.

"The old rope trick," Bill said, and now I'm sure he was quite right. At the time, I thought he was being overly cynical.

Wendy, who had managed the difficult feat of keeping both feet in both camps, told me a story that illustrated the spirit of things in the League as she had known it:

During an early meeting after the Ashram had moved into the Big House, Tim had proposed to move the entire League to Europe, where they would proceed to march across the continent on a "journey to the East," gathering adherents as they went. For seasonal reasons, it would be necessary to get this show on the road in a matter of ten days or something like that.

Everyone had thought this was a groovy idea, sort of, but

Allan Marlowe raised a crucial objection which sank the whole project then and there:

"But Tim," he said, "my robes won't be ready by then."

Most of the talk in the common room was about money. The idea of conserving what we had on hand never seemed to enter Haines' mind, although it is possible to live on a modest income once you have a roof over your head, if you are prepared to give up all luxuries, smoke Bugler, and adopt a Hitlerian diet. The Ashram had been 100 percent vegetarian at Ananda, and I had found the meals to be surprisingly edible. For some reason, this practice had been dropped and, except for brief interludes, we had as many meatballs on our spaghetti as anyone else.

There was also lots of ice cream and candy for the children. When money was particularly low, Haines would make a point of blowing the Ashram's last $20 on a big bash for the kids, and some cash would always turn up from some surprising source shortly thereafter.

Nevertheless, Bill usually had everyone convinced we wouldn't last another week. Although the food problem was largely self-imposed, the fuel bills were not. Heating a fifty-room house during a winter in New York requires big bucks, as Tim had pointed out to me when he urged me to go to Alabama. Every visitor with any loose cash in his pocket had to be tapped, and we often had to rely on the fireplaces, which, however cozy in their radiant proximity, barely gave off enough convective heat to keep the pipes from freezing.

There were several projects under consideration. For one thing, a guy named Al Bonk had been visiting from Woodstock with samples of his pottery. It was charming and fanciful stuff, which he said he sold to local stores with no trouble at all.

I have met several potters since. Every one of them, talented or not, managed to make a modest living by it. The ideal legal craft for potheads of moderate intelligence may be making pots. Once you get your hands in that gunk, they say, you never get them out. This simple craft might have propped up the place, but Haines was no more of a businessman than I was. As almost all of those who do it will affirm, business administration is a full time job which requires special skills and hard work.

There were also jewelry-making, printing and, presuming this and that, the Neo-American Church, as possible sources of income. The only occupants of the Bungalow at the time were Jack and Mary Petrie, the butler and cook. Billy, Aurora, Tommy, Suzanne and Peggy were all working on their tans or enjoying the seasonal attractions available in Europe or New York City.

I wrote and Haines approved the following proposal to present to the millionaires when they reappeared on the scene. (Bill, by the way, later changed the spelling of his fake name from "Samkara" to "Sankara.")

THE SRI RAM ASHRAM AND THE NEO-AMERICAN CHURCH FINANCIAL POLICY AND PROBLEMS

Nature of the Relationship

At present Mr. Kleps is living at the Ashram, where Sri Samkara is the Guru, and has no plans for establishing an independent community, since the Neo-American Church is primarily concerned with householders and with the economic and political defense of the psychedelic religious movement rather than Yoga life per se of the Ashram. This does not, by any means, exclude the possibility of the Neo-American Church acquiring a permanent headquarters on the estate or elsewhere (see section on Cranberry Lake below), but the matter is not at all essential to the continued efficient operation of the Church.

Sri Samkara and Mr. Kleps find themselves in very happy agreement on most of the great issues which exist within the psychedelic movement; they seem to share the same tastes and prejudices and to favor highly complementary styles of expression and teacher-student game playing. On all levels, the combination seems most happy and fortuitous.

Both Sri Samkara and Mr. Kleps regard Timothy Leary with the greatest respect and admiration, and consider him to be a teacher in the great tradition. Both men, however, have grave reservations about the League for Spiritual Discovery and the capacity of the Leary household to function as an efficient organization headquarters. Both men are willing to be members of the League; that is, to assent to the principles for which it stands, but neither is willing to center his creative or managerial energy within the organizational framework of the League.

The opinion of both is that Timothy Leary's great energies and unique talents are wasted in managerial and organizational activities. It may be that no teacher of his stature can be efficient in ordinary practical terms since everything is seen in terms of its instructive possibilities and discriminations between individuals simply cannot be made by ordinary standards.

Whatever the case may be, however, it has clearly become necessary for the Ashram to occupy separate quarters, and this move, to the complex of buildings behind the Main House occupied by the Leary household, is already underway.

On the level of practicality and self-support, Sri Samkara and Mr. Kleps envision the Ashram directly managing and operating the press facilities which have been acquired through the generosity of Mr. Hitchcock and Dr. Leary, with the Neo-American Church and the Sri Ram Ashram using these facilities to publish books, pamphlets, catalogs, and so on; the income from which will be used for the support of the entire community.

The *Neo-American Church Catechism and Handbook*, including a catalog of items which will be sold by mail order, is now in final stages for printing. Many of the items offered in the catalog will be designed, made and manufactured by members of the community on the estate. Mr. Kleps intends this book to go through constant revision and expansion. A detailed and complete catalog will probably be offered separately, in time, with only the major standard items, such as rings, decorative objects, meditation tapes, and posters and prints listed in the handbook.

The book itself will sell for three dollars, and, if properly distributed, advertised and promoted, may be expected to return a large amount of working capital to the Church within the next few months. Application blanks for membership in the Church are included, and since an initial contribution to headquarters from new members of five dollars is requested, a considerable income from this source may also be reasonably anticipated.

Other Projects

1. The Kriya Press has already brought in $375 from the publication of poetry broadsides. There is no reason why the press should not make a very decent income from ordinary contracted printing jobs, and through our publication, leaving the income from Neo-American work aside.
The Neo-American Church plans a two week seminar for

boo hoos and the Ashram plans a two week seminar for the study of Yoga on the Millbrook estate this summer. Students will live in tents and provide their own food and for other needs. Fifty students times $100 fee equals $5,000.
2. The Sri Ram Ashram, a Yoga community, may develop an intensive program for weekend visitors, for which a not inconsiderable contribution will be expected. In any event, the entire problem of visitors will be treated in a reasonable and consistent manner.
3. Members of the Ashram will either work hard or pay their own way, or both. Idlers will not be tolerated. Yoga is a life of action.
4. Ashram craft and art shops of various kinds are being set up; jewelry, pottery, art (silk screen and photo offset) printing, weaving and textiles; with the products of these shops sold through the Neo-American catalog and possibly through a community store on the grounds.
5. Morning Glory Lodge. MGL is presently in the hands of Carl Newton, a very turned-on and tuned-in young psychiatrist friend of Kleps. This property could probably be bought back for $2,000 to $3,000 leaving $100 a month payments to be made. Birch Island, a small but scenically ideal property directly across from MGL might be purchased by the Church or Ashram for $16,000 to $18,000. The combination of MGL and Birch Island would make a "mythic" property of incomparable value for initial psychedelic experience. A cadre of three or four commonsensical people could manage the place all summer and produce enough income from visitors to, at the very least, make the mortgage payments and pay the bills.

Long Range Needs

All long range needs can be met out of income provided by the projects outlined above.

Immediate Needs

1. Working capital for paper, binding, advertising, distribution, and so on of the *Neo-American Church Catechism and Handbook*, $1,000.
2. Working capital for Ashram shops: Jewelry, $300; Pottery, $200; Silk screen, $200; Weaving, $100; Sandals, $100. Equipment: (a good used Ampex costs $500 or so), and

working capital for the production and sale of meditation tapes, records, and eventually films.
3. Appliances, office furniture, typewriters, mimeograph machine, and so on for the Ashram are needed.
Our experience in centralizing the editorial work in one room of the main house has been very instructive. People like to work around other people who are working. By having the press room, the editorial room and probably most of the shops all in one building and properly integrated and furnished, production WILL take place, without coercion or even much external reward. The production and creativity problems which have existed in the Main House have not been due to a lack of talent and willing hands but to a refusal to organize things along these lines. Any donation would be helpful; please specify the department you wish to assist.
4. The Neo-American Church is already incorporated pro forma in California as a non-profit religious organization. We can put anyone we like on the Board of Directors. Mr. Kleps would like to have the Board made up of one California resident (already on the pro forma board), Sri Samkara (he has agreed), Timothy Leary (he has agreed), Dr. Newton, Mr. Hitchcock, and any two persons nominated by Mr. Hitchcock. This will insure Mr. Hitchcock against any possible misuse of property purchased with his capital or on his credit or leased or rented from him. If Mr. Hitchcock agrees, we can proceed to make the necessary arrangements.

A Word About the Spirit of the Ashram and the Church

It is not impractical to approach the problem of giving direction and organization to the psychedelic religious movement in a humorous and entertaining manner. We are not "selling ourselves" to the "holy mothers" of former times, but to young, vital, educated, sophisticated people. It is not gaiety and laughter which are mistrusted today, but solemnity and sanctity. The ancient forms and rituals have their place, but it is no longer a crucial place. We must develop our own forms, and, as one might have suspected, those forms which seem to have survival value are the ones least calculated to have that result, those springing from spontaneous invention or accident.

Jokes pass the acid test, as sermons never will.

Only a few of these schemes ever amounted to much, partly for lack of money and partly for lack of organization. Only Sheatsley held a regular outside job, slinging corpses at the morgue.

Later, in Arizona, where pottery did support the place for a while, Haines would force some people to take outside jobs, but they either failed to hold them or, if they held them, failed to contribute their earnings to the Ashram and either left voluntarily or were driven away. The life of wage slaves, of any income or collar color, conflicts in all kinds of ways with the tempo and tenor of community life among stoned people.

Work itself is not the problem. Not working at all is incredibly boring for most people, stoned or unstoned. Intra-mural projects, even those involving considerable drudgery, get done if the leader of the gang wants them done badly enough to spend his authority. This Haines was willing to do. Tim was not. A reputation as a stern taskmaster would have done terrible things to his chosen public image.

The voluntarily poor and the idle rich have a lot in common. Both are on a kind of endless holiday with an unwritten future. Large, blank spaces await. There is lots of freedom and self-determination, and both the rich and the voluntarily poor have a chronic what-do-I-do-next problem, although the poor, since they must devote time and trouble to finding food and shelter and transportation and entertainment, may be less threatened by boredom, and more threatened by anxiety.

There were times when I suspected that Billy Hitchcock became a little jealous of the poverty of his ragged companions. In the comfortable Millbrook setting, even our occasional desperation had a kind of romantic quality, which contrasted favorably with his own boring capacity to solve almost any routine problem with his magical checkbook. The fact was that there was more emotional distance between Billy and, say, the editor of his newspaper, than there was between Billy and Charlie Hitchings from the Ashram, who occasionally earned a couple bucks by helping Jack and Mary at the Bungalow.

Charlie was just an average kid, but he nevertheless thought of everyday life in a way unknown to his working-class ancestors. "What am I going to do today?" he would ask himself when he woke up in the morning. Billy often asked himself the same question.

Artists, craftsmen and intellectuals who manage to make a living by doing what they would probably do even if they were rich, are envied and respected, even by their patrons, much more than most of them realize.

As mentioned in our plea that a few crumbs from the Mellon billions mill be brushed our way, we had already started work on the *Catechism*. The IBM variable-space typewriter necessary for justified right-hand margins for photo-offset printing was set up in the music room along with a drafting table and some desks.

Shortly thereafter, we moved the two photo-offset presses from the basement of the Bowling Alley to the unused garage in the Gray Buildings on the hill behind the Big House. Sheatsley built a two-by-four and plywood darkroom for the camera in the middle of this space.

Our right to do this was questioned by those few Leaguers who were politically perspicacious enough to recognize that the Ashram's independent control of any space with a roof over it went a long way towards splitting the community and ending Tim's hegemony, but Tim's loyalists were greatly outnumbered by dissenters and those who just didn't give a shit or thought karma would take care of it.

There was a distinct possibility, however, that Tim would "take care of it." Tim had told Bill he intended to be back by winter's end, now that Rudy and Jackie had been disposed of.

Wendy, Michael and I spent most of the day in the music room of the Big House working on layout and typing. The view from that room was lovely when snow was falling, a hushed surround both brilliant and subdued, which, for all its detail, gave little hint of what century or country we were in.

When the Hitchcocks returned from their various watering holes a short time later, I think they appreciated the change in the general tone of things. It was lighter than it had been, but more industrious also.

The visit of our lords and ladies (let's be realistic!) to the Big House was brief but pleasant. They seemed to like what they saw. I stayed in the background, and made no attempt to join in Bill and Billy's first talk about the future of the place, which didn't last long. Bill gave Billy our typewritten proposals, Billy promised to read them and "let us know," and that, according to Bill, was that.

This was my introduction to Billy's twin brother, Tommy, who seemed to be a darker and handsomer version of his brother; to Aurora, Billy's wife; and to Suzanne, Tommy's wife. Aurora was a neat little Spanish package, to be sure; and Suzanne, an ectomorphic blonde who seemed uptight, or just shy, in contrast to Aurora's ebullience, was hardly an aesthetic disaster area either. They looked exactly the way they should have looked, as did everyone at Millbrook, now that I think of it.

With the Hitchcocks back on the board and Tim still off of it, Bill and I assured each other, anything could happen. On the other hand, we had no idea what Tim might have been saying to the Hitchcocks by phone or letter. It wasn't at all impossible that we would find ourselves following Rudy and Jackie into outer darkness.

Our most important problem at that time, which Haines saw clearly but I didn't, was that Tim saw our ups as his downs. According to Haines, we would either establish ourselves in the Hitchcocks' good graces before Tim arrived, or we would be "screwed, blued and tattooed" before we knew what was happening.

"But Tim made a deal with the D.A. to stay out of Dutchess County," I objected, when Bill voiced these dire apprehensions. "Maybe he will figure there's safety in numbers, or something. Maybe he'll chicken out and never show up at all."

"Are you kidding?" Bill growled. "He's sitting there in California sweating his balls off worrying we'll get more out of the millionaires than he did. Why do you think he sent you down to Alabama? It's all right to have respect for your guru, Kleps, but you haven't learned one thing I have. Don't carry it too far."

The psychological atmosphere of this period, when we all lived in the Big House under the benign tyranny of Haines, and the Hitchcocks were close enough to be on friendly terms but not so intimate as to be embroiled in every detail of our daily lives, or we in theirs, was more philosophic-minded and romantic than it would be later. When Tim was present, we were always somewhat entangled with his public persona of the week and whatever media-oriented definition of the community and what it stood for he happened to favor at any given moment.

This added interest in some ways, amusement frequently, and suspense, but a lot that was good, and also fragile, was lost in the show-biz excitement of it all. If no special public attention was directed our way, it was easy to think of the place as a pleasant, contented, sometimes even drowsy, community of like-minded people. A minute later (Have you heard? Have you read? Did you see what was on TV last night?) we all seemed to be playing roles in a television documentary whether we liked it or not.

As a social critic, Tim usually didn't say anything in public that was blatantly false or that the rest of us sharply disagreed with. On the contrary. Most of the time, we applauded every word and admired the theatrical skill he employed to get his points across. Even his most hyperbolic political pronouncements, if they proved indigestible to the folks back home, could usually be dismissed as chicanery in the service of a higher good.

When, however, in his "high priest" mode, he pronounced edict after edict of metaphysical smarm, loaded with abstract nouns and alwayses and everyones and musts, it was frequently a bit too much and sometimes much too much.

The word "we" was forever on Tim's lips, and when his utterances passed beyond the routine hyperbolic imagery of the day and became seriously crazy (unserious craziness was OK), many of us would have greatly preferred that he speak for himself. As is usually the case with "we" abusers, Tim rarely made any effort to explain what he meant by the word, but if we, the people he lived with, were not "we," who was?

"Another thing," I remember Billy Hitchcock saying, as he complained about being defined in the public mind by such pronouncements, "is that I don't get all this constant love, love, love stuff. I mean, maybe some people need to hear that all the time but I was brought up that way, weren't you?"

Well, yes, as a matter of fact, I had been, with certain reservations, and so had almost everyone else around. And what was more important, we (usually) acted that way. We were, with few exceptions, if any, "nice guys." Actual malice was a great rarity on the place. But what about Tim himself? Was he a "nice guy?" One could come up with all kinds of evidence that he wasn't (Haines didn't think so) and that all of that "love, love, love, stuff" was in the "protesting too much" category. So why didn't the rest of us protest enough, so to speak? Why did we allow Tim to define the situation?

Because Tim made Psychedelianism pay off and we didn't. The basic "philosophy" he preached has always gone over very well in the American moronocracy because it's good for business: radical pragmatism of the Dale Carnegie school of non-thought; try real hard to believe what you want to believe and it will all come true. Have confidence in confidence alone. Climb every mountain and cross every stream, and dive into a few bottomless pits while you're at it. It's exactly the frame of mind every con artist wants his customers to have, so, in a nation ruled by con artists, it is promoted as widely as possible.

Tim was radical only in a very limited sense. In spirit, he was more like P. T. Barnum than, say, John Jay Chapman. He compromised his stated principles again and again to promote his immediate interests. I would say he took a kind of pride in doing this and delighted in leading a "double" life. He had wider horizons than the rest of us. He had the dreams of the true salesman. Millbrook was his home office but his territory was out there and his people, the people he thought about in the middle of the night, the people he cared about, were out there also, the voters of tomorrow.

As far as the rest of us were concerned, the voters of tomorrow could go piss up a rope. We were functioning. The place wasn't exactly wide open, but it wasn't hidden either. Let the electorate of the future come to us, behave in a semi-civilized manner, kick in a few bucks, take their dicks out of their ears, and they might learn something of lasting value or, at the very least, enjoy a vacation from the rat race on the treadmill in the jungle out there.

Had our First Amendment rights been protected instead of trashed, this attitude would have worked just fine. We could have openly turned on every sane person who showed up. Our community in general, and all three sects in particular, would have become rich and powerful in no time at all. Instead of money problems we would have had logistical problems. But we were not allowed to promote our religious practices to those in the market for new religious practices in a natural, open and honest way. In our fortunate case, we could have provided a magnificent physical setting, a neat little menu of philosophic sets/sects to choose from, and the best LSD money could buy in return for donations from satisfied pilgrims and enthusiastic converts. This normal, healthy and correct course of development had been made impossible by the powers that were, and because it was impossible, we could barely support ourselves, even with the free rent.

The times did not call for the natural and the normal. They called for speechifying in the classic cant of mob politics; for smarm and lots of it; for exaggeration, fraudulence, hypocrisy and the deployment of any arguments and inducements, however fallacious or illusory, of any possible utility; the relentless pursuit of celebrities; mutual back-scratching orgies with virtually any influential person willing to participate; fund raising by all of the standard, sleazy means and lots of silly slogans.

Tim seemed to have been born for the job.

Bill, despite his conviction that the crushing burden of our monstrous fuel bills gave us no choice, was full of conflicted feelings about Tim's return.

"We're a couple of amateurs, Kleps," Haines said to me at one point, after he had asked Tim to send money to help pay for our latest tank of oil (possibly extracted from Mellon wells). "I can't help it. I know what happens to the neighborhood once you let the Irish in, but the simple fact is that nobody around here can do what he does. We've got to lower the moral tone of this place, or we will all freeze our balls off. So unless you have any more bright ideas, I'm going to have to tell him I think he should come back here, that we want him back here. If he kicks us out, I think we can get the Gray Buildings out back."

No, I didn't have any more "bright ideas," if one meant by that, as Bill did, a fast way to raise a few thousand dollars. The "Irish" would have to be welcomed back, for the sake of the blarney.

Chapter 28

DRILLING THE KING

Intellectual "work" is misnamed; it is a pleasure, a dissipation, and is its own highest reward. The poorest paid architect, engineer, general, author, sculptor, painter, lecturer, advocate, legislator, actor, preacher, singer is constructively in heaven when he is at work; and as for the musician with the fiddle-bow in his hand who sits in the midst of a great orchestra with the ebbing and flowing tides of divine sound washing over him—why, certainly, he is at work, if you wish to call it that, but lord, it's a sarcasm just the same.

"Well, Kleps," Haines announced with great satisfaction one morning, "we are invited to the Bungalow this afternoon for drinks and to make our pitch. I think he's out of his mind, but Billy, particularly, seems to like your style. I think we are very fortunate to get this chance before the Mad Scientist gets back."

I agreed. Tim's track record was clear. There was every reason to expect that he would try to kill our projects and evict the Ashram.

It wasn't difficult to understand. It was, after all, local energy lost to him. As I had said in the "viruses meeting," as long as I was Tim's guest I would try to follow his rules, or leave. On the other hand, if I, or the Ashram with me in it, had a private arrangement with the landlords, all bets were off. We could go our own way without worrying about the shifting sands of Timothy Leary's priorities.

My first look at the Bungalow left me a little stunned. Reading stories and viewing dramas set in posh country houses can make one more familiar with poshitude than is good for one's mental health. The American mass media mobsters have made a lot of people think there is something wrong with them because their actual living standards contrast so unfavorably with the affluent suburban or exurban image which is routinely depicted on screen as if it were a kind of norm, the automatic reward of keeping your nose to the grindstone, which it isn't by a long shot, and never has been. Envy, identification, guilt, admiration and resentment are all mixed together in the minds of ordinary people by TV shows and movies set in posh surroundings, with mostly negative consequences for the viewers, I would say. It's a witch's brew at best. Posh soup. I'm sure that setting up these artificially high standards motivates some people to work like dogs in the hopes of attaining to broad lawns and three car garages, thereby serving the interests of the ruling class, but I bet it also encourages hordes of others to throw in the trowel so far as housing is concerned.

The granite-walled, copper-roofed Bungalow was oriented by way of its terrace and pool and lawns toward Millbrook, town of, to the south, over a vista of gently descending fields and woods, but one entered on the other side, from a circular drive in the trees. Passing through a marble-floored and glass-enclosed portico that stretched the length of the main building, one entered the living room, which had a bar (aha!) at its east end and a huge fireplace in the west wall.

An opening to the right of the fireplace led to the billiards room, which had an ornamental fountain set in its back wall. The dining room and a pantry were right-front, off the main room, overlooking the pool and lawns, and a split level down from the pantry were the kitchen and servants' quarters, which occupied what amounted to a building of their own. The library was to the left front, off the main room, overlooking the tennis courts. A gently curving hall with a black and white tiled floor led from the main room. Its doors were all on its south side and opened first on the library and then on five large bedroom suites.

The French doors from the living room which opened on the terrace were guarded by two, five-foot-high, Chinese temple dogs.

Below the balustrade of the terrace was a swimming pool, and below that, off to the left, were the tennis courts, by means of which Tommy, Suzanne and Aurora kept in excellent shape, in contrast to Billy, who was a little overweight. A few turns in the pool, in season, were about the extent of his routine exertions; but he made up for it by being about ten times more mentally active than the other members of this golden ménage, as well as being generally in motion from morning to night, if not from morning to the next night, both on terra firma and up in the clouds.

Jack, the butler, let us in and showed us to the bar and the library, in that order. The Hitchcocks would join us shortly. I looked us over. A strange crew. Because he had some kind of theory at the time about the desirability of remaining in physical contact with Mother Earth, Michael was barefoot. Haines was in his full, yellow-robed splendor. I was attired in Ross's charitable donations and the gold toad necklace Jill had given me.

"Christ," I said, and downed my drink. I got up to get another.

"Take it easy, Art," Haines said, "these people may have a hundred million among them, but they're just as crazy as we are."

"I suppose so," I replied, "but I can't help being impressed by so much power. I'd feel the same way if we were having drinks with South American dictators or Merlin the Magician. Just think of what they could do with this kind of dough if they wanted to."

"I have," said Haines. "You don't run across young millionaires very often."

Everything went well. I read my "How to Guide a Session" article (it's in the *Boo Hoo Bible*) and everyone laughed at the right places. At one point Tommy said, "Yeah, just the opposite of what Leary says."

Hmmm. Tommy, it seemed, was no Learyite. Hmmm. We spent a couple of hours in pleasant conversation.

"Hmmm," I said in the car as we drove back to the Big House.

"Exactly my feelings also," said Michael Green, who had been quiet during our visit, except when he had been asked by Suzanne to explain his bare feet. His explanation was simple: He wanted to stay in contact with Mother Earth.

"One might say," I said, "that they are just plain down-home country folks like you or me."

"One might say that," said Haines, "but one would be wrong. Let's not get carried away because we got a couple free drinks. We have one thing going for us, and that's that we know how to handle the acid. At least I do. Whether you can or not remains to be seen and frankly I have my doubts. Remember what Fitzgerald said about the rich?"

"Yeah," I replied. "'The rich are not like you or me.' Then Hemingway said, 'That's right, they have more money.'"

"Well, I agree with Fitzgerald," said Haines. "They may act like children but they have hearts of stone, Kleps. Hearts of stone. But I've got to admit this is the best lot I've seen yet."

(Fitzgerald, I learned later, had been a drinking buddy of Billy's father.)

A couple days later, our impression that we had made a good impression was confirmed. Haines, Bali Ram and I were invited to the Bungalow for a trip. As Haines outlined the coming engagement to a wide-eyed Ashram, it appeared that I was in for an adventure that would make my trip at the Meditation House look like miniature golf.

Besides the three of us, Billy, Aurora, Tommy, Suzanne, and a Eurasian fakir named Sham Dowley would be present. Bill, who had had some previous contact with him said that his first name suited his act. (I don't remember Sham's last name, so I have used the name from *Connecticut Yankee* that will pop up shortly.) Suzanne and Aurora's brother, Marco, and his wife, Beatrice, would be having their first trips.

Marco was the Finance Minister of Venezuela, and next in line to become President or to be assassinated, depending on which faction got to him first. What was it I had said about South American dictators?

"Christ," I said, upon hearing this list of people I was scheduled to trip with.

"Take it easy, Kleps," said Haines. "After all, they are just plain, down-home country folks like you or me."

"What about Peggy?" I asked.

She had returned to her town house in New York, Bill said. She had recently married a doctor who was said to be a clod and opposed to acid. The marriage was doomed, according to what Bill had heard.

I lifted my eyebrows.

"She's not your type, I'm sorry to say," Bill said. He was right. I liked her, but she wasn't. "Besides, from what I hear, she's gaga about Timothy. She married the good doctor on the rebound when Tim latched on to Rosemary."

Bill could have gone far as a gossip columnist. He was always ready to jump to conclusions, a habit which didn't always pay off, as we shall see.

The appointed day arrived. We were to have dinner at the Bungalow before the trip. I went to Bali's room and took a shower.

Bali put on his gold costume. Bill packed his trip bag, which contained everything necessary for minimal life support during periods of "ecstatic nongame experience," as Tim would have put it, including handfuls of fake jewels, paper, pencil and so on. I also made my preparations: three packs of Tareytons and plenty of matches.

As we drove up the pretty birch-bordered road, now broadened into a magnificent avenue by a heavy, steady, gentle fall of giant snowflakes, I had all kinds of "here I am doing this" thoughts of the "nostalgia for the present" type, which are a pretty good sign something important is happening or about to happen.

I thought I was fortunate to be driving up that road accompanied by the two strange but benevolent beings beside me, who were at once so close to me in spirit and yet so distant in experience, to such a wonderful and beautiful destination where I would die and be reborn without pain, in comfort and in warmth, secure in a setting of established power and casual magnificence, and I thought it was better to live this way than to take the 5:45 bus every morning to go to work as a bagger in a fertilizer factory in Birmingham, Alabama, in order to earn my daily bread.

These thoughts, materialistic though they may have been, helped a great deal to erase from my mind the unworthy fears which arise at such times over the impending loss of one's personality, life, mind, soul, or whatever you want to call it.

Chapter 29

THE SMALLPOX HUT

He carried my trespass to his betters; I was stubborn; wherefore, presently upon my head and upon all heads that were dear to me, fell the curse of Rome.

Everything glittered and gleamed at the Bungalow. The place seemed stoned although it wasn't yet. I noted that a good fire was going and there was plenty of wood. Music played from concealed speakers, controlled from a closet panel of great complexity off the library, and a tape machine had also been set up on the rug in front of the fire. The three women were wearing evening dresses, Aurora wore a blazing red dress, which suited her perfectly, but Tommy, Billy and Marco were informally attired. Sham, who looked pretty uptight but not actively malevolent, was in a Nehru-style outfit.

I hardly tasted dinner, which was served by Jack and a jumpy little Irishman named Jimmie, whom I hadn't seen before. The Petries had Scottish accents so thick I often couldn't understand them, and Jimmy's Irish brogue was almost as heavy. More classics. "Central casting," as Tim often put it, "was on the job."

Marco looked like a tough customer all right, the very model of a modern major general. He entered into an intense discussion with Bill and it developed he was apprehensive about the trip because he had been responsible, as a magistrate, for the execution by firing squad of thirty or so of his political opponents in the last year. That was consistent with venerable customs in his part of the world but, as with a kid just back from Vietnam, there was good reason to suppose he might have a rough trip, and to feel apprehensive as well as virtuous about turning him on. In Venezuela, according to Billy, he was surrounded by armed guards and had a submachine gun at his side at all times, possibly manufactured by Numerich Arms.

We would now find out what happened to a tyrant on a trip. A common fantasy of Psychedelians, myself included, was to bomb a fascist politician in the hope of making him more aware of the nature and consequences of his actions and perhaps more humane on that account.

Well, here one was, and a volunteer at that. How would he react?

After dinner, while Suzanne and Aurora went to a bedroom to prepare the drinks (*Suzanne* and *Aurora* are preparing the drinks??), Billy set up a movie screen to one side of the room and focused a light projector on it. Pretty, shifting pastel colors appeared. Good. Bill put on a raga. Good for him. The drinks were passed with much giggling, since, tee hee, the hypodermic used for measurement had leaked and neither waitress could tell for sure who was getting what. Unthinkable to object under the circumstances. In for a dime, in for a dollar. Down the hatch. Within ten minutes I knew it was at least 500 mics of Sandoz, the original and the best.

Marco and Beatrice took possession of the bear rug. Bill, Bali and I squatted around the tape recorder. Aurora and Suzanne curled up in facing couches on either side of the fire. Tommy, who was the only person present not on acid, sat in a chair facing away from us and smoked a joint.

Sham sat on the floor in the lotus position, near the light-show screen. Next to him was a roll of cloth which I had not noticed before.

Bali rose, went over to a peripheral rug in front of the bar at the far end of the room, and started to dance, very, very slowly.

Chapter 30

THE TRAGEDY OF THE MANOR HOUSE

At midnight all was over, and we sat in the presence of four corpses.

Sham got up after Bali did, unrolled his cloth, and hung it up on the screen. The pastel clouds were now passing over what looked like a black dumbbell standing on end, over which crawled a horde of ants. It was a black tanka, the most sacred of the Tibetan Lamaist religious flags, which is said to represent time, death, and the progression of the generations. I don't doubt it a bit.

And I didn't like it at all. It was turning the pretty, pastel colors into murk.

I got up, with considerable deliberation, and went to the bar for a drink. Bali, I noticed in passing, was now poised on one foot like a statue of gold and bronze. He wasn't blinking and he didn't seem to be breathing. As a matter of fact, he was the only thing in the room that wasn't blinking and breathing, including the furniture. Take a piss? The curving, checkerboard tiled hall led the eye to no conclusion. I went into the only bedroom suite on the left, which was for common use. The room seemed pleased to see me. There was no longer any such thing as reflected light. Every glitter now had a life of its own, every gleam a distinguished place in the scheme of things.

Ripples and swirls of something or other were moving through my body. Gold, marble, glass, silk and running water. Mirrors everywhere. It was the ruling class of two continents out there, plus a couple of funny-boys from the mysterious East and Bill Haines and, when I got back, me.

Chapter 31

MARCO

Well, there are times when one would like to hang the whole human race and finish the farce.

I was OK. I like to move around while going up. There is nothing to think about or not think about, so one might as well just screw around with minor details, get a drink, take a piss, or whatever, until the transition is complete; then enter into the spirit of the thing. The faster you go up the better. The bigger the dose, the easier it is to go up, and the harder it is to come down.

Marco was standing a couple of feet away from Bali, the human statue, looking at him intently. Tommy had taken a chair facing away from us and the fire, and had his head in his hands, as if some tragedy too heavy to be borne had just occurred.

Marco beckoned me over to him. I couldn't understand a word he was saying, because he spoke Spanish. He handed me a walkie-talkie, one of a pair he held in his hands, about the size of a pack of cigarettes, and motioned me over to the couch which contained kittenish Aurora, cute ruler of two continents. Sure enough, Marco's voice was coming over the device in my hand, and I could see him where I had left him earnestly delivering into his machine, probably the best distributed by the CIA, a stream of vowels with a few consonants floating in it. I recognized some

English words like "police" and "arrest" and so on. "Sorry, but I don't speak Spanish," I said. I turned my tiny radio off, and put it down on an end table.

I was standing behind Aurora's couch. Billy Hitchcock, sprawled out on the floor, was looking up at me through a large fake emerald which he had picked up from the hundreds of shiny fake stones Haines had scattered around. The entire scene boomed with arcane energy. Decor is not philosophy.

Which is not a bad mantra at this point on big trips, when many paranoid episodes take place, due to premature categorizations and speculations about the meanings of events. One is tempted to exclaim, "Holy shit, this can't be happening. I must be out of my mind. What are these people really doing? Are they deliberately trying to drive me crazy?"

To which the voice of experience should reply, "Shut up, you jerk. Internal and external are false distinctions. Everyone here is acting out his archetypal role using the means at hand. Those roles are, and these people are, elements of the psyche; your psyche. Call me anytime. If there's no answer, keep trying."

When you see this clearly and fully accept it, you are "dead." The introductory part of the trip is over. You are now "in the realm" of universal archetypes, where people say and do things you wouldn't expect to hear or see at the corner bar on Saturday night.

Tim thinks of this state as being "at the cellular level." As with many of his other inventions, this metaphysical image has Fazzmic appeal and utility. Everything takes on a certain golden liquidity. One does not see events as occurring in a regular cause and effect or linear way but rather as being contained in some kind of "eternity capsule" outside of space-time.

As philosophic concepts, "time capsules" and "cellular levels" are every bit as rubbery as "arcane energy." These philosophically useless terms, however, convey the feel of things very well, and can be called good Fazzm on that account.

Bali, frozen into his classic pose in his shining costume, represented this condition in a manner sanctified by art and tradition, and Marco was just as accurate a representation of his way of looking at things, as was everyone else present.

My own introductory act was to go to the bar, make a drink, take perhaps one small sip, set the glass down somewhere, forget where I had put it, go to the bar, make another, set it down, go to the bar again, and so on. After a while, I realized what I was doing. Powerful, icy highballs were standing all over the place, gleaming wetly in the firelight. Well, I thought, at least anyone who wants a drink can get one without exerting himself.

Another classic was being enacted: The tape machine was screwed up, and Billy and Bill were untangling reels of tape which had spilled out on the floor, or at least trying to perform this classic task. Bill finally dumped the whole tangle in his bag and put on another tape. He got behind the machine, put his arms around it, and announced with mock solemnity and relish, "He who controls the tape recorder controls the world."

How true, sort of. Could be, in a sense. Suddenly, everything, although still just as fantastic as it had been, seemed pretty amusing also. The mood of the room changed, except for the Tommy and Sham regions, which seemed to stiffen as people began to talk and laugh. The constructions I am obliged to use in describing this are driving me crazy. A region of mood is something one might identify spatially in a painting, right? A stage setting might have two regions of mood. I am not talking metaphysics.

Sham had his eyes closed and began rapidly mumbling some mantra or other to himself. I could now identify my proper place in the room. It was with Bill and/or Billy, so I settled down near the tape recorder next to them. Bali joined us. Bill was drawing an Om symbol with his finger in a field of tiny garnets on the carpet. Bali added a flourish, a sweeping line coming up from the intersection of the lesser and greater curves, but Bill shook his head impatiently and erased it. Great symbolism in there. I felt that pure light was streaming in and out of the top of my head.

Chapter 32

DOWLEY'S HUMILIATION

Yes, Dowley was a good deal wilted, and shrunk up and collapsed; he had the aspect of a bladder-balloon that's been stepped on by a cow.

The only thing in the room that I didn't want to look at was the damned black tanka. What the hell, I was already dead, wasn't I? This was a heavenly room with beautiful people in it. No grim and terrible symbols were required. Unfortunately, the black tanka is regarded with superstitious awe by the lower, laboring class of Tibetan Lamaists, feelings carefully fostered by the upper, priestly class of Tibetan Lamaists, who live off of them. One must carry the artifact in a special container and go through a tedious ritual when crossing water. Curses for mishandling, and so on.

To hell with that. I interrupted Haines at his Om drawing and directed his attention to the tanka. "Doooo yoooou waaaant that thiiing up there?" I asked. My voice sounded like it was coming from the bottom of a barrel.

"Nooo. It's just one of Sham's little tricks," Haines mooed.

I turned to Billy, who was watching Bali draw another fancy Om in the garnets, and asked him the same question.

"Whooooo, me?" Billy asked, startled. "Noooo."

Billy was somewhat out of it at that point, to be sure. Bill later told me that Billy had asked him, early in the trip, if he, Billy, was "really" Billy Hitchcock, who owned "this place." "Boy, was I tempted," Bill laughed when he told me about it, "but I patted him on the shoulder and told him of course he was."

Bill heard Billy's reply. "Do you want that tanka up there, Bali?" he asked.

"Are you kidding?" Bali asked, flashing a look of great disdain at both the tanka and Sham.

"Come on," Bill said. Bali and Bill both got up and made it over to the screen, where, with what seemed unnecessary violence, they tore the tanka off its moorings and tossed it in a corner.

The look on Sham's face, as he witnessed this act of desecration, was one of horrified disbelief, but the mood of the room immediately went up another notch, as the screen regained its original clarity and lightness. Decorations and music are the closest thing on a trip to "control board" functions. Every little variation has an enormous and immediate effect. Art is magic.

The next act was put on by Marco and Beatrice, who started rolling around on the bearskin rug growling and pawing at each other like a couple of bear cubs. Kind of cute. This went on for some time. Billy and Aurora were talking to each other. Haines was telling one of his hilarious anecdotes to me, Bali, and Suzanne, who had joined us on the floor. Tommy and Sham remained in place.

I heard a car door slam outside, and went out in the still falling snow to see what was up. A pretty young girl was lost in the maze. She was looking for someone I didn't know, whom she thought was staying at the Gatehouse. Tommy came out, and gave her directions. I went back in. Haines was in full form. He was making comments on everyone else's trips. Marco and Beatrice were getting most of the heat.

"Go get her, Marco. Atta boy. Claw her eyes out," and so forth.

Aurora, who seemed lost in the music most of the time, and content to be there, urged Haines to "relax, reeelax." Bill responded by saying, with mock ferocity, "Don't tell me to relax. I don't like to relax. You relax." Aurora laughed.

Tommy, Haines noticed suddenly, had disappeared.

"Where's Tommy?" he asked.

"I don't know," I said. "The last time I saw him he was outside talking to the girl who wanted to go to the Gatehouse."

"Aha." Haines had missed the whole incident. The situation, however, was instantly clear to him. Tommy was down at the Gatehouse fucking merrily away with the girl, while poor Suzanne was abandoned to her fate. He insisted she move in closer.

"Don't worry, Suzanne," he said. "These Mellons are all alike. We'll take care of you."

"What do you mean?" Suzanne asked. She looked frightened.

"I mean you shouldn't worry about Tommy being down at the Gatehouse with that girl."

"Oh." A few minutes later, Suzanne got up and went to her room. When she returned, she said nothing, but listened attentively to Haines' line of chatter with a drawn face and haunted eyes. The next day we found out why. Tommy hadn't gone anywhere with the lost girl. After giving her directions, he had gone to bed. When Suzanne looked in their room and saw him lying down with his eyes closed, she thought he was a dummy placed there by Haines to test her faith, or something. This had not made for an enjoyable trip from Suzanne's point of view, to put it mildly.

Every big-dose group session will produce one person who will make most of the definitions and generalizations, whether you plan it that way or not. Haines usually played this role very well, despite occasional slips. It took some pretty inventive paranoia on Suzanne's part to convert Bill's error into a full-scale bummer. The field for misunderstandings is wide when the trip's participants have only recently been introduced to one another, and it is important to avoid literal-mindedness and to remember that many words and expressions have more than one meaning, and things are often said in a joking and ironical spirit or on the supposition that you know something that you don't. Names can cause endless complications: "Hope is useless." "Dawn will never come." "Where is Charity?" "Have Faith." "Let's do it on Tuesday."

Never agree or disagree with anything unless you are sure you understand what is being suggested. Is it is OK to "let go"? Before you reply in the affirmative, consider all the possible implications of such a request, or stand back.

When a true paranoiac is doing most of the generalizing and defining, the number of covert operations and devious intrigues one may see all around can quickly reach critical mass, and the scene may degenerate into a tangled web of truly bizarre machinations. Experience, per se, doesn't necessarily prevent this kind of thing. Anyone fixated at the occultist level will inevitably put the people he "guides" on paranoid bummers. Marco, a strong personality, would have done exactly that with his walkie-talkie and growling animal acts if he had been tripping with a bunch of inexperienced kids instead of hard-bitten veterans of the Psychedelian wars such as ourselves.

Suzanne was the only "kid" in the room. Everyone else, including the novices Marco and Beatrice, was a full-blown "character," and not about to change his or her ways to suit anyone else's convenience, acid or no acid.

As dawn was breaking, I took a stroll around the house and was joined by Marco. When we came to an open door leading to the cellars under the house, Marco, with a sinister chuckle, suggested that we "go in there." I just laughed, shook my head, and we moved on in the crisp snow.

The conversations I had with Billy during the trip were all most pleasant and instructive. His line amused me and my line amused him. Everything seemed to be out front. At one point, Billy asked me to come over and look at a large painting which hung on the wall next to the French doors to the patio. It showed Henry VIII on his throne, sternly ordering Sir Thomas More, with dogs yapping at his heels, out of the royal presence. The painter's name was Pott.

"I want you to remember that, Art," Billy said with a big grin.

"I should think we could improve on some of these old routines, Billy," I replied, in the same spirit.

His favorite stories were of the incredible fuckups of the past two years at Millbrook.

"Yeah, we have had some real con artists around here," he concluded, after a story about the inventor of a diamond-making machine he and Tommy had installed, for a while, in the basement of the Bungalow to do his stuff. (This isn't as silly as it sounds if one assumes a conspiracy between DeBeers and General Electric, as many do.) Then a sudden realization seemed to hit Billy hard.

"... but I have a feeling that maybe we haven't seen anything yet."

"I certainly hope not," I replied, and so it would be.

Aurora danced up to me and said, "Arthur, I understand you. It's all a dreeeem." She flung her arms wide to include the whole room.

"Right," I said, giving her a hug. It seemed to stick, too.

The night's anticlimax was provided by Sham. I think he realized that everyone would ignore him unless he spoke up, so he became extroverted in the early morning hours. He went out in the hall and brought in a some small carpets which he unrolled for Billy's inspection. Billy was polite. Haines, however, was offended.

"What do you think this is, Sham? The Calcutta bazaar?"

Sham chose to interpret this as a joke, and laughed nervously. Then he invited Billy and me, Bill and Marco having gone to the library, to come back to a bedroom and see something "really rare, for men only."

What Sham had to offer next were several prototypical "Little Dirty Comix" in the lowest aboriginal shamanic tradition. All the women were butterballs. My favorite showed one of them being lowered in a basket, with her elephantine rump bulging out of a hole in the bottom, over a grinning fool lounging below. We were by no means completely straight at this point, and the contrast between this part of Sham's act and his former imitation of a graven image was too much for me and too much for Billy also. It was impossible not to laugh in the poor bastard's face. Billy told me he bought some of the stuff later. He hated to make anyone feel bad, and although he would frequently lie his head off, I never saw him behave with other than the utmost politeness to any desperate beggar or seemingly sincere pitchman who got within range.

When the sun cleared the trees, everyone went outside to

appreciate the brilliant landscape. The sky was clear. It was lovely outside. We all strolled around for a while, and then came back in to have a buffet breakfast. Mary was busy vacuuming the living room. Bill's fake jewels were all neatly gathered together on a piece of paper on a coffee table.

On the way back home Bill said, "Well, you and Billy seemed to hit it off quite well, Kleps, and naturally, I got stuck with dear old Marco."

I told Bill about Marco's suggestion that he and I explore the dark cellars instead of enjoying the sunshine and the snow, which Bill thought was pretty hilarious, a good example of the comic-book villainy Marco had projected on the trip.

"That's what gets me about him," Bill said. "I had to keep reminding myself; this guy is for real. But, he's really sort of a nice fellow, despite all the paranoia. What am I saying?"

"He like Otto," Bali said.

Yes, that was it. Marco was like Otto. We didn't see much of Marco thereafter, but later Billy told us about his further adventures. Marco had returned to Venezuela, but wasn't willing and/or able to play the political game the way he had before. A kind of reductio ad absurdum seemed to set in. After a frantic phone call from Beatrice, who was convinced her husband was about to be assassinated, Billy flew down and brought him back to the States, where Marco had another trip and decided he didn't really want to be in politics after all. He went into business instead.

While walking down an ordinary suburban street with Billy one day in Venezuela, Billy reported, Marco had illustrated some point he was making by shooting a hole through the front door of a house they were passing with his .45. By leaving South American politics for business, Marco moved up a notch to a more honorable life, unless he dumped radioactive baby food on the market or something like that.

Mythically, Billy didn't have anywhere to go on the Fazzm up-side. He was already doing a fine job as an aristocrat, just by providing the setting for something new and important to happen naturally, without paying any attention to the customs, precedents or even laws which restrain the powerless. A high and creative function. Too bad more rich people don't have the courage or imagination to do it.

Back at the Big House, I went right to bed. When I woke up, in the early afternoon, I felt fine. No hangover, no fatigue, no regrets. The world in general looked like it had "taken a bath," as Psychedelians often remark the morning after.

The usual post-mortems were being held in Bill's room. First Bill would tell a story and then Bali. The kids were delighted.

"Well, Kleps, what now?" Bill asked. "We're in," I said. "If we're not, I'll turn in my psychologist's badge. The key to the whole thing is not to think in terms of conning Billy. He's no fool by any means, and he is just as whacked out as we are. I think we should be completely out front with him. If you ask me, Tim and the League people in general have screwed themselves up with Billy by trying to put moralistic pressure on him. They try to make him feel guilty for being rich. Just because they see things that way when they get stoned doesn't mean Billy does. You heard some of those stories he was telling me?"

Bill nodded. He was attentive. This was serious business.

"Well," I continued, "he's never really been conned by anyone, including Tim. He just plays along for the fun of it. If he likes us, and I think he does, and if we put on a good show, I think we are secure here for the foreseeable future, but appealing to his idealism or his conscience won't get us anywhere. He's just as cynical about human nature in general as we are, if not more so. As for big money, I don't know."

(I was wrong about one thing, Billy was snookered constantly, particularly by Tim. He did not, however, stay conned for long and passed on easily to other things rather than waste the fleeting hours on pointless recriminations.)

"Well, does he believe in psychedelics?" Wendy asked. Wendy, I noted, was looking a hell of a lot better than she had the day before. Apparently, the trip had cut a few of the bonds I had woven around my libido.

"Yeah," Bill added. "What about that? I must confess I couldn't figure out what any of them thought about it. Could you?"

I had to admit that I didn't know either. It seemed to me Billy had a profound distrust of abstractions, and made his decisions on the basis of intuition and feeling, but it seemed incredible that anyone could take so much acid without having some kind of philosophic theory about what was happening to him when he took it.

"Do you think he's enlightened, Kleps?" Howie Druck asked.

I couldn't answer that question then, and I can't answer it now. Billy occupies a peculiar place in my private hierarchy of important people; sort of off to the left in a private box of his own. I think I can usually see the world pretty clearly as others see it. In Billy's case, I can do this up to a point, and then: zilch.

Later, as I was sitting in the common room looking over some art Michael Green had finished, Wendy came over and asked if I intended to work that evening.

"Yes," I said, "as a matter of fact, I need someone to strip for me."

"Stripping" was tedious work in those days, accomplished with razor blades and rubber cement, to replace errors with corrections in the photo-ready copy, and to justify the right-hand margins, and Wendy hated to do it as much as anyone else, if not more so.

"Arthur, you know I will strip for you any time," Wendy said, with a charming giggle, followed by a nice, old-fashioned blush.

Well, here we go again, I thought to myself. That night, despite a brief lecture from me on how little she should expect from her new roommate in the way of Eternal Devotion, which condition I had come to view as a form of insanity that had almost finished me off, Wendy moved in. My views on this subject, she professed, were also her own.

Some lucky and/or fast-moving single got Wendy's room in the servants' wing.

The synchronicity of losing a wife to a guy named Green and then appropriating a mistress from a guy named Green made me wonder later if money wasn't the key factor in both events. Could be.

A few months earlier I had been a penniless emotional wreck in a Florida jail. Now, thanks to the Supreme Sacrament, I was living on a 2,500-acre private estate in a fifty-room mansion, with a pretty and charming young lady, who had exactly the skills I needed for the work at hand, and rich parents besides, and I was surrounded by jovial and fascinating friends and companions, some of them zillionaires, who were eager to help me do exactly what I wanted to do—produce a book.

I didn't have a worry in the world.

Chapter 33

SIXTH-CENTURY POLITICAL ECONOMY

But no; you see I was an unknown person, among a cruelly oppressed and suspicious people, a people always accustomed to having advantage taken of their helplessness, and never expecting just or kind treatment from any but their own families and very closest intimates.

On the night Tim returned, I had an experience that was pretty damned weird, even for Millbrook. I was stoned on the lesser sacrament and was sitting in the music room, in the dark, by myself, enjoying the moonlit snowscape. I heard a car coming and went to the French doors that led to the porte cochère to see who it might be. A sedan passed by. Tim was sitting next to the driver. I could see Susan in the back seat. I went around back to greet them.

Nobody was there. The people in the kitchen hadn't noticed anything. Weird. I went back to the music room and watched more snow fall. About an hour later, the big bell started ringing. Someone had been alerted from town by phone. I heard a car and went up to the French windows to the porte cochère just as I had before. Exactly the same scene I had witnessed an hour earlier was repeated, but this time it was most assuredly Tim in the flesh, and Jackie, Susan and a couple other people. Joyful and genuine greetings. What the hell, politics or no politics, it was nice to see them all again.

"Timo!," I said.

"Arturo! I have been hearing all kinds of good things about you," said our glorious leader. Susan was beaming, but Jackie looked uneasy.

"Well," Wendy said to me that night, "I bet things get pretty heavy around here now."

When Tim appeared in the music room the next day and found it converted into a place of industry instead of meditation, with Michael, Wendy and I busily picking away at our various tiny tasks over light tables and drawing boards, he seemed torn by a variety of conflicting emotions. Haines had predicted instant disaster, which seemed reasonable since most of the League members regarded our sequestration of what I had to admit was one of the most beautiful rooms in the house as an act of piracy if not impiety. I had wedged the door to the back stairs closed to keep out the dogs, and there was a sign on the French doors to the library warning idlers and monologuists to keep their distance during working hours.

I showed Tim around. Ordination certificates. Membership cards. Nearly completed mechanicals for the cover of the *Neo-American Church Catechism and Handbook*. Michael had just done his original drawing of The Great Seal, showing a three-eyed toad with the motto "Victory Over Horseshit" below it, and Wendy was whiting out ink spots and smudges.

"I don't like your motto, Art," Tim said, looking over her shoulder. "Victory? Over? Horseshit?"

"What's wrong with that?" I asked.

"It isn't a gentle love message," Tim replied, with a straight face.

"Well, I'm going to add this explanation," I replied, trying to keep my face straight also. I showed him a paragraph I had written describing the difference between horseshit and bullshit:

> Our victory is over horseshit rather than bullshit. Bullshit is a rare and valuable commodity. The great masters have all been superb bullshitters. Horseshit, on the other hand, in the common parlance, refers to downright crap. The free, playful

entertaining flight of ideas is bullshit; and more often than not will be found afterwards to accord perfectly with universal truth. Horseshit is contrived; derivative, superstitious, ignorant. We might take Gurdjieff as an example of a master bullshitter and Meher Baba as an example of a master horseshitter.

Tim was amused. His private tastes were not always bad, by any means, and if he saw something good, he couldn't help appreciating it, even if he wished it wasn't there.

"What are your objectives, Art?" Tim wanted to know.

"Money and power," I replied, very much off the cuff.

Tim laughed, threw up his hands, and walked out. There were no attempts to kill our projects. Instead, Tim gave us all the help he could, so far as intramural matters were concerned.

If Tim had asked me the same question when I had first visited Millbrook, I would have replied differently. At that time I was looking for Enlightenment, for the Truth with a capital "T."

But I had found it, so now what? Did I want to tell the world? Certainly. Solipsistic nihilism has been given a bum rap by people who don't know what they are talking about or, often with great effort and tongue biting, not talking about. It's natural that I would champion the doctrine I knew and loved but which was routinely picked on by the other kids on the block and pooh-poohed in the schools they went to. Paternal love came into play. I wanted to see my pride and joy vindicated and treated right.

Am I consumed with a passionate zealotry to bring all and sundry to worship, as it were, at the same shrine, as it were? No. It isn't like that at all.

I feel no obligation to drag people into the woods, through the woods, and out the other side. If they follow my advice, they can leap over the woods in one mighty bound, like Superman. Or they can stay where they are if they like. I don't care.

Those who honestly confess to confusion and sincerely want Enlightenment excite my sympathy. Aside from the Supreme Sacrament, what they usually need are a new set of concepts to think with. I try to supply this.

As Confucius said, "The first thing that is necessary is to call things by their right names." True in every Zmm.

I'm indifferent to those who are indifferent, or who think it's all a lot of crap but don't pass laws that savagely punish us for being the fools that they declare us to be. I would have little interest in convincing them otherwise if they would leave us alone. In many ways, it has been the enemies and adversaries of the Church who have kept it alive, not me.

Nothing unusual about that, historically speaking.

What I wanted for the Church, when Tim asked me, was what I wanted for myself then and now: a congenial setting, minimal economic restraints and the power to defend myself and my fellow religionists against the assaults of our enemies. In other words, I wanted the best shelter, services, tools and weapons I could get, just like everyone else. What I was willing to give up for those outcomes was and is another matter entirely.

Despite Tim's bland attitude toward my activities, it didn't take long before he announced that he wanted to bounce the Ashram, which may have explained his bland attitude towards my activities. The old "one enemy at a time" trick.

"He says," Bill reported to a glum group, "that he made it clear when he invited us here that it was just temporary. He doesn't want us to move into the Gray Buildings, either. What he thinks we ought to do is move into Art's place up in the Adirondacks. How we are supposed to swing that sweet little deal escapes me."

"Hitchcock, I suppose," I said. "I'm sure Karl would sell if the price was right."

"We're not going anywhere," Bill said, "I want to be here when this place falls apart to get my share of the kiss-off money. And so should you, Kleps, if you know what's good for you. I can see it all coming. The parties are going to start upstairs and you're going to have total insanity around here again very quickly."

"But we can't stay here, and the Hurdles are living in the Gray Buildings," Betsy said.

"The Hurdles can move," Bill said. "What about that stone house up by the barns?"

Haines convinced Billy and Tommy to move the Hurdles to the empty stone house adjoining the barns, by offering the Ashram's services as house cleaners and painters to make it habitable. The barns could be seen from the public road which enclosed the property, and were such outrageous examples of conspicuous consumption that they often stopped those few motorists who were sightseeing or had taken a wrong turn. Jeez, is that a cathedral over there, or what?

I helped paint the interior of the house, which turned out to be as much fun (it all depends on the spirit which prevails) as it was work. As the Hurdles neared completion of their migration to these much more sumptuous quarters, Wendy and I moved our office into a room on the first floor of the Gray Buildings. Our new office had one door opening on a small corner porch and another to the large concrete-floored space which we now called "the press room." We carried our completed work back and forth to the Big House, where we slept with it.

In unstable, unpredictable social situations, those who make no effort to guard what they value are often the most paranoid. They either think they are divinely protected or suppose themselves so efficiently persecuted that caution is useless.

"Heaven forbid that we should appear paranoid, Wendy," I said. "We shall therefore protect the *Neo-American Church Catechism and Handbook* as if everyone in sight wants to destroy it."

Wendy, from whom a party or parties unknown had recently stolen about $600 worth of jewelry, readily agreed.

The soft-headedness of many of our fellow residents was demonstrated by a spectacular event that happened at about that time: Gigantic blossoms of glowing color appeared in the early night sky. Everyone ran out on the porch. Flying saucers! God! Shiva's aura! "I'm ready," Karen Detweiler cried, "come and get me!"

When the show was over, Wendy and I wound our way up the hill to our place of work, as usual. Hurdle and family, soon to move out, were seated on lawn chairs, drinking beer and eating potato chips. They were the only people around with accurate information. It had been a NASA experiment, sodium bombs in the stratosphere, or something of the sort, and they had read all about it in the *New York Daily News* that morning.

Haines shrewdly and smoothly negotiated the Ashram's

migration, including two public confrontations with Tim over the issue when both were on large doses of the Supreme Sacrament. During the second of these powwows, the second floor hall became impassable, so great was the audience gathered to cheer on their respective champions. Having already decided to make a bid for the Gatehouse, I stayed in the background, although I made it clear that I supported the Ashram.

One of Bill's ploys during this period, when the issue of the Ashram's right to stay on the property at all was still considered debatable, was to sneak into Tim's room and find out what book he was reading that day. If it was, say, *The Magus*, a silly novel which Tim seemed to find highly inspiring for a while, Haines would play the role of a solemn, moralistic and traditional yogi. If, on the other hand, Tim was reading Krishnamurti, Haines would become jocular, irreverent and nonchalant.

No matter how fanciful these debates became (at one point, Tim invited Bill to fly down to the Caribbean with him to "get a fresh slant" on the situation) or how profound the philosophic depths, Bill would terminate the exchange by pounding his cane on the floor and saying, "I want those Gray Buildings." He got them.

Occasionally a mild, contrarian remark, such as, "Well, after all, he did invite us here in the first place," or something of the sort would be voiced in the Ashram, probably just to keep Haines rolling.

"And what would this place be like without us?" Haines would reply. "Why don't you ask yourself that sometime? Besides, it's my understanding that the Hitchcocks didn't give the place to Timmy alone but to Timmy and Dickie and Ralphie all together, right? What do you suppose happened to the other two members of that sweet little trio? Do you think for one moment it wasn't the good doctor himself who eased them out of the picture? Well, I am not so easily conned."

The real battles took place at the Bungalow, where Tim and Bill went to plead their cases. I stayed out of that too. Tim had already let me know, in an assurance which I knew I could rely on as much as any other politician's promise, that he would be happy to have me stay in the Big House with Wendy if I wanted to.

Bill's tirades of rhetorical questions were one of the foundations of his authority. He knew how to make people feel morally right in situations which otherwise would have made them feel guilty and weak. After one such morale-boosting session, Haines and I were left alone for a few seconds. Bill winked at me and said, "There's nothing like a little self-righteousness when you're trying to get your hands on someone else's real estate, Art."

Truer words have never been spoken.

Susan Leary, much to Haines' delight, enlisted in the Ashram shortly after the move. She stayed about three weeks. She said she wanted to get away from Rosemary, whom she thought to be a witch of darkest pitch. Bill was confident that a period of "healthy living" with "normal kids her own age" would fully renovate and disinfect her polluted psyche.

I employed Susan, who was famous for her blank stare, to keep Michael Green's nose to the grindstone. She would track him down and gaze at him until he fled to work. Haines was impressed, and said I had made a major contribution to managerial science.

One day, while Susan was placidly awaiting her next assignment, I asked her what it was all about. Did she really think Rosemary was a witch? Her expression abruptly descended to about 50 degrees below zero, and she proceeded, in flat, sing-song tones, to lay Rosemary out in spades. She was an "evil woman." She was trying to destroy "Timothy." She hated Susan and Jackie. She was frigid and barren and did not love Tim. All she wanted was to destroy everything she could lay her spells on.

I wasn't exactly crazy about Rosemary myself, but this seemed somewhat harsh. On the other hand, what did I know about it? And yet again on the third hand, it took two to tango. One thing's for sure; Rosemary's replacement, Joanna Harcourt-Smith, who "latched on to him," to use Bill's characteristic phrase, in Switzerland, was worse. She coincided with Tim's most lunatic intellectual phase, while Rosemary coincided with mere opportunism and amorphousness.

Wendy announced that she needed a vacation. Since we had been working about twelve hours a day, every day of the week,

I could see her point. Her parents were paying for it, so, with no objections from me, she flew off to Florida to visit "an old girlfriend" for a couple of weeks. "Girlfriend," shit, but I didn't care, and I had never pretended to Wendy that I did.

Shortly after Wendy left, I got an engraved card in the mail. I was invited to a "psychedelic seder" at Peggy Hitchcock's house in New York, as were Bill, Tim and a few others from the League and the Ashram. It further developed that Tim and I were to read the service, or part of it. I had never heard of a "seder," psychedelic or otherwise, but Ted Druck set me straight. "Oh, Passover. Yeah, right. Celebrate killing the first-born sons of all Egyptian families. Sure, why not? Give them gnats first. What will God think of next?"

The kids of Jewish origin in the community were greatly amused by the idea of a seder on acid, and thinking of, say, an Easter service conducted with the Supreme Sacrament as Eucharist, I could see why.

I went down in the Ashram's van. Our excursions to and from New York on the beautifully landscaped and noncommercial Taconic Parkway, one of the many lasting achievements of the semi-socialist '30s, always put me in a good mood, which was improved on this occasion by the absence of twerps in either the League or the Ashram vehicle. Peggy had been selective. It wasn't that I didn't like our twerps, or, it was clear, they me. The problem was their incessant moralizing about almost everyone and everything. It tended to put a damper on the free flow of conversation.

The band of brothers communal ideal, and the endless list of rights and wrongs which followed from it, were assumed by the twerps to measure the moral worth of all conduct on the place. This attitude was alive and well despite the authoritarian guru systems firmly in place, and the fact that most of us were unemployables living on the charity of the rich.

As the only avowed elitist around, I was in many ways immune to the pressures exerted on Tim and Bill. I got a lot of flack for this at first, before it became generally known that I was a hopeless case.

"Meritocracy doesn't have anything to do with the Church,

or with religion, or with psychedelics," I would say, "or with who is the better person, or the more likable person, or the more trustworthy, or whom I want to hang out with," and the list would go on and on.

Well, what did it have to do with?

"The franchise. I think how many votes you get ought to be graduated by IQ and achievement test scores and stuff like that."

End of discussion, almost always. None of the band of brothers moralists and egalitarian primitivists I'm talking about, and in those days there was one behind every ornamental shrub, wanted to discuss their favorite subject in such blunt, blood-curdlingly factual terms. They wanted to vent spleen and make all who didn't conform to the latest totems and taboos squirm and confess and tear their hair out and cover themselves with ashes and throw themselves into hideous contortions, thereby evening the score, as it were, for the crime of enjoying any distinction of any sort.

I just wouldn't play.

Neither would Bill Haines. He wouldn't explain himself, he would just threaten to kill, or seriously injure in some picturesque fashion, anyone who attempted to lay this kind of crap on him. "Nitwit" was one of his most favored terms.

Tim, on the other hand, was inextricably enmeshed in the egalitarian mystique, and was obliged to repeat and endorse and appear to observe in actual practice all the kid-culture political dicta and moralistic formulations "our" media ordained. It's the classic price extorted from those who seek prominence in this field of endeavor. The French radical politician Alexandre-Auguste-Ledru-Rollin succinctly summed it up to a court trying him on the charge of joining in the aborted revolution of 1848:

"I had to follow them," he said. "I was their leader."

Chapter 34

THE YANKEE AND THE KING SOLD AS SLAVES

The law is clear: it doth not require the claimant to prove ye are slaves; it requireth you to prove ye are not.

Laying on an Israelite tribal ceremony at the beginning of the band-of-brothers phase of the Psychedelian revolution was most appropriate, in a reverse kind of way, in Fazzm terms. Big Daddy was in for a hard time of it.

"Go home and kill your parents," Jerry Rubin had said at one point, probably the nadir of the phase of which I speak. Jerry and his buddy, Abbie Hoffman, had been promoted to leadership status in "the movement" by the media moguls of the day, who appreciated the political services rendered to the forces of reaction by Abbie and Jerry's egalitarian, rabble-rousing style. Like Tim, who was always well aware of who owned what, and the official roster of media-certified "anti-establishment" geeks in general, they never violated the grisly icons of Judaism while trashing everyone else's icons with gleeful smirkitude.

Such genocidal advice made the Neo-American Church look pretty decorous and old-fashioned. We weren't with it anymore. What was all this "Enlightenment" shit? Whatever it was, it was counterrevolutionary.

Well, we still had Millbrook, so I wasn't worried. The gathering at Peggy's house, a five-story job just off Fifth Avenue, was no meeting of the rabble to plot pillage and rapine, nor of the rich to figure out new ways to tread them underfoot. I doubt if anyone present spoke one word about politics all night.

Maybe I shouldn't call it "Peggy's house," since, strictly speaking, it wasn't. When Peggy had divorced her pill-pushing husband, the story went, she gave him the house and a million in cash to show there were no hard feelings, or something. "The family" had reacted by putting her on an allowance for a while. When I asked her to confirm this she replied, "Well, yeah. I knew how much he loved that kind of stuff."

But all of this was treated as mere paperwork which would be taken care of down in Pittsburgh. Everyone continued to call it "Peggy's house," and Peggy continued to use it as a place to flop and throw parties in just as she had before.

A bar had been set up in the second-floor hall, at the top of a curving, marble staircase. Peggy's butler poured and stirred, and a dozen people, drinks in hand, were milling around in a large sitting room to the right of the stairs, most of them looking pretty uptight. Within an hour or so there would be about a hundred, and nobody would look uptight.

Peggy led Bill and me up to the third floor where, in a closet bar in a paneled office, she showed us a large punch bowl, the cups that went with it, and a small bottle with a dropper, all on a silver tray. "250 mics a drop," she said, "but I don't think there's enough to make it 250 a cup. I'll let you guys figure it out, OK?"

Peggy returned to greeting her guests. Haines and I measured the number of cups of punch in the bowl and the number of drops in the bottle. It worked out to about 40 mics a cup, which we both thought was about right, considering everything. A low enough count per cup to make novice freak-outs unlikely, or at least manageable, and there ought to be enough, assuming no heavy guzzling, so those who wanted boosters could get them.

"Did you recognize anyone downstairs?" I asked, as Bill poured and stirred with mock-dramatic gestures and chortlings.

"They look like a bunch of deadheads to me," he said. "I didn't see anyone I knew, but there was one fellow in a round collar. That may be promising. Wait until you get a taste of this. I wonder if Peggy is telling everyone what's in it?"

"Oh, I think so," I said. "What the hell. It said 'psychedelic seder' right on the card."

Peggy's ex, wearing a dark suit with vest and a wooden expression, entered the room during our preparations. If he said anything to us, I can't remember it. He sat behind his desk as if turned to stone. Watching the demonic forces at work? Conveying disapproval? Guarding his lair? Letting us know we had a witness? I couldn't figure it out.

Very slowly, because the glittering crystal punchbowl was almost full, I carried the tray downstairs and set it on the bar in front of the butler.

"So, this is the real stuff, huh?" he asked, in tones implying he was not impressed.

"There ain't nothin' realer," I replied. "You can tell those who ask that one cup of this should leave them standing but in the right frame of mind to appreciate the philosophic meaning of it all. Why don't you have a cup yourself?"

"I think I'll stick to Scotch," he said.

I poured myself a cup and went into the main salon. People were seated and standing all around the room, talking in small groups. New guests arrived in a steady stream, and I noticed a few taking cups of punch.

Bill and I went around telling everyone the sacraments were served. Dutifully, they trooped off to get their rations, but quite a few looked like they were going up the Amazon, against their better judgment, to wrestle alligators. I saw Tim talking animatedly to the young Episcopalian priest whom Bill had noticed earlier.

I went over and sat next to Bill. I could feel the acid coming on and I wanted to get over the hump in the company of someone I knew. I had never taken LSD with so many novices and strangers around, and it made me apprehensive.

"Don't worry about it," Bill said. "It's a party. You're supposed to act funny. By the way, I just got a new sidelight on dear old Timothy."

"What's that?"

"When he came in he came up to me right away and asked, 'Where's the acid?' He really looked nervous. I never saw him act like that before. I think he really needs the stuff to do his stuff. He's an acidholic."

At the time, this seemed like a strange idea. It was the function of booze and other downers to relax tension in social situations. Acid was no tranquilizer.

True, but with experience, I learned that, with experience, it's possible to be dexterously extroverted on the stuff, if that's the way you want to go. At the Ashram in Arizona, I sometimes took acid with Haines, who made a habit of it, on Sunday mornings, although Sunday was open house, and we had all kinds of visitors, including the local sheriff's deputies and square tourists who were there to view the weirdos and buy some pottery.

One time, on a pretty heavy trip, I had to get rid of three armed and drunken cowboys who had fallen prey, sort of, to Bali Ram. It's an interesting way to trip, the main lesson being how unbelievably stupid and blind straight consciousness is most of the time, but I don't recommend it to novices.

The ceremony, conducted in the dining room, went smoothly. Tim and I, seated together, got up to read our respective parts of the service, which was printed in booklets. Tim was the old geezer and I was his youngest son. A young rabbi, extremely Reformed, I assumed, was seated next to Peggy. He said a few unmemorable words.

While we were having after-dinner brandy, Haines, who had left the room a few minutes earlier, bustled in, stuck his head between me and Tim and put his hands on our shoulders.

"Listen, you guys," Haines said in a heavy whisper, "I want your advice."

Well, that was a switch. Tim and I both grinned.

Haines had gone up to the library for a few moments of "quiet meditation." He had been sitting in a corner of the library in the dark when the priest had come in and telephoned his bishop, unaware that Haines was present to hear him.

"He kept saying things like (Haines fluttered his hands) 'Oh,

Bishop, it's so terrible, you have no idea. They are all drinking LSD and everyone is talking in a perfectly insane way' and stuff like that. I think it's an insult to Peggy that one of her guests should sneak behind her back to squeal on her like that."

"Well, what can we do about it?" Tim asked.

"I think we should bomb him," Haines said. "He deserves it."

Haines was not reluctant to bomb those he thought merited the honor. He didn't do it to politicians, cops or ordinary people but only to those whom he thought were "asking for it," so to speak.

A BBC television crew had recently visited the property to make a documentary. The director had blandly informed us that he was "naturally stoned." He wasn't afraid of taking LSD. Heaven forbid.

He didn't need it.

This line of shit will drive all but the most saintly Psychedelians who hear it up the wall, across the ceiling, and down the other side. It's an insult, and such blatant self-deception it's almost unbearable to listen to it.

The spiritual four-flusher visiting a Psychedelian community should avoid saying things like "the vibrations around here are terrible" or "I'm a witch, you know" or, "oh sure, I talk to trees all the time myself," but of all the comments likely to enrage his hosts, "I can do anything you can do but I don't need LSD to do it," or words to that effect, are provocation in a class by itself.

It's like saying, "the law can't touch me, baby" while drunk and disorderly in a Chicago police station at 3 a.m. It's an insult to the honor of the group, and something has to be done about it. Haines let the director have it in his coffee one morning, and he went bounding and sprinting all over the woods and fields for about four hours, bellowing like a moose. When it was over, he admitted he had been afraid of it all along and didn't understand anything about it. He then packed up his staff and stuff and left. We never saw the documentary, if there ever was one.

"That strikes me as a happy idea," Tim said, in response to Bill's suggestion that we bomb the priest.

I also gave my blessings. This was clearly a case of the exception which "proves" the (shows that there is a) rule. With great aplomb, Haines walked around behind his target's table and deftly demonstrated that the hand is quicker than the eye. It became evident, an hour later, that the priest loved the stuff. The transformation was abrupt. One moment he was grimly sitting in a corner sipping his gin and the next moment he was on the dance floor with Peggy, putting on an exhibition of pelvic-thrust, head-jerk dancing worthy of the most primitive teenager. You can take the boy out of the country but you can't take the country out of the boy.

Or, as Gotama is said to have said:

> The conduct of the passions and attachments is the same as the conduct of a bodhisattva, that being the best conduct. (*Guyasama Tantra*)

Or, as Lui Pa is said to have said:

> What use is meditation? Despite meditation, one dies in pain. Give up all complicated practices and hopes of attaining siddhis and accept the void as your true nature.

Or, as Sahara is said to have said:

> The childish Yogins like the Tirhikas and others can never find their own nature. One has no need of Tantra or Mantra, or of the images of the Dharanis; all these are causes of confusion. In vain does one try to attain Moksa by meditation. All are hypnotized by the system of the Jhanas but no one cares to realize his own self.

You can say that again, Sahara.

As the festivities were winding down, Billy invited me to stay over at his apartment and go up to Millbrook in the morning with Fred Blacker, who had not been invited to the party, but was scheduled to drive the Cadillac back to Millbrook. The Hitchcocks, a couple other people and I then gathered together, why I don't know, on the curving stairs in front of the bar, with the result that the other guests had to weave among us to get downstairs as they departed.

We probably would have stayed on the stairs for some time, since all present were in a mood of hilarity and clarity which a combination of psychedelics and booze will sometimes produce, but Peggy's butler, who was hovering unsteadily above us, started injecting put-downs of Billy into our conversation; incredibly stupid insults, like those I remember exchanging regularly with my friends in junior high school. Furthermore, he dropped his New York prol dialect and started sounding more and more like Jack back at Millbrook. Another Scot, evidently.

Billy was not amused. The butler had him cornered. In company, if some jerk says, "You always were full of shit, Hitchcock," you can't ignore it no matter how rich you are, if your name happens to be Hitchcock. The butler was on a mean drunk, probably felt one-upped by all of us acid heads, and was looking for trouble.

When he said, "You may be rich, Hitchcock, but I have character," Billy seemed to be at a loss for a words but finally said, "So's your old man."

We all got up and left.

In a general McPozzm way, I interpreted the psychedelic seder as a demonstration of the abrupt high status I had somehow acquired in Psychedelian society and in the eyes of the powers that were. According to the program, I was Tim's junior, his "son," but I was also trusted and accepted more than he was. It seemed natural and correct to me that this should be the case, but it had happened incredibly fast, and with no machinations on my part intended to bring it about, which probably explains, to some extent, why it had come about.

There were all kinds of heavy Fazzm meanings floating around like lead balloons, as one might expect at a psychedelic seder.

When Peggy cooked up the party, she was probably thinking of Fazzm ideals, with "Ecumenism, spirit of; LSD, enhancement by" at the head of the list. This fantasy, then as now, was a popular concept. It sounds good but it doesn't float.

In contrast to what I think Peggy intended, the thing about the party I liked best was the spirit of hilarity and irreverence that LSD produced in the teeth of one of the world's most savage celebrations of tribal vengefulness, primitive supernaturalism and cruelty to children.

I don't see Psychedelianism as blending and refining supernaturalist religions into some higher and finer froth. They are all rotten to the core. Nothing can be done with them. The garbage disposal is called for, not the blender.

A week or two after the seder, Noel Tepper came over to the office that Wendy and I used in the Gray Buildings, with the New York State incorporation papers for the Church. Billy, as a charter member of the Board of Toads, was on hand, and so was Tommy. It seemed like the right moment, so I asked the twins if it would be OK for the Neo-American Church to take over the Gatehouse. After a brief private consultation in the press room, Billy and Tommy agreed.

Whew. Not only did the Church now have a private setting, Wendy and I would soon have a whole building to ourselves. Since the "great migration" of the Ashram from the Big House to the Gray Buildings we had been sleeping in a cranny above our office which hardly deserved to be called a closet. And, since the seder, Tim had become increasingly hostile. While it seemed that Wendy and I might remain in the Big House, he had referred to our work on the *Catechism* as "a labor of love" and "the only constructive thing that's being done around here." Now, I was frequently informed, I had joined Bill in the doghouse. My appalling alcoholic intake, rather than my admirable literary labors, was what Tim usually mentioned when my name came up.

And how long could I depend on Haines? I had been politically useful when the Ashram was in serious danger from Tim but my continued utility to Bill, now that he had prevailed, was another matter entirely. I was a potential competitor for both Tim and Bill in various ways. What if Billy did donate "real" money to the Church? In what way would that be good for the League or the Ashram? And what if Peggy made me an offer I couldn't refuse? I knew that nothing was happening, or likely to happen, on that front, but Bill and Tim didn't know it. What then, for Christ's sake?

I could clearly see the bumpers flashing in both noble craniums and small steel balls with my name on them going for wild rides, somewhat wilder on Tim's machine than on Bill's, and then dropping into the "watch out" slot in both cases.

It was a big relief to cut out both middlemen and deal with

the Hitchcocks directly. I was now an independent power on the place for sure. Things were looking up.

Otto attended this pleasant gathering, and since Noel was present, I mentioned Otto's complaint that his father was draining his trust fund. Otto went down to the Big House, where he still lived in the cellar, and returned with his papers. Billy and Noel looked them over. Sure enough, Otto's capital was rapidly withering away instead of flourishing and sprouting new growths, despite the manifold benefits of the wonderful invasion of Vietnam all capitalists should have been enjoying at the time. He had every right to be suspicious. Score another one for Otto?

A little later, we got expert testimony which seemed to confirm one more highly implausible Otto story. He had long claimed that his Oriental rugs, on which he and Winnie slept, were unique examples of something or other and really belonged in a museum. An importer friend of Bill's, stopping by for a visit, took a close look at them and said they were "priceless."

"Where does he get this stuff?" Haines, who already had his eye on the Black Buddha, asked in bewilderment.

It wasn't much use asking Otto. If the circumstances of his life were hard to believe, the explanations he offered were more so, and went on forever, and strayed from the point the way Alice traveled through Wonderland.

The next day, Otto and I went down to the Gatehouse to clean it up and to turn on the water and electricity. Otto wanted to fix up a cubbyhole for himself next to the furnace in the cellar. I didn't expect Wendy would be enthusiastic about it, but I told my troglodyte companion that it would be OK with me if it was OK with her. Until she returned, in any event, he was welcome.

The Gatehouse was a mess, but after a couple days of hard work, we had running water and electricity and had repaired all the broken windows. We thought we had the portcullis mechanism figured out pretty well, but it seemed that a large and oddly-shaped crank needed to turn the winch had, wisely I'm sure, been removed to some other location.

In the days of the Fergusons, a fire in the top tower room had charred or covered with soot everything on the third floor. I decided to leave it as it was. Someone I liked would probably come along who would be willing to clean it up as the price of occupancy. Our living quarters would be on the second floor, which had a tower bedroom with a fireplace, a bathroom, a small guest bedroom, a pantry, and a living room, with an open kitchen built into a counter attached to the inside wall. Small but quaint. The windows faced toward the bridge on one side of this room, and toward the outside world on the other. In the summer, looking inward, one saw the bridge and masses of green leaves; in the winter, the bridge and a tracery of twigs against the sky. A door led to a stone porch, over the grotto-like sitting room for the grooms with its pedestrian gate.

In Dieterich's day, the story went, these grooms not only raised and lowered the portcullis and shoveled horseshit but also raked away all the tracks made in the white gravel roads to the Big House. On the inside of the porte cochère, three steps above ground level, a heavy, arched, plank door, into which I drove a new lock, led to the entrance hall, and up a step, to a half-paneled, parquet-floored, circular room at the base of the tower, which I later furnished as an office.

All the walls were made of stones and boulders, some of which must have required a steam crane or lots of horses and blocks and tackle to lift into place. They fit the romantic picture, however, with the curved clay tiles above and the portcullis in the middle and the wrought-iron hinges and light fixtures here and there. Right behind the Gatehouse itself, two stone walls defined the perimeter of a large parking place and then became the walls of the bridge over the inlet between a small lake and a large pond.

On the bridge, a fanciful stone tower incorporated a winding staircase which led up from the road to a small porch, and down from the road, in two-and-a-half turns, to the pond. Descending these corkscrew stairs while on LSD, as almost everyone did at one time or another, seemed to take much longer than it should have, causing an enjoyable, amusement-parkish kind of uncertainty about where one was in relation to the water level, exactly.

Otto and I spent as much time drinking and shooting the shit about this, that and the other Ottoish kinds of things as we did working. My excuse, which I think any fully informed jury would have applauded, was self-defense.

During this period, while Wendy was away and the *Catechism* was being printed by Sheatsley and the Drucks (even Howie lent a hand, and seemed to enjoy it), I got to know Billy and some of his outside friends, notably Charlie Rumsey and Sam Clapp. An awareness, if not a full appreciation, of the diplomatic situation between Tim, Bill, Billy and me began to supplant, or at least amend, what had been a sentimental set of attitudes.

Easter came. Although we were now dispersed in three distinct centers, everyone got together again for a three-day party in the Big House and on its sunny porch roofs. A variety of psychedelic sacraments were available, many manufactured and distributed by Owsley, a California underground chemist who was visiting Tim at the time. Owsley was a Narad-style paranoid, but with a more organic flavoring. His Weltbild was of a universal abattoir. An ecological sausage chain of cosmic gobblers, in which mankind was situated as the most bloated link, comprised the All. To properly conform to his status in the Great Lunch, he ate only meat, for breakfast, lunch and dinner.

Tim held court, relaxed enough by the fine internal and external weather to swap funny stories with Bill and me instead of arguments and accusations. One story concerned his ex and her husband, the bald-headed Tantric. She was expecting, and Tim had offered congratulations when he ran into them on the streets of New York. "You know what the baby will be, don't you?" asked the husband.

"No," said Tim.

"The Messiah, of course," he replied.

Of course. What else?

Even Dick Alpert showed up for a while. He was sitting in Jean's room, one of the windows of which was serving as the main door to the porch roof, wearing a bed sheet and beads and generally looking holy. I couldn't take it. Not again. I waved, received a nod in return, and avoided him thereafter, as, I noticed, did almost everyone else around.

Then I relented. I had him down as "Protector of the Youth" in the *Catechism*. Was that OK with him? It was.

I didn't know it at the time, but he had not only switched his attire, from J. Press to bed sheets, but his name from Dick Alpert to "Baba Ram Dass." This additional fraudulence was too much for me. In both the *Neo-American Church Catechism and Handbook* of 1967 and the *Boo Hoo Bible* of 1971, he appears under the name his mother gave him. *Be Here Now,* the book Dick produced in his new persona, is a farrago of good, bad and indifferent selections from eastern religions. The omniscient, omnipresent and omnipotent God Almighty is frequently mentioned. Evans-Wentz would have loved it.

Oddly enough, for years our inventory of the *Boo Hoo Bible* and Dick's inventory of *Be Here Now* were stored in the same ranch outbuilding in tiny San Cristobal, New Mexico. (Dick's "Lama Foundation" supported a community of Slobovenoid Blobovenoidalists nearby.) Even more oddly enough, my rooms in San Cristobal were on the same site Aldous Huxley occupied when he was visiting D. H. Lawrence and wanted to maintain a prudent distance from Frieda and Mabel up the road. I included a photograph of his old shit house, a two-holer from the rough and ready days of Elmira's original motel, in the *Boo Hoo Bible*.

Later, in Burlington, Vermont, the newly minted Middlebury graduate who was to become my wife, best friend, chief bee hee, and mother of my youngest daughter, and I went to see a film at the University of Vermont in which Dick presented his philosophic and religious illusions, delusions and hallucinations. After about fifteen minutes, we couldn't take it anymore and drove to the nearest Dunkin Donuts for first aid.

We had met on a trip, her first big one. Having gotten it right the first time, she not unnaturally asked, "Boo, what is wrong with that man?"

Before I could frame an adequate reply, a kid across the U-shaped counter from us accidentally spilled his net bag of marbles on the floor and they rolled all over the place, to the great amusement of all present. Her question had been answered in the best way possible. No gloss was necessary.

As time passed, I understand, Dick became more of a standard supernaturalist Sado-Judeo-Paulinian, maybe even a genuine Christian, to some extent. That's a step up from the likes of Meher Baba, I would say, so I hope it's true.

Owsley, a scrawny specimen, walked around naked, although his two dim and dusty-looking girlfriends did not. One night, Wendy and I, driving back to the Gatehouse in a used, but very reliable, car her father had recently donated, found Owsley wandering along the road, clothed, toward the west gate. He was looking for "Hitchcock's house."

"I thought it was one of those houses over there," he said, after we picked him up, swung around, and headed up the road in the other direction. He pointed to the lights of a couple of small houses which were located outside the sacred precincts, and just barely visible from the Big House. Conclusion: This guy tends to jump to conclusions.

"No, he has a little place up the road this way," Wendy said.

"He owns the whole scene, huh?" Owsley asked. He sounded much less confident than usual.

"Fifty-fifty with his twin brother," I replied.

"Really?" Owsley asked. "They're twins?"

That was all the opening Wendy needed. A natural fan of all celebrities, great and small, good and bad, she was in her element. It was an opportunity to tell one of these sublime beings all kinds of things she knew and he didn't know about two other celebrated beings even more celestial than himself. The twins were fraternal, not identical. Billy was light-haired, Tommy was dark-haired; Billy was right-handed, Tommy was left-handed; Billy was an extrovert, Tommy an introvert, and so on. She ticked off all these differences on her fingers, while Owsley, so to speak, licked them off with tail-wagging gratitude.

Little things can mean a lot, after all.

When we stopped at the entrance of the Bungalow, which seemed even more enchanted than usual in the moonlit, scented, spring night, Owsley froze and his mouth fell open for a moment, but he pulled himself together quickly, bounced up the steps, and rang the bell. I could see Jack coming to open the door, so we drove away.

Wendy and I exchanged the knowing smiles which seemed to constitute the foundation of our relationship.

"What are you going to say to Billy if he goes for it?" Wendy asked.

Since the name "Hitchcock" had escaped Owsley's lips, I don't think either one of us had any doubts about what "it" was.

"I hope I won't hear anything about it," I said. "If Billy can't tell that guy is a fruitcake, well, we're just going to have to wait until he acquires the rudiments of human wisdom, or something." Wendy thought that, as a friend, it was my duty to warn him.

"That's what all the other fawning sycophants are always doing," I replied. "They spend half their time warning Billy against each other. So far, I stand out as the lonely exception. If he wants to play cops and robbers, let him. I'm not going to compete with every con artist who comes along, God damn it."

When Owsley left, his car, a veritable rolling laboratory, was stopped on the Taconic by Guardians of Virtue from the Place of Overflowing Shitholes. It was widely reported that he had pulled $10,000 in cash from his boots to get free. Based on my experience, this would mean that he had probably donated one or two thousand, which he happened to have in his pockets at the time, for benevolent police purposes.

With Tim's blessings, the Ashram settled down in the old common room of the Big House they had recently officially vacated, for what everyone thought would be a one-night trip on STP, the new wonder drug Owsley was pushing. He had recommended 30 milligrams per person, so that's what they took. The consequences, as those of us who declined to try it had feared, were much crazier and more unpredictable than trips on the New Reliable.

For three days and two nights, meals had to be served on trays, because no participant could do anything much more complicated than visit a toilet and return. Even on such short excursions, they often strayed, got lost, and had to be led back by whomever was playing nurse. Haines, who held up better than anyone else, nevertheless claimed at one point that he was sitting at a table with some old crone while the sea rose slowly all around them.

Bali, off and on, was transformed into the evil Hindu goddess Maya. With flashing eyes and a cackling laugh, Bali-Maya slithered through the halls, freaking out everyone who crossed his or her path.

"I don't know how to explain this stuff, Kleps," Bill said to me as things were winding down. "The main problem is it comes and goes. You think you're down and then three seconds later you're high as a kite again."

I tried it later, with Bill and Wendy in Arizona. Sure enough, that's the way it was, even at half the dosage. Why did Owsley push the stuff? I have no idea.

In Asa Elliot's *The Bloom Highway*, which includes a pretty funny interview with me while I'm smashed and stoned, there is an account of a Neo-American Church wedding party which is an accurate and, for experienced Psychedelians, hilarious, description of what's likely to happen when a bunch of neophytes get together and take large doses of LSD.

Note the desperation with which Elliot's friends seek some kind of pseudo-philosophic generalization, or slogan, to explain what is happening to them, in order to make it stop happening. It's the uncontrollability that's terrifying. The hand holding and chanting of the "we are one" mantra have a palliative, anti-high function.

It's all defensive and repressive. Almost nobody wants to learn anything. On the contrary, if the heaving masses do encounter any new information, they try desperately to arrest learning as quickly as possible and by any means available. In a way, one might say, they will "throw him Ernie" rather than face the facts. Sacrifice a goat. Buy off God. Propitiate. Repress.

But one must face the facts before one can see through the facts. If the reader is not familiar with the standard "mechanisms" of repression, by all means read Freud's *The Interpretation of Dreams*.

At the peak of a major death/rebirth experience, one should see everything in terms of synchronistic dream themes based on solipsist-nihilist epistemological assumptions, or not try to interpret anything at all. As a general rule, "Why?" is probably the least productive question one can ask on a trip. Time will tell. Leave the interpretations for later. Not accepting the situation as it is is dangerous for the same reasons that ignoring one's surroundings is always dangerous. To deny on a big trip that one is "living in some kind of dream world" is to refuse to face the facts as they are presented.

"What's the rush?" is often a much better mantra than "We are all one."

But Enlightenment is exactly what freaks most people out the most, no matter how readily they may entertain correct ideas about it in an abstract way when straight or on grass.

A death/rebirth trip almost always involves a few moments of stress or even panic, as do all major transitions. One must try to get past this phase with a minimum of fuss instead of prolonging it by trying to shorten it. Be polite. Don't upset your friends with your transitory anxieties. Most likely, they have their own foolish apprehensions to deal with.

If you refuse to discard your usual McPozzm assumptions and hang on to the first clump of "metaphysical" trash that floats by, you will come to shore imagining that the junk you grabbed was the central meaning of the trip rather than the means you employed to avoid and deny it. Your new mental set, if any, will be determined, not by the truth, but by the repressive ideas to which you clung when the truth was too close for comfort.

Chapter 35
A PITIFUL INCIDENT

Confound him, he wearied me with arguments to show that in anything like a fair market he would have fetched twenty-five dollars, sure—a thing which was plainly nonsense, and full of the baldest conceit; I wasn't worth it myself.

"Jeezums," Sheatsley exclaimed, using the most ribald expression of astonishment in his repertoire. Haines was chuckling and snorting and the Ashramites were laughing and giggling and casting quick glances my way to check out my reactions.

We were all gathered around a tape recorder on the picnic table in front of the Ashram on a fine summer morning listening to Tim's recorded "review" of the *Neo-American Church Catechism and Handbook*.

A freshly printed copy had been delivered to him the day before at his camp back in the hills, along with a request from Bill for a taped review which the Kriya Press would print for promotion.

Haines had rejected a cash offer from the owner of a chain of head shops in New York to buy the entire edition of 2,000 copies for about the cost of production. The pitch was that, having made the plates, the Kriya Press could use the money to print more books at a much lower unit cost, and make a profit. Assuming the *Catechism* sold well, this made sense, but Haines had decided that he didn't need middle men, although neither he nor any of his followers knew anything about book distribution. Knowing virtually nothing about it myself, I didn't object. For all I knew, it would be duck soup.

Over the tape recorder came the following outrage, delivered in Tim's usual dry, light, precise and charming voice, which the Kriya Press transcribed as follows:

THE NEO-AMERICAN CHURCH CATECHISM AND HANDBOOK
A Review by Timothy Leary

The psychedelic revolution has (with miraculous swiftness) won the hearts and capped the minds of the American people because (like any religious up-heave-all) it uses the ultimate weep-on, humor.

Psychedelic guerrillas, disorganized bands of wise goof-offs, creative fuck-ups, and comedian chaplains, have in six quip years effortlessly taken over the most powerful empire in world history.

With music, clowning, laughter, the psychedelic revolution has passed through the classic socio-political stages of every great human renaissance:

1. The philosophic preparation (Alan Watts writes the Zen introduction).
2. The underground swell of the masses hungry for freedom (Allen Ginsberg Howls).
3. Accidental flare-ups of trigger incidents (Laredo Texas: by this rude bridge that arched the flood, their flag to customs seize, unfurled here the embattled ...).
4. Widespread guerrilla tactics (Ken Kesey's Merry Pranksters).
5. The turning-point victory (the publishers of *Time-Life* get turned on).
6. The mopping-up operations (in charge of Sgt. Pepper).
7. The writing of war memoirs, prayer books, manuals, catechisms, new testaments, grandiose biblical versions in which the accidental-inevitable is made to seem planned blueprint.

The evangelists and social historians of the psychedelic revolution have a delightful roster of hero-comedian-clowns available for legendary canonization.

Alan Watts is the smiling scholar of the Acid Age. For thirty years he has been converting the most complex theories of oriental philosophies into jewel-like up-levels, wry epigrams. Cool, gracious, never ruffled, chuckling to share with us his amused wonder at God's plans for the planet and, with quizzical eye, glancing to see if we will catch on.

Alan Ginsberg. The celestial clown. Giggling, posturing with complete insight, histrionic, shamelessly direct. No one, not even J. Edgar Hoover, can be with this nearsighted, rumpled, worried, hysterical, lyrical, furry bear for ten minutes and not giggle back because he tickles and hugs you when no one else dares.

The Leary-Alpert-Metzner-Harvard-Mexico-Millbrook Circus backed and lurched into history making every mistake except taking itself too seriously for very long. (Someone was always high enough to laugh.) The name of our prisoner rehabilitation project was "Break-Out." The Good Friday religious experiment became the Miracle of March Chapel, to the dismay of Boston University. And it worked. The initials of our research organization, the International Federation for Internal Freedom, spelled out the conditional paradox of the atomic age.

Institutional titles, creeds, were invented and outgrown monthly. Conversions, excommunications, schisms, could never keep up with the changes at Millbrook. You couldn't resign from the Castalia Foundation and denounce its methods because it had already evolved into the League for Social Disorder which in turn couldn't be sued for its theatrical proceeds because the money and the slide projectors had been given away and everyone was dropped out, camping in the woods, and how could the police get a search warrant to raid a sacred pine grove or a promontory known as Lunacy Hill?

The psychedelic yoga is the longest and toughest yoga of all and the only way to keep it going is with a sense of humor. This has been known to seers and visionaries for thousands of years.

For me, the model of the turned-on, tuned-in, dropped-out man is James Joyce, the great psychedelic writer of this century. Pouring out a river-run of pun, jest, put-on, up-level, comic word acrobatics. The impact of Joyce via McLuhan on the psychedelic age cannot be over-estimated.

Bill Burroughs is the Buster Keaton of the movement. He was Mr. Acid before LSD was invented. The soft-bodied answer to IBM. Unsmiling comedian genius.

Twenty years ago today Sgt. Pepper taught the band to play. The classic ontological vaudeville routine.

The Buddha smile.

The laughing fat Chinese sage.

The flute of Krishna tickling the cow girls.

The dance of Shiva.

Om, the cosmic chuckle. The sweaty belly guffaw of a Hasidic Jew.

Where are the laughing Christians? Something twisted grabbed the Christian mind around the third century. Is there any tender mirth left in the cult of the cross?

Mystics, prophets, holy men are all laughers because the religious revelation is a rib-tickling amazement-insight that all human purposes including your own are solemn self-deceptions. You see through the game and laugh with God at the cosmic joke.

The holy man is the one who can pass on a part of the secret, express the joke, act out a fragment of the riddle.

To be a holy man you have to be a funny man.

Take for example Art Kleps, founder and Chief Boo Hoo of the Neo-American Church. Authentic American anarchist, nonconformist, itinerant preacher. A pure-essence eccentric paranoid in the grand tradition of bull-headed, nutty men who stubbornly insist on being themselves and who are ready to fight at the drop of a cliché for the right of others to be themselves.

For five years this Art Kleps has been a wandering guerrilla monk in the psychedelic underground.

When he first showed up at Millbrook, in 1963, Kleps was a school psychologist, a big blond, loud-voiced, bar room intellectual. He roved around Castalia one weekend; grandiose, blustering, reverent, deeply intelligent and too drunk to take LSD.

Then the oldest son of a Lutheran minister wrote a 1,000-page Pilgrim's Progress epic about his three-day non-trip to Millbrook, running off fifteen typed pages a day and coming back to Castalia weekends as Christian H. Christian crawling painfully up the kitchen floor, splashing in the toilet bowls, filled with whiskey, throwing out an endless monologue of corny psychological-psychedelic paranoia, and making feeble passes at Castalia's soft-eyed marijuana goddesses whom he hallucinated to be thirteen year old virgins. Like Dylan Thomas, so high, so juiced on his own cerebro-spinal fluid, he accused us of slipping LSD into his food.

Then he got fired by his school board for some series of honest, rebellious, adolescent antics (he is one of the most creative psychologists in the country), and, naturally, started his own religion.

"We maintain the psychedelic substances are sacraments, that is, divine substances, no matter who uses them, in whatever spirit, with whatever intentions. We do not employ set rituals, make conditions for membership other than agreement with our principles, or regulate the frequency or intensity of the sacramental experience. Many of our members are damned fools and miserable sinners; membership in the Church is no guarantee of intellectuality or of spiritual wisdom; it may even be possible that one or two of our boo hoos are opportunistic charlatans, but we are not dismayed by these conditions; it has never been our objective to add one more swollen institutional substitute for individual virtue to the already crowded lists."

Art Kleps, the Martin Luther of the Psychedelic Movement, even when drunk, spraying blindly from his ink pot, the most courageous theologian of our time.

While the academics play word games about God's medical condition, Art Kleps, staggering insane in his study at three in the morning, tackles the real gut issues like: are marijuana and LSD really God's sacraments? Then, if yes they are, and I say they are, then anyone who uses them, gives them, is involved in a divine transaction no matter how gamy, how nutty, how sordid his motives, so it doesn't matter who or when or how or why you turn on, it's still a holy cosmic process whether you are a silly thirteen-year-old popping a sugar cube on your boyfriend's motorcycle or a theatrical agent giving pot to a girl to get her horny, or an alcoholic Catholic priest carrying the Viaticum to a hypocritical sinner or even a psychiatrist giving LSD to an unsuspecting patient to do a scientific study.

"It's all God's flesh," shouted Art Kleps, "no matter what your motives may be."

Oh yes, let Art Kleps be given the credit. While the rest of us were still involved in research foundations and poetry conferences, and trying to demonstrate that LSD was a nice healthy productive medicine for virtuous docile Americans, Art was roaring around in a turquoise convertible with a suspended driver's license, drinking bad wine from a bottle and shouting,

"Don't bother trying to curry favor with the establishment; it's a losing game. We aren't American Indians who can be patronized and isolated. Congratulated on our sobriety, and all that. We have the right to practice our religion, even if we are a bunch of filthy, drunken bums. Try not to degrade rights into mere claims based on evidence of virtue and lack of vice. We do not stand before the government as children before a parent, the government stands before us as the corrupter of our God-given human rights, and until the government gets its bloody, reeking paws off our sacred psychedelics and ceases to harass and persecute our members, until, indeed, every poor wretch now suffering in prison because he preferred the mystical uplift of pot to the slobbering alcoholism of the politicians is set free, our attitude must be one of uncompromising hostility."

Pageant magazine reporter: "You call your local ministers boo hoos. Why do you use such a ridiculous title?"

Father William Kleps: "We realize this title does have its absurd connotations but we have intentionally chosen something with absurd qualities to remind ourselves not to take ourselves too seriously."

Pageant magazine reporter: "You claim to be a church, but you don't take your own religion seriously. What do you take seriously?"

Kleps: "A lot of things. But one of the things we take least seriously is institutional life, the thing most people take more seriously than anything else. We think this is one of the faults of modern man: elevating institutional forms and structures to the level of eternal verities."

The wit and wisdom of this great psychedelic bull is collected in a soft-cover book, the *Neo-American Church Catechism and Handbook*. The table of contents reflects the flavor of this mad, disorganized masterpiece:

Pronouncements of the Chief Boo Hoo on: LSD, Marijuana, Sex, Revolutionary Politics.

Articles: Synchronicity and the Plot/Plot, With LSD I saw God, The Bombardment and Annihilation of the Planet Saturn; the Reformation of the New Jerusalem, Morning Glory Lodge and Millbrook, Neo-American Church Gives 'Em Hell, the 95-Item Test of Neo-Psychopathic Character, Free Advertising at Government Expense, Up-to-Date List of Boo Hoos, Catalog, Cartoons.

Readers of the *Neo-American Church Catechism and Handbook* will learn that the Seal of the Church portrays a three-eyed, turned-on toad rampant over the motto: "Victory Over Horseshit."

Tim Leary: "Art, I don't like your motto. It's a whiskey trip. It's not a psychedelic love message. Victory? Over? Horseshit?"

Art Kleps: "It's my trip. Take it or leave it."

And then Art flipped out into typical political paranoia:

"Our victory is over horseshit rather than bullshit. Bullshit is a rare and valuable commodity. The great masters have all been bullshitters. Horseshit, on the other hand, in the common parlance, refers to downright crap. The free, playful, entertaining flight of ideas is bullshit; and more often than not will be found afterwards to accord perfectly with universal truth. Horseshit is contrived; derivative, superstitious, ignorant. We might take Gurdjieff as an example of a master bullshitter and Meher Baba as an example of a master horseshitter."

You ask Art Kleps what his goals are and he tells you, "money and power." To that silly end the last twenty pages of the *Catechism* are designed as a Monkey Ward catalog of items available from the Neo-American Church, cash in advance, including for $30, a destruct box ("If opened improperly, contents go up in flames"), and, for $100, a certificate stating that "The Chief Boo Hoo never even heard of you and regards you with indifference."

Kleps' *Catechism and Handbook* is that rare commodity, an original, personal, unashamed, naked unveiling of a man's mind; the Art Kleps head trip. At times padded, at times so involutely paranoid that you lose the thread, at times sloppily falling down, but always manly, coarse, stubble-bearded, shouting, praying, and in touch with central broadcasting, the original, two-billion-year-old, Sunday-night comedy show.

Art Kleps came on the scene before the cool, gentle love-heads. He can't stand flowers. He hates rock and roll. He has absolutely no sense of beauty. He is a clumsy manipulator, a blatant flatterer, a bully to the weak, the world's most incompetent con-man. He is, in short, a sodden disgrace to the movement.

Oh pilgrim, if you come to visit the Chief Boo Hoo you will see a sign on his door, "Parsonage, Neo-American Church, Art Kleps, Chief Boo Hoo." You ring the bell and await your spiritual teacher. The cover of the book flies open and there, reeking of the fumes of a smoky, sweaty, 21st Century Martian waterfront saloon is the Chief Boo Hoo himself: glaring, unshaven, wrinkled shirt, sloppy pants.

Reading this book is a revelatory laugh-cry trip for those who are ready for it.

Last night Rosemary was lying by the camp fire on a bed of pine needles, reading the *Catechism*. When she finished she looked up, her face beautiful in the red shadows and said, "Art Kleps is a funny man." Rosemary is right. Art Kleps is a not-wholly holy, funny man.

Jeezums H. Christ, indeed. Of course, we all laughed like crazy while this bullshit was being played. Wendy managed to squeal "that's not true! that's not true!" several times, which I appreciated, but I was amused as much as anyone else if not more so. It was pure, undiluted Leary, that was for sure. The questions and comments which followed concerned my sadistic attitude towards the lilies of the field, all those hallucinatory virgins, my alcoholic and paranoid inclinations, my insensibility to beauty, my squalid quarters, my slovenly attire and so forth.

"Well, Kleps," Haines asked, after we had recovered our composure, "should we print this?"

I surprised myself by not saying "No" right away. Hmmm. Tim probably figured I would demand deletions and amendments. He would play along with this, no doubt, and we would end up with ... what?

On the other hand, if we let it stand as recorded, Tim's ferocious animosity towards anything the public might think was admirable and original ("Sergeant Pepper" was a "vaudeville routine"?) would be exposed for all to see.

Well, that was a good thing wasn't it? If the moronic hordes took it seriously, so what? If it kept the stupid bastards away from me, all the better.

"Yeah, print it," I told Haines. "Let him have his fun. It may not say much about me, but it sure as hell says a lot about Timothy Leary."

As a matter of fact, it's the clearest example, in print, of the Freudian mechanism of projection I know about.

Haines liked this move. I think we both thought of it as a finesse, or "the old rope trick, self-administered," or something of the sort, but our attitude mystified the troops, Wendy included.

There was another factor, namely, the *History of the Psychedelic Movement Coloring Book,* the project I had started working on after finishing the *Catechism.* It was not yet in print, but I had shown Tim a few pages. He had seemed genuinely amused by them. So was Sam Clapp, who put up $1,000 to have it printed. As one might expect, many of the pages in the coloring book were irrelevant, frivolous and immaterial insofar as the actual history of the "psychedelic movement" was concerned. I converted things that were pretty grim for the people who had gone through them, such as the expulsion of IFIF from Mexico, into slapstick. Almost everyone I met in the years to come who had both an ankle-biter and a copy of the coloring book, Gai Duncan included, told me that it was the kid's favorite crayon target.

The way I pictured Tim was no more reverent than the way I pictured everyone else in the book, including a fictional boo hoo of the Neo-American Church. This was in sharp contrast to my comments about Tim before the Senate subcommittee, and a step away from the generally respectful treatment I gave him in the *Catechism*. It was likely that Tim had written his "review" in what he thought was the same spirit. It was all in fun, all good-natured raillery.

Yeah, well, sort of. But no matter how sortofish the comparison, I wasn't going to open myself up to the accusation of being the kind of person who could dish it out but not take it. Why, that was almost as bad as being called a "sissy." The horrors of it all. When I did get around to publishing the coloring book, I printed Tim's review of the *Catechism* right up front, word for word. To some extent I'm sure, I did this in the spirit of "everything you say bounces off me and sticks on you twice, so there."

I have reprinted it several times. It may be the least self-conscious thing Tim ever wrote. Like the drawings and stories of children, it has the charm of transparency.

But this was not to be the end of the matter. In a strange move which showed that Haines and I probably had the politics of the situation figured out right, Tim reprinted the review in *The Politics of Ecstasy* (College Notes) but removed all mention of my name and my book, although still quoting me at length, sometimes correctly.

In Tim's new version, the drunken theologian being trashed is "Lisa Lieberman." The essay is entitled "The Mad Virgin of Psychedelia."

The Neo-American Church became the "Neo-Marxian Church," the motto of which was represented as "Victory over Sexuality." The card tacked to the door reads "Art for Art's Sake." (Little play on words there, I guess.)

This was bitter, calculated and nasty stuff, and ruined the off-the-wall goofiness of the original.

Sometime in the early '70s, I ran across a piece in the *Village Voice* by Jill Johnston, their house lesbian feminist of the day, in which she accused the media of suppressing female spokespersons for various causes, and cited that tough broad "Lisa Lieberman" as someone Tim Leary, with the help of various hired scriveners and media thugs, managed to upstage right into total obscurity.

"Elbowing," Otto called it.

I think Ms. Johnston got it right, basically. Tim's intent throughout, unmodified by any concern for veracity or consistency, was to picture anyone whom he thought might shadow his brilliance as the leading light of Psychedelia, including Lennon with his shopworn vaudeville act and Watts with his decipherings of "God's Plan for the Planet," as imitative reruns and self-deluded diddlers and piddlers, while promoting himself as a magisterial, all-knowing figure serenely orbiting above and beyond it all, making the rules.

The next item published by the Ashram was a pamphlet Tim whomped up called *Start Your Own Religion*. In it, Tim advocated cooking up your own cute cult instead of joining anything of the "mail order" variety, meaning the Neo-American Church, of course. The membership of one's cute cult should be limited to "essence friends." Nothing was said about doctrine.

This pamphlet, and everything Tim said and did on stage or screen, gave the impression that the League for Spiritual Discovery and the vague place known as "Millbrook" among most Psychedelians, were identical. Every day or two he would escort visitors through the Ashram and refer to "our" potters, "our" presses, etc. We all knew what he was doing, and we all just laughed it off, but Tim was dead serious.

As a solipsistic nihilist, I can't very well be a sincere "theologian," but what kind of "theologian" was Timothy Leary?

The quotations coming up pretty soon, with my comments appended, are from *Neurologic*. Tim sent me a pre-publication copy when he was in Switzerland and I was working on the first version of this book. Then he was trapped and sent back to prison in California. I had not mentioned (what I knew of) Tim's crazy ideas or subjected them to the deprecation they merited in the *Boo Hoo Bible* mostly because he had been either a prisoner or a fugitive while I was writing it.

"He may have changed," I told myself, whenever it seemed appropriate to fire a few rounds in his direction. Not only was I reluctant to distress him further while he was enduring these trials and humiliations, but I did not want to give aid and comfort to our mutual enemies.

This also distorted and diluted the first version of this book.

After reading *Neurologic,* I thought Tim had switched to Jimson weed, or something worse. Smelling water a mile away, he had lowered his nose into the dirt and was plowing a furrow towards it, as a cowboy once told me his horse had done after eating the stuff. I did not respond to the book at all, hoping Tim would come to his senses and canter along with his head up once again, even if he was going in the wrong direction. Later, on reading Aldous Huxley's *Collected Letters,* I discovered that Tim had been harboring these notions since the beginning of his Psychedelian career. "The most awful rubbish about the genetic code," Huxley, in a letter to Humphry Osmond, called Tim's private maunderings to him on the subject.

Although imprisonment had not improved Tim's capacity for ratiocination, the experience hadn't given rise to the "awful rubbish" either, but may have helped to expose it to public view. Being locked up tends to encourage "jive," and to blunt one's sense of discrimination.

It seems clear that Tim developed his delusional system early in the game, but hid it, as Lisa Bieberman hid her Paulinian supernaturalism, whenever it seemed convenient to do so, which was most of the time. This peculiar combination of firm beliefs and an adamant refusal to state those beliefs except through hints and oblique allusions is typical of paranoid ideation, and runs a meandering, shifty course, often through caverns measureless to man, in much of Tim's writings and "New Age" writings in general. In any asylum run by me, Tim and Lisa would be housed together in the well-defended ward of the paranoids wing, treated gently and encouraged to attempt to convert each other.

I think this shit ought to be out in the open. My comments are within brackets:

The theories presented in this essay are Science Fiction.

[The opening line of *Neurologic* and classic Learian smoke and mirrors. Tim suggests throughout the essay that his theories are to be taken seriously, that they are valid and philosophical and he gives reasons for believing in them.]

They are scientific in that they are based on findings from physics, etc.

[Tim's fantasies are "metaphysics," that is, Fazzm speculations about things which cannot be defined or observed or inferred or validated or tested in any way in the terminology appropriate to that which can be. Science, as distinguished from "Science Fiction," is not "based on" empirical findings. It is the empirical method of inquiry and analysis itself. It isn't the findings that are empirical, it's the reasoning and the methods that are empirical or not empirical. The McPozzm world isn't scientific or not scientific. It is what we can say about the McPozzm world that is scientific or not scientific.]

They are fictional in the Wittgensteinian sense that all theories and speculations beyond the propositions of natural science are subjective.

[The application of the term "subjective" is very subjective, and that's probably why Tim was so fond of it. Speculations about natural science are not subjective? Since when? Some speculations, about anything, are more subjective than others, that's all. What Tim is really saying here is that all metaphysics, which he confuses with philosophy in general, is sheer fancy, and his fancies are therefore just as good as the next guy's. Even this doesn't follow, and let's leave Wittgenstein out of this. Tim never quotes him; he just invokes him.]

Such theories ... are equally fictional.

[Equally fictional? This can only mean they are all fictional. Even among theories propounded without any regard for experience or internal logicality, some will be supported by observation better than others. According to Tim's formulation, the theory that a superhuman entity known as the Tooth Fairy leaves dimes under pillows for little boys and girls who have been to the dentist is no more or less "fictional" than the theory that Mommy and Daddy do it. Tim, bent on the obliteration of all meaningful distinctions in a miasma of rhetoric, never uses homely examples such as the above, or examples of any kind, because they tend to clear the air.]

It gives us pleasure ... to believe that the species ... evolves ...

[This is radical and infantile pragmatism. Believing gonorrhea is no worse than a bad cold has made a lot of people feel good until they stopped feeling good. Believing in the "Seven Stage Life Cycle" serves a similar function: What, me worry?]

... a theory of what is subjectively true and consensually fact.

["Fact?" "True?" Wasn't all of this "fiction" a few pages ago? So, if 51 percent of the population vote in favor of the Tooth Fairy theory, it's a fact. And if that isn't startling enough, some of these fictions are, although subjective, "true," and some aren't. Some must be false, or what does "true" mean? Your guess is as good as mine.]

... a theory of the seven levels of reality and their interaction.

[This "reality" chopping, Tim asserts, is "ontology." But "ontology" has a well-established meaning as a form of "metaphysics" concerned with "being" and presuming "essences." Whether these terms are mere noises or actually refer to anything is debatable. I think they are all hot air. But, assuming they have meaning, if "ontology" is philosophy rather than mere maundering, it is not concerned with relations within or between particulars such as "child-rearing" or "the species" but is about the nature of "being" itself. Mental? Physical? Both? Neither? Mutable? Immutable? ... and so on. This is the most naïve error amateur philosophers make: Large sizeoids, such as comets and "the species" are thought to be in the same class as universals. Propounders of Scientism, in its various guises, make this silly mistake all the time, and are hailed in the mass media as intellectual giants for doing so. Oh well. Throughout this essay, Tim consistently misuses philosophic terms. He doesn't know what he's talking about, and what's worse, doesn't want to know, and what's worse, tries to convince everyone else that they shouldn't want to know, either.]

The hazard of this philosophy is that it is tangible.

[Holy shit. Now we have a philosophy that is not only fictional, but tangible as well. Does this mean one can stumble over it in the dark, but only on television? A "tangible" philosophy is a round square, or noise. The word "hazard," in this lunatic context, is a little alarming, I'm sorry to say.]

The Neurology of Dying. A few minutes of clock time ... experienced as millions of years.

[How many million? Are there any other people around? If so, is it "millions of years" for them too? Or do they die like flies, strictly by the clock? Then what? No worse than a bad cold?]

The Mission of DNA.

[Aha. The metaphysical hog emerges from the ontological tunnel, and it's on a "mission." Tim goes on to declare that his genetic code God is "omnipotent" and a "super-brain." Where is this "Brain?" Is It omniscient and omnipresent as well as omnipotent? Is prayer to It efficacious? Is there a Purgatory? Do indulgences cause the remission of sins? Is Tim Its Vicar, here below?]

Dying is merging with the life process. Consciousness returns to the genetic code. We become every form of life that has lived and will live. We become the DNA code and leave the planet with the DNA code.

[A code takes off from a planet with a load of ectoplasmic passengers? A code is an abstraction, a set of relations between particulars. Neither the Morse code nor the DNA code nor the code of silence nor the code duello can "leave the planet," or even buy a ticket to Hoboken. A bunch of wires and keys, or an organism, or electrical charges or marks or sounds can travel, but not a code. All supernaturalist imagery is of this kind, namely, Globular Blobovenoidalism. Abstract concepts and large, impressive appearances like planets and species are "merged" and have "missions," and send "messages" to their minions and favored prophets such as Tim here below.]

There is no death.

[Tim's DNA Code God is independent, in other words, of genes, chromosomes, protein, carbon and all other things subject to deterioration.]

When the body stops functioning, consciousness advances to the nervous system ... goes out to work in the larval circuits and to play in the body of rapture. Neurological existence within a ... system becomes "infinite" as chronologged by a third circuit verbal mind.

[This is an attempt to preserve personal identity, after the excesses of the previous generalization wiped it out. Tim is trying to say he has a soul (an infinite Neurological existence) of his own, after all. Neurology without nerves.]

It's all pretty crazy and pathetic, and almost certainly originated in the standard Irish-Catholic ghost and corpse worship and mock cannibalism in which Tim was raised, compared to which almost anything is an advance.

And Tim isn't the only well educated person to suffer from the general Blobovian conviction that abstract concepts can have a location in space, zoom around, bite each other on the ass and so forth. It is a commonplace in institutions of the Higher Learning to take questions such as "Where is the meaning?" seriously, as if a spatial location for "the meaning" could be found (the text, my head, your head, our heads). Strictly speaking, "the meaning" is nowhere or, along with everything else, "in" my mind. There would be no mind/matter problem for philosophers if this was not the case.

I think Blobovianism is given a big boost in the primary grades when kids are taught that "3 goes into 6 two times" or something else along these lines. The fact is that 3 isn't anywhere and can't go anywhere, nor does 6 have the ability to absorb other numbers, or send them packing, however much it may seem that way. All such expressions are merely conventional shorthand idioms for abstract arithmetic operations which would be tedious to spell out every time they are used. Treating them as if they were anything else is silly and profoundly irrational.

The thought of an innocent, barefoot lad or lassie with cheek of tan reading *Neurologic* as preparation for his or her first big trip down the mental Mississippi makes my blood curdle. In terms of encouraging a healthy mind set for the occasion, *Neurologic* may be even more disorienting than the *TBD* or *Mind Games*.

Tim and I were always able to talk to each other in a civil manner in private, no matter how uncivil things got in public. But Haines always said exactly what he felt like saying, no matter how civil or uncivil or just plain silly it was, both in public and in private. As a result, during the "Summer of Love," Haines and I were often not on speaking terms.

It had nothing to do with Psychedelian doctrine and everything to do with Haines' overly suspicious nature. The fact that King William and I were actually close friends who hung out together, got stoned and smashed together, pursued the world's most dangerous bipeds together and so forth caused him to imagine all kinds of sinister things we might also be doing together, like arranging a "sweet little deal" for the Church which would force the League and the Ashram to submit to my imperious domination or go pick shit with the crows on Route 44.

This vision of my intentions had no foundation in my actions or inclinations. Nevertheless, if the reports I constantly heard from primary sources were to be believed, it was a vision that flitted in and out of Bill's capacious cranium for most of the long summer months and sometimes nested there and laid large, crazed eggs. Eventually, Bill realized that I didn't want what he suspected I wanted and that I genuinely liked his act and wanted it to succeed, but this light didn't dawn until after the final raids began.

And what about King William himself, the reader may well ask. If I was really the court philosopher, why didn't I manage to form a more productive alliance with this powerful person, who had the wherewithal to make things happen? Billy was a founding director of the Church, and my best friend. Because of the tax laws, he was virtually forced to give away hundreds of thousands of dollars every year. One would have expected a normal zillionaire, given these facts, to have blown some "real" money our way.

The Church, and its leader, were not merely poor at this time but frequently flat broke.

Rich people do not usually understand what "broke" means. They see it as a transitory and even whimsical misfortune, like a stubbed toe, locking oneself out of the house, a flat tire and a flat spare on a back road, and so forth. It can't be serious. If it is, how come you're alive?

In my case, and many other cases on the property, this view actually had some merit. We were not a good example of what it meant to be poor, because the bizarre circumstances in which we lived made it OK to be poor. Most of the time, I hardly noticed. Unless I ran out of cigarettes or something like that, I didn't feel broke.

Did Alice have any money in Wonderland? Did she feel broke?

I have all kinds of good reasons (most of which are too boring and trivial to spell out here) to believe that the rich Psychedelians often became confused about those of us who, although poor, seemed generally content with our lot. It was an attitude which stood in sharp contrast to the conduct of most poor folks who had gotten close enough to them to insert a tap and drain off a dram or three. Why didn't we do this, that and the other thing; that is, all the things they thought they would have done had some cruel and monstrous twist of fate placed them in similar circumstances? It wasn't that I didn't bring up the subject. I did, but then I just let it lie there, and I wasn't the only economic basket case at Daheim (Dieterich's original name for the place) who appeared to take this ho-hum attitude.

Consider Sam Clapp. I had ordained him, at his request, Boo Hoo of Nassau, Primate of the Bahamas, Patriarch of the Caribbean and Protector of the Lesser Antilles. I really liked this title. It had rhythm. And Sam, it seemed, genuinely wanted to "do something" for the Church but somehow couldn't figure out "how to do it," exactly. This was also what I heard from Billy. The great problem seemed to be the avoidance of taxation. Sam was a

Harvard Law graduate and one of the original organizers of what is now the Resorts International company. I had been around while Sam and Billy and a couple other guys had pulled this off, using the Mary Carter paint company to do it. Was it my job to tell Sam or Billy how to avoid or evade taxation? It was clearly their area of expertise, not mine.

Sam was extremely wealthy, and seemed to enjoy spending his money, as he had made it, in imaginative ways. He told me that whenever his children from a previous marriage visited him at his private island in the Caribbean, he arranged to have them arrive by boat after the sun had set so he could greet them at the dock and then lead them up a long flight of marble stairs flanked with rows of uniformed footmen holding flaming torches. I thought that this, like the Neo-American title he had invented for himself, showed a nice flair for the dramatic, and I didn't like it at all when Sam resigned because his liege lord in the neo-feudalistic scheme of things, Bernie Cornfeld, insisted on it. It was, Bernie said, bad PR for Investors Overseas Services, in which Sam and Martica were major players.

I couldn't get mad at Sam. Money was his life, and defying Bernie would have cost him millions of dollars. Nor did I have anything against people living in the grand manner then, and I don't now. My socialist principles were not offended. Not only are there all kinds of sound practical reasons for encouraging a private economic "sector" to flourish, but life in general would be much less interesting if there were no rich people around to amuse the rest of us with their follies and, every now and then, to adorn the world with genuinely original and beautiful things on the grand scale. On the other hand, these rich bastards should not be allowed to form gangs and run everything.

As of the date of this writing (1994), I would say that the European Union has a pretty good balance. I would crank things another quarter turn to the left but do it slowly. The American system, on the other hand, is capitalism gone berserk and a demonstration of how right Karl Marx was about so many things, as well as a demonstration of how stupid and manipulable most people are, about which Marx had nothing to say, as far as I know.

Once, over dinner at the Bungalow when Billy was away (Sam

had insisted that I sit at the head of the table), Sam asked Wendy and me how we "liked the idea" of living in a "small castle" on a private island off the coast of Scotland. I thought this was a very interesting concept, indeed, but Wendy didn't, so the subject never came up again.

Sam casually offered me the use of his suite at the Regency and his car and driver whenever I happened to be in the city during his absence, but I never took him up on it because I had no cash to get back and forth with, to buy clothes with, to tip with, and so forth, and there was virtually nothing I wanted to do in New York anyway.

I loved Millbrook the way it was and, basically, was happy as a clam. Clams don't worry about accumulating wealth. They live on whatever plankton happens to pass by and are happy as oysters to get it.

I think Billy, most of the time, and this was quite an achievement for an owner, understood, and to some extent, sometimes, shared this bivalvian frame of mind. He also loved the place the way it was as did Otto and many of the troops.

And Billy and I both knew, although we rarely talked about it while things were going well, that it could not last. It was an outrageous violation of every rule in the book that it had come into being in the first place, and had survived as long as it had.

The main reason I didn't kick, scream, foam at the mouth and chew on the rug when company came over was that I didn't want to spoil it all. Every now and then, I would have the equivalent of a petit mal seizure, but nobody seemed to take these minor fits of mine about the economic situation seriously and neither did I.

I know that all of this is hard to believe, but it's true. Remember, I'm a preacher's kid. And, to top that off, my parents usually spoke German when they discussed money, as they did when they discussed the latest peccadilloes of particular members of the congregation. They thought gossip and money both too indelicate for the tender ears of children and maybe they were right.

"Hennenwetter, noch einmal," my beautiful mother would

customarily say to conclude such conversations, which usually took place in the car on the way home from church.

Historically, mavericks born to the ruling class of plutocratic societies, like Billy (one does not automatically become a member of the "establishment" by being born to this class), and the intellectual iconoclasts they sometimes patronize, like me, do not get along well for very long. The fact is that Billy and I probably did better than most in this respect.

The fortunate few who can live and prosper on unearned income develop enthusiasms for a doctrine or a style or a personality or a combination thereof just as we unfortunates do, but the rich are much more wary of organized religious and philosophic novelties than those of us with not much to lose.

Wealthy people rarely become wealthy, or grow up wealthy, without learning how dangerous organizations can be and without learning how much hostility is generated by the exercise of economic power, which, in most circumstances, is indistinguishable from military and police power. I think it would clear the air if all money pictured bombers, tanks and cops in action instead of famous and distinguished alumni, since those are the things that actually make the paper worth something. Ownership is only a legal claim to a set of rights, and if those rights can't be enforced they're meaningless. The power invoked by the deeds and currency and whatnot is the power Mao Tse-tung referred to as coming out of the barrels of guns, not the power of reasonable argument or of truth and beauty to sway the human heart.

The more deeply one becomes involved in something, generally speaking, the fewer illusions one will have about it, and this is as true of capitalism as it is of anything else. When a capitalist, for whatever reason, rocks the boat (the "system") occupied by himself and other capitalists, he risks social exclusion and expressions of extreme displeasure from his fellow travelers, at the very least. That can be expensive.

It was one thing for Paul and Mary Mellon to support the Jungians, the Eranos group and Joseph Campbell, and to set up the Bollingen Foundation and publish the Wilhelm translation of the *I Ching,* and so forth. It was another thing entirely for William and Thomas Mellon Hitchcock to support criminalized religious associations led by Tim, Bill and me.

The latter conduct resembled the Elector of Saxony's harboring of Luther. It was dangerous as hell. The former are mere cultural deviations that the public expects of the rich every now and then—and the rich expect from the rich every now and then.

By failing to promptly throw us all overboard and close the place down as soon as the laws against our religious practices were in place, Billy and Tommy came close to engaging in an insurrection, or something on that order of magnitude, in the boat rocking department. To find close parallels to this kind of conduct among plutocrats in American history, one would have to go back to pre-Civil War days, or even back to the starting line. (Prohibition? I don't think so, but I'm not a professional historian, and maybe I don't take that era seriously enough.)

Billy and Tommy made it pretty clear that they thought my style and philosophic orientation suited them, and fit the Psychedelian case better than anything else on offer, but I think that the idea of a financially secure and independent Neo-American Church set off alarm buzzers and caused red lights to blink and rotate in their rich-kid heads. They knew, at least in an intuitive kind of way, that I would fight if the Church became the dominant organized Psychedelian power, that I would escalate rather than compromise, that the conflict would inevitably involve them and that they would lose control over the course of events. Furthermore, I drank too much and I liked teenage girls. Easy to blackmail.

So, OK. I no longer had any serious expectation of getting "real money" from our landlords, and had become adjusted to the idea of selection #2 on the fight or flight menu. But why was Billy so cheap about a few thousand here and few thousand there, enough to keep me writing instead of struggling to survive? And why did he have to be so perfidious about it all? Was he a Neo-American or wasn't he? No man can be blamed for declining to create a monster that might destroy him, but what about some reasonable degree of loyalty to, and support for, one's (freely chosen) cause?

Well, for starters, I wasn't the only one.

"Billy is known as a welsher, Art," Charlie Rumsey blandly informed me one time after I had expressed my disgust that a firm promise from Billy to donate "$40,000 in two weeks" had been broken with no explanation, under the worst possible circumstances, leaving me adrift in Washington, D.C., without a pot to piss in. (Pissing in the park is illegal in Washington, D.C.)

"Why, I saw him crawling out of a restaurant on his hands and knees one time when we were kids, so he wouldn't have to pay the bill. He's the only guy I know who could get away with the kind of stuff I've seen him pull. It's all charm, you know. A hollow shell, what?" Charlie grinned. "But who knows? Maybe you're the one to break the bank."

Unfortunately, although he was always polite to strangers, it seemed that one of the ways Billy defined a close personal friend was that with such a person he could express, and manifest by an inability to write his name, his genuine attitude towards money, which held that it was a sacred substance circulating in his veins instead of blood, the letting of which, particularly in driblets, was a serious matter. Major losses didn't seem to bother him all that much.

"I know what you're going to say, 'penny wise and pound foolish,' right?" Billy said to me one time, at the conclusion of the strangest of all his adventures in the field of redistributing the wealth I ever witnessed.

We were having breakfast in Billy's second house in Sausalito. It was a nice morning, both out on the bay that I surveyed from a table in front of a large window and back on Wall Street, which Billy, still in bed, checked out by phone between bites of pancakes and eggs and swigs of orange juice. Priscilla was up (things are a little topsy-turvy in Sausalito's hillside houses) in the kitchen. There wasn't another soul in the place, although there certainly had been the night before.

Suddenly, a thunderous sound of descending footsteps came from the stairwell. "Jesus, cops?" I thought to myself, and I think Billy asked himself the same question. All the people we knew, including "Terry the Tramp," managed to get around without causing unseemly commotions, even when they were seriously agitated.

Two obese "Hollywood Heebs" burst into the room, babbling crazily and gesturing wildly. Since both of them seemed to be screeching, moaning and blubbering at the same time, I couldn't understand much, except maybe "the trucks are waiting," or something like that. Something about a pig? I couldn't be sure. Billy sat bolt upright and asked, "How did you guys get in here?"

"The door was open," Hollywood Hopeful #1 answered, as he flung himself on Billy's bed, and waggled a paper and a pen under Billy's nose. He begged Billy to sign. No rational arguments were put forward, only an incoherent tale of things gone wrong, interspersed with cries of anguish and despair. It was a note for $50,000, I found out later. With every indication of extreme displeasure, Billy co-signed this instrument. As soon as he did, the motion picture producers fled. The entire drama had been played out in a matter of seconds. Billy had met these guys in a bar only the week before, on a trip to Los Angeles. They were making a movie about a guy who fucks a pig, or wants to but is scorned by the animal, I don't remember the exact scenario. The movie was called "Futz," or something like that. I don't know if Billy got stuck for the 50 thou, but even if he didn't, this deal did not accord with textbook descriptions of what investment bankers do for a living. When good old whatshisname and Jane Fonda's brother asked him to invest in *Easy Rider* he turned them down flat.

So, who is to say? The economic aspects of it all may have been so loaded with neurotic warps that trying to figure out what Billy was trying to accomplish in any particular situation, mine included, was a waste of effort. Tommy, talking casually to Haines and me one time, said that his brother was "crazy." He wasn't using the term loosely, and I don't think he meant Billy's drug use or his philosophic concepts. Neither Haines nor I asked for details. I don't know about Bill, but it seemed to me that discussing Billy, an intimate friend, with his brother, a not so intimate friend, as if Billy were any crazier than the rest of us, wasn't right, even if he was. I have no idea what Miss Manners would say about it.

"Why don't you buy that place?" I asked Billy one day, gesturing backwards, as we left Millbrook's charmingly old-fashioned bank and walked up the street on our way to Eddy's Liquors.

(Eddy, believe it or not, would sometimes leave the door open on early summer mornings so his regulars in desperate need could come in and help ourselves, while Eddy was around the corner having coffee with his cronies.)

"It would improve our public relations around here enormously," I continued. "A friend in need is a friend indeed."

"We looked into that," Billy replied.

"Well, what was the story?"

"They didn't want to sell," Billy said.

Such terseness was typical of Billy's style when the specificities of financial matters came up, unless he happened to be smashed, when, on one or two occasions, he gave us an earful.

We frequently went out for dinner, to the Old Drover's Inn or to another joint closer by on Route 44. After one such jaunt to the latter rendezvous, with Peggy and Ron Rakow and a female visitor whom Billy had freshly picked off the Big House front porch, it happened that we drove home with Billy and his girl in the back seat and Wendy and I up front, with Peggy and Ron following in another car.

We were all smashed, but Billy, Peggy and the female visitor had really distinguished themselves. The freshly plucked visitor, who had a wild look about her from the start, had ordered bottle after bottle of Lancers wine, for which she admitted a long-term fondness bordering on reverence, and Peggy and Billy had seemed determined to match her rate of consumption or pass out trying.

Conversation at our table had become so loud and reckless of offending the staid decorum which pertained at other tables in the room that I thought the manager was going to come over and admonish us at one point, but he never made it. "These are my neighbors," he probably thought to himself, "Christian forbearance is called for."

Peggy had emphatically pronounced the word "fuck," or one of its variants, about fifty times between the first bottle of Lancers and the last cup of Irish coffee. Perhaps she was trying to demonstrate something to Ron. Billy told funny acid stories, but Miss Lancers' monologue made no sense at all. She seemed to be simply babbling like a victim of acute malarial fever.

As soon as I drove out of the parking lot, Billy, in the back seat, started telling Miss Lancers how fond he was of her. Was it true love, or just moonlight madness? He would be really pleased if she would stay overnight at the Bungalow as his guest, and so forth. Wendy started giggling uncontrollably at the utterance of the words "moonlight madness," and I could not understand a word Miss Lancers was saying.

"To the Bungalow?" I asked. "Or should we go over to the Ashram and drive Haines crazy?"

"Oh, let's go to the Bungalow, Art," Billy replied. "I'm pretty sure Jack has some Lancers stashed away somewhere."

A few minutes of muttered conversation and the thrashing around of bodies followed in the back seat and then the girl finally said something that made sense. She didn't believe Billy was really a millionaire. All men were after only one thing, and they would tell any lie to get it, and so forth. This was all expressed in very maudlin terms.

"Listen, baby," Billy said, "if you knew how rich I was you'd piss in your pants." More struggling in the back seat, but this time, Wendy told me later, it was mostly a struggle on Billy's part to prevent the girl from scratching his eyes out. When things settled down, Billy suddenly started talking to me.

"Speaking of money, Art," he said, "we really have to sit down some time and figure out exactly how to get you some."

Before I could reply to this startling announcement, Billy was off on a monologue about exactly how It All Worked, how much he had, where It came from, what form It was in, exactly how much of the income from It he could give away without it costing him much of anything and so forth.

Unfortunately, I wasn't exactly sober at the time myself and I can't recall all the details, but the main theme was the extreme difference between the value of his shares when they were put in trust by the original thieves, who plundered the public weal through the Mining Act of 1872 and similar rip-offs, and their present value, which meant he could give the Church $100,000 at a cost of 40 cents or $40 or $400 or something like that. Something with a four in it.

As Billy gushed on about this fascinating subject, Wendy and I made sincere and appropriate comments of encouragement and interest in the right places, but Miss Lancers was uncharacteristically silent. When we pulled into the circle drive in front of the Bungalow she said, "You live in that place? How come you ride around in this crummy car?" It was my car.

"My Cadillac is in the garage for repairs," Billy replied, with austere dignity. The girl started babbling again. We all went inside. Peggy remembered that she had a present for me. She disappeared down the curving hallway. "You're going to love this!" she shouted. She returned with a gaudy necktie. I think it had a hula dancer on it. I did like it, but the trouble was I didn't own a shirt with a collar to hang it on.

Suddenly, I realized what a bunch of bums we looked like. Miss Lancers was wearing stockings and high heels and all that, but Billy, Peggy, Ron, Wendy and I all looked like we shopped at the Salvation Army. Ron's car happened to be an oldie also. No wonder Miss Lancers was suspicious. She had every reason to believe she was being kidnapped by a gang of psychopathic liars, led by a deranged lecher, who had broken into a house owned by real rich people. Loud voices could be heard coming from the pantry where Billy and Miss Lancers were having another altercation. She refused to believe the house was his.

"Er, I think Wendy and I will go home, Peggy," I said. "I don't want to cramp Billy's act."

The next day I asked Billy how it had all turned out.

"You know what that fucking broad did? She started throwing plates at me! She thought I was hiding my Lancers stash on her or something. That was the craziest broad I have ever gone out with in my life, and I've gone out with some pretty crazy broads."

True enough, but I would call Aurora (and, later, Priscilla also) fine examples of female human nature and neither primarily a gold digger, either. Billy could and did attract the sincere affection of many nice people, myself included.

And the Mellon millions?

"Oh, yeah. I did get off on that subject for a while, didn't I? Listen. I'm definitely going to work it out. It will take a little time but we will definitely do it. Listen, did I mention any figures?"

I nodded solemnly. He had, although I couldn't remember a single one of them and neither, I had determined, could Wendy.

"Well, keep that kind of stuff under your hat, OK? I mean, it's in your interest as much as mine that we should keep the other people around here in ignorance, right?"

Right. Oh, well. Poverty motivates. Poverty strengthens your character, sometimes. Poverty teaches many lessons unobtainable at any other price.

In moderation, poverty may even be good for your health, in that it can force you to simplify your diet, walk instead of ride, cut wood, do all kinds of jobs around the shack, dig slit trenches, drag frozen moose carcasses over the tundra, etc. Even so, when all is said and done, I would trade my poverty for gold at a moment's notice. It may be foolish of me, but there it is.

The score is, let me see here: around $14,000 I guess, plus rental value, free meals, free drinks, free acid, free pot, free nitrous oxide and whatnot. And minus a $10,000 welsh on money owed for business services rendered and another $2,000 or so I blew in the expectation of the maturation of various sterile seeds of hope. For anyone who understands the tax laws of this crazy country, the above accounting will provide a laugh and a half.

Legally, it seems to me, the responsibility of the Hitchcock Cattle Co., and Billy and Tommy as individuals, to compensate everyone rendered economically useless on the property over which they had undisputed governance, is unlimited and virtually eternal as well, because this responsibility should also apply to the progeny of the victims of their machinations.

People who had already rendered themselves unemployable before they got there, such as Leary, Alpert, Metzner, Hollingshead, and so forth, have no grounds for compensation, but my case could well serve as a benchmark for hundreds of other claims. (My not having sued yet shows how crazy I am.) Despite my mescaline trip in '60, when I first set foot on the sacred soil in '63 I was being paid $1,000 a month as a school and clinical psychologist, and when I left I was unemployable, not to mention indictable and committable.

By all of the normal standards which the law recognizes (for which I have an indifferent respect, if any, but what difference does that make?), my life since has been that of a wretched fugitive and helpless derelict, unable to sustain any kind of stable existence or provide security for my dependents, except through activities contrary to the best interests of the military-industrial complex of the American imperium, that is to say, through the cultivation and dispensation of anti-hypnotic, emancipating substances.

I estimate the total amount which Billy and Tommy should be ordered to put in trust for us lunatics and our descendants, not to mention the conversion of the estate into a luxurious asylum for our perpetual maintenance, at \$444,444,444,444.44, which should be just about enough of a hit to put both of them on welfare or into honest jobs as gas station attendants, filling up the tanks of ordinary folks with the best refined that Gulf, or whatever it is calling itself these days, produces, as Billy once claimed to me he would do if ever cleaned out.

All ex-Millbrookians who can show they were functioning economic units before being derobotized for life at the hands of the demonic duo should be compensated with an income of a million a year at the very least, and all of our dependents and descendants likewise, since they ought to be presumed humanized by contagion, and thus rendered incapable of integration into an inhumane society, unto the umpteenth generation.

In those days, we all believed we were part of something new which was of colossal importance and which had developed such a powerful dynamic it could not be suppressed by its natural enemies forever. I still think so. If anyone seemed to forget the enormously important social and historical implications of what we were doing, Tim was always there to remind us of them in the most hyperbolic terminology imaginable.

Many of the conflicts and rivalries between leaders and factions within the Psychedelian community were generated by stupidity, ignorance, infantile jealousy and sometimes downright dementia, but they did have content, usually, and the content isn't trivial at all if one looks forward a few generations and thinks in terms of the eventual outcomes of these conflicts.

Small distinctions at the beginnings of new and important things can lead to vast differences in the institutions and customs which millions of people may have to live with for a long time, whether they like it or not. These institutions and customs may be called "vulgarizations" but what kinds of vulgarizations?

A child born to some kinds must struggle to escape; in others, he is virtually invited to escape.

I put Judaism and Judaical Christianity and Brahmanism in the first category. I put genuine Christianity and genuine Buddhism (not Lamaism) in the second. The different forms of Psychedelianism that we represented at Millbrook may be seen, Fazzm, as variants of these and other classic divisions.

I enjoyed the intramural contests. I did not want to eradicate the differences, but to make them glare forth as a lesson to all.

I could have screwed Tim up in all kinds of ways, particularly in the media. I could have competed directly with Bill in community building and probably emptied the Ashram in a matter of days.

My vanity stopped me. Being a cheat and a spoilsport was not consistent with my image of myself. I didn't want to win by getting rid of the competition. That was Tim's way of doing things. I wanted to win because I was right, and by demonstrating that I was right by making my case and beating the competition to a pulp in print, which seems to me to be a sane and healthy way of looking at things.

Chapter 36

AN ENCOUNTER IN THE DARK

Still, I had one comfort; here was proof that Clarence was still alive and banging away.

One day when Wendy, who was pregnant, was in New York having her hair dyed or her legs waxed or some similar office performed at her mother's expense, I went over to the Bungalow to see what Billy was up to. I found him seated at a wrought iron and glass table next to the swimming pool, looking bored.

It was mid-morning of a fine, breezy, summer's day and the other Bungalowites, Aurora included, were away in New York.

"You're just the maniac I wanted to see, Kleps," Billy said, brightening up considerably at my appearance. "Let's raise a little hell around here, what?"

Do ducks go barefoot in the park?

I made myself a Bloody Mary at the bar between the two dressing rooms at the end of the pool, and joined Billy at the table.

"The way I look at it, what's the use of having a place like this if you can't have any fun in it, what?" Billy asked.

Good point.

Margaret, who was always gracious and composed no matter how crazy things got, appeared with some breakfast for Billy, and asked me if I would like some, too. I said I would, thanks, and told Billy about an invitation, which I had received and accepted the preceding day, to appear on the Alan Burke TV show. Billy was delighted to hear about it, and said he would invite everyone on the property over to the Bungalow to watch the show on his new color set.

"We'll make a party out of it," Billy said. "Too bad you won't be here to enjoy it."

Any excuse would do for a party that summer, as we shall see. While I ate breakfast, I thought of several, and so did Billy.

Priscilla Ashworth. An ex-girlfriend of Ted Druck's, Priscilla, a tall, brown-haired beauty of the Gibson-girl variety, in her late twenties, was visiting the Ashram for a few days. I had met her briefly and had been favorably impressed. Besides being gorgeous, she had that telltale look in her eyes that means a high IQ and a lively sense of humor. I didn't know what kind of relationship she had with Ted, or exactly why she was visiting.

"She sounds like my type," Billy said. "Maybe I can beat Ted's time. All's fair in love and war, what?"

Good, that took care of Billy's gonads. As for my own, there happened to be three unattached "marijuana goddesses" at the Ashram at the time, any one of whom I would gladly have crowned Queen of the May if we had been having Druidical ceremonies in the woods. The notion of ravishing all three of them in a row, in the manner of a traditional Mormon bishop or a king of Israel, entered my head.

"Little Lisa" was eighteen or so, a lithe and lovely raven-haired doll type who, although she looked the picture of virginal innocence, had, so she had told me during a previous brief encounter aborted by my being arrested for not having a helmet while taking her to town on Tord's motorcycle (fine: $50), embarked on a career of dissolute and sensual living at the age of fifteen, as a regular at Bobby Baker's club in Washington, D.C.; the same den of iniquity pointed out to me by the secretary from the Juvenile Delinquency Subcommittee the day before the hearings as a "high old times" kind of place.

Little Lisa seemed to be vaguely attached to the Bhavani-Sarasvati-Susan Shoenfeld axis. She had been sleeping, the last time I noticed, with a sixteen-year-old named Ginger, in a room at the Ashram. Little Lisa might have been somewhat "femme," but during a skinny-dipping party she had demonstrated, to my satisfaction, that she wasn't hostile to the "seed-bearing" faction of the population, at least not in my case.

Ginger, a pretty, strawberry blonde of the standard American type, was, I knew, fighting with her boyfriend, a crazy and violent boy of twenty or so whom Haines seemed to be tolerating because he had a small private income, most of which he was turning over to the Ashram every month. He later split, joined the League in the woods, and became a fake Indian of both continents, a wearer of buckskins and also a worshiper of Yama, the Hindu god of death.

"Big Lisa," an extremely blonde blonde, also sixteen and not so named because she was tall or fat but because she sported a pair of jugs that just wouldn't quit, was a contender. This girl, a daughter of the foremost female leader of the old-fashioned Vedantist contingent in upstate New York at the time, had conned her mother into believing that the Ashram was straight and was actively resisting the evil, drug-soaked influence of Leary and his crew, so that she would be allowed to spend the summer with them as a student. The only virgin around over the age of twelve, Big Lisa got a lot of kidding, particularly when she exchanged a few words with me.

"Watch out for that man, Lisa," Haines boomed on one such occasion. "He likes them young. I don't know how Professor Freud would explain it, but personally I think it's because he's a lousy lay. I have been told as much by people who should know." When I asked for the name of his misinformant, Bill said he was "not at liberty to divulge that information," which he claimed to have received "under seal of the confessional."

When Billy and I had completed our list and a couple joints, a couple drinks, and breakfast, there was no question about how we intended to spend the balance of the day.

"Listen, Art," Billy said, "let's go down to the Ashram and have lunch there. I'll bring some wine and flowering Vietnamese tops that just came in." This was the name given to sinsemilla in those days.

Haines treated Billy's and my activities, such as dispensing wine and joints to one and all, engaging every girl in sight in frivolous banter, and so on, both before and after lunch, which was served outdoors, with increasingly obvious intimations of displeasure. Billy had not been coming up with the kind of contributions to the Ashram he had not been coming up with to the Church, and Bill was primed to explode.

"Well, I hope you boys have enjoyed your free lunch," Haines announced. "But I want you to realize this is a yoga ashram, not the Copacabana." Haines was full of dated references to show biz in the '40s and '50s. He continued in the same vein for several minutes, much to everyone's amusement. At this point in Bill's tirades it was usually possible to interpret the whole thing as a first-class comedy act, and if fuel wasn't added to the fire it would usually remain at that level. The temptation to add fuel to fires is not the easiest one for me to resist. I got a fiver from Billy and handed it to Haines. "To pay for the lunch," I said politely.

Haines got out of his rocker and walked to the center of the rough circle we formed in front of the house. Ceremoniously, he struck a match and burned the five-dollar bill.

He shook his fist at Billy and me.

"That's what I think of cheapskates," Haines bellowed. "And as far as I'm concerned I don't want to see you around here again, Hitchprick, unless you bring your checkbook. And you can take your pimp with you when you leave!"

Haines' attitude toward lewd and lascivious conduct was not as simple as this instance might make it appear. On other occasions, he would dilate at length on how desirable it was for all and sundry to "get laid" and trace the source of all human error and unhappiness to "not getting any." In dealing with relations between the sexes, it often seemed Haines had only one rule: Whatever was happening was wrong. When he was stoned all of this usually evaporated, along with almost every other abrasive characteristic, and Haines, from the viewpoint of his own celibacy, seemed to regard the various sexual and romantic gyrations around him with amused tolerance and sympathetic concern.

Haines, as a personality, bounced up and down in place like a yo-yo from straight to stoned and back to straight again. Stoned,

Bill was a wise and lovable rogue; unstoned, as often as not, he was not much better than a common scold.

With a flick of his robe, Bill swept out of the scene and up the stairs to his room on the second floor. Sheatsley, Ted, and Howie and a couple of others, shaking their heads, went back to work in the press room. The rest of us proceeded down to one of the lakes for a swim.

"What more can one ask?" I asked Billy at one point, as we lounged on a grassy bank sipping wine and smoking the best money could buy while several glistening, jiggling creatures of the female disposition played in the water before our bloodshot eyeballs. "And many a girl with her virgin breasts encircled with gold comes forth to the inward joys of lovely spring," Milton wrote at the age of twenty-one. Good for him.

"Art, I think I'm going to drop out," Billy said. He was serious. He was fed up with New York. Aurora didn't understand him. Millbrook needed him. He only had to go to New York once a week and his job, first at Lehman Brothers and then at Delafield and Delafield, was good for $300,000 a year, but who needed chickenfeed like that? He already had $300,000 a year for being born right. (I'm not sure Billy used these exact words, but "born right," along with "undeserving rich," are idioms which have always appealed to me as suiting the case very well.) He wanted to buy a helicopter, but maybe he could get E-Z payments, and so on and so forth. I think he actually did say "E-Z payment." Billy could be pretty witty, whacked or unwhacked.

During this Lucullan disquisition, other versions of which I had heard before and had come to realize were straightforward presentations of Billy's day-to-day money problems, however bizarre that might seem to those who thought of "money problems" in an entirely different context, Priscilla, who was getting dressed nearby, started giggling instead of freezing up. Most people went blank when they first heard Billy discuss the perplexing economic choices that confronted him. It didn't seem "real," I guess. Was this guy "jerking everyone off," or what?

But Priscilla appreciated the ludicrousness of it all. During all the time I knew her, she took all the unexpected Byzantine twists of plot and improbable combinations of characters that life at

Millbrook and with Billy afforded in a spirit of tolerant and intelligent amusement.

Perhaps, as a student of English literature, Priscilla was able to find a parallel for almost everything that happened in some literary context. So could I, up to a point.

Big Lisa, with whom, by some concatenation of circumstances, I found myself up at the Bungalow along with Billy and Priscilla later in the evening, was a different story. Since her impressions had been produced by the pop Vedantism of her mother, the pop education of the public schools, and a few weeks' exposure to Bill Haines and his crew, I found it hard to imagine what, if anything, was going on in her head.

After Billy and Priscilla disappeared down the curving hallway, leaving Lisa and me sprawled out on the bear rug in front of the fireplace, I found out what I should have known all along: No matter how fantastic the setting or distinguished the company or expensive the drugs, Lisa was not about to come across until she heard a few protestations of undying affection. Things hadn't changed that much. Nothing short of certain key words, which I found it impossible to pronounce, would do the trick.

I would get the traditional booby prizes, and that would be it.

We listened to *Carmina Burana* for a while (the best recording, an old Decca, seems to be out of print) and then I drove Lisa back to the Ashram.

Sure enough, as I had expected, the lights were on in Bill's room. He was waiting up for her.

"Oh, God," Lisa said. "I hope Bill doesn't throw me out. He probably won't believe nothing happened."

I assured Lisa that, if necessary, I would defend her honor by swearing she had repulsed my advances by citing the spiritual teachings she had learned at both the feet of her mother and the pair attached to Bill Haines.

"OK," Lisa said, brightening up considerably. "I'll come down and see you tomorrow morning, right?"

Is the Pope a Catholic on Easter? As I drove down the crumbling, moonlit road to the Gatehouse, I congratulated myself on my sportsmanlike conduct, and anticipated the delightful reward which, it seemed to me, Lisa's parting words suggested that I might enjoy when the sun dawned. Surprised again by "instant karma"!

I parked the car under the shadowy arch of the Gatehouse and got out. Could it be?

Yes, Little Lisa and Ginger were sitting on the steps, with a duffel bag and camping packs beside them.

"My cup runneth over," was all I could think of to say, as I showed them the way to the guest bedroom.

Haines had kicked them out of the Ashram, but they didn't seem terribly worried about it. If I couldn't put them up they would just move out in the woods with the League. I instantly made it clear I was delighted to have them for the night, bears being known to shit in the woods when it's raining, but we would have to discuss a more prolonged invasion with Wendy, who was expected back late the next day.

The precipitating factor in their expulsion, according to Ginger, who, like Lisa, lost no time in getting her clothes off and making herself at home, was the behavior of her ex-boyfriend, David, the Yama lover. He had struck her in a violent rage because she wouldn't let him fuck her anymore. She saw herself as just a typical American teenager who liked to take a lot of dope and screw around, but her boyfriend was on a weird, if common, occultist trip in which he saw her as some kind of evil, but irresistible incarnation of seductive forces which sought to mire his soul in the toils of carnality. She had made him fall in love with her just so she could torture him later, etc.

Nothing she could say would make him believe she just wasn't interested in a "heavy trip" with anyone at that stage of her life. Then, on top of having to contend with that kind of crap, she and Little Lisa were subjected to a constant barrage of obscene insults from Haines, who poked his cane in their crotches and told them to get their "filthy coozes" out of the room while he was talking about yoga, and suggested that they buy bicycles and go to Poughkeepsie to "peddle ass" to contribute to the support of the community.

I laughed, but Little Lisa pointed out that, although it was funny when you told about it later, it wasn't so funny when it was happening.

"How would you like it if someone was always grabbing you by the cock?" Lisa asked, giggling as she suited her actions to her words.

After the orgy, I got the rest of the story. My appearance on the scene with Billy, and the resultant day-long party of skinny dipping, boozing and dope smoking, had apparently set off all kinds of emotional bombs and sent Haines into a frenzy of "house cleaning" during which he had ejected these two charmers and had attempted to throw out David, a paying student, as well. That had convinced everyone that Haines meant business.

When the girls had last seen him, David had been crouched in his room sharpening a knife and threatening all and sundry with bloody murder if they didn't keep their distance. David moved out to the woods a few days later, after I arranged to store his belongings, which he professed to fear Haines would steal, in the basement of the Bungalow.

The next morning I awoke, with a clear head, to a charming scene, a materialization of many a fantasy in my youth: two stark naked girls of my very own, so to speak, dusting the furniture, making breakfast, collating my latest bulletin to the Neo-American membership, and unabashedly assuming as many provocative poses as possible in an enthusiastic spirit of lewd and lascivious cohabitationalism.

There's no use denying it. It isn't true love, but it's nevertheless impossible to place any monetary value on this kind of thing, because it isn't prostitution either. What is it? It's impossible, that's what it is.

"Jesus," I said, as we sat around the table out on the porch, having wine coolers. "Here comes Big Lisa."

Sure enough. Over the brow of the little hill made by the bridge appeared, in a regular series of magnifications and escalations as her steps brought her both closer and higher, Big Lisa in all her splendor, wearing a bikini, sandals and nothing else.

When she got upstairs, Big Lisa put a good face on the matter. She may have been relieved to find her intentions, which I'm pretty sure did not involve an audience, frustrated. She hung around for a while, told us the latest developments of the great purge, which did not involve her, since Haines had expended his animosity on much more serious malefactors, and then left, after politely declining my invitation to doff her bikini and join the group.

"Boy, those people up there are going to flip when they hear about this scene," Ginger said. Ginger held a low opinion of Haines and of most of his followers as well.

"So will Wendy," added Little Lisa, not one to beat around the bush.

Yes, much as I hated to think about it, certain questions were begging to be answered. Exactly what the hell did I think I was doing? Wendy was pregnant. To the best of my knowledge, she was devoid of the bisexual inclinations which would have made a ménage à quatre possible.

If I insisted on the girls staying, Wendy would leave, and it would make her unhappy. Also, I would miss her. She wasn't the greatest passion of my life, but I loved Wendy in my fashion, and Little Lisa and Ginger would forget the whole incident fifteen minutes after reaching Lunacy Hill. In fact, they would probably forget their own names and nationalities within fifteen minutes after reaching Lunacy Hill.

On the other hand, here was the solution to the stalemate on the property, jiggling around right in front of my eyes. My seraglio was at hand! I could turn the place into a kind of girls' dorm.

Millionaires by the dozens would flock to the banner of the three-eyed toad! With solid financial backing for a change, the Neo-American Church would reign supreme as the Great Whore of Babylon, just as foretold in the Scriptures. I loved the image. Wendy was the only problem.

When Wendy returned, she coolly surveyed the scene with a tight smile and narrowed eyes. The girls had dressed, and their belongings were in the downstairs room that I used as an office. "I would like to let these devoted and industrious parishioners move in, Wendy," I said. "What do you say? They can help you with the dishes and cleaning and whatnot besides doing church work."

"No," Wendy said flatly. "It's either me or them. Take your pick."

"Sorry kids," I said.

"Oh well, I guess we'll go live in the woods with the League," Little Lisa said, picking up her pack. "I think you're wrong, Wendy. We could have had a lot of fun together."

"Yeah, I bet," Wendy said. She started rattling pans around in the kitchen. "I don't want to discuss it. Just go away."

And that was the end of that one.

(The phrase "that one" was used constantly at Millbrook to refer to any episode, argument or game which presented a coherent conceptual organization, and was most often employed as I have employed it here—in dismissal. "That ones," one might say, were the great benchmarks of our social existence.)

This abrupt termination of my efforts to broaden my horizons while lightening Wendy's domestic obligations by two thirds at least, didn't cause resentment to burn in my breast or anything like that. What the hell. A few thousand years in the past, Wendy might have beaten off similar assailants on the family cave with the jawbone of an ass, if necessary. It was all too elemental to complain about.

But my failure to take the matter seriously went to her head. One would have thought I had given her a license to kill.

I was taking a bath one afternoon when I heard, indistinctly, more than one feminine voice in the hall. Jean Lewis and her sister, Meg? No shit? Far out!! I turned off the tap and shouted that they should make themselves at home. I would be right out.

When I emerged, after maybe five minutes, neither Jean nor Meg was anywhere in sight.

What the hell?

"Where did they go?" I asked Wendy. "I don't know. They didn't tell me," Wendy answered, in her most plonking tones.

Probably went for a walk, I thought. I hung around the bridge for a while and surveyed the lovely landscape from the tower. I could hardly wait to see Jeannie again. Should old acquaintance be forgot? I wanted to show her off to Billy and Bill, who were capable of appreciating the finer gradations of the finer things. Jeannie, besides having a kind heart, intelligence, good taste and genuine curiosity about all manner of things, possessed an irrepressible, effortless, almost solemn, whimsicality (Nancy and

Jessica Mitford come to mind), a trait which suited life at Millbrook perfectly.

Hell, even Bali would have liked her.

My favorite '50s-style paragon and her kid sister never showed up, and I didn't learn until much later that Wendy had given them, as Otto would have put it, the "big freeze."

This pissed me off a lot, when I found out about it. I then learned, through Noel Tepper of all people, that Meg was living with her current admirer on a small farm near the estate. We went to visit. It was a goat farm, that is to say, a tax dodge. Let us draw the curtain on this beastly scene.

Let's draw the curtain on the Jean Valier scene which followed also (although, if this were a commercial book, I wouldn't). Two Jeans and a Meg sacrificed to the green-eyed monster, and Wendy's career as a big time doe hunter had just gotten off the ground.

Millbrook was recognized by all who lived there as a mother of misalliances, to such an extent that it became a standard comedy routine to speculate on which improbable disassortive mating would be next. Endless Fazzm theories may be advanced as to the whys and wherefores.

Psychedelianism tends to make people more tolerant of the failings and faults of others, up to a point. In general, the variations of human nature seem amusing instead of threatening. Wendy and I, one might say, had both gone on vacation from our normal stamping grounds when we had shacked up together. At the same time, psychedelic experience acts as a powerful bonding agent and, if you are so inclined, an aphrodisiac. And, in my experience, if and when you do hit it right on a trip, putting the resultant alliance asunder is almost impossible, no matter what.

All Psychedelian communities should seriously consider term marriages. They are permissible in the OKNeoAC.

Chapter 37

AN AWFUL PREDICAMENT

Sleep? It was impossible.

In late June, I invited Tord Svenson to move into the third floor of the Gatehouse and he promptly accepted. After a reorganization of his company, he had suddenly found himself out on his ear. His former employer, a right-wing libertarian, had told the FBI to shove it when they called to voice their apprehensions about the notorious Keeper of the Divine Toad of the Neo-American Church being allowed to work for a living, but New England Nuclear, the new owner, saw the matter in a different light. When Billy heard about it, he seemed greatly amused.

"What's so funny?" Tord asked. We were all breakfasting on the porch on perch I had caught in the lake that morning.

"You're going to love this one, Art," Billy said. "Guess who owns stock in New England Nuclear? Tim Leary. I bought him in just a month or two ago."

Was that so? Maybe Haines wasn't so crazy after all. Nobody was buying me stock in New England Nuclear or anything else.

"Listen, Billy ..." I started to say.

Billy waved his hands as if brushing away flies. He knew what I was going to say. I shouldn't worry. He had all kinds of plans. He had to work out a tax deductible way of doing it.

OK. I changed the subject.

Tord, from the beginning, was bemused and morally offended by the feudal realities of life at Millbrook. His Scandinavian, populist principles were constantly violated right in front of his eyes. Every day, after visiting around the property, Tord would return to the Gatehouse with hilarious reports of a new outrage of Tim's or Bill's he had witnessed, but his sense of humor abandoned him when it came to the Bungalow and its inhabitants. Those pills were too fat to swallow. As we shall see, Tord's social ideology eventually proved stronger than his psychedelic experience.

Tord remained in contact with Lisa Bieberman, although she had viciously and unfairly attacked Tim and me in her Psychedelic Information Center Bulletin. When The Group Image and a couple other egalitarian primitivist "tribes" moved into the round barns in the woods at Tim's invitation later in the summer, Tord identified with their attitudes more than he did with mine, Tim's or Bill's, although he had to admit that these groups were composed, generally, of stupid slobs and led by bumptious oafs.

If the place had lasted, I think Tord would have developed into a natural leader of a group of somewhat higher-class egalitarians on the property, which would have been interesting and OK with me. As for my philosophic conviction that all of my experience was a hallucination and that was that, Tord, once he caught on, didn't want to hear any more about it.

"I know what you think, Art," he would say, cutting me off when the subject came up, "but I just can't buy it. Don't you realize it's completely insane?"

This reaction did not make me angry. At least Tord saw what was involved, and didn't give me the usual song and dance about how right I was, followed by a demonstration that not a word I had said had penetrated.

The 2,000 *Catechisms* came back from the Roman Catholic monastery across the Hudson, where Haines had sent them to be bound. Without commenting on the contents of the monstrously heretical document in their hands, the monks had done a good job. And they had done it with cheerful demeanors to boot, Haines maintained. If so, good for them. It's been my general experience that you never can tell about monks.

Now the *Alan Burke Show* had to be dealt with. It was a clone of the *Joe Pyne Show* in Los Angeles, with New York characters instead of Californians.

Purveyors of outlandish doctrines of all kinds were invited to appear and then subjected to their host's ridicule. An on-screen exchange which occurred between Paul Krassner, the editor-author of *The Realist,* and Joe Pyne, a fascistic lunatic, who happened to have a wooden leg, demonstrates the spirit of these productions:

> Pyne: Tell me, Mr. Krassner, do those acne scars of yours bother you much?
>
> Krassner: Not much. Tell me, Joe, I have always wondered, do you take off your wooden leg before you make love to your wife?

The decorous conventions which applied to exchanges in Senatorial hearings did not apply.

I went up to the Big House, where Tim still maintained an office and a bedroom. Although he and Rosemary had an expensive tent on Lunacy Hill and the best camping gear money could buy, they spent a lot of time, including sack time, at the Big House. This didn't go over very well among his followers, whom Tim had firmly rusticated, rain or shine, or worse, under intermittent drizzles from sullen skies, beneath plastic tarps and mildewed canvas for the entire summer.

(I have one piece of advice for any readers who may find themselves, through necessity or by design, tenting out for any protracted period of time: Make a platform. One can usually find scrap plywood and two-by-fours at the local dump or a construction site. Ask around. If necessary, make the platform in sections and bolt them together. Support it with as many bricks or cinder blocks or empty paint cans as you can find or transport, but make it level and raise it off the ground. A flat, level, stable floor under a tent makes all the difference in the world.)

I found Tim, spic and span as usual, in his spacious, elegant room and at his desk, typing away with a jug of burgundy at his side. He seemed undisturbed to hear that I would be on TV again, and pleased that I had come to him for advice.

"Smoke a joint to make you high, Arthur," he said, "and take some speed because it will make you feel good. Stay away from booze. That's what I always do."

Old rope trick? I don't think so. It was excellent advice. Tim wasn't always "on the job," so to speak, and we were genuinely fond of each other, sort of, each after his own fashion. And this conversation was private.

Wendy, Tord and I drove down to the city in Tord's old Citroen. Wendy's parents, whom I hadn't met, were out of town, but we would use their apartment to get ready and to watch the show later. One of Tord's jobs was to round up some speed from one of our members in New York. I had to buy some clothes. Mike Duncan had called, and I had invited him and Gai, who were now married, to come over to the apartment to watch the show.

Wendy's parents' apartment, which overlooked the Planetarium on the Museum of Natural History grounds, was just what I had expected, based on Wendy's descriptions. It was hard to believe that anyone actually lived in the place, which closely the resembled the "rooms" of furniture set up in department stores. There wasn't a book in sight, except for some kid stuff in Wendy's old room. They meant well. Just ignorant, that's all.

After I had taken it all in, Wendy said, "Well, maybe now you understand me better."

Her tales of life at the old homestead had been chilling my bones for some time, but she was right, one picture was worth a thousand words. It was incredibly impersonal and cold.

Wendy's father had just concluded a deal with Sears Roebuck to sell them his shirt factory in South Carolina for a flat $1,000,000. They planned to sell the apartment and move to Palm Beach in a year or so, which they did, after first going to England to buy a white Rolls Royce. All very innocent. I never felt any serious hostility from either one of them, or very much of anything else either.

Before we entered the studio, I absorbed a joint, as Tim had recommended, and bought two miniature bottles of brandy. I was nervous as a squirrel, and since I was cold sober, it seemed to me that one or two nips wouldn't make me unintelligible.

While we were standing around in the lobby with Tord waiting for our contact to appear, the "personality" who would precede me as a "guest" swept through, surrounded by her entourage. It was Dagmar, the big-boobed girl of the *Jerry Lester Show* from the early days of TV. The receptionist had just told us Dagmar would go on before I did.

"Well, what does that mean, Art?" Tord giggled, as this apparition swept by.

"It's obvious, Tord," I replied. "She represents the past and I represent the future."

Tord groaned, then cackled.

Our boy showed up and handed me a folded paper. When I asked him what it was, he said, "Never mind, just snort it. I guarantee you won't have a worry in the world five minutes later."

OK. We went up to the guest waiting room and sat down. There was a monitor on the wall. Dagmar came on. Babble, babble. As I had been prior to the Senate hearings, I was so nervous I couldn't understand a word of what was being said. I was out of touch.

I went to the men's room and snorted the pinch of white powder in the paper and then downed both bottles of brandy. When I was directed into the studio during the intermission to take my chair, Burke had disappeared, probably for his own favored refreshments. I had to sit there for a while, silently staring at the audience, which contained a grinning Tord and a winking Wendy.

Burke came in and introduced himself. As soon as he did, I got the same sensation of being slightly lifted up in the air that I had felt just before the Senate appearance. I chatted merrily away with Burke as if we were neighbors meeting at the corner bar. After I had concluded an amusing anecdote, Burke suddenly looked apprehensive.

"Listen, Art. I don't know if you're familiar with the format here, but I should warn you. Have you ever seen this show?"

"Sure," I said. "It's simple. The guest gets advertising at the price of blood, right?"

Burke looked even more dismayed than he had originally.

"Well, I guess you could say that, but it isn't always that way."

As soon as the interview got rolling, it became obvious that

I had charmed Burke. The guy simply liked me and he couldn't do anything about it. His attempts at insults turned into twisted compliments. My cause was bad, but he had to "admit" I was an "attractive person, and an effective missionary for what you believe in," as he said at one point.

Later, Tord told us that two old ladies behind him in the audience had been deeply offended by the entire proceedings, particularly the breaks, when Burke and I, obviously not angry with each other over the sharp words we had exchanged about the issue at hand, engaged in friendly conversation off the mike. "Look at that. They're laughing together. This whole show is a fake!" he reported one of these venerable vultures saying to another.

Meat Hook, deranged as ever, was in the audience by special invitation. He initiated the question and answer period at the end of the show by citing "scientific" research results of the "of 13 alcoholic, junkie-prostitute speed freaks who smoked an ounce of hashish a day for 13 years, seven reported feeling nauseous" or, "of 47 stark-naked human chromosomes hosed down with a solution of LSD and Drano, 42 were wounded, and five gave up the ghost" variety.

Following this recitation of the latest hokum, Baird delivered his standard line of paranoid, rambling, and frequently incoherent denunciations of all who dared to touch anything not blessed and thus sanctified by the American Medical Association, as he, Meat Hook, had been. Bishop Fulton Sheen, whose crazy sermons were televised in the '50s, may well have been Meat Hook's model and inspiration. (Offhand, I can't think anyone else in the same class. "Fundamentalist" TV preachers don't even come close.)

I called upon "our chemist," Tord, to reply with his analysis of the scientific evidence on the subject, which Tord did with great aplomb, causing a minor sensation also, I suspect, because of the contrast between his learned mini-lecture and his appearance, highlighted that day by a light-blue, fluffy, synthetic fabric vest, which didn't close over his broad chest. He probably impressed some members of the audience as a Viking throwback, intent on new crimes even more dreadful than those practiced by his notorious ancestors.

As for Baird, who for years ran a "cold turkey" drug clinic in Harlem and once told a reporter he thought all "drug pushers" (any kind of drug not controlled by the AMA, and in any amount) ought to be "hung from a meat hook, live," my calling him "deranged" is not just an idle insult. I mean it the way I meant it in the old days, when I had to make everyone understand that the kid or prisoner or patient in question was not merely peculiar but seriously nuts.

Later, Carl and Bernie told me Meat Hook had told them, in describing the way he ran his drug clinic in Harlem, that he didn't "fool around with these characters." He took them to a darkened back room and examined their cocks by the light of a candle to make sure no drugs were concealed under foreskins. He also sang the *Star Spangled Banner* at football games, my favorite sidelight on this incredibly demonic personality. With enemies like Meat Hook, one might ask, who needed friends?

The show had been taped for later broadcast. Back at the apartment, I had the narcissistic pleasure of watching myself on television for the first time. It seemed to me I had done OK, and everyone else thought so too. In fact, I was warmly congratulated by one and all at Millbrook. Billy said that the party at the Bungalow had been a big success. Sam, who attended, wanted to know if he could buy a film of the show for the edification of his guests in the Caribbean.

Tim was astonished. "I didn't think you could do it, Art," he admitted, and then told me a story about how a Vassar girl he had met on a train the next day had bent his ear about me. She wouldn't believe I was in my late thirties. I had looked about twenty-three on the tube, she said. That impressed Tim, who later walked off a TV show when the interviewer told him he looked old.

I was saddened to learn, however, that my pet crow, Swami, tenderly raised from infancy at the Gatehouse, and left at the Ashram while we were away, where he ordinarily played raucously and happily with the cats (a fast peck at the tail, and a strutting retreat) had kicked the bucket and joined the choir during our absence, after taking a short snort of Al Bonk's ceramic glaze. In Arizona, Bill shot Wendy's cat, Trenton, daughter of Philadelphia, whom Wendy had left at the Ashram when we went to Vermont. The sinister implications of these events, I am happy to say, have not preyed on my mind much ever since.

When things at Millbrook started falling apart, so did my public performances. Tim's original estimate of my ability along these lines ("unreliable") was not far off the mark. Tim had the same problem.

On one show we watched at the Ashram, Tim, eyes glittering, seemed to be a virtual superhuman manifestation of pure intelligence and truth, laying waste the opposition's arguments like an avenging angel. On another, a "Playboy Penthouse Show" or something like that, he came off like a rambling, disconnected old man incapable of reading a timetable. It all depended on "where his head was at" that day.

As our Psychedelian community withered under the attack of the Sado-Judeo-Paulinian mind police, my interest and willingness to participate in these inherently corruptive rituals rapidly waned and then vanished. I was never good at it. Those levitations were a lift, sort of, but I now look down on them.

Chapter 38

SIR LAUNCELOT AND KNIGHTS TO THE RESCUE

We were being made a holiday spectacle.

The next great scene at Millbrook was the Fourth of July party of 1967. Every Psychedelian resident of the estate was invited to the Bungalow. Fireworks! Music by the Grateful Dead and Aluminum Dreams! Girls in hootchy-kootchy costumes! Many guests were expected from the upper reaches of New York stoned society.

Liberty forever! Equality and Fraternity, to my way of thinking, did not ring with the same clear note, but what the hell, to each his own poison. The general mood at Millbrook was still too stoned, despite our quarrels, to poop parties. Most of us, most of the time, saw our differences as entertainment and variety rather than sedition or subversion. We were all, after all, Psychedelians, and our enemies had not yet stormed the gates in force. We still lived in a pleasant little world we could honestly call our own, and most of us were determined to enjoy it.

Joe Gross, the psychiatrist who had joined the Church in Miami, showed up early in the day with Cathy Elbaum, a thin blonde of thirty or so, who had vague connections in the publishing world and with Sam and Martica Clapp. Joe, who had already visited once or twice, was in his usual state of confusion and apprehension over the coming festivities. He had not yet taken LSD, although he "believed in it," and couldn't make up his mind whether or not to take the plunge at the party.

Everything about Joe was confused and contradictory. A Gemini, he was alternately or simultaneously on both sides of every question, but never genuinely committed to anything. He hated New York, but lived there because his mother, with whom he had dinner twice a week, did. It was a standard case of the Jewish mother's relentless grip so well-publicized in song and story.

Still a bachelor in his late thirties, he was strongly attracted only to women he couldn't get: young, blonde, preferably Scandinavian girls whom he would spot on the streets and who would invariably "disappear" when he followed them. The ones he could get, and there was a constant parade, were all smartasses as crazy as he was who would inevitably muck up his mind. Whenever he could manage it, he would take trips to Scandinavia and Canada in search of his ideal, but "something" always went wrong.

Joe's living arrangements illustrated the stark dualities which seemed to afflict every aspect of his life. His office, in the penthouse of 4 East 89th, overlooking the park and the Guggenheim Museum, was a little disorderly but comfortable and warm. Most of his patients were on Medicaid. Joe couldn't refuse anyone with any kind of sob story, and the word had spread.

His apartment, a few doors down the street, was cold, barren and dirty. No curtains, no rugs and no furniture except two inflatable plastic chairs and a huge, round bed that was never made.

Considering all the other incongruities in his life, it probably seemed natural to Joe that he should join the Neo-American Church and hang around with me and the other Millbrookians but never take any of the stuff that was the point of it all, except a little grass now and then, which, he said, always made him "feel paranoid."

If you "feel paranoid" every now and then you are almost certainly not a paranoid, at least not in any serious way. Meat Hook, I'm pretty sure, never "felt paranoid" in his life.

Joe, in the language of the day, was always "going on his patients' trips." Many of them must have thought he was faking approval of their enthusiasms for professional reasons, but those of us who knew him well knew he wasn't. Every time I saw him he seemed to have new favorites: a guy who was "into" the Kabala, a girl who was "into" Sokka Gakkai, food nuts, sex nuts, spiritualists, flying saucer telepathic communicationists. The list seemed endless. It is endless.

Joe looked his part, too. He resembled a bearded and soiled version of the Pop'n Fresh dough man in the TV commercials, with thick glasses, and usually had an expression of diffident, quizzical acceptance on his pleasant face. Joe wanted to understand. He assumed everyone knew something important he didn't. Unfortunately, as is often the case with nice guys, he was also afraid that he would turn into a ravening monster if he took acid, and perhaps murder his mother and rape the nearest Scandinavian blonde, or vice versa.

While Cathy and Joe were dressing for the party, Wendy took me aside and confided a deep, dark secret. She and Joe had decided to take "lots of tranquilizers" as soon as the festivities commenced. Since neither Wendy nor Joe could drink the way I did and remain upright, they both thought that this expedient might "allow them" to get "as stoned" as I did. Could be. It stands to reason that anything disinhibiting will encourage boosting to the point where dosage doesn't really matter anymore, which was my standard pattern. What, me worry?

Tord and Joe instantly hit it off. Joe was fascinated by Tord's nonchalance. Tord was planning on taking 40 milligrams of STP for the party. And the Keeper of the Divine Toad, who loved nothing better than a session of what might be called superficial depth analysis, was delighted to rake over his various theories about the Millbrook scene and its leading lights with a professional shrink. Wendy enjoyed this indoor sport also. I left them happily maundering away at the Gatehouse and went up to the Bungalow to help the Hitchcocks with the preparations.

Charlie Rumsey, who would have died a thousand deaths if he had missed anything like this, was on hand, and I helped him prepare several pitchers of the Supreme Sacrament in the pantry off the dining room before Suzanne dragged me off to help her hang up paper streamers.

Charlie, "that flunky" who didn't show up at the "get my furniture back" meeting, was an old buddy of Billy's and became, for a while, a frequent companion of mine also. While still in his early twenties, Charlie, an offshoot of the Harriman family, which had a nice little place down river from the Place of Overflowing Shitholes, had become well known in New York for treating the daughters of wealthy families to safaris in Africa, and for heavy gambling on sporting events. He seriously depleted his income with such adventures, and then, in an effort to recoup, lost the farm in cranberry futures. The year's crop he happened to bet on was banned by the feds as too poisoned by pesticides to be marketed. He had enough left over from this debacle, however, to maintain a roomy apartment in New York and live the fabled "playboy" life without recourse to onerous employment.

When the Psychedelian Age dawned, "Champagne Charlie" came into his own. Although the general public never heard of him, he became as famous among the rich of New York as Dr. Jake. If Charlie supplied one's sacraments, one could be sure that they were the best available, and that the vanguard of the jet set was stoned on the same stuff, a clincher sales point. Charlie knew "everybody" and "everybody" knew Charlie.

Psychedelianism will truly have triumphed on the day when the sun's early light dawns in Central Park on a statue of Charlie, a characteristically impish smile creasing his boyish face, eternally pouring a glass of fortified bubbly for Human Nature Itself, as it were. It could and should be done. The wealthy children and grandchildren who did not inherit familial sociopathy because Charlie was on call when he was needed ought to feel an obligation to do it in remembrance of their spiritual father.

"Hey, Charlie," Billy asked at one point, "can you think of anyone else we should invite?"

"How about Hunt?" Charlie immediately suggested. "I already invited Cathy."

Cathy Hartford, who later became a dedicated missionary bee

hee of the Church and Transultrametasuperpanhypersebastocrator of the Virgin Islands, was Huntington Hartford's eighteen-year-old daughter.

"But he never turns on," Billy objected.

"Well?" Charlie asked, with a wink in his voice.

"Right," Billy said, after biting his fingernails for a moment or two. He made the call. Sure enough. Good old Hunt would try to make it.

By the time the outside guests started arriving, we were mostly zonked. Wendy, wearing her "ecstatic clothes," had come up with Tord on his motorcycle, but Tord, at someone's suggestion, had gone back down to the front gate to give people directions to the Bungalow. Peggy, who had just arrived from the city, approached me with a cross expression on her face.

"Who is that awful man down at the gate?" she wanted to know.

I explained that the awful man was my buddy Tord, Keeper of the Divine Toad, and that he was under the influence of 40 milligrams of STP, despite everything I had said to warn him off the stuff. Peggy was mollified, but not by much.

She had come up in a regular car with friends in informal attire who would don their costumes at the Bungalow. The driver had stopped to ask Tord how things were going.

"Oh, the usual with these rich bastards," Tord had replied. "They're all wearing costumes and showing off for each other and everyone's stoned out of his gourd. Just go up and help yourselves to whatever you want. Eat the rich!"

From a factual standpoint, this was pretty accurate, but the tone was wrong.

"Give him hell when you see him later, Peggy," I said. "There's no excuse for that kind of stuff. If Tord finds all of this so distasteful he shouldn't be living here."

Later in the evening I saw Peggy wagging her finger in Tord's face, followed by an intense exchange of views, followed by an embrace. So much for class warfare when one is plummeting through the *Mysterium Tremendum* and encounters another plummet. Compared to the plummeting, nothing else matters much.

I found Joe next to the swimming pool, holding a weak highball, looking like a lost sheep, standing out like a sore thumb, being a specter at the feast, and so forth. He was surveying a throng of costumed merrymakers (Billy was a turbaned pasha, Aurora a harem dancer) with undisguised bewilderment. Nothing Joe did was ever disguised.

His incomprehension arose from seeing almost everyone present knocking back cups of acid-spiked punch and then dancing, talking, laughing and swimming around in the pool as if they were enjoying themselves.

That's what bothered Joe. If we had been wandering around pontificating in unknown tongues while pointing to non-existent objects in the sky, Joe would not have been worried. If we had stripped off our garments and fallen into a writhing heap of anybody-fuckers, he would have accepted this as explicable, and likewise if we had all squatted down and examined our navels for hidden mantras, or whatever.

He would have been impressed, but I don't think he would have freaked out, if we had all sprouted wings and flown away cackling like geese, but to see everyone happily chatting away and bouncing around as people usually do at a good party profoundly violated his preconceptions. Joe was out front about it, as always. Looking particularly sheepish, he said, "You know what I want to know, Art? You aren't going to believe this."

"What?"

"What are they all talking about?"

Exactly. It was, after all, not a frame of mind with which I was entirely unfamiliar. Despite my mescaline trip, when I first visited Millbrook I assumed the residents knew all kinds of important things I didn't know.

Joe thought of psychedelic experience as synonymous with visionary experience. He thought he could imagine what it would be like. He would have hallucinations, or something similar, which meant he would be psychotic, or something similar, for a while, and perhaps forever.

All the nice things Psychedelians told him faded away before this vivid and alarming concept.

It followed from this that the more trips we took, the more

territory, so to speak, we covered, and so we would accumulate information in pretty much the same way lonely lechers would accumulate information on visits to Copenhagen to chase blondies. We would have quite an accumulation of information to pore over with other visitors to the same places.

The uninitiated would not be welcome at such discussions. That was why Joe was standing there all by himself. He didn't want to intrude on the "mysteries," which everyone who knew about them seemed to treat so lightly, thereby making them seem even more mysterious.

I took a pill from my pocket.

"Joe, will you for Christ's sake take one of these things and forget about all that shit?"

"What shit?" Joe wanted to know.

"Oh, all those unfounded speculations. You don't know what you're thinking about, or, to put it another way, I know what you are thinking about better than you do."

Joe was horrified. Was I reading his mind? But after a lot of heavy drug pushing from me, he finally swallowed half the pill.

I couldn't stay with him because Billy had asked me to spell Jack and Jimmy at the bar while they prepared the fireworks. I ducked out half an hour later to check and found Joe standing in the same spot and looking at the crowd with the same expression, except now his pupils were dilated.

"How's it going, Joe?" I asked.

"Well, how do you manage things sexually?" he asked.

"What do you mean?" I asked, genuinely startled.

"Oh, you know, how do you decide who gets who?"

In my condition, I couldn't take it. I went back to the bar after saying, "Oh, come on, Joe, relax," and patting him on the back.

Why should I go on Joe's bad trip? Do the strictures of decent and honorable pastoral conduct include a responsibility to wrestle with the bummers produced by people you have turned on? On the one hand it would seem so, and on the other hand it would seem not. By paying attention to it, you imply it's worthy of your attention and if it's worthy of your attention, it's worthy of the attention of the nervous wreck who came up with it in the first place.

On the other hand, if you don't pay attention, your behavior may be interpreted as callous indifference and cause resentment and bad feeling all around. Tim usually did what I had done with Joe, and I think he was right. Make some gesture of friendliness and play the whole thing down.

Joe's trip confirmed him as a true Psychedelian, instead of someone who "believes in it" the way some people believe in the Angel Moroni, but it did not bring about any major changes in his style of life or way of thinking. While I knew him, he remained an extremely eclectic supernaturalist, and continued to hope and grope for pie in the sky, as did almost everyone else.

"What do you want?" I asked him one time.

"I want to see a miracle," Joe replied.

Exactly. He wanted confirmation of the beliefs he already held, and had held since childhood. Joe didn't want to change. No, far from it.

I could urge Joe to discard his preconceptions and keep an open mind, but there was no way I could do it for him or even teach him how to do it. In order to relax and enjoy himself, rather than manufacture and multiply an endless series of pseudo-problems and quasi-solutions, Joe would have to combat his own repetition compulsion, and transform himself. Aside from all the supportive, tolerant and friendly people around him, Joe had a magic kingdom, Millbrook, he could visit where a magic potion, LSD, was available and there was even a magic book, the *I Ching*, to assist him in this noble project. The fact was that Joe had more miraculous help available than he needed.

A wholesale transformation is only possible when one is willing to start over completely with a clean slate, and few people have any genuine desire to do it. The enemy is always the repetition compulsion. Nothing new will ever happen to anyone who always knows what to expect.

The fireworks display, something I had never witnessed before on a trip, was everything the various light shows then becoming popular tried to be but weren't: absorbing, dazzling, "mind blowing." The after images were just as good as the originals. As soon as it was over, the bands began to play. I alternately danced and tended bar. Bali Ram and Aurora put on an exhibition of fancy dancing on the porch by the flashing light of a strobe, and it wasn't long before Charlie and I had to mix up a couple new pitchers of refreshments.

People kept pouring in the front door, including the Hartfords and friends, and I was delighted when Jack appeared to take over the bar. It was more fun to wander around with a pitcher and top off all the drinks standing around. Things were taking on that timeless quality. Various tableaux developed and faded to be replaced by others. Three girlfriends of Wendy's showed up from the city, and we showed them to the first bedroom suite, which was being used as a coat room. I could see they were terrified out of their wits by the scene they had just passed through.

Wendy tried to reassure them.

"Where's the acid, Arthur?" she asked me. "These girls have never had anything stronger than grass."

"It's all in the glass pitchers. Just stick to drinks out of bottles at the bar and you won't have any problems," I said to the trio of wide-eyed Jewish princesses. "Tell you what, I'll go and get you some grass." I went off in search of Billy, whom I found in his bedroom, talking to Charlie. A misunderstanding had developed. Hunt had just told Charlie he was barred from Paradise Island for life. Hunt, although he no longer owned the island in the Bahamas outright, apparently still had enough control over it so he could bar people who had offended him.

"He accused me of giving acid to Cathy," Charlie said. "The unbelievable thing is I didn't give her any. She didn't trust ours, so she brought her own. I couldn't tell Hunt that."

"Well, is she freaking out or anything?" Billy wanted to know.

"No, nothing like that," Charlie said. "She's probably had more trips than anyone in the room. She's just stoned out of her gourd, that's all. But so is everyone else here except Hunt. He won't even let Jack pour his drinks for Christ's sake."

Hunt remained the odd man out all night. He would step into rooms where stoned gatherings were taking place, and simply stand there, rigid, glaring balefully. Then he would suddenly wheel around and march out again. This performance, once people got used to it, caused gales of hilarity. According to Billy, he was "always that way," which I found hard to believe.

At an entirely different kind of stoned party in California, which I attended eighteen months later with Charlie, Cathy and two of her girlfriends, Cathy told me what I thought was an interesting story.

Just before the Hartford party left the Fourth of July party, someone had managed to bomb Hunt's highball with a small dose. A few miles down the Taconic, Hunt, who was sitting up front next to his chauffeur-bodyguard-companion, had suddenly swung around and said to the stoned kids in the back seat, "You know, those people were really having fun up there. Maybe we should go back."

"I've never heard him say anything like that in my life," Cathy said. Unfortunately, the chauffeur talked him out of it. Hunt's chauffeur, everyone said, was also his closest friend. Too bad, indeed. When I had been introduced to Hunt by Billy, I had immediately said, by way of openers, "Listen, why don't you give Paradise Island to the Neo-American Church?" He had immediately disappeared in front of my eyes. If he had returned and taken a large blast, who knows? Maybe he would have paid the necessary bribes, gotten his bridge, and saved the family fortune. The guy he really needed to talk to was Sam.

That later party in California was a classic of the paranoid-occultist genre, and worth describing. The place where it was held was called Harbingers, home to a group of 100 or so classic California Slobovenoid Blobovenoidalist simpletons led by a visionary occultist who claimed that his entire home state would fall into the sea any day now, that he was communicating with flying saucers and his unborn child, and so forth.

A Narad type, and a tarot-cards kind of guy, he had made several tapes explaining his system. Joe had the complete set and thought they were wonderful. The group had published one edition of a newspaper named *Harbingers* which was highly thought of on the West Coast. Formerly a hot springs resort, the setting was ideal for a party. At least 500 people showed up.

The idea was that the Harbinger people, by "getting their heads together" and "sending out the right vibrations" and "calling on the powers of the group mind," or whatever, would in one night bring all the rest of us, which included almost every

Psychedelian power on the West Coast as well as straight representatives of government and academia, over to their way of thinking. They would show us where it was "really at." It didn't quite work out that way, or in a way, it did. At that party, Joe Gross' expectations would have been gratified. It rained in slashing, thunderous downpours all night. The place was raided, and in the ensuing panic, one person was killed and another injured in auto accidents. The leader's wife miscarried, and it turned out the fetus had been dead for some time, which instantly disproved everything he had been saying about his telepathic powers.

All of us were held for hours in whatever room we were occupying at the time of the raid, while a search was conducted. Only two people were arrested, however. The cops, believing the Kool-Aid to be safe because they saw ten-year-olds drinking it, had helped themselves while they stood watching naked couples cavorting around the dining room demonstrating their liberation from sexual inhibitions, as was then the fashion on the West Coast. Those cops who indulged quickly became, from the viewpoint of law and order, part of the "problem" instead of part of the "solution." There were 500 boo hoo blacks in the Kool-Aid I knew about. Half a cup had elevated me nicely.

During the chaos, Charlie managed to escape with Cathy and one of her friends, Cynthia Hoag, but the other girl and I were trapped in a wood-frame dormitory with about fifty other people all night. Since she was seventeen and closely resembled Deanna Durbin at the same age, I didn't really mind. All three of these girls had signed up as bee hees when Charlie had brought them over to meet me. But it was a horror-show production, and we were both happy when we were able to hitch a ride to Sausalito in the morning.

Every occultist-supernaturalist group I knew about which attempted to integrate the use of LSD into its communal delusional system self-destructed like Harbingers, although not in such a dramatic fashion. They disintegrate because psychedelic experience cannot be made to conform to consensual expectations or indoctrination or peer pressure. Set and setting are important because they can make things easy or difficult, but they are not determinant, which is one of the great virtues of psychedelic experience.

Nobody can control it.

In terms of pre-Psychedelian religious traditions, once Haines and I were in at Millbrook, radical "Buddhism" was also in and everything else, except as window dressing, was out. There was always someone, most notably Tim, trying to fold us into some version or other of the Giant Omelette, but Tim kept his DNA Deity in the closet at Millbrook, as far as I know. To expose it would have clashed with his act at the time, which was to present himself as floating freely above all of us who "wrestled" here below with "problems" he transcended.

Paranoid systems vary along various dimensions. A few are fairly harmless and even entertaining, but most are so dull and ugly it seems incredible anyone should believe in them unless forced to do so by irrefutable evidence, logical economy, and predictive perfection. Yet millions of people do believe in dull and ugly paranoid systems for which there is no evidence at all.

No apparition which fit neatly into one of these systems would change my solipsist-nihilist epistemology in the slightest. All appearances, no matter how routine or how fantastic, are, Snazzm, simply matters of plot development and scenic design within the dream.

But being aware that it's all a hallucination doesn't mean that I'm not interested in how things work out. I hope for agreeable, believable and dramatic developments, but with plenty of comic relief also.

Where was I? Oh yeah, the Fourth of July party. I was trying to locate some lesser sacrament for Wendy's old chums.

Billy rummaged around in a drawer and came up with a brick of Vietnamese sinsemilla, which I carried back to the living room. No girls, New York from, friends Wendy of. They had fled, Wendy said. The scene was "too much" for them. "Let's go swimming," she suggested.

I put the brick down on a coffee table and we joined the skinny-dippers in the pool. Joe, who seemed to have relaxed a little, had moved to the other end of the water from his original station and was now avidly ogling the naked bodies. Gradually, the crowd thinned out. Bill Haines, looking reasonably gruntled, and Tim, looking disgruntled, probably because he had not been the center of attention, went home with most, but not all, of their respective retinues.

As the sky lightened, passed-out people could be seen scattered about the floors and lawns, including little Jimmy, neatly laid out in his red jacket, and who can blame him? The survivors stopped swimming and dancing and gathered in the library to listen to classical music, sip brandy and talk. Back to the mood worlds. Coming down somewhat sloshed is easier than coming down sober.

While we were having bacon and eggs in the kitchen later, Billy said, "You know, this is incredible. There hasn't been one freakout or fuckup all night and this party is almost over."

No sooner had the words escaped his lips, than Len Howard and Teresa burst into the room with pained expressions on their faces. Their Corvette, they asserted, had been stolen.

"What were you saying, Billy?" I asked.

As bummers go, it didn't amount to much. We found the car later, only slightly damaged, in the woods near the Gatehouse. Susan Shoenfeld had ditched it there after taking Sarasvati and Bhavani on a joy ride along Route 44 that had culminated in a 120-m.p.h. chase by a cop cruiser. The festivities had not gone unnoticed by the police. Cars had been lined up all along Route 44 to watch the fireworks. Susan paid for the repairs.

One of the few uninvited guests remained a problem for two days, however. This young woman tried to move into the Bungalow, by means of the same evasion of the question of permission or invitation employed by less adventurous primitivist wanderers who were willing to settle for a hut in the woods and a free meal at the Ashram every now and then.

She calmly sat down at the Bungalow dinner table whenever there was food on it, flopped on any unoccupied bed when she felt like a snooze, and was in the process of calling up friends in New York and inviting them to join her as a fellow Stranger in Paradise when Tim, who had been rushed to the scene by Billy, took her firmly by the arm and threw her out. Ejected from

Heaven by the Archangel himself. Quite a tale for the folks back home in the East Village.

This sad creature aroused both pity and indignation as do importunate beggars everywhere. She was not one of the beautiful people, or even one of the interesting people. She was a "sad sack," as Bill put it, a professional victim, a "passive aggressive," to use the jargon, who knew the whole time she pretended not to know, exactly what was going on, what game she was playing, what she was spoiling, and how it would all end.

She would make those she envied feel guilty by forcing them to reject her, and thus give some meaning and emotional intensity to her otherwise meaningless and dim existence. She would be a reproach, a curse, a blight. A ghoul's life, to be sure, but at least this particular example of the species was brave enough, or crazy enough, to attempt her emotional rip-off on the rich. Usually, they only practice on those as weak and poor as themselves.

Of her own class, she was a star performer.

Billy was enormously pained by the whole incident.

"Don't look so glum, Billy," I said. "Just another archetype."

"But I just feel so sorry for people like that. But what the hell am I supposed to do about it? Turn my house over to them and go live in the East Village?"

I assured Billy that, in the opinion of the court philosopher, nothing of the sort was required of him. His passage through the eye of the needle was going wonderfully well, etc. Every now and then, I would tell Billy what I thought he ought to do, but my instructions were not nearly so well received as my indulgences. Leaders of religious associations who detect the tiniest ember of guilt in a patron should blow on it and fan it until it produces some life-giving warmth. Tim routinely performed this basic survival procedure with theatrical expertise and Bill did it sometimes, but I was a hopeless case.

I had lost track of Joe Gross, and when I saw him a few weeks later, he seemed to be back at the same old stand. It would take more than half a pill to extract Joe from Purgatory, where almost anyone is welcome, no matter how he acts.

Chapter 39

THE YANKEE'S FIGHT WITH THE KNIGHTS

I was a champion, it was true, but not the champion of the frivolous black arts, I was the champion of hard unsentimental common sense and reason.

One day, while I was painting the walls and varnishing the paneling in my office, Tim, bearing a jug of wine, walked in and sat down. The weather was fine, and I had opened all the doors and windows to air the place out. Tim was amused by the mouse traps, boxes of rat poison, and spray cans of insecticides which I had collected, out of harm's way, on the mantelpiece.

"I've always felt I could judge a person by the way he decorates his mantelpiece, Arthur," Tim laughed.

"Could be," I replied, setting out glasses on my writing table.

"Have you visited the Ashram recently?" I asked.

"No," Tim said, pouring. "I have given up trying to talk to that crazy son of a bitch. He's really out of his mind."

I mentioned Haines' latest move: getting rid of the pretty girls and moving in the Lumbering Behemoths.

"I just don't trust broads who let themselves go like that," I said, sipping. "They must be filled with grievances as well as fat globules. We can't afford to have people like that around. We're not geared for it."

"Yeah, I talked to one of them. Karen something. Pretty bad."

Sure enough, this particular lardass, a graduate student at SUNY New Palz where she was preparing to become a psychologist, later volunteered to testify against us in the conspiracy case just for the glory of it all, or something. Girth appeared to have become Haines' main test for the admission of camp followers to his family circle.

We talked awhile about the usual stuff, and then Tim abruptly changed the subject.

"Did I ever tell you what happened to my first wife, Arthur?" Tim asked. It was a grim story. He had come home one afternoon from work at the Kaiser Psychological Clinic in San Francisco, where he was director of research, and found the corpse of his wife lying on the floor with a note next to it reading, "I cannot live without your love." I was shocked. It was the first time I had heard Tim volunteer anything about his personal life that wasn't self-congratulatory and exemplary.

"Jesus, Tim," I said. "That's one of the most terrible things I've heard in a long time. Well, at least things like that never seem to happen around here, whatever other problems we may have."

In order to expiate guilt, Tim had to act as if he loved everyone, and try to make everyone love him. The LSD experience had to be interpreted in a manner consistent with these requirements. From which, in standard psychoanalytic twists, followed much of Tim's history, including the return of the repressed, the cyclical build-ups and let-downs of his supposed loved ones and much else, if you want to push it. Yeah, sure, and so what? It didn't mean Tim was right or wrong in anything he said or did.

We chatted a while and then Tim went out to fish off the bridge and I went back to my interior decoration. A few minutes later, Billy Hitchcock walked in.

"Kleps, I just heard one of the most incredible things I have ever heard on this property and I have heard some pretty incredible things. I can't believe it."

Billy almost always built up his stories in advance. A true salesman.

"What, what?" I asked.

"Well, Tim's outside fishing off the bridge. When I stopped the car to say hello, he turned around and lifted his finger like this (Billy demonstrated) and said, 'Art Kleps is the only sane person on this property.' Come on. Let me in on it. What the hell did you say to him?"

Nothing special that I could remember. I was just as surprised as Billy, who had driven over to invite us to the Bungalow for dinner. Aurora, who was spending more and more time in New York because of Billy's increasingly non-domestic habits, was back. Sam and Martica were in attendance. He also wanted me to meet a business associate, Seymour Lazar. I called Wendy from upstairs and we took off in Billy's car. As we crossed the bridge, I saw Tim paddling out towards the center of the lake in the small boat I kept tied underneath the bridge. Tim and Susan were invited also, Billy said. It would be quite a mob.

"I still don't believe it," Billy kept muttering as he plowed his big Cadillac through the narrow, leafy tunnel of the shortest gravel-road route between the Gatehouse and the Bungalow, flushing small game and one or two deer (there were two herds on the property, whitetails and a small, red German variety) right and left as he went.

"Oh, come on, Billy," I said. "If it suits his purposes, he'll say I'm hopelessly insane tomorrow. You know Tim."

"Besides," Wendy added, "saying someone is sane around here may be a left-handed compliment."

True. I think it was just a matter of Tim taking a break from the Slobovenoid Blobovenoidal nonsense and amateur psychologizing he had to listen to back in the hills. Every now and then, he had to get loaded, relax, and say what he thought, whether it supported his political agenda of the moment or not. On the other hand, maybe he just wanted to get me drunk before dinner.

Later, I found out I had won a "sanity contest." The kids had put up a list of candidates in the Big House kitchen and I had won, hands down. Tim had neglected to mention this.

As promised, we had a full table that evening, including a

straight and snotty cousin of Billy's who made comments like "sure, we know, Tim" whenever Tim made a cryptic or quasi-paradoxical remark. The cousin had the look of a man who has just discovered shit on his shoes.

This character seemed to consider himself a genuine Mellon of Pennsylvania and/or Virginia, as distinguished from these semi-civilized Hitchcock half-breeds who tolerated the likes of us.

Everyone except the legitimate Mellon was stoned and half-smashed on grass and wine, and merrily yakking away in consequence. The unadulterated Mellon's waspish asides acted as a sort of contrast or counterpoint or punctuation to the rest of the talk. I was sufficiently spaced so I could actually appreciate this, in a way. Added depth or resonance or something, sort of.

Tim finally took notice of the authentic, true, pure, holy and fully documented Mellon's hostile commentary. "Well, I'm perfectly willing to admit I'm a charlatan," Tim said, grinning and opening his arms in acceptance. "We're all charlatans aren't we? Don't you agree, Susan?" He swung around to face his daughter, who was seated at the foot of the table.

Susan had her head down. She shook it abruptly and negatively and ran out of the room, clutching her napkin. Tears glistened. It had been a mistake to invite Susan to the dinner. Tim got up and followed, to explain what he meant, I guess.

Did he say it was all a game and we had assigned ourselves different roles to play? Maybe. But why call that charlatanry? Did Tim mean, Snazzm, that one can do nothing but delude oneself, that is, "have" a dream? I doubt it. That isn't charlatanry either.

Charlatanry, which is deception, requires the appearance of a world of particulars about which one can tell the truth or lie, and this is true in any Zmm. Dream figures may lie to one another, and mythic beings tend to lie like crazy, with some specializing in the profession. There are truth tellers and liars in dreams, just as there are good guys and bad guys in dreams.

One good way to define veracity is to say it is what telling lies isn't. Truth is a characteristic of some sentences, that's all. One tells the truth about one's impressions and ideas to the extent that one gives an accurate report of them and does not intentionally mislead. Fictions are neither true nor false, per se. Fictions and errors remain distinct even if, as sometimes happens, a fiction turns out, in whole or in part, to be factually correct about something or other.

These distinctions, so important to beady-eyed philosophers, Tim brushed aside. Words were to be used to soothe or stun, and to paralyze reason, and above all else, to prevent Tim from being fingered for anything. All usages had to be made vague and safe instead of sharp and dangerous in order to provide a cloud-shrouded littoral where he and other pirates could not be distinguished from honest fishermen, at least not from a distance.

Explicit, systematic rationales for intellectual charlatanry are hard to find, although the sentimental glorification of professional and pathological liars and crooks is a major theme of what might be called the cumulative Hollywood *House-Tree-Person* test. This Judaical neurosis has also played an important part in American literature, good and bad, for a long time and has now (1994) reached a blatantly psychotic level in the mass media. Not only are professional swindlers glorified, as usual, but so are serial killers and brutal cops. The rest of the world should erect every barrier possible against this shit and "quarantine" the United States if necessary.

The philosophic justification for making fraudulence and mendacity one's guiding stars in life, such as it is and as best as I can make out, seems to go something like this:

If, as it seems, it is all an illusion, then it's all a fraud which means that you are a fraud and I am a fraud so let us all freely lie to one another, each in his own charlatanic fashion, and may the best pretender prevail. The underlying premise is the supposed equivalence between "illusion" and "fraud."

But there is a great difference, obvious to most nine-year-olds, between an illusion or a fiction or a dream on one hand and a lie on the other, a distinction neither Tim nor his hero Aleister Crowley nor a lot of other con artists seem able to grasp. Appearances are appearances for naive realists and solipsists and dreamers and the awake and the enlightened and the unenlightened alike. They are all one has. Superior theories, those that get us anywhere, about how particular things work, "save" (explain) the appearances they deal with, while inferior theories leave all or some of the same appearances out in the cold.

> It will be seen that among the objects with which we are acquainted are not included physical objects (as opposed to sense data), nor other people's minds. (Bertrand Russell)

The central liar in Mary McCarthy's *The Groves of Academe* is a lot like Tim in lots of ways. Here are some quotes, run together from different places in this minor masterpiece:

> And at bottom he did murkily consider all attainment, idealism and so forth, to be a sort of speciousness; the upper world, for him, was divided into admitted frauds, hypocritical frauds, unconscious frauds: this fraudulence, in fact, to his glazed-pottery-blue eye, constituted the human, and below it was the only animal activity, which was of no interest or amusement to the observer. Every relationship, therefore, propelled itself for him toward confession and mutual self-exposure; the slurrings and elisions of his voice conspired toward this end; even in his ingratiating mood, his talk had a sidelong motion, suggestive of complicity ... One begins by persuading *oneself*, and this germ of persuasion is infectious. [He] has a remarkable gift, a gift for being his own sympathizer. It's a rare asset; it would be useful to him in politics or religion ... He's capable of commanding great loyalty, because he's unswervingly loyal to himself. I'm not being sarcastic. Very few of us have that. It's a species of self-alienation. He's loyal to himself, objectively, as if he were another person, with that feeling of sacrifice and blind obedience that we give to a leader or a cause. In the world today, there's a great deal of free-floating, circumambient loyalty that fixes itself on such people, who seem to offer, by their own example, the possibility of a separation from the self that will lead to a higher union with the self objectified in an idea. It's [his] fortune or his fate to have achieved this union within his own personality; he's foregone his subjectivity and hypostatized himself as an object ... The criteria of truth and falsity, as we know them, don't exist for [him]. He doesn't examine his statements from the point of view of the speaker but from the point of view of the listener. He listens to himself as you or I

might listen to him and asks himself, 'Is it credible?' Even in private soliloquy, credibility is the standard he applies; that is, he looks at truth with the eyes of a literary critic and measures a statement by its persuasiveness. If he himself can be persuaded he accepts the moot statement as established. This is real alienation. In the critical part of his mind, he's extraordinarily cold with himself, cold and dedicated. Hence his incessant anxiety, like the anxiety of a military commander or an author or a stage director; he's busy with problems of reception, stage effects, cues, orchestration; his inner life is a busy rehearsal and testing for activity on the larger stage of tomorrow, where the audience, as usual, will miss the finer points. Immersed in all these difficulties, hung up on the little snags of production, he's impatient, understandably, with outside interrogation. 'Is it true?' you want to know, but the question's irrelevant and footless. Do you ask an amber spot whether it's true? Or an aria? At bottom, he doesn't give a damn ... what you or I think, any more than a general cares about democratic opinion. We're not his critics or even primarily, his audience; we're amateurs whom, unfortunately, he must use in his production, green troops whom he has to put up with since the great Commander we all act under saw fit to send him no better.

Jeezums!

The day after the Great Pretender vs. the Magnum Mellon dinner, Wendy and I went to Millbrook, where I got a haircut and a marriage license from the same person. Wendy would take the bus to New York and return on the appointed day with her parents, sister and brother-in-law. I sat with her drinking coffee in the Millbrook Diner until the bus came.

I walked back to the Gatehouse from the barbershop. It was a walk I always enjoyed, past the supermarket, and then uphill past an old-fashioned drug store, several modest but well-tended houses, and the Episcopal Church. Once I was over the brow of the hill, an uncluttered prospect of fields and woods opened up with "my" charming Gatehouse, looking like a toy construction in the middle distance, occupying center stage.

On my next visit to the Bungalow during my vacation from the marital condition, I walked in to find a political harangue, of all things, in progress. Since every Psychedelian I knew on the estate disbelieved and/or despised the official line on almost every subject, there usually wasn't all that much about politics to talk about. This seemed to be as true at the Bungalow as it was at the Ashram. Maybe it was different back in the hills but I doubt it.

Billy owned a Spanish-language newspaper in New York called *Il Tiempo,* which had a wide distribution not only in the city but in several Latin American countries, particularly the Dominican Republic. His editor, who was holding the floor in front of the bar, had apparently come up to Millbrook to give Billy and anyone else in earshot the benefit of his views on the latest political crisis in that country.

Billy, Tommy, Sam and Seymour Lazar, who had impressed me as quite a pain in the ass the night before (a "feisty" little prick with lots of "chutzpah," I suppose one might call him), were sprawled around the living room looking bored and sullen while the editor shook his fist and delivered a rapid-fire series of pronouncements. The women and the children, I could see, were outside by the pool. The editor had his coat on and seemed about to leave. Judging by the number of empty glasses and cigarette butts in view, it looked like the editor had been holding forth for some time.

His speech was straight, hard-line anti-Communist ranting of the old school. "They" could do no right and "we" could do no wrong. The monstrous American genocide then under way in Vietnam was too restrained, we could kill twice as many of the godless commies if we really tried and so forth and so on. When the editor uttered the name of Fidel Castro, a tremor passed over his swarthy features and his eyes popped out a little. He didn't just disapprove of Castro, he hated his guts. It was the only time I heard anything like it at Millbrook.

Billy responded with a series of half-hearted uh-huhs, yeahs and mmms and sank lower and lower into the couch, and Sam and Seymour behaved pretty much the same way. I could hardly believe my ears. On the few occasions when Billy and I had talked about South American politics, usually in reference to Marco, he had expressed the usual liberal wisdom on the subject. Sure, he participated in the big rip-off in various ways, as did anyone with 50 cents in the bank although few knew it, but he didn't deny for a moment that it was a rip-off.

"Come on, it's obvious isn't it? Have you ever seen how those people live down there? Anyone who thinks things are going to go on forever as they are is kidding himself," Billy had said. "Of course they're going to go communist or socialist or whatever you want to call it sooner or later. I've taken that for granted for a long time."

Billy, like most of us in those days, tended to underestimate the power of the Euro-American cosmopolite oligarchy to manipulate its tame and timid captive moronocracies through monopolistic control of their mass medias. At the time, because of the good coverage given to the war in Viet Nam, it was actually possible to think that TV made it harder for the establishment to deceive the public, and many of us thought exactly that.

And Billy, like most people, overestimated the intelligence of the average voter, here and abroad. If I, an experienced tests-and-measurements psychologist who should have been fully aware of how dumb most people were, made this error, as I often did ("Jesus Christ, they can't be that stupid," I would say to myself), how could I expect anyone else to not make it? On hearing the Tories had won an election in England, where the Mellon family had many close connections in ruling-class circles, Billy had slapped his hand on his forehead, and laughed explosively. "What? Those fucking thieves got in again? I can't believe it! Where's the phone?"

So why all the uh-huhs, yeahs and mmms?

When the editor left, Billy went up to the bar and poured himself a stiff one.

"Schmuck," he said.

"Yeah, I hate to listen to that shit," Sam added.

"Well, what the hell, Billy," I asked. "If you didn't like what he was saying, why didn't you tell him he was full of crap? You have a controlling interest in the paper, don't you?"

"Yeah."

"So this creep is your employee, right?"

"Sometimes I wonder."

"Does he write editorials like that?"

"Worse."

"Well, why don't you fire him and hire someone who represents your views? Why not be social-democratic and libertarian?"

"You don't understand business, Kleps," Billy said.

How true, but as time went on I learned a few things. Although the paper consistently lost money, that had nothing to do with it, and may even have been a plus. As a matter of fact, Seymour tried to get control away from Billy a year later. It was worth having because of its political influence in the Dominican Republic and in other Spanish-speaking American "client states," and for no other reason, except possibly that it was the best kind of "write-off," that is, an asset that appeared to lose money as far as the public and the IRS could or wanted to see, while actually making a lot of it. If the paper told stories agreeable to those who owned and managed the client states, and did not tell stories disagreeable to them, the owners of the paper would be rewarded in various ways.

When Billy visited the Dominican Republic, he didn't stay at a hotel, he stayed at the Presidential Palace. If, for example, the concession to rent out seat cushions at soccer matches was to be sold off to make a fast buck, President Baleguer, or whoever, would not tell Billy to go stand in a corner with his face to the wall, but instead would allow him to make a bid on an equal footing with the other capitalist parasites who were hanging around. The right to "wave the kapok" was worth big bucks to those leeches who had wormed their way into the core.

No newspaper representing Billy's actual views would be worth anything, because it couldn't have been sold in the Dominican Republic or anywhere else in the region. The newspaper represented the system in virtually the same way Federal Reserve Notes represented the system. Billy could no more alter the political orientation of the paper, in which resided its true value, than Hugh Hefner could print a picture of a syphilitic sex organ on the cover of *Playboy*. He would have been sued and he would have lost.

Chapter 40

THREE YEARS LATER

I said, name the day, and I would take fifty assistants and stand up against the massed chivalry of the whole earth and destroy it.

I n the summer of '70, when I was living on the property as a private guest, after doing time in the Northampton, Massachusetts, jail for possession of the sacraments and lewd and lascivious cohabitation with a Smithie, I got another lesson in politics. Billy and I were flying down the Hudson in the helicopter right after the Kent State murders. Even Bennett College in Millbrook, a junior college for girls, which had been given its library by Billy's mother, as he informed a stunned librarian who had asked us what connection we had with the college one day, was in an uproar. I happened to know one of the leading firebrands, Susie Werneke, very well. Billy was angry also. The Kent State murders and Kissinger's insane bombing of Cambodia had succeeded in arousing his normally torpid sense of civic responsibility.

"Listen, Art," Billy said, after making his usual detour to view Pocatino Hills, shake his fist, and yell some expletives down at the Rockefellers below (the Governor was apparently entertaining some nuns at a garden luncheon), "Why don't you write an editorial right now, and if I like it I'll print it in *Il Tiempo*. I mean, what the fuck, what? If a bunch of Bennett girls can get out and do something, I feel I can too, and the way things are going now, what do I have to lose?"

I wrote out an editorial as we flew along. There was nothing in it which would have caused the slightest lifting of eyebrows at the *New York Times* or even at the *Poughkeepsie Journal*. My emphasis was on the danger of antagonizing an entire generation by shooting them at random, and so forth. The usual stuff. I can't usually write the usual stuff, but I guess I was angry enough to do it then. Billy thought it was wonderful.

The apoplectic, anti-Castro editor had been replaced by a more businesslike type who didn't write the editorials, but who followed the same general policy as his predecessor. While we were having beer and sausages at "21," Billy handed his new boy my editorial, saying, "By the way, I would really like to see this printed."

The editor put my paper in his pocket without reading it and went back to explaining how insiders could make a fast buck in collectors' issues of South American postage stamps. The editorial identifying Nixon and Kissinger as war criminals was never printed. When I asked how the editor had justified this insubordination, Billy shrugged.

"He said it wasn't right for our audience," Billy said. "I guess he has a point."

And that was the end of that one.

Back to 1967.

Wendy and I both had doubts about tying the knot, but there was no doubt at all that an infant was aimed straight at us, head first, we hoped. Another factor was the difficulty prosecutors faced in trying to force spouses to testify against each other. Considering everything, holy wedlock seemed like the right thing to do.

We went every day to the post office in Millbrook, where, with a couple exceptions when $100 bills brightened the day, causing the birds in the trees to sing more melodiously, there would be $10 or $15 at most; enough to buy cigarettes, wine and groceries and, perhaps, to mail out *Divine Toad Sweat*s to those who had asked for them and do the laundry.

Nobody paid regular dues and very few of our members, most of whom were students who spent every spare nickel they had on the lesser sacrament, had stable addresses or stable incomes. I might have been able to come up with another book or a magazine but there was no way to produce either without capital. The irony of our prime patron owning a foreign-language newspaper during this period, when we were entirely at the mercy of an establishment media, seemed pretty routine by that time.

I still hadn't met Wendy's parents, but she assured me they would cover the expenses of her having a child, if nothing else. They did. Tim was enthusiastic about the marriage, and readily agreed to perform the ceremony, which would be held outdoors in front of the Big House.

"It's one of the most sensible moves you have ever made, Arthur," Tim assured me. Well, maybe.

Tim's own domestic situation was deteriorating. It was pretty clear that the tent in the hills was not going over much better with Rosemary than the mud hut in Nepal had gone over with Nina. Tim ejected Susan Schoenfeld on a charge of turning Rosemary on to some junk, which always finds a market among those leading the simple life involuntarily. It was the first time I had heard of any heroin being around and, although no one appeared to be hooked on the stuff, Tim's reaction, if founded on fact, made sense. If any of us had been busted for narcotics possession, it would have done more political harm than a thousand pot or acid busts.

Opiates are not nearly as dangerous as the official propaganda maintains, and if it were up to me I would restore the days of yore when most farm families routinely bought a pound of opium around Thanksgiving to see them through the chills and ills of winter (I have seen the evidence). For most people, it's much safer to smoke opium than to down a few martinis.

It's all a genetic roulette-wheel trip, and some predispositions are demonized while others are tolerated or even subsidized for reasons which have nothing to do with health and everything to do with furthering the interests of the owning and ruling classes. Is drug x easier or harder to control than drug y? Is drug x more profitable than drug y? These are the only questions that really matter in the capitalist scheme of things. What is good is bad and what is bad is good.

You say that drug x stimulates the imagination, encourages critical thought and provides ordinary people with a cheap source of home entertainment?

They feel no guilt over their criminal conduct?

Some of them grow their own?

Well, if such be the case, no profits are being made and no taxes are being paid. These considerations, on top of the Sado-Judeo-Paulinian terror of anything that changes people for the better here on this earth, is more than enough to do it. The sky is falling and the end of the world is at hand. Call out the troops.

Prior to the introduction of the powerful psychedelics, I think the American drug laws were best understood in Marxist terms. Since then, I think religious combat underlies it all, but Marxist logic still applies and is good enough to explain things to the satisfaction of most lawyers and shallow thinkers in general.

Unlike psychedelics, however, it is true, opiates and coca are highly addictive in the incredibly concentrated forms in which prohibition forces producers to deliver these drugs to their markets. If it wasn't for the laws, most people would smoke a little opium for their aches and pains and chew a few coca leaves for a lift now and then and never become addicted.

Neither substance, in any concentration except an extreme overdose, does any direct physical harm. Many addicts, including thousands of physicians, function better on the stuff than off it. W.C. Fields, speaking of booze, had it right: "In my experience, it is most often the absence, rather than the presence, of the substance in question that causes all the problems."

The property crime and general physical debility associated with opiate use in the United States is entirely the result of the high price that most addicts must pay to obtain their daily ration, and the highly refined form it comes in, and both the price and the potency are direct consequences of prohibition.

As has been clearly demonstrated by the humane and rational European ways of dealing with the problem, an addict who is allowed to obtain what he needs at little or no cost will often eat three meals a day and trudge off to work in the morning just like everyone else. If anything, he is less likely to commit crimes than his non-addicted contemporaries because, once he has his fix, and no worries about getting the next one, he is generally content with a quiet, modest existence and not about to go roaring off into the night in search of cheap thrills the way boozers and speed freaks do. Addiction, per se, is not all that serious a problem. The problem is addiction in a context of high prices and criminal sanctions against use.

It's an American problem, deliberately created by the stonehearted American capitalist oligarchy to crush working-class people under as many capricious and arbitrary burdens as possible, to turn them against each other and terrorize them and prevent them from thinking straight about anything.

My wife, my daughter and I lived in "Nieuw Amsterdam," a huge housing development southeast of Amsterdam, from the spring of 1988 until January of 1991, when we were forced to return to the United States because of crimes committed against us by a DEA agent named D. O'Neill and his co-conspirators in the Dutch police, Mossad, and American Express, who stole our mail, burned our money and attempted to fry our brains with subsonic vibrations, or something. I got this stopped by calling in the fire department to investigate (a little tip there for all you folks having your brains fried), but we were never informed about what kind of infernal machine had been at work, just as we expected we wouldn't be.

Most of this happened after the Dutch Ministry of Justice, fully informed by me of my criminal record in the United States, had granted us residence, and on liberal terms at that. The American mind police intervened, and had the decision reversed, asserting, along with other lies, that the Neo-American Church (about one-third of the members of which always have been and are now racially Semitic) had a "Nazi basis." We didn't have any proof of this until it was too late to do anything about it, and then we got copies of the incriminating documents by accident, or so it seemed anyway. (See *Kleps v. The Netherlands*, ECHR 19551/92.)

"Love it or leave it?" Not anymore. You will stay on the

plantation you were born on, unless drafted to put down insurrections on other plantations, and grin from ear to ear when massa passes by with his lash. Oh yeah, maybe they will let you move if it will help depress wages somewhere else. I always forget about that one.

Putting aside the guardians of law and order, Holland in general compared to the United States as fresh air from the North Sea compared to industrial pollutants blowing up into Texas from the nightmarish industrial slums along the Mexican border. Our spacious, high-ceilinged, three-bedroom apartment, which overlooked a small lake with lots of fish, ducks and swans in and on it, cost us about $200 a month. The finest Moroccan hashish, available from over 250 coffee houses around the city, cost $7.50 a gram. We were surrounded by Third-World immigrants, many of whom were on the dole and many of whom were "illegals" supported by those on the dole and by individual initiatives of various kinds.

The guaranteed annual income for all legal residents included a vacation allowance sufficient for a month in Spain every year. The powers that were had decided that people who don't have jobs need vacations as much as those who do. I agree. We do.

Opiate addicts were common, but there were also all kinds of services for these unfortunate folks. The community was peaceful, pretty and well-tended. We bicycled around in the genuine parklands between the buildings, even in the late evening, without apprehension. The atmosphere, both physical and social, reminded me of Westchester during the '30s and '40s. What more can I say?

Long live the Queen!

The Wendy-Arthur wedding went off pretty smoothly, although for a while it looked like Tim would refuse to preside and we would have to ask Haines to do it.

The problem was Susan Shoenfeld. While I was up at the Bungalow early in the morning getting dressed in some of Billy's finery and having a couple Bloody Marys, Susan, our most recent outcast, walked in.

Billy, who, like Otto, ranked Susan in the highly attractive category, and did not know about her recent expulsion from the

League, immediately asked if she was staying for the wedding. "Sure, why don't you, Susan," I added. I had nothing against Susan, and appreciated her style. Although, like Peggy, she was too boyish for my tastes, her voodoo nonsense amused me greatly.

Heretofore, oddly enough, most of my conversations with Susan had been about self-defense. She claimed to have burned Doc Duvalier's Chief of Police in Haiti a year or so earlier in an acid deal (it was typical of Susan not to bother making excuses for this conduct) and feared the Ton Ton Macoute might find her and carve her heart out, or something. When she asked me for advice, I suggested that she might buy a .22 semi-automatic rifle in town and keep it under her bed.

If any crazed zombies covered with blood and chicken feathers tried to break her door down in the middle of the night, she could fill them full of holes, which might slow the ungrateful dead down long enough so she could jump out the window or take some other evasive action.

Susan, who hadn't known it was legal and easy to procure a firearm in the land of the free and the home of the brave, immediately bought a Ruger, with a little clip and lots of ammunition, at the Millbrook hardware store. She didn't hunt with her rifle, but enjoyed shooting at targets in the woods, which was enough to alarm and offend Haines, who eventually seized the weapon and threw it in the smaller lake behind the Gatehouse. Just as he was pitching it in, he told me, a carload of Bungalow visitors passed over the bridge where he was standing (in his robes, as it happened), with his arms upraised and the rifle in his hands, thereby creating an intriguing subject for dinner table speculation, no doubt.

Leaving Susan at the Bungalow, I drove down to the Big House to check on the arrangements. Banners and streamers and shrine areas were all over the place. The black tanka hung from a line strung over the stone steps to the Big House front lawn where the ceremony would be held. I didn't have the heart to take it down. No matter what the intentions of whoever put it up, it was, Snazzm, a black cat case. Perhaps I should have called off the wedding, but removing the warning sign wouldn't have accomplished anything.

Tim was not ready to preside. I found him on a tractor cutting grass at the west side of the house, dressed in a pair of old shorts. I drove the Cadillac up to him. What in hell was going on?

"Art, did you invite Susan Schoenfeld to the wedding?" he asked, after shutting off the engine. His face was set in stern lines. Jesus Christ! News traveled fast at Millbrook.

"Well, yeah, Tim," I said. "Billy and I did. We didn't invite her back to live here, just to stay for the ceremony."

"Unless you have her off the property in half an hour I won't perform the wedding," Tim said, not betraying the slightest hint of amusement. He was dead serious. Tim had decided Susan was a "downer" and Tim had no mercy on "downers."

"OK. I don't care much either way," I said. "You had better get cleaned up, though. I'll be back in fifteen minutes."

"Just get her out of here," Tim said, his face relaxing somewhat. "I don't want that girl anywhere near me. She's pure poison."

"I just don't worship him anymore," Susan said, when, back at the Bungalow, I asked her what the trouble was.

"I'll take care of it," Billy volunteered. "Tell Tim I took her to the station."

Who performed the ceremony didn't matter much to me, but when I called Wendy about it, she was insistent that I persuade Tim to do it, as he had promised. The invocation of the name of William Haines (who?) would not have improved her status among the Jewish princesses of New York nearly as much as the invocation of the name of Timothy (no shit?) Leary.

I drove back. All was well. Tim was in his office on the third floor having flowers stuck in his hair by Rosemary. I gave Bhavani, who was standing by, a box of ladyfingers and a small bottle of Sandoz LSD in solution from the large reserve of crystal that Tommy held in a safety deposit box in Barclay's Bank in London. When Tim saw the bottle, his mood altered abruptly from mild resignation to eager anticipation.

Haines appeared, caught the mood instantly and, after a few

coarse remarks concerning the consummation of my forthcoming union, fell with relish to assisting Bhavani in the preparation of the sacraments. Since some straight visitors were already on hand, and more were expected, including Wendy's family, we agreed that only 25 micrograms per ladyfinger would be a good idea.

Michael Green, wearing only a pair of shorts and a lei, walked in. Wendy and her family had arrived, he reported. Her mother was crying, and her father looked "sort of stunned." I drove back to the Bungalow and returned with the Hitchcocks, the Clapps, and another car carrying Jack and Jimmy and several cases of champagne, which Jack and Jimmy put down on the porch by a table with the traditional cake. All was in readiness. Tim and Tambimutto were standing under the tanka.

About fifty people, many of whom I didn't recognize, were sitting on the lawn. To the sound of bongo drums and flutes, Billy, my best man, and I walked to the summer house where I had my first sight of my parents-in-law-to-be. Classic bourgeois Jewish in appearance, they looked as stunned as Michael had described them. But most of our visitors looked stunned when they first arrived, even if they were not there to see their daughters wed to an alien from "inner space."

Wendy's sister, Jill, smiling brightly in the sunshine, looked like one of Joe's Scandinavian blondes. Billy muttered an appreciative comment before we got within hearing range. Her husband, Wally, who operated a company that handed out annual awards for the best TV commercials of the year, looked like the classic MadAveExec that he was. Their four-year-old daughter, beaming like her mother, clutched a bouquet.

We all walked back, appropriately paired and tripled, to the steps under the black tanka. Tim uttered some typical Timisms, Tambimutto read from the *Vedas,* cymbals clashed, and pipes played. Ladyfingers were passed, and I noted that Tim's identification of them as "the sacrament of our religion" had not made any impression at all on the straight segment of our audience. Mrs. Williams was eating one and so was the little flower girl.

As soon as the ceremony was over, and everyone was up on the porch sloshing down the bubbly, as Otto put it, and eating cake, Wendy steered me over into the far corner of the porch and anxiously asked, "Arthur, how much did you put in those ladyfingers?" She was relieved when I told her it wasn't much. Jill's daughter played happily with the resident kids, who were enjoying the opportunity to have a small dose in an outdoor party setting. Mr. Williams and Wally, both mildly stoned, joined enthusiastically in a baseball game that Tim organized.

Mrs. Williams, however, tossed her cookies and passed out, but regained consciousness quickly. She wasn't able to describe her symptoms and seemed relieved when we told her she was on a very minor LSD trip and would return to normal consciousness in a few hours. I suspect she had two, maybe three. We put her to bed in the Gatehouse. Later, Wendy said she thought this little trip had loosened her mother up somewhat.

Well, legally staked out once again. At least this time nobody could accuse me of leading an innocent maiden into perdition. I had found her there, and the term "innocent maiden," in any sense, did not apply.

Surprisingly often during the 1967 "Summer of Love," considering how many visitors we had and how threatening the political situation came to be, not much would happen on any given day. It was possible to relax and converse, drink, putter around, read, go fishing or swimming, drink, or whatever.

I retain in my memory an unusually detailed recollection of one low-key scene of this kind, probably because it has such a mild, mellow P.G. Wodehouse flavor.

Billy and Tommy and I were drinking beer and discussing the foibles of mutual acquaintances, on lawn chairs in "Swami's corner," an alcove in the stone wall that traced the perimeter of the Gatehouse-bridge region. Swami was present only in blithe spirit, but plenty of his more colorful and tuneful relatives were around, chirping it up.

There were no women, rivals, children, servants or courtiers present, just the four of us birds, one ectoplasmic. I'm pretty sure it was a Sunday afternoon. If not, it felt like it.

Things had become so relaxed that, despite the character flaw to which I have already alluded, I was about to bring up the financial condition of the religious institution for which, in one way or another, we were all responsible, present balance zero, when there was a soprano "hello" from the gate.

"Naturally," I moodily muttered to myself, as I ambled over, glass in hand, feeling more relieved than disappointed, if the truth be told. It was fate. Did I harbor an unconscious dread of the almighty dollar? Should I wear a T-shirt with "Born to be Broke" on it? Could be.

It was the mother of a kid from town who was a schoolmate and close friend of Jackie Leary. The boy had recently been busted for growing a couple pot plants in a window box in his bedroom. The connection with Jackie had not gone unremarked in the press and it was not now going unremarked by the lad's mother, who had obviously had a few, and who can blame her?

"Well, come on over, have a beer and tell us all about it," I said, ushering her through the pedestrian gate. What else could I do? And it would be a good idea if Billy and Tommy got this kind of story from a primary source, for a change.

I introduced her, and Tommy gave up his chair, moving to a concrete bench built into the wall. I didn't introduce Billy and Tommy, thinking our guest already knew them, such was the seeming familiarity of the friendly greetings exchanged.

She was a pleasant sort and, although justifiably pissed off about the situation in general, not really hostile to the community.

I was OK, Haines was OK, but Timothy Leary was a different story altogether. She went on in this vein, one not entirely unwelcome to my ears, for some time.

I noticed that Billy and Tommy were both grinning, and that Billy was egging her on. Suddenly it dawned on me: She hadn't recognized the twins. For all she knew, they might have been Bertie Wooster and Bingo Little.

"Well," I said, when the flow slackened for a moment, "what about the people who brought Tim Leary here in the first place? Don't you think they have some responsibility for what goes on around here?"

"That's a good point," said Billy.

"There's no question about it," Tommy added. "After all, it isn't Tim Leary who owns this place."

Chronic worrier though he was, this situation was just too fraught with comedy for Tommy to resist. Like Billy, he was bursting with suppressed merriment. The junior pot farmer's mother was pretty merry also, oddly enough. The mood was infectious, I guess.

"You mean that Billy Hitchcock?" she asked. It was evident it took some effort, but if her congenial hosts at this impromptu gathering were inclined to dump on Billy Hitchcock she would add her two cents' worth.

"Why, that Billy Hitchcock is probably the worst of them all," she declared, with great emphasis. I poured her another glass of beer. Billy vehemently agreed with her generalization about "Billy Hitchcock's" location on the moral totem pole, and pressed her for more details about her son's case, and for anything and everything she might have to say about anything and everything on the place. It went on for quite a while. Rarely, I think, has any woman been given a better opportunity to bitch to a more receptive audience. When the flow threatened to end, I put in a word about how "rich people think they can get away with anything" which restarted the conversation as if I had administered benzedrine to all present.

"I've noticed that," said Tommy.

There are few subjects upon which people with ordinary incomes are more eager to animadvert, particularly when they are in their cups, unless someone rich is present, in which case not a word is ever said about it.

It was good for another fifteen minutes at least. An atmosphere of uninhibited frankness prevailed. If it hadn't, Milwaukee would not be what it is today.

"Um, if you don't mind my asking," the townswoman asked, "who are you two guys? I know Mr. Kleps here, but ..."

"Call me Art," I interjected.

"I'm Billy Hitchcock," said Billy, with the exact degree of mirth appropriate.

"What? You're kidding me!" Her startled eyes swiveled to Tommy, who also confessed.

She took it well, considering everything. There was only one, faint-hearted recrimination, and she couldn't even manage a frown for that:

"You've all been teasing me."

"No, no," Billy said. "Honestly, we wanted to hear what you had to say."

Tommy and I chimed in along the same lines. It had been too good a chance to pass up. Yes, it had been pretty funny, but also most informative and interesting. Billy and Tommy were eager to help her solve her problem in any way they could. No lawyer? What about Noel Tepper?

Amidst mutual expressions of esteem and calls for a replay sometime, our little party broke up. Our visitor departed, with a great story to tell back home.

Dinner at the Bungalow tonight? Sure thing. "Now, that was fun," Tommy said, before he and Billy took off in Tommy's Chevy.

I think the kid got a year suspended or something like that. If so, it may have been enough to keep him out of Vietnam. Getting busted saved quite a few kids from getting mangled or killed in those days.

I can't remember exactly when the startling event took place, but sometime in the summer of 1967 Mummy made what amounted to an inspection tour of the property. When the news of her presence at the Bungalow came in, I happened to be at the Ashram, and on good terms with Bill, so I guess it was around the time that the *Catechism* was being printed. Maybe the *Catechism* had been printed, and she had seen a copy, which would help to explain what happened and did not happen.

Bill, who may have been on a light dose at the time, was electrified by the news. He seemed to interpret her visit in an entirely positive light, although nobody else did, and rushed to get cleaned up, don his robes, commandeer a car and driver, and dash off for the Bungalow, although no invitation had been extended.

It was clear that visions of sugarplums were dancing in his head.

He was back in ten minutes, looking about as shell-shocked as I have ever seen him look. "You had better get down to the

Gatehouse, Kleps," Haines muttered in an aside to me as he swept past. "She is only here to look the place over and you are definitely on her hit list."

Questions were asked but none were answered. Bill vanished into his room, and I took off for the Gatehouse.

"Mummy is coming!" I announced to Wendy, who looked properly galvanized by the news. We both rushed around like maniacs, trying to make the dump look semi-inhabitable. I mopped the stairs and dusted as much of the surrounding wood as I could reach, while Wendy concentrated on our barren quarters themselves. Sure enough, about an hour later, while we were both still frantically attempting to make a sow's ear look like a silk purse, why I don't know, a Rolls pulled up in the parking lot and a woman attired entirely in black, accompanied by a man attired in similarly funereal garb, alighted.

I swung open a window.

"Hi," I said. "Mrs. Hitchcock?"

"Yes."

"I'm Art Kleps. Please come up. The door's open."

Mummy never cracked a smile, and declined to sit. She stood on the second-floor landing in the doorway, while her companion hung back a little, and shot questions at me and Wendy in drill-sergeant tones. She was obviously a woman accustomed to command, and I must confess to being somewhat jolted by the experience.

Who were we? What were we doing here? Who invited us? Isn't that illegal? Good-bye.

"Holy shit," I said to Wendy, as the Rolls rolled over the bridge.

Had we played it wrong? Probably. Would it have made any difference if we had played it right? I doubt it, unless suddenly stabbing the woman in the ass with a hypodermic full of acid would be considered "playing it right." That would have galvanized a lot of people into action, and made some kind of difference, but exactly what kind of difference it would have made is a whole other question.

And that was the end of that one. I don't remember ever saying a word to Mummy's sons or daughters-in-law about her visit or hearing a word about it from them. We didn't even talk about it among ourselves. It was like one of those minor earthquakes in California. The day it happens, nobody talks about anything else. The day after, people are strangely uncommunicative. The day after that, it's as if it never happened.

Mummy, according to Billy, did not exactly revel in her status as a prime specimen of the Mellon zillions on the hoof. "Oh, I don't know, boys," she would often say as they rolled past Levittown or some other '50s development of modest new houses, "sometimes I think I should give all the money away and we should go live in a house like one of those over there," causing little Billy and little Tommy to laugh so hard they fell off their jump seats.

Nor did she approve of Billy's undisguised greed for more, more and yet more. "Why, you're nothing but a fast-buck artist!" she told him one time.

Well, we all have our crosses to bear, I guess, as my mother often remarked.

Speaking of mothers, the Arthur-Wendy wedding seemed to stimulate Betsy Ross, who had been opportuned by Howie Druck for some time to make their liaison legal, to make his dreams come true. Their marriage was celebrated a couple weeks later, but this time at the Bowling Alley with Bill Haines doing the honors instead of Tim. Haines had just the right voice for this office: deep, resonant, assured.

It was a pleasure to listen to Haines recite, but it did seem strange to hear Max Müller's translation of the *Prajna-Paramita* at a wedding ceremony, which, after all, is addition portending multiplication, rather than subtraction.

But, then again, why not? What better time to remind people of the illusory nature of the world?

I have it on tape:

Everything passes, things appearing, things disappearing. But when it is all over, everything having appeared and having disappeared, being and extinction both transcended, still the basic emptiness and silence abides, and that is blissful peace. Thus, oh Saraputra, all things having the nature of emptiness, have no beginning and have no ending. They are neither faultless nor not faultless. They are neither perfect nor imperfect. In emptiness there is no form, no sensation, no perception, no discrimination, no consciousness, there is no eye, no ear, no nose, no tongue, no sensitiveness to contact, no mind. There is no sight, no sound, no smell, no taste, no touch, no mental process, no object, no knowledge, no cessation of ignorance, there is no noble Fourfold Truth, no pain, no cause of pain, no cessation of pain, there is no decay and no death. There is no knowledge of Nirvana, there is no obtaining of Nirvana. Why is there no obtaining of Nirvana? Because Nirvana is in the realm of no thingness. If the ego, soul or personality was an enduring entity it could not obtain Nirvana. So long as man is seeking highest wisdom he is still abiding in the realm of consciousness. In highest Samadhi, having transcended consciousness, he has passed beyond discrimination and knowledge, beyond the reach of change or fear, he is already enjoying Nirvana. The perfect understanding of this and the patient acceptance of it is the highest perfect wisdom, that is, the Prajna-Paramita. All the buddhas of the past, present and future, having attained highest samadhi awake to find themselves realizing Prajna-Paramita. Therefore, oh Saraputra, everyone should seek self realization of Prajna-Paramita, the transcendent truth, the unsurpassable truth, the truth that ends all truth, the truth that ends all pain, the truth that is forever true. Oh Prajna-Paramita, oh transcendent truth that spans the troubled ocean of life and death, safely carry all seekers to the other shore of Enlightenment. Listen to the mantra, the great mysterious mantra: Gate, gate, paragate, parasamgate, bodhi svaha! Gone, gone, gone to that other shore, safely passed to that other shore. Prajna-Paramita. So may it be. Wisdom, hail!

Ladyfingers were also distributed at the Betsy-Howie wedding, but they had much more of a kick to them than ours had had, and Haines made sure that everyone knew about it.

As a result, most of the straight guests present didn't take any, although quite a few put one or two away for a rainy day. All, however, were treated to a demonstration of what is meant by the expression "freaking freely" which will probably remain indelibly engraved on their memories for life. During the reception, someone shouted, "Hey, who's that up on the roof?" and all eyes turned skyward.

Pat McNeill, naked as a jaybird, was prancing around on the

porch roof in front of Tim's room. Beatles music floated down to us, as well as Pat's voice.

She was shouting, "Yoo hoo, Timothy Leary, come on up here. I want to get fucked" and other requests of a similar nature, interspersed with snatches of song and girlish giggles. Someone stepped out of a window and pulled her in. Conversation at the party, which had been somewhat strained, became highly animated.

Tim told me later that getting clothes on Pat had been quite a struggle. Finally, she agreed to put on a pair of Tim's pants, but nothing else. Two boo hoos from Philadelphia who happened to be visiting that day told me that they had been quietly "meditating" (watching goldfish) in the music room that evening when Pat had appeared and sat down next to them, bummed a cigarette, made some idle conversation, and then asked, in a matter-of-fact tone, "Hey, would you guys care to fuck?" They didn't, perhaps because they were not attracted to women in general.

"Let's fuck" trips are pretty common, although Pat's was more dramatic than most. Her ideation, if any, probably went something like this:

Now that I'm stoned, what do I want to do?

What I really want to do is get humped by Timothy Leary, my sterling guru.

Why not ask for it? It's natural, and nothing to be ashamed of.

After all, should I be secretive, sneaky and hypocritical about this or come right out with it?

Nobody has the right to criticize me for expressing a natural wish. Dishonesty is one of the greatest curses of mankind.

Why shouldn't women say they want to screw just like the men do?

Come to think of it, why shouldn't I take my clothes off and dance on the roof? That would be fun, and men like to look at naked women, don't they? If I want Tim to fuck me, I should show him what he's getting.

What about Rosemary?

To hell with Rosemary. All's fair in love and war.

What about embarrassing my husband and children and Howie and Betsy and so forth?

I'm setting a good example. They should all take off their clothes too, and announce whom they want to fuck. Everybody wants to fuck. Why don't they take their clothes off and go at it?

If this was, indeed, the way Pat thought, it would have been difficult to refute her at any point.

She wasn't waving a gun around. She was waving her ass around. Was Pat's ass injuring anyone?

If Pat had behaved this way in Macy's basement instead of on the Big House roof, it would have been a different matter altogether. "Location is everything," as they say, or, as Blake put it, "One law for the lion and the ox is oppression."

Shortly after the Howie-Betsy wedding, Haines kicked Sarasvati out into the cruel, Sado-Judeo-Paulinian world once again. Perhaps the burlesque show on the Big House roof had reminded him of what his most ardent female admirer really wanted: to be hosed down with his precious bodily fluids. Immediately after getting the heave-ho, Sarasvati appeared at the Gatehouse, sobbing and simpering and asking for my advice.

Since Haines and I were, once again, not on speaking terms, I suggested that she borrow some of my camping equipment and hide out in the woods on the hill overlooking the Ashram, so she could spy on the object of her affections from a safe place. She did, and it drove Haines into a frenzy, as I had expected.

Reports came back to me of Haines blundering through the brush brandishing his cane and vowing to suspend his vows of "ahimsa" (nonviolence) if he caught her. Eventually, much to everyone's astonishment, Sarasvati, instead of creeping quietly back into the outer circle during a trip, as was her usual tactic, left the property, and wasn't heard from for about two weeks. When she returned, beautifully dressed and carrying expensive new luggage bulging with presents for the kids, Haines was too flabbergasted, and probably too happy to see her again, to offer any objections. I happened to be present at the Ashram at the time, my latest difference of opinion with Bill, whatever it was, having been resolved or, more likely, totally forgotten.

Her story was incredible even by Millbrookian standards. She had pried $100 out of Susan Schoenfeld's ribs before she left, and had taken this sum to the nearest race track where she placed the entire amount on the nose of a 100-to-1 shot named Swami, which won. With the proceeds, she flew down to British Guiana where Dr. Mishra, the Ashram's original guru, was living, his visa to the United States having expired shortly after the Ananda breakup. Mishra treated her with the greatest civility and invited her to stay as his house guest for a few days.

When she left, Mishra gave her a present to take to Bill: a bottle of Scotch whiskey. "What the hell did he give me this for?" Bill asked, turning it around in his hands and then passing it to me. "He knows I almost never drink."

The rest of us, however, did, and it wasn't long before Sarasvati was back in her usual rags, rolling around on the floor, giggling and muttering to herself while Bill gave her an occasional friendly poke with his cane.

Probably because the chicken coops, where kid visitors often spent the night, were located there, the worst freak-outs seemed to occur in the ruined gardens below the farm manager's house, where stern Clum and his brood might hear them, or, if they were really lucky, see them. In one instance, when I happened to be nearby and was called upon to help, the Clum family, if they were watching, were treated to the sight of a Chinese boy screaming and writhing around on the ground as if entangled with an invisible boa constrictor, while a baby-faced, teenage American girl slowly removed her clothes in front of him, as if performing some kind of weird sex-cult ritual. That's the way it looked when I arrived.

Diana, eighteen, a frequent visitor who had shared some LSD with the Chinese boy and a couple other kids up on Ecstasy Hill a few hours earlier, solemnly explained that she thought the Chinese boy was screaming for her pussy, since that was what he had wanted earlier, but I managed to convince her that this was an unlikely motive for flailing the ground with one's arms and legs while howling like an animal.

"Come on, Diana," I said, as I yanked her jeans up, "You're cute, but you're not that cute."

Using the usual soothing syrup, I talked the Chinese boy down. When he came out of it, he didn't remember his freak-out at all, or anything leading up to it, only the happy parts of the trip up in the hills earlier, looking down on the misty vistas of the Hudson Valley and talking to the other kids about the inner meaning of it all. But he had caused distress in the household of a benefactor, and the way he had been brought up that was a cause for great shame. No problem, Chinese boy. It's all part of the game. Try it again some time.

Diana later became a full-time Ashramite in Arizona, where she and Betsy and a living doll named Jane did a lot to help relieve the aridity of it all. The Chinese boy, too embarrassed to return, wrote us a nice note apologizing for his conduct and saying he had benefited greatly from the experience. It sure as hell didn't look like it at the time, but this is often the case.

Otto punctuated the final months with two bursts of gunfire, neither one of which hurt anyone or was intended to. The first burst burst when Sam and Martica Clapp, Billy, Aurora, Wendy and I accompanied him to the small town near Woodstock where, sure enough, he showed us his submachine gun factory under the maple trees in a quiet residential neighborhood. He introduced us to the boss, who praised him as one of their most trusted advisors on difficult technical problems. As a fitting climax to our tour of the premises, Otto, while twitching, sweating and muttering as usual, loaded a few rounds into the drum magazine of a freshly fabricated 1921 model Thompson and fired a fusillade from a back door into a mud puddle in the parking lot. None of the assembly-line workers even bothered to look up from their work.

The second burst burst after Otto appeared one evening at the Gatehouse with a brand-new North Vietnamese army rifle and an equally pristine wooden box of Chinese ammo, and asked to sleep on the floor of my office that night because he had had a premonition that we would need protection. How, in the midst of America's maniacal invasion and brutalization of Vietnam, had Otto acquired these samples of the ordnance with which these brave Buddhists defended their homeland against the demonic power of the Pope and the Pentagon? I didn't bother to ask.

Sure enough, at about 3 a.m. some drunks (we presumed) showered the place with firecrackers and Otto scared them off by firing two sharp, socialist shots into the earth near the wall. When the State Police arrived, the noise no doubt having been reported, Otto boldly presented himself, explained his conduct, and showed them his weapon.

They left without even writing anything down, perhaps because they didn't feel up to an exercise in calligraphy at that hour of the night, or because they had heard as much of Otto's surreal and detail-filled monologue as they wanted to hear, and didn't feel like getting all of that down on paper either.

The parties went on.

Aluminum Dreams, a rock group in which Billy had taken an interest, probably because of the female vocalist, who would soon move on to greener pastures, took over the second floor of the Big House. They never made it, and didn't deserve to. Tim, Bill and I did our best to ignore them, which wasn't easy if you happened to be within earshot. Billy wrote off thousands of dollars which he had put into equipment and expenses, and almost lost his servants also, because of the imperious demands the three male musicians made when they were at the Bungalow.

Tord found a girl, appropriately Amazonian in appearance, who had come to the property in search of a lost horse. She never seemed to say anything, at least not when I was around, and Tord became increasingly incommunicative himself. They lived together on the third floor for a while and eventually married, off the property.

The "Third World" egalitarian-primitivist group erected a "Tepee Town" back in the woods. Another group, loosely associated with them, came in to make a movie. They had professional equipment but little capital. The general idea was to represent heads as noble Indians and narcs as depraved sheriffs and drunken lawmen of the Old West, but I don't think there was a plot, as the term is normally understood. There was no script. There was a pink horse, ha ha, but after you've seen one pink horse, you've seen them all.

Tim, naturally, did his best to convert these extremely amorphous cinematographic concepts into The Life and Times of Timothy Leary. As the producer said to me just before he left, broke and with almost no usable film, "Well, I've discovered one thing. You either go on Tim's trip around here or you don't go on any trip at all," which I thought summed up the general situation very well.

If he had simply recorded, without serious interference, snippets of everyday life on the property it might have made a good flick.

A visitor with a shortwave radio set, which he kept in the trunk of his car, showed up one day. Since a small island in the Caribbean was at that time threatening to declare its independence of the U.K. and casting about for support, we all thought it would be a good idea if Billy had a chat with the island's Prime Minister by radio, to see how he would react to the idea of naturalizing a community of acid heads, some of whom, presumably, would be filthy rich.

Since Billy, greatly amused, said he thought it was worth a shot, the radio was set up in the Bungalow's library, and a mildly stoned and jovial group gathered to watch the visitor twirl his knobs and tweak his toggles; a waste of time, as it turned out.

All the ham could get over his device were hilariously synchronistic snatches of this, that and the other thing from the Caribbean region, none of which had any practical utility for any of us: communistic denunciations of the rich, homilies on "communication problems," news of drug busts, etc. The island was unreachable, possibly because the CIA or MI6 or the BVD had jammed the local frequencies.

Billy and I and almost everyone else in the audience enjoyed the farce for what it was, but the best Tim could manage was a tight smile. Leaving the ham aside, he seemed to have been the only person present who had taken the project seriously.

Afterwards, because Tim asked to try out our new used car, I found myself in the back seat with the ham, a young guy with slicked-back, black hair and aquiline features, who looked like the model for a line drawing of a radio enthusiast I had seen many times in my youth, in advertisements in my favorite magazine of those days, *Popular Science*. Here he was, in the flesh.

Wendy sat next to Tim, who proceeded to take the worst and

longest way back to the Big House over the most rutted and pot-holed roads, at an unsafe speed, while twisting his head around to carry on a conversation about radio with the guy next to me.

"For Christ's sake, Tim," I finally said, after the car had suffered its third or fourth wrenching shock, "slow down. You're driving like a maniac."

"You think I'm going too fast, Arthur?"

"I have complete faith in you, Tim," said the ham at my side, before I could answer.

"Well, I wish you would slow down a little," said Wendy.

Tim slowed down. To show all was forgiven, I made a comment about how much of the radio chatter we had heard had been synchronistic with the project or with life at Millbrook in general.

"Yes," Tim said. "Amazing, isn't it? You know, there are times when I am convinced there is someone or something up there writing the script."

"That's what I think," said the ham, who then proceeded to deliver a series of routine speculations about how LSD might enhance "outer space communication," and allow us to contact "higher powers" and such, all of which all of us had heard before ad nauseam from other visitors intent, not on learning anything, but on securing our subscription to their favorite fantasies of deliverance from above. Tim, however, lapped it right up, dropping in a comment here and there demonstrating that he too, could read Sunday supplements and science fiction magazines.

Later, because the car would be needed early the next morning to take someone at the Ashram to the dentist, Wendy and I walked back to the Gatehouse in the pale moonlight and dark tunnels made by the overhanging roadside trees.

I made what I thought was a most disillusioning suggestion.

"Wendy," I said, "let's face it. Tim's a supernaturalist science-fictionalist or something like that. He thinks something up there (I pointed to a patch of stars in the roof of our leafy corridor) is doing it. He doesn't understand synchronicity."

"I never thought he did," Wendy said.

If I had not deluded myself about Tim I might not have come to understand synchronicity myself. There was another strange aspect: It seemed to me that many of the "troops," who rarely said anything philosophical, had a better general appreciation of the subject, just as Wendy did, than their supposed leader and teacher. At least, in the case of the kids, when they talked about "God" they usually meant something vague, abstract and Emersonian. At best, they were Deists. Transcendentalists. Pantheists. What the hell. That's about the best one can expect from most people.

Tim, in contrast, believed a gigantic "cosmic" entity of some kind was "doing it." This, to his way of thinking, was more "scientific." In the land of the partially sighted, a man who was blind was king.

Otto Preminger visited the community, prior to making one of the least Psychedelian of the commercial "psychedelic" movies which appeared around that time. Tim and Bill brought Preminger down to the Gatehouse to meet me, but I was in town buying booze. In this instance my vice may have saved me from a fate worse than death, but in general, my drinking was getting to the problem stage.

Everything constructive that I wanted to do cost money, and I didn't have any. All I had were promises and parties, sometimes two of the latter a week. As for developing the place into a self-supporting mecca for Psychedelian religionists, the flaming handwriting was on the wall, and the message was dire.

Tim's group became increasingly disorganized, disgruntled and diluted with transients. Haines, in self-defense, ceased to concern himself with anything other than the Ashram and its immediate surroundings, as did I in regard to the Gatehouse. It became clear the place was headed towards anarchy and there wasn't much Haines or I could do about it. If the influx continued, we would merely hold enclaves in what amounted to a public park.

This was dangerous in all kinds of ways but particularly threatening to the owners. "Use easement" and related legal concepts were not part of what might be called the "conceptuaries" of us peasants, but the Hitchcock Cattle Corporation and Mellon family lawyers were aware of such things. The risks that the twins had already taken of torts and criminal defenses blaming everything on them were buffered by an intimate knowledge of what kind of people they were dealing with, that is, nice people, or at worst, harmless—to zillionaires—nuts.

Now, all of that was changing. For all they knew, some Uriah Heepish person they had never seen had already knitted himself a shack of twigs and wattles in their woods and was busily hand lettering page after page of perfectly drafted legalese which would make the surrounding acreage a legal leper colony or a port of entry when filed with the county clerk, and tie them up in court for the next 400 years if they didn't pay him off through the nose.

Photographs? Tape recordings? There was a boundless scope for apprehensions of all kinds.

Every time Tim went to New York he would get drunk and invite everyone he met to come up to Millbrook. It was clear he was deliberately demolishing the tripartite organization of the place which, for a while, had seemed so natural and promising. Either Tommy, who now made no secret of his dissatisfaction with the swelling population statistics, would revolt or we would be raided again or both. A wide-open Psychedelian mob scene would not be tolerated for long in Dutchess County.

Given the enormous potential political clout of our patrons, and assuming three relatively small and stable groups, a scene which could have been written off by the powers that were as just another whimsy of the rich might have survived much longer, but hordes of anonymous fake Indians from the gutters of New York represented a virtual guarantee of disaster in the near future.

We were up against long-entrenched local Republican ruling families of such reactionary and downright fascist dispositions that they had hated having Franklin Delano Roosevelt, "the Squire of Hyde Park," living among them. To use Aldous Huxley's apt characterization of Tim's much milder earlier conduct, Tim was now "snoot-cocking" these mass murderers and serial killers (warmongers and capital-punishment freaks) in a way they could not ignore.

Tim knew, in a general kind of way, what would happen. Since it would happen anyway, he wanted it to happen sooner rather than later and in a form that suited the wave of populist political rhetoric that he was riding at the time. He wanted to milk it. "It's all a matter of timing, Arthur," he earnestly informed me several times.

It became clear that the modest, domestic, essentially reclusive practice of Psychedelianism, which we had enjoyed for a while at Millbrook and which suited the Hitchcocks and Bill and me and almost everyone else around just fine, appeared of little account and eminently expendable to Tim, who cared little for the gods of the hearth, especially when those commonplace deities were contrasted with the newly risen and enormously powerful gods of television, the mass media, and the popular culture in general, with whom, at the cost of considerable personal sacrifice and unremitting effort, he believed he had achieved an "in."

As Tim saw it, our values led nowhere, which was true because they were all ends in themselves, which we already were enjoying and merely wished to preserve, as one would wish to preserve for as long as possible the pot of gold at the end of the rainbow.

The assumption that the whole scene would collapse in a few years, at most, was almost certainly correct if nothing changed radically for the better. I don't think Tim saw any future in the elitist, defensive, xenophobic enclave concept. Our community was not located where strange things were done under the midnight sun, or where an influx of a million a year or so would bedazzle the local peasantry with visions of down payments on mobile homes, but right smack in the middle of one of the most exclusive residential areas in the United States, which our most powerful and determined enemies considered their own private parkland, more or less by divine right. After all, they owned most of it, didn't they?

In contrast to the pointlessness of trying to hang on under such unfavorable circumstances, making a "photo op" out of it all and pandering to the kid culture by pretending to be the most communistic egalitarian-primitivist around, would help bring Tim fame and fortune and perhaps support him in his old age. It would keep his show on the road by keeping his name in the papers and his face on the tube.

There was nothing unreasonable about this analysis, but the question that bothered me was: If Billy Hitchcock, Tim Leary, Bill Haines and I (and the core community in general, which had demonstrated many signs of life when given half a chance), with our various assets and complementary talents, couldn't maintain a stable Psychedelian community, who could?

Well, what reason was there to believe that, at that time and in the United States, anyone could? Even so, if Tim, Bill and I had ever approached Billy with a reasonable (xenophobic enclavish) plan, in which our roles were defined in terms of our demonstrable talents, it's not unimaginable that Billy (and maybe Peggy and maybe even Tommy) would have funded the community the way it needed to be funded. Maybe it would have been necessary to move the whole works somewhere else, maybe offshore, but was a total crack-up absolutely unavoidable?

Why, in an effort to straighten things out, didn't Tim, Bill, Billy and I ever take a trip together without having fifty or so other people around at the same time? If it hadn't done any good, at least we would have had the satisfaction of knowing we had tried.

History is full of these almost unanswerable why didn'ts. The craziest aspects of human nature are often better illustrated by what isn't done than by what is.

The history of science and technology, which one might suppose to be relatively free of them, is in fact full of these seemingly inexplicable lapses. What kinds of beings are these who waste millions of man-hours by not inventing the cotton gin, for example? It's said that Whitney first got the idea by watching a cat trying to snatch a chicken by clawing through a fence. Is it really that much harder to imagine the cotton being pulled away from the seeds than to imagine the seeds being picked from the cotton? Why were all those seafarers allowed to perish from scurvy when the efficacy of citrus to revive almost-dead men was common knowledge among sailors for centuries?

There is no shortage of current examples. Why, to cite one, doesn't every fire engine and emergency vehicle on earth carry a portable tank of dimethyl sulfoxide to spray on burns and wounds? You tell me.

Few people can look back over their lives, after they have been around a while, without thinking of all kinds of simple, obvious things they could and should have done to solve their problems, but didn't do, for which there seems to be no explanation other than to say "I was blind."

I don't think the problems of which I speak can be eliminated, at least not directly, by reforms in the social order. They are manifestations of a universal mental disability caused by imprints and the repetition compulsion (or just plain "habit," if you prefer), which knows no borders and is stronger than any ideology.

The power of imprints, which are simply one's original impressions of how things are related, to persist in the face of overwhelming contrary evidence, is illustrated in my case by a "belief" I hold that the city of New York is north of Westchester County. Notice the present tense. Knowing about a manifestation of this mechanism may weaken, but rarely eliminates, the affliction.

I must have acquired this image at about the age of five, when my family moved from the city to Crestwood. I have been in and around and under and over the city and its environs off and on ever since, but to this day, unless I make an effort to see it otherwise, the island of Manhattan points north.

The East River is on the West Side and like the Hudson, which is on the East Side, flows north. I recall being vaguely concerned as a child, when the family car would turn left on the Bronx River Parkway for our annual trip to Vermont, that we were headed in the wrong direction. "Well, Dad's probably going around the city somehow," I would say to myself, and return to elbowing my brothers for my fair share of space in the back seat. At some point, when the landscape became unfamiliar, the entire world would make a gigantic 180-degree turn, and both Crestwood and New York City would be behind us, firmly to the south but, in my mind's eye, with the city closer to us than the suburban county.

Why? It was my original impression, that's all. The city seemed cold, I guess, in every sense of the term, and Crestwood seemed warm in every sense of the word. Crestwood was therefore south of the city.

Returning from New York in the helicopter one clear and almost windless day, Billy decided to go straight up and hover for a while. The entire landscape of which I speak was spread out beneath us like a relief map. I could see the actual state of affairs in great detail. Billy and I had been talking about the contrasts and similarities of our boyhoods and we both tried to locate my old boarding school in Bronxville. No luck. I suggested that we swoop down and follow the Bronx River but, on consulting the gas gauge, Billy decided we had better be on our way.

Did this experience correct or even diminish this ludicrous mental problem?

Not in the slightest. The Battery's up and the Bronx is down. I still have two maps of the area in my mind's eye, one correct and superficial, the other false and powerful.

It's an irritant when I'm reading fiction set in the area. I know my imagery is warped, and I struggle with it for a while, and then give up. How can I possibly enjoy a good story while twisting maps around in my mind at the same time? It can't be done. At least it's conscious. I can, if I must, as when driving in and out of the New York area, force myself to see things right side up, as it were.

Could I get rid of this troublesome imprint on a trip? Certainly, if I insisted on regression to my early childhood for that purpose, and found someone willing and able to assist me in this usually boring and frequently laborious process. It has never seemed worth the effort. If repeatedly jailed because of a compulsion to turn road signs in the area backwards, or something of the kind, I probably would think it worth the effort.

It may all serve a useful purpose, in that I am reminded, whenever the terrain of my birthplace is brought to my attention, which is pretty frequently, of the power of imprints in general. Without these reminders, I might forget why it is so many people believe in so many crazy things. It encourages tolerance, of which combative people can always use an extra shot, and pity for lunatics, of which almost all of us need as much as we can get.

I'm not talking about indoctrination as it is ordinarily understood. If, during my childhood, the doctrine that New York City was north of us had been constantly propounded as what everyone ought to believe, the way supernaturalist "Christianity" was, in our home in Crestwood, and I had been obliged to bow my head and affirm that the city was in a "space warp zone," or something similar, and to listen to bizarre anecdotes and patently fallacious arguments denying the validity of magnetism and condemning Rand McNally as an agent of the Devil, I think I would have resisted.

Since the subject never came up, there was nothing to resist.

Catholicism is more powerful than Protestantism in this way. The Roman Catholic Church does not, except as almost emotionless mental exercises, trouble to make out any kind of rational argument to its captive audience of little kiddies. Instead, it simply hammers in the images as early as possible and reinforces the habits as often as possible.

The Sado-Judeo-Paulinian zombies who have criminalized Psychedelianism and destroyed the Bill of Rights in an effort to stamp it out were brought up on a vast array of lunatic imprints and are blind slaves to the repetition compulsion. Most of our persecutors are so crazy about so many important particular things that they might as well be called crazy in a general way. For people loaded with the classic American Sado-Judeo-Paulinian religious imprints, the whole world is turned upside down.

This mental derangement, involving, as it does, so many self-destructive compulsions, will eventually polish the place off if it goes uncorrected. Americans are not simply European transplants or the descendants thereof. They are a different breed altogether, and the rest of the world ought to keep its guard up.

Americans, in general and unless pushed too far, are willing to disregard what is staring them right in the face in favor of believing authoritative pronouncements or the standard cant or popular myths on any and all subjects. Compared to Europeans, they are just plain gullible. They "have faith," faith in anything they want to have faith in. There is no need to "have faith" in what seems obviously correct, or probable. The necessity for faith only arises when one wishes to believe in, or cannot help believing, things that are inherently fantastic or "unbelievable."

In Vermont, in 1972, I got some plans for a plywood dinghy, and discovered what seemed to be a serious error in the drawings of the bow. I wrote to the company, one of the two largest in the nation, and asked about it.

"You're quite right," the reply came back, "the line drawing [sic] on the bow is in the improper position. Over the past couple of years, more than 3,000 Eight Balls have been made, but you are the first one to make a comment on this fact."

Only a week or so later, I received a letter from the art director of Portal Publications, one of the biggest art print houses in the country. I had complained about the quality of a Maxfield Parrish I ordered; it looked murky to me.

I quote a few lines:

"At last! A real live opinion. I've had to contend with oceans of praise. We've sold hundreds of thousands ... no attempt was made to correct the color. I feel embarrassed and infuriated ... disgusted ... ."

People who build boats and order art prints are not, generally speaking, stupid. The various generals who repeatedly assaulted virtually impregnable positions with inadequate forces in the Civil War before Grant came along were not stupid. All those cotton planters who never once considered that you could pull the cotton away from the seeds instead of pulling the seeds away from the cotton were not stupid. All those sea captains who failed to include a couple barrels of dried lemons in their list of stores before sailing weren't stupid.

The builders of the great Near Eastern civilizations who invented astronomy, mathematics, writing, and law, but took 2,000 years to think of making wedge-shaped bricks for arches and vaults, were not stupid.

They were not sufficiently disenchanted. The psychedelic experience is not the spell, but the lifting of the spell, the transformation of the toad, the maiden's salvation; not the sword in the stone, but the sword out of the stone.

Was there any way we could have prevailed at Millbrook against the monstrous forces of evil arrayed against us? I don't know, but the first thing required would have been a "united front." If Haines, Hitchcock and I had set a date for a trip and invited Tim to join us, it's hard to imagine him staying away. It would have been impolitic, the one and only cardinal sin in Tim's book. He would have made difficulties about time, place and circumstances so as to give himself an edge, and these manipulations probably would have aroused Haines to a fury, but a meeting to discuss the proposed trip could have been arranged at which, perhaps, Billy and I could have bombed Tim and Bill and, at minimum, things would have lightened up a little.

My memory is hazy about it. It seems to me Haines and I discussed the possibility once or twice. I recall Haines flatly saying, "He won't do it," and changing the subject, but I never talked to Billy about it, or did I? I'm sure I never suggested it to Tim. I let it slide. I never made a project out of it, never allowed the subject to fully engage my imagination.

By the time such a trip became a necessity if we were to survive as a community, I was dispirited and exhausted, ready to throw in the towel. The thought of trying to persuade Tim, Bill or Billy to do anything they didn't want to do made me shudder, quiver, vibrate, flinch, flutter and roll. I had been over that trench top too many times. I was groggy and shell-shocked. It is said victory in battle often goes to the side that makes one last effort when neither side has any heart left for fighting.

At Millbrook a last charge of the forces of right bows and bright dawns was never made.

So we lost the battle. The war goes on.

Chapter 41

THE INTERDICT

The vast castle loomed black upon the hilltop, not a spark visible about it.

Late in July, the Republicrat, Voodoo-Papist gang lords of the Place of Overflowing Shitholes demonstrated for all to see that they had even less respect for the law than we did.

Their minions blockaded the property, stopping everyone coming from, going to, or merely attempting to get past it. Any male motorist who was casually attired or not recently barbered was ordered to park on the side of the road while he and his vehicle were searched for proscribed substances. One of Jackie's friends from town was arrested for possession of a few shreds of the lesser sacrament after he exited the pedestrian entry under the Gatehouse. Several drivers whose cars didn't come up to the sheriff's exacting standards were arrested on such charges as "dirty license plates" or "obscured windshield." I was at the Big House when the first reports of these events came in, and Tim and I rushed down to the Gatehouse to see for ourselves. Sure enough, It looked like a military operation. Cars were pulled off the road all around the T-junction of Route 44 in front of the Gatehouse, and every vehicle that came along was halted for inspection by sheriff's deputies standing in the road. Radios crackled. Police cars came, picked up prisoners, and left. Where was Wendy? Our car was parked under the Gatehouse arch, but her bicycle was gone. Tim was worried about Jackie. He was out there somewhere too.

"Listen, Art," Tim said, "you call Noel Tepper and keep on calling him until you reach him. And call the papers and the ACLU. I'm going out there and find out what's going on."

Tim then demonstrated consummate theatricality under pressure by picking a flower in Swami's corner and sticking it in his hair before he opened the gate and crossed the road into enemy territory. After a brief exchange with the cops, he was ushered into a patrol car which then sped away toward Millbrook.

I went upstairs and called Noel. He would be right over. He would call the ACLU and ask them to send observers. I called the *Poughkeepsie Journal*. They would send a reporter and a photographer right away. I went out in front of the portcullis, but not over our property line, to wait for Noel. Some of the cops waved to me. I waved back. They were, after all, merely working stiffs doing their jobs as ordered. If they went no further than that, I bore them no personal animosity.

When Noel arrived, he had his wife Elly with him and an ACLU friend. Two more ACLUers pulled up next to them in another car.

"This is unbelievable," Noel said. "I stopped at the courthouse in town and it's an absolute madhouse. Apparently they're just arresting anyone whose looks they don't like. Did you know they got Wendy?"

"What for?" I asked. I was stunned. Wendy never carried anything illegal with her, and she didn't have the car.

"No visible means of support," Noel said. "She was just riding her bike and they arrested her because she didn't have any identification papers or money on her."

"What?"

Noel nodded. I had heard him right. And Tim had been arrested on a bad check charge. Two or three other residents had been picked up, but most of the arrestees were strangers who just happened to be passing by. Tim's bad check, for $8.11, had been provided by an ex-cop who owned a sporting goods store in the

Place of Overflowing Shitholes. We needed about $300 for bail, Noel estimated.

I drove up to the Bungalow. Billy and Tommy and Aurora were all, hmmm, away. Suzanne, who looked terrified, and who can blame her, wrote out a check for $300. Noel and I circled the property to survey the ACLU posts. We saw one "squirrelly liberal" with binoculars perched on the branch of an apple tree just inside the west gate. Then we drove to town.

A small crowd surrounded the courthouse, a one-room, storefront affair on a residential side street. Noel went in and I walked over to Merritt Books with Suzanne's check. The always genial owner cashed it and vehemently expressed his disapproval of Sheriff Quinlan's conduct, as did several other wide-eyed locals who were standing around. Was this Russia, or what? A sixteen-year-old bicyclist, daughter of a prominent local family, had been stopped and questioned at length. Several other town residents had been given the same kind of treatment.

I handed Noel the cash. Wendy pleaded not guilty and Noel put up the $50 bail the judge had ordered. On the following Tuesday Wendy pled guilty and was fined the amount of the bail, as were most of the other people against whom kangaroo-court charges had been laid. Tim was discharged when he showed that he had covered the check.

The blockade continued until evening. When it was over, Tim, Rosemary, the Teppers, Wendy and I drove to the Place of Overflowing Shitholes and had dinner at Howard Johnson's. It was clear to all of us that this was just the beginning. We had to make plans. When drinks were ordered, I passed, much to Tim's astonishment.

"I'd better lay off," I explained. "Who knows what the morrow will bring? But you people who can handle it should go ahead and slosh it down to your heart's content."

There was unanimous consent to all the principles Haines and I had advocated for months. One would have wondered, listening to the unanimity that prevailed, how we could possibly have become so disorganized in the first place.

From now on, only invited visitors would be allowed on the property. We would put a sign on the portcullis saying so. Tim,

Haines and I would meet regularly to check people out. All sacramental substances would be stashed outdoors. We would try to convince Billy to put Noel on a retainer to represent all of us. We would try to convince Billy to make judicious "campaign donations" at the county level. We would try to convince Billy to do all sorts of things.

"But Billy is ... at sea," Tim said, grinning at the double appropriateness of the expression. Billy was at sea. A little yacht trip in the Caribbean, as a matter of fact.

Chapter 42
WAR!

War, and the knights of the realm divided into a king's party and a Sir Launcelot's party.

Defending oneself against governmental tyranny in the United States is always primarily a financial problem, unless you're rich or have the backing of someone who is. The conviction rate in federal prosecutions is close to 99 percent, higher than what it was in Nazi Germany.

The whole system would collapse if the vast majority of those arrested and jailed were not forced by poverty to plead guilty because of an inability to do all the things which members of the oligarchy regard as routine: to make bail and hire genuine lawyers, private detectives and witnesses; to bribe the police and judges and media and/or finance and support their rivals for election or appointment; to blackmail and intimidate and sue and expose and entrap everyone on the other side; to get them fired and/or force them into debt and buy and call all their paper; to issue threats or offers of more lucrative employment to cause them to defect and inform and sabotage their own cases; to appeal all adverse rulings to higher courts and, all else failing, to lower one's problem into those Stygian depths where the laws themselves are made and unmade, and the word "corruption" is meaningless, there being nothing with which to contrast it.

The Hitchcocks had the kind of money it takes to hire the most devious extortionists produced by the most prestigious law schools in the country to do all of the above. Had they done so, "Sieg" Heilman, the district attorney, and Quinlan, the county sheriff, might have ended up shoveling shit in the Hitchcock Cattle Company cow barns and tugging their forelocks when Billy and Tommy, their lords and masters and probation officers, passed by on horseback.

An apprehension of such unwelcome outcomes was the reason why the owners' magnificent residence on the hill was treated as if it were a mysterious phantasm during all the invasions of their domain made by the forces of law and order during the period that is covered by this book. The Bungalow could be seen by everyone else around, but it was invisible to the police. It wasn't that the cops avoided the place, no, they almost always came in by way of the east gate, right past Hurdle's house, and sometimes exchanged jocular remarks with him, and then went right past his employer's house.

By pretending that the Bungalow wasn't there, Sieg avoided stimulating powerful, instinctive defensive reactions in those who had the means to squash a scuttling little political roach like himself, and might even have been able to injure his masters.

Despite all the complaining that went on, those of us taking the heat put very little pressure on Billy and Tommy to do more than they did during the final months.

The rich, to a large extent justifiably, tend to equate the preservation of their capital with their health, safety, peace of mind and self-esteem, and by an unjustifiable extension, with all good, true and beautiful things in general. Wealth isn't everything, but it seems to support, nourish and protect everything. When it came down to the wire, Billy and Tommy put the conservation of their wonderful magical powers ahead of their recently formed and inchoate religious convictions and the protection of their vassals, friends and fellow fanatics, however one cares to sort us out, just as Sieg Heilman knew they would.

And what price would the rest of us have paid? If someone had handed me a million dollars, how much would I have risked on the defense of Millbrook as it was then constituted? The laws being what they had become since '64, not a dime. I would have emigrated to The Netherlands, or fled with my loot to some other relatively sane and safer place. Tim had a house in Berkeley. Did he sell it? Of course not.

The reluctance of Psychedelians in general, rich or poor, to pledge their lives, property, and sacred honor for the cause can make us appear to be mere dilettantes and triflers, compared to our barbaric ancestors.

Supernaturalists have generally displayed a willingness, if not an eagerness, to suffer and die, and to cause others to suffer and die, to defend, maintain and extend their doctrinal dominions against all enemies, foreign or domesticated, actual or hallucinated.

Based on the history of Western religion, one might have expected that Psychedelians, upon having our basic human rights so flagrantly trashed, would have done a little more in the way of retaliation.

Psychedelianism is not in this evil historical tradition. Violent reprisals would only escalate and prolong the conflict. Why should we respond to our persecutors in their own terms? The power of the experience itself is so great that we will eventually replace all competing religions with the same relentless efficiency displayed by the noble cane toad in its conquest of Northern Australia, and by means of similar techniques: through indigestibility primarily, but also by gathering together under streetlights at night to eat bugs and by sucking ourselves up through our own assholes when we are run over by cars.

When it's all over we can say that that karma took care of it. "Real" wars "really" are hell.

If any human beings are still around, or if, as I advocate, a new, genetically engineered species of similar biochemical configuration has replaced us jerks, the Supreme Sacrament will work just as well 1,000 years from now as it did the day it was discovered.

On the Tuesday after the blockade cases were settled, I typed up a public notice, with a map attached, defining the division of authority on the property. Tommy signed without hesitation.

Although I had talked briefly to Tim and Bill about trying to do this, and both had agreed that it would be a good idea, I don't think Tim or Bill expected anything would come of it. When it was published, Bill was delighted. Tim said nothing about it, which probably meant that he was displeased. Copies of the original documents are reproduced in this book.

The "Donation of Thomas," as I like to call it, was published in the next edition of the *Millbrook Round Table*. This public definition of the areas on the property governed by the leaders of our three Psychedelian sects, on Neo-American Church stationery, signed by Thomas Mellon Hitchcock as a director of the corporation that owned the place, and published in the town newspaper for all to read, has never been mentioned in any of the pop "social histories," published during the following thirty years, which purport to cover the subject.

If the hired scriveners who produce these fakes did any genuine research and referred to actual documentary evidence about anything, the sociological smarm, metaphysical cant and delivered "opinions" they depend on for a living would be unfavorably contrasted. Can't have that.

The Ashram provided a plywood, four-foot-square sign, which I nailed to the portcullis. "Private Property" it announced in rude red letters on a white background. "No Trespassing, Visitors by Appointment Only, Warning Grounds Patrolled, Trespassers Will Be Prosecuted."

When Billy returned from snorkling in the pellucid waters of the cerulean sea, Tim persuaded him to pilot his "Mixmaster," which had engines and props fore and aft of the cabin, a feature I liked a lot, to Caesar's Palace in Las Vegas with a load of select excursionists. This trip, he claimed, would provide those on it with a desperately needed opportunity to "get a fresh perspective" on the situation. Those left behind, Tim did not mention, would then have an obsolete and useless perspective on the situation. Rosemary would remain at the Big House, but Peggy and Ron would go. Tim might return from this vacation or he might not. He wasn't saying.

Since Tommy and Suzanne planned to be in New York for an indefinite period, Sam and Martica Clapp would occupy the

Bungalow until Billy returned. I was not offended by this but Billy apologized. He had offered the use of the house to the Clapps instead of to the Klepses, because he knew Sam and Martica would "take care of" Jack and Mary. Good point.

With Rosemary in the Big House would be Jackie and Susie Leary, the three Aluminum Dreams boys and a newly installed "caretaker" named Gregg Roland, a carpenter and all-around handyman who had recently appeared on the scene with a huge, very pregnant Negress and five brown kids at his side.

This was the official roster. Unofficially, many members of the League were filtering back into the Big House and the Bowling Alley.

One evening, shortly before his scheduled departure, Tim appeared at the Gatehouse, bearing a gallon jug of burgundy and wearing an expression of amused expectation.

"Art," Tim asked, after we had settled down in my office with glasses, "what am I supposed to do with all those people?"

I was somewhat surprised to hear this. When I asked, "What people?" Tim waved northwards and said, "Oh, all those people up there."

We both knew that he meant the League members, particularly those who believed they had established a special and sacred relationship with him. They expected, not unreasonably by normal standards, that their spiritual leader would attempt to preserve their religious community in some other location. Were they not his "essence friends"?

I had no interest in exploring the moral dimensions of this problem with Tim. It had been obvious to me for some time that he wanted the League to disperse.

"Damned if I know," I said. "Why, are they any worse than usual these days? I suppose they're a little uptight because you're leaving."

"They're absolutely helpless," Tim said. "Apparently they expect me to support them for the rest of their lives. I'm not their guru, I'm their nursemaid."

Of course, Tim had said all kinds of things which encouraged his people to take a completely impractical view of their situation at Millbrook, but I had learned that it was pointless to remind

Tim of anything he had said in previous incarnations, such as the day before yesterday.

I also assumed that many of the Leaguers had been attempting to "materialize" the "group spirit" or something of the sort in order to solve their problems. They hoped to produce a miracle by "getting their vibes together," and all of that kind of rot. People who have been gathering around a campfire night after night for months getting seriously stoned, and very often smashed as well, with the moon floating above and shadows dancing, and the metaphysics of Timothy Leary percolating in their brains, can't be blamed for thinking that way instead of figuring out how to find a lawyer courageous enough to bring suit on their behalf for hundreds of millions of dollars in compensation against William and Thomas Mellon Hitchcock and the Hitchcock Cattle Corporation for driving them and their children crazy with illegal drugs, thus criminalizing them and making them unemployable for life.

As far as Tim was concerned, the League, like the Castalia Foundation and IFIF before it, had been a mere plot line in a script for a show starring him. What might be called the "Millbrook Saga" had required that such groups exist, with Tim at the head of them. The set was now being demolished and the books closed on this miniseries. Like bit players and extras in a movie, everyone should now go home, make scrapbooks, and either retire from the business or look for employment elsewhere. Their services were no longer required.

All of this was entirely consistent with Tim's general way of looking at things, which he had stated and restated and overstated and had flagrantly practiced for years.

Could he help it if a sucker was born every minute?

Various aspects of the situation, new to me, came out as we continued talking. Gregg had built a kitchen for Rosemary on the third floor. The servants' wing was to be closed off completely for the winter. The Aluminum Dreams had half of the second floor and were driving Rosemary crazy with their practicing, which took place at any hour of the day or night when they happened to be awake and capable of wielding their instruments.

"What about the rest of them?" I asked.

Tim shrugged and lifted his arms.

Well, that takes care of that, I thought.

"Listen, Art," Tim said, "would you type something out for me? Use official Neo-American Church stationery. I want you to sign this too, if you will."

I snapped on my nice new electric portable, a gift from Sam Clapp, which Tim greatly admired. Back in the hills, he was obliged to disparage all such "unnatural" devices. Tim's statement was a sort of bequest to Marshall McNeill, granting him absolute suzerainty over the regions of Lunacy and Ecstasy hills, hunting and fishing rights, and so on. We both signed it.

"Good," Tim said, folding the document and sticking it into his pocket, "maybe this will satisfy him but I doubt it. Of course, what I'm doing is giving away something I never had in the first place. Those people don't seem to understand that Billy and Tommy Hitchcock own this place, not me."

Good point. Too bad he hadn't made it earlier and to a more general audience.

We had more wine.

"Art, why don't you take over the Big House?" Tim suddenly asked.

I laughed. Tim, who had appeared at least semi-serious when he made this ridiculous proposal, joined right in.

"I thought that would be your reaction," Tim said. "Well, you will look after Rosemary, won't you? Let's go up to the house and put up some SPIN signs, anyway."

Why not and why not. I called up the stairs to Wendy to tell her I would be back in a couple hours, and followed Tim up to the house.

If some soothsayer had told me, back in '64, that Timothy Leary would some day offer me control of the Big House, and that I would refuse it without hesitation, I would have concluded that I was dealing with a pretty sorry excuse for a soothsayer, indeed.

Tim could no more give me the Big House than he could give the woods behind it to Marshall, but putting that aside, and thinking of such a move as a replay of Haines and the Ashram moving in, even at this late date, well, hmmm. As Tim knew very well, he had given me a concept which, although inherently crazy, I couldn't help toying with. After all, I had pulled off some other extremely improbable things at Millbrook.

The most important negative factor was that Billy had not contributed a nickel to me or to Haines since he had put $1,000 into the *Catechism* project. Things were working out exactly as Haines had predicted. The Hitchcocks clearly hoped that without help from them, other than free rent, we would all be forced to leave to earn our daily bread by the sweat of our brows, as God intended.

Like hell we would, but it wasn't time to expand by trying to take over the Big House or anything else. It was time to contract, dig in, hang on, and all that kind of stuff. How, during the winter to come, I would heat the Gatehouse, which had what amounted to a refrigerated wind tunnel whistling under it much of the time, was something I didn't even want to think about, but it was a trivial problem compared to heating the Big House.

Aside from the economic problems, there was an almost endless list of other discouraging facts. Would Jackie respect my authority? No, he would resent me like crazy. Could I bring myself to kick him out of the family homestead if he continued to leave samples of the lesser sacrament lying around his room? Jackie had been busted for possession six or seven times altogether, being a firm believer in the "if your head is right you can't get hurt" theory. No. Could I kick Gregg and family, including a newborn babe, out in the snow? No. Would Rosemary subordinate herself to Wendy, as the leading female influence? In a pig's ear she would. Even if I could manage those currently in residence, could I reasonably expect to control the guests any of these people might bring in? No.

There was also the matter of the Donation of Thomas. The move Tim suggested would scramble the precise division of territorial authority and responsibility set forth in that sacred document, which might be exactly what Tim wanted to accomplish by "giving me" the Big House. Clarity and precision were his enemies, as they are of all natural-born hornswogglers. In the public mind, "Millbrook" was "Leary's place," and Tim wanted to keep it that way.

"No fucking way, Kleps," I was obliged to instruct myself, as I followed Tim's car up the road to the Big House. "Let him horn in on someone else's swoggles." But I was grinning. There was a lot about this one that was highly amusing, if I resisted the temptation to take it seriously.

"How can you turn down all this, Arthur?" Tim asked in a heavily ironical manner, as we closed the front door of the Big House behind us and switched on the hall lights. The ravages of amateur movie makers and hordes of egalitarian primitivists were everywhere to be seen. The place was a mess.

"Better to rule in Hell than serve in Heaven," I said to Tim as we climbed the stairs, which set him off on a series of similarly semi-apropos quotations. Rosemary, whom we found in her new kitchen, accepted a glass of wine but did not join our mood, which had by this time become decidedly effervescent.

Tim then suggested that I join the League for Spiritual Discovery. Since I was now the "official protector" of Rosemary and the Big House, it would "be only proper" if I did so.

"Why not? How can I take an organization that wants me as a member seriously?" I said, or something like that. Things had definitely reached the "If we can't kid each other, who can we kid?" stage of the drunkard's progress.

Tim then started putting me through a rapid-fire series of hocus-pocus questions to which, as one usually does when plastered, I thought I gave highly amusing and original answers, but Rosemary interrupted this age-old form of home entertainment:

"You realize you're breaking all the rules of the League by doing that, don't you?" she asked, in a tone appropriate to Duty, Stern Daughter of the Voice of God.

Tim sighed resignedly, and desisted.

"It's just a game for the benefit of outsiders, Rosemary," he said. He turned to me. "I keep saying that to everyone and they just keep on taking it seriously anyway."

This I believed.

Then Tim lit into Rosemary. It was quite a display of mind

over matter, or something. He had, he told me, his eyes glittering in an impish way, as if we were discussing an intricate political maneuver, been trying to explain to Rosemary that all games had to come to an end sometime. Now it was time for the Rosemary-Tim game to come to an end. Constant change was the rule of life. One must avoid, as if it were the fifth horseman of the apocalypse, getting trapped in outdated routines. They had had a wonderful trip together and now they should part before their relationship deteriorated any further.

Rosemary responded by saying "Yes, Tim" and "I understand," and things like that. I said nothing. If I hadn't been smashed I would have been acutely embarrassed. According to my standards, Tim and I had been close enough for long enough so we could put our doctrinal and political differences aside and discuss our private lives with each other as friends, but I hardly knew Rosemary. Tim was humiliating her in front of me, and I was sure this was producing a seething distillation of indignation and resentment behind her bland exterior. After all, my type or not my type, Rosemary wasn't Sarasvati. I doubted very much that abuse was the best she expected from the object of her affections.

Although, according to Tim, Rosemary thought I was "funny," I was sure she was a standard, Giant-Brain fantast, and thought of me as a rival or even an enemy of her belief system and of her leader and lover as well. Haines and I were, basically, poachers on what was rightfully Tim's territory. His attempt to "give" me the Big House was therefore an incomprehensible betrayal of his true friends and of her. If he had to transfer authority, why didn't he transfer it to one of his loyal followers?

There were politically sound but Machiavellian answers to this question, but Tim could no more reveal them to any of his followers, Rosemary included, as explanations for his conduct, than he could present them to me as reasons why I should do what he wanted. To do the former would have been political suicide; to do the latter would have been absurd.

It's a little problem Machiavellians tend to have. Not only do they have to cook up devious plots, they have to cook up devious plots to explain the devious plots they just cooked up, and so on ad infinitum.

To hell with it. Tim suggested that we go around the house tacking up "Warning. Protected by SPIN" signs, which we did, and then I went home. Wendy was highly amused by the whole affair, and so was I.

The next night we had an informal farewell party at the Big House, during which Billy, his usual polite self, took me aside and assured me that he would have invited me along also, but there just wasn't room for two more. But if I wanted to leave Wendy behind ...

No. Thanks but no thanks. I couldn't do that.

"Yeah, I knew you wouldn't, Art," Billy said.

Wendy and I spent the night in Jean McCready's room on the third floor since Jean was still camped out in the woods. In the morning, the entire crew of jolly travelers appeared at the foot of our bed to say good-bye. Tim, radiating good spirits in all directions, jumped in and embraced us both, a classic Learian display of affection which put Wendy in a good mood all day.

The view from Jean's room was beautiful. It was a warm, buzzing, Indian summer day. The windows were wide open yet there was no sound of traffic. On the third floor, you could easily forget the physical devastation and social disorder below.

"You know, Wendy ..." I started to say.

"Forget it," Wendy replied.

We went back to our humble home with its immovable portcullis and empty heating oil tank in the basement, which stayed empty all winter.

Peggy called up one evening. What did I think about having a Halloween party at the Big House?

"I think everyone is too bummed out for any kind of party, Peggy," I replied, without thinking about it very much. After Peggy hung up, I had second thoughts and called Bill. Peggy was a notorious soft touch, which was probably the main reason I had never asked her for a dime. But perhaps I was depriving the deserving poor of an opportunity to beg for airplane tickets or whatever.

"A Halloween party?" Bill responded. "Is she out of her mind? Jesus Christ, Kleps, if you're in the mood for a dance macabre, go ahead, but I think I'll take a rain check."

Yeah, well, that was how I felt about it also. The subject was closed. I filed the incident under "Rich People, Incomprehension Of," along with quite a load of other stuff. Now that I have opened this bulging file, however, I see that I should admit that it contains several embarrassing recollections demonstrating that yours truly, a libertarian socialist of the old school, can also forget what it's like to be broke and homeless, if given half a chance. Nothing to it. (Easier done than said, one might say.)

Otto was having a bad time of it. Tim and Bill were "cold-shouldering" him. A mad passion he had conceived for Susan Schoenfeld had not been reciprocated, to put it mildly. Indeed, before Otto left the property to go back to his house in Woodstock, he had suffered many emotional wounds because of this infatuation, directly and indirectly. Perhaps the most serious element in this complex of psychological conflicts was the undeniable fact that his hero, Billy, had shacked up with Susan in the Bowling Alley for a few days, but since Otto thought of Billy and Susan as so elevated as to be beyond all criticism, he could not permit himself to feel consciously jealous or resentful about this interlude of "lust in the dust" between these two ethereal beings. All he could do was "eat it" and it didn't go down very well.

When Tim kicked Susan out, Otto's mythic vision was devastated. Billy was the king, but Tim was the Pope. (Exactly what place I occupied in Otto's scheme of things was always something of a mystery.) Romantic passion had been brought into terrible conflict with reverence and esteem.

Otto's love for Susan was entirely genuine, as demonstrated by the completely idiosyncratic idea he had formed of her character. His vision did not even vaguely resemble anything anyone else thought about her, whether they liked her or not. She was, according to Otto's dreamy-eyed descriptions, a kind of compound of all the sappiest heroines of the silliest novels ever written. Whenever he talked about her, which was incessantly, his face took on an expression of beatitude in startling contrast to his normal appearance. "Gentle, delicate and pure" were typical of the adjectives he employed to describe this tough broad. These claims were so fantastic it was impossible to even try to contradict him.

When Otto left, with a $100 check from Tim, he was in sad shape, and when he returned after the tourists had departed for the West, he was worse. Not only did he look beaten and drained, his description of his adventures was not merely eccentric but delusional.

What he wanted from us, he told Wendy and me, were the two small rugs he had left with us for safekeeping. During his wanderings between the Ashram, the League, the Gatehouse and the Bungalow, Otto had left behind a confused trail of odd but often valuable possessions. Among these was a gigantic, ebony armoire which he had shipped to the Bungalow. Tommy, Jack and I had wrestled it into a corner of the billiards room where, to the amazement of all present, it seemed to fit in perfectly, as if it had been born there. He also had given a large statuette, called "the Black Buddha," to Tim, Haines and Billy in turn. Haines had treasured this object, and the mixture of amusement and exasperation with which he normally reacted to Otto's conduct soured greatly when Otto had taken it back.

Otto's adventures in New York, as he related them to Wendy and me after we invited him upstairs, where we gathered around a catalytic heater in the bedroom, started out funny enough. Since Tim's check had been drawn on an out-of-town bank, he had spent hours trudging from one financial institution to another trying to cash it. All the tellers he had approached had declined to honor it until he tried the Bank of Tokyo, where it had been promptly cashed with the utmost politeness.

He had then paid a visit to "the Mafia's doctor," an "old and trusted friend," which had led to various complications that didn't make any sense at all. Exactly what Otto had been trying to accomplish in New York was extremely unclear. As a result of this, that and the other misadventure, he felt he had received "the kiss of death" and was being pursued by various agents of the underworld bent on his destruction. He could identify them by the particular color and design of the cowboy boots they were all wearing.

The last "agent" he had seen had been on the bus which had brought him home, where he found that his friends at the machine gun factory had been "paid off" and turned against him.

To top it all off, a bunch of "fake hippies" had invaded his house, making it impossible for him to live there. No, he couldn't call the police. They were in on it, of course.

(I hadn't known, until I heard this story, that Otto owned a house.)

"Oh, God," Otto moaned piteously, head in hands, slumped against the curved wall of our bedroom. "What am I going to do? I only have one hope left."

"What's that?" Wendy asked.

"I just hope I don't get bumped off by an underling," Otto replied with the utmost earnestness. "It would be a disgrace to the name of Albenesius."

Oh, well. As best I could determine without my bag of tricks, he wasn't hallucinating. He retained his pride in his name. Given a measure of tender, loving care, he would probably snap out of it in a few days, if not hours.

We took him up to the Ashram, where Wendy and I had been invited for a spaghetti dinner, the sauce of which turned out to be much more inspiring than usual. Along with a little TLC, Otto was being offered lots of THC as well. But Otto refused to eat anything. His loss of appetite was unfortunate, since a good dose of cannabis at that point might have made his paranoia more romantic and digestible, so to speak. In fact, after his second or third meatball, he might well have snapped out of it completely. Haines was sympathetic, as he usually was when someone was in genuine trouble, but he wouldn't take him back.

"Why pick on me? Will you take him back?" Haines asked me.

No, I had to admit that I wouldn't. For one thing, I couldn't afford to be drunk twenty-four hours a day, and I wasn't pretending that the Neo-American Church resembled the Salvation Army either. Something that might be called a "holy fortress," perhaps along the general lines of Lambeth Palace and Disneyland combined, was more what I had in mind in those days. It was Haines, it seemed to me, who was doing the General Booth imitations, so let him live up to his act!

Otto finally agreed to a self-commitment, which I had recommended. (A complete loss of appetite really is a bad sign, and very dangerous.) It wasn't his first and it wasn't his last. One time, after Billy and I got him out of Bellevue and we were driving away, I asked him if he had learned anything during this, his latest stay in a loony bin.

"Yes," he earnestly replied. "I learned how to levitate." I didn't ask Otto to prove this assertion. His track record was too good. Perhaps, if Billy or I had requested a demonstration, we would have been rear-ended by a bus and all three of us would have "levitated" right through the roof of the car.

In 1970, Otto achieved what I'm sure he considered a most enviable status in the general scheme of things: Shortly before I moved into Little Jimmy's house up the road, he became Billy's chauffeur. Unfortunately he also got a small inheritance at about the same time, which he promptly invested at Eddy's Liquors in several cases of fine wines. He consumed this treasure at such a rate, Priscilla told me, as to render himself incapable of leaping to his wheel at a moment's notice, or doing much of anything else on any kind of notice. Billy, who hated driving, particularly in New York City, and who can blame him, then used his influence to install Otto as a handyman in an egalitarian primitivist commune in northern California which had a reputation for being more down to earth than most. I hope this worked out, and that the name of Albenesius has not been disgraced in any way.

With Tim and all the Hitchcocks away, life at Millbrook became even more discontinuous, ambiguous and episodic than usual. A garrison atmosphere prevailed. Gregg Roland came down to see me to talk about the state of our defenses.

His first words were: "Art, if you need another gun, just call me at the Big House." He pulled a .38 out of his belt to show me he meant business. Should have kept Otto, I thought to myself.

Yet, as Gregg went on to tell me what was happening up in his neck of the woods, the brandishing of a weapon began to seem a most appropriate and welcome gesture. Tim hadn't told me the whole story, not by a long shot. His precipitous departure for Las Vegas, according to Gregg, had been the result of days of pressure on the Big House by a contingent of disaffected dwellers in the woods led by a heroin dealer from Harlem and his three-man cadre of fellow hoodlums.

They had beaten tom toms and shouted war whoops at night and then moved into the Big House and tried to take over. The leader had said to Tim, "Listen, you may think you're running this place but you're not. I am." Tim had gone into a song and dance about how the Big House was his "tepee" and people should respect each others' tepees. This sermon had not gotten him anywhere. The only argument they respected was Gregg's .38. They were being held at bay on the first floor, Gregg said, but only barely.

I didn't know whether to laugh or cry.

"What about the League guys?" I asked.

"Pffish," Gregg said, making a motion of contemptuous dismissal.

A few days later, the hoods departed, using a pair of bolt cutters to get through the door under the Gatehouse, after abandoning what I assumed to be a stolen car behind the tower. Jack and I towed it off to our private dump, where it joined a collection of other discarded vehicles.

It wasn't until early in 1975, as I was typing up the first, tabloid incarnation of this history, in a small house near Jay Peak, Vermont, that I realized that Tim never mentioned the invasion of the African savages, during our talk at the Gatehouse or at any other time. His motives in posting those SPIN warning signs at the Big House, and many other things that had happened during that period suddenly became clear. I should have put it all together when Gregg told me the story, but I guess it exceeded the limits of my cynicism at the time.

A *Daily News* reporter and photographer showed up, hoping to do a series of articles on the place. Haines at first refused to cooperate, but changed his mind when I argued that he would probably get better treatment if he did than if he didn't, the standard excuse for submitting to the hazard.

I intended to because I genuinely liked the reporter, who was a fiftyish, cigar-smoking, Damon Runyan type who quoted Aristotle in a heavy Brooklyn accent. Sure enough, the series turned out to be as sympathetic as anything we ever got in the underground press, if not more so. When the article on me and the Church came out (it's reprinted in the *Boo Hoo Bible*), I called up to thank him, and he told me his editor had killed the last installment, which was supposed to sum things up, because it was "too nice."

At least his editor cleanly killed the last installment instead of distorting it. At *High Times*, a magazine which is almost certainly a Drug Enforcement Agency front, any interview deemed "too nice" or "too rational" is mutilated until it conforms to the prevailing standard of blithering idiocy. Is it true that the ink with which this moronic rag is printed contains a slow-acting poison? I don't know, but it wouldn't surprise me. Maybe the staples are radioactive. Remember Waco.

It wasn't long after the great blockade that Noel informed us that a grand jury squatting in the Place of Overflowing Shitholes was considering charges against several people on the property, notably including William Mellon Hitchcock. This news cleared out the remaining uninvited egalitarian primitivists in a matter of days.

Chapter 43

THE BATTLE OF THE SAND BELT

The Church, the nobles, and the gentry then turned one grand, all-disapproving frown upon them and shriveled them into sheep!

On the morning of December 9, 1967, half a dozen cops, at least, barged through the Gatehouse door when I opened it. I was arrested and hustled out to a waiting van where I was handcuffed to Bill Haines, who was already seated inside.

We both laughed. We hadn't spoken to each other in some time. Pretending to be in charge of the whole works, and in my capacity as "protector" of the Big House, I had written a satirical "Orders of the Day," in which I had mentioned that the young women of the Ashram would be permitted to eat one or two cookies with every meal since they were "wasting away to mere shadows." Bill had taken umbrage at this, and sent word that I was not to darken his doorstep again.

This had been at the beginning of the Lumbering Behemoth phase of Bill's unending battle with the opposite sex, which had caused a serious aesthetic degradation of our surroundings, as far as I was concerned, and showed a callous indifference on Bill's part to my refined sensibilities in this regard. If he had decided to run a fat farm, how come only young women were invited?

"Well, Kleps," Haines rumbled, "it's nice to see you again although I must say I would have preferred different circumstances."

"Likewise, I'm sure," I replied.

I blew my nose and tossed the Kleenex out the back of the van.

A young deputy, standing there in the winter sunlight, pointed to the Kleenex and shouted to one of his superiors who was out of my view.

"Hey, the boo hoo just blew his nose in this. What should I do with it?"

"Put it in a vial," the reply came back.

Sure enough. He took a plastic vial from his pocket and stuffed the Kleenex in it. Then he wrote something on the label. Haines was in stitches.

At the same time, I later learned from Wendy, other deputies were cleaning out everything in her kitchen that didn't look familiar to them: wild rice, tamari, tahini, miso, bulgur, kelp; camomile, ginseng and sassafras bark tea; anise, fennel and other herbs and spices which might be something sinister, particularly since all of these items were in glass bottles instead of the standard commercial containers. Everything in our medicine cabinet was confiscated. Every inhabited building on the place except the farm buildings and the phantasmagorical residence of the owners was raided.

Wendy's account of these events is in the *Boo Hoo Bible*, as is a reprint of Tim's article called "The Great Millbrook Snot Bust," which he wrote for the *East Village Other* after he returned from California to give himself up on the grand jury charges. Also included are some clippings from the *Poughkeepsie Journal*, one of which is a picture of Billy being fingerprinted while the great moose-like face of the sheriff hovers behind him, glowering righteously at this fake evidence of the law's impartiality in action. The heading reads, "'Outrage' Says Socialite."

Fake, I say, because Sieg would quash the warrants charging Billy with conspiracy to violate the narcotics and public health laws, criminal facilitation and maintaining a public nuisance.

When the indictments came down in March, his name was not on the list of indicted persons. The Hitchcock Cattle Corporation had been substituted as a "pinch punching bag," I guess one might call it. There was no picture of this event in the newspapers. Sieg did not remove my name and substitute that of the Neo-American Church, Inc., nor was this courtesy extended to the guru of the Sri Ram Ashrama.

Not having bail, Haines, Jackie, Gregg and I were locked up in the Dutchess County jail, a sinkhole in which accused persons who can't buy their way out await trial, sometimes for months, in barred cells with only a narrow corridor to pace up and down in during the day.

In keeping with the great American principle of Trial by Incarceration in Stinking Holes, the un-rich are expected to plead guilty to something sooner or later, even if guilty of nothing, to attain the relative comfort of prison, and in almost all cases we do.

"Well, Kleps," Haines said that night from the cell right next to me, "if I have to be arrested at all I can't think of anyone I would rather have standing next to me than William Mellon Hitchcock. We'll be out of here tomorrow, or Billy will be in the cell right next to us."

He was right. Billy's lawyer arranged bail for everyone. In the morning, we were put in a van and driven back to Millbrook, where we signed statements agreeing to appear in court when ordered. Then we were freed.

When Tim returned, Rosemary, of all people, was with him. A few days after Tim had terminated her services she had fled to Ralph Metzner's hideout in California. Ralph had welcomed her with open arms. Billy had bought a house in Sausalito for Priscilla and himself. One night, while Billy was away, Tim had appeared in Priscilla's bedroom in a distraught condition.

"Priscilla," he had asked, "what am I going to do about Rosemary?"

"Go get her," Priscilla had answered, with typical straightforwardness. He had done so, and they had been remarried in a mountaintop ceremony in Arizona, which, according to Billy, had been a serious flop since a cold and heavy fog had moved in at the crucial moment, Tambimutto had gotten falling-down drunk and several people, totally spaced, had become lost and had freaked out among the crags. Screams, moans, and cries for help, as well as unearthly echoes of these sounds, could be heard during the ceremony, which culminated in Tambi's throwing up all over his vestments immediately after pronouncing Tim and Rosemary man and wife. To clean up after this, as it were, and also to engender positive publicity following the raid, Tim wanted to hold another ceremony, with both Haines and me officiating.

Well, why not? Tim said he had an OK to use the Bungalow, and it was too chilly to do it outdoors anyway, so we all got dressed up and went over to the landlord's house. A television crew who had come up from New York had already set up their equipment. Tommy and Suzanne had moved back to their New York apartment, and Billy was still in California.

Once again, I was amazed at the facility with which Tim produced exactly the right kind of scene for public consumption on short notice. Surrounded by masses of flowers, Tim and Rosemary sat on a couch at the sunny end of the library, attired in their most "ecstatic" costumes, with the rest of us looking like members of their court, or something of the kind. In the adjoining living room, the TV crew looked around in disbelief at all the evidence of couth and wealth. An enormous mandala, painted by Aurora's brother Roberto, hung above the mantelpiece and flashed away by the light of a hidden strobe. To top it all off, Jack was expertly and cheerfully dispensing the best that money can buy from behind the bar. (How had Tim managed that?)

The public was getting an impression of Millbrook as a place where beautiful people did interesting things in a luxurious setting. And we all were all congregated in the only place on the property which hadn't been raided and the occupants arrested— the landlord's house. And Tim and Rosemary were the stars of the show. Haines and I were bit players.

Was Tim consciously building a case against Billy and Tommy? I don't know. It never entered my head at the time.

Bill performed the main part of the ceremony in his pleasantly unctuous public voice. All I did was give a blessing: "May the Lord bless you and keep you and make His face to shine upon you, forever and ever, amen." I figured it couldn't do any harm and I even gave the old Paulinian Boy Scout salute. They were both hopeless cases, so why not tell them what they wanted to hear in the inmost recesses of their souls, as it were? (I became harder to get along with later.)

Bill and I signed the marriage document, a long scroll of unmistakably Learian smarm beautifully lettered by Michael Green, which Tim and Rosemary thereafter displayed in their bedroom. When it was time for the interview, the television reporter was extremely polite and even deferential. What Tim said was that the laws being used against us constituted religious persecution, and that we would fight to uphold our First Amendment rights to the end. That was what we all said, but only Tim could arrange to say it on television just about any time he felt like it.

The information on which the search warrants had been based, it turned out, had come from one Fintan O'Hare, who had been encouraged by his brother, a Sado-Judeo-Voodoo-Catholic priest in the Place of Overflowing Shitholes, to visit the property and insinuate himself into our community in order to collect evidence against us. I didn't remember ever having seen Fintan, who was a pudgy creep with a Vandyke beard according to the newspaper photos, but Haines remembered him and so did a few Leaguers. He had hung around for a day or two, claiming to be a freak on the inside even if he was a creep on the outside. Someone may have passed him a joint; nobody knew for sure. Tim seemed genuinely outraged over the sectarian-warfare aspect of the thing and sent a telegram to the RC archbishop of New York complaining about it. There was no response.

We could have burned down a cathedral or two in revenge, I suppose, but not having been brought up in the Emerald Isles, we just didn't think of it.

Outside in the driveway, after the TV crew left, I turned to Haines and made some remark about how smoothly everything had gone, and how fortunate we were that the reporter had not insisted on visiting the Big House, where the camera would have provided the public with a much grimmer and grimier picture of things.

"Yeah," Haines said. "I just hope this theatrical production doesn't get me in trouble with my probation officer."

"Wha-a-a-t?"

Haines was greatly amused at my startled reaction to this revelation. What probation officer?

Well, it was a family problem. His father claimed Bill had stolen some money from him and he had to make payments every month or go to jail. I remembered that Haines had replied with, "I'm not," to my ritualistic, "I'm sorry," when he had told me he was going to New York for his father's funeral a few months earlier. The next question was: Where had the money for his monthly payments come from? I knew better than to ask.

Tim and Rosemary went back to California.

Billy returned, gave himself up, was fingerprinted and photographed, spread some soothing syrup around, invited me and Wendy to visit him in Sausalito, and departed. When the first-class tickets arrived from a travel agency Aurora owned in New York, we boarded a jet at Kennedy and six hours later were comfortably ensconced in a magnificent house overlooking the bay, wondering what all this was about. It wasn't about anything, it turned out. Just another demonstration of the magical power of money.

Tim attended most of the parties which ensued. During the first of these, I asked him if he had read *Ficciones*.

"Yes," Tim answered. "Incredible." Then he changed the subject from my latest literary enthusiasm to his latest literary enthusiasm: none other than that old fraud, Aleister Crowley. This is insane, I thought to myself.

There was a toothsome South American girl present, to whom I had been expressing my views on the prominent literary lights of the era, Borges included, to her evident pleasure. (I had a higher opinion of Borges then than I do now.) Tim, in effect, informed us that we should stop discussing the talented but trivial works of Nabokov and Borges and move on to higher, finer things, namely, the occultist fantasies of Aleister Crowley. I have never been able to discover in the writings of this jerk anything memorable or admirable, although, unlike most occultists, he was, like Tim, literate. (Jerking off, he said in a deathbed confession, was the secret of his success.)

I retreated to the porch with a fresh drink and a fresh joint to look over Moonlight Bay, listen to the Moody Blues, and groove on the limpidity of the shining night, and all that jazz.

"How the fuck any self-respecting intellectual acid head can get all excited about a fucking idiot like Aleister Crowley, for Christ's sake, and ignore Nabokov is beyond my fucking comprehension, God fucking damn it to hell," I said to Wendy, who had joined me.

"He doesn't want other people to see how smart you are," Wendy said.

"You mean it's still the same old story, a fight for love and glory?" I asked. Wendy giggled and I relaxed.

I relaxed too much, which might well have been what Tim intended. How do I neutralize Art Kleps? That's easy, throw lots of horseshit in his path and drive him to drink.

A week later we returned, no richer and no wiser. Haines was disgusted with me. Why hadn't I asked Billy this, why hadn't I asked him that? Why hadn't I gotten some money? How would we defend ourselves?

"He says not to worry," I replied. "What was I supposed to say to that?"

As I described our hectic and mostly alcoholic adventures in further detail, Haines calmed down considerably. It was all clear to him. Tim had manipulated the situation from A to Z to drive me to drink and prevent me from talking privately to Billy about anything that mattered.

When I got to the part about the professional jewel thief, a graduate of Tim's "Acid for Inmates" project at Harvard, who was also the worst driver I had ever met in my life, and had almost taken Billy and me into San Francisco Bay with a particularly mindless swerve in the wrong direction, Haines cracked up and waved the subject away. As any fool could see, I was no match for Tim, especially on his home ground. Any negotiating with

Billy, as long as Tim was anywhere in the vicinity, would have to be done by Bill. I moodily agreed that he probably had something there, and hung my head in shame.

Haines and I assumed that the illegality of the attack would be matched by the illegality of the defense. Someone in Albany would get paid off. Perhaps the charges would be dropped because of "technical" faults. At the worst, some fines would be paid, but nobody would go to jail. Nobody did, as it turned out, but the cases dragged on much longer than we had expected. They were not swept under the rug.

On March 12, 1968, the grand jury indicted the Hitchcock Cattle Corp., Bill Haines, Tim Leary and me for permitting the premises to be a public nuisance, maintaining a place where persons gathered for unlawful purposes, criminal facilitation and, of great legal importance, "conspiracy" to permit the property to be used for the purpose of unlawfully using, dispensing and distributing narcotic and hallucinogenic drugs. Tim was charged with distributing LSD. Tim, Bill, Jackie, Greg, Len Howard and I were accused of possessing marijuana, and Haines and I were accused of possessing amphetamine. The latter, in my case, I presume, was a small amount of prescription Ritalin from Joe Gross, clearly marked, or a trace of speed in one of Maynard's old syringes from Dr. Jake/Max. If I had known of any marijuana in the house I would have smoked it, but it's virtually impossible to defend oneself against the charge of "possessing" small amounts of anything illegal in any dwelling, since people tend to hide small, illegal things in strange, hard to reach places, and often forget they have done so. And, if every roach that has accidentally fallen into a crack somewhere were exposed tomorrow, and charges brought, millions of people, cops, prosecutors and judges included, would be subject to the majestic force of these lunatic laws, all of which presume guilt and have been upheld by the Supreme Court many times.

Although, according to Billy, I was supposed to be "coordinating" the defense, I had no lawyer. Noel Tepper represented Haines. Billy hired a local insider, which irritated Noel and made Haines extremely suspicious. Tim had Mike Standard, a prominent civil rights lawyer from New York. The fact that Sieg had taken Billy's name off the conspiracy indictment and substituted the Hitchcock Cattle Corporation made Haines seriously apprehensive. A large cash bribe in a paper bag had undoubtedly been handed to Sieg or one of his confederates. Since you can't put a corporation in jail, all real pressure was off Billy, according to Haines' analysis.

"Not really," I said, during one of the interminable discussions of the subject at the Ashram. "He still can't afford to have us rat on him like giant squealing stool pigeons, and with no money to defend ourselves, how else can we get out of this? It's a balance of terror. If we don't hang together, we will all hang separately."

Comments of this kind coming from me eased Haines' chronic fear of my making a "separate deal" with Billy and Tommy considerably, but a fertile field for endless, and largely pointless, speculations remained. When Tim's possible "separate deal" and all the conflicting lies which might be told to the grand jury by all the minor players being summoned to testify were added to the mix, the whole situation became a murky stew of darkest hue.

Wendy was among those who had been summoned to the grand jury hearings, but she had been excused because of her advanced pregnancy. Haines did not take even this at face value, and he may have been right. It's possible that Wendy's father may have threatened to send an unpredictable and uncontrollable "street-wise" lawyer from New York City up to Dutchess County who, although he would not have been permitted to be with her during her inquisition before the grand jury, might have possibly arranged a deal to have all of us plead guilty to lesser charges in return for testimony against William Mellon Hitchcock and Thomas Mellon Hitchcock, depicting them as ruthless and insatiable voluptuaries who had enticed us into their den of iniquity to satisfy their twisted needs. But would Heilman have gone for that? It seemed unlikely.

Maybe this, maybe that. There wasn't any end to it.

Only lawyers are allowed to have lawyers (themselves) do their talking for them if they are called before a grand jury. All others are forced to testify under oath in whatever state of ignorance of the law they may be in at the time.

Anyone, even a lawyer, subpoenaed to appear as a witness before a grand jury can be jailed for refusing to testify against his mother if the prosecutor decides to "grant" him immunity from prosecution, whether he wants it or not, for any admissions of his own violations of the law that he might be forced to make while sending her to the electric chair, and the "immunity" thus granted is often much less of a protection than it is made to appear.

This legalistic evasion of the Fifth Amendment in grand jury proceedings was originally intended, so it is said, to allow the public to expose corrupt officialdom, but in almost all cases it is used by corrupt officialdom to degrade, enslave and defraud the public.

Both the grand jury rules and the conspiracy laws destroy the annoying Bill of Rights provisions of the Constitution, such as freedom of religion, press, speech and assembly. When the grand jury method and the conspiracy laws are combined, your goose is cooked and the Supreme Court doesn't give a fuck, and has said so repeatedly in a series of We Don't Give a Fuck rulings which anyone can read in *Title 18, U.S.C.*

Anything we had written or said to each other, indeed, the mere fact that we associated with each other at all, was evidence of criminal conspiracy. The list of members in the *Catechism* and the identification therein of Tim, Bill, Billy and me as members of the Board of Toads of the Church was cited as evidence of conspiracy in the indictments. It all followed logically if our religious practices were defined as crimes, which they were.

Most of those called before the grand jury lied their heads off, or so they said, thereby risking perjury charges, which was morally correct and highly admirable, but Jean McCready, often referred to among us as "Clean Jean," refused to testify at all on the grounds that doing so would violate her religious beliefs. Judge Jiudice, scorning her citation of the First Amendment as irrelevant since no Roman Catholic priests or nuns were involved, gave her thirty days in the slammer to think it over, so Jean and Rosemary now shared this honor.

Jean pulled ahead in merit points however, because when the thirty days were up she refused again and Jiudice sentenced her to another thirty days. This barbaric practice can go on forever.

American citizens have no more right to refuse to answer questions in grand jury proceedings than suspected heretics had during the Spanish Inquisition.

It's just one of many rights most Americans think they have, but don't.

Jean's boys moved into the Ashram. Prior to her second appearance, the assistant D.A. in charge of the case allowed me to take Jean out for lunch with the kids. I slipped her a ball of hashish which she promptly swallowed with a spoonful of ice cream.

Unfortunately, the jurors and their choir director couldn't see the halo which formed over her head in court but Jean knew it was there, which was the important thing, I suppose. Tim was feeding the slots in Vegas during most of this, but when he returned one of the first things he did was go to the jail and let Jean off the hook. He told us he told her to tell the truth. I suppose he probably did and she probably did. It would be interesting to read the transcripts, if only to find out what questions she wasn't asked.

The classic summary of the situation given by lawyers is that the typical grand jury would "indict a ham sandwich" if asked to do so by the prosecutor.

This fact helps to explain why anti-establishment communities which grow and prosper are always brutally destroyed by the established power in the United States, no matter how inconvenient explaining such murderous atrocities may to the public may be. If allowed to develop normally, they might convene grand juries and bag the wrong kind of sandwich.

How far the loathsome creatures of the Place of Overflowing Shitholes were prepared to go was demonstrated by two follow-up raids which occurred a few weeks after the big one. The Gatehouse was left alone, but the Big House and the Ashram were entered without warrants. When the thugs knocked on the Ashram door and were refused entry because they had no warrants, they smashed the door down and arrested two Ashramites who had refused to open it for "failure to cooperate with a police officer." Jean's ten-year-old son, Cliff, was ordered to appear before the grand jury, although he was considered "too young" to visit his mother at the jail. He refused on religious grounds, and nothing was done about it.

Were Jack and Mary and Jimmy called up before the grand jury to testify about their employers, William and Thomas Mellon Hitchcock?

Certainly not.

Questioning servants would constitute discrimination against the rich, since the rich are the only class which can afford servants, and would discourage rich people from investing their money in bribes for legislators and judges in order to get richer, thus striking at the foundations of Freedom and Democracy.

Sieg also knew that Sado-Judeo-Paulinian values forbad any interference in the ancient, inviolate and sacred relationship between masters and servants, which is a reflection of the relationship between God and His toys. If he had forced a ten-year-old boy to testify against his mother, rich people might have wondered if the hallowed confidentiality which existed between their servants and themselves might be crushed beneath the iron heel as well.

Sieg did not wish to cause any uneasiness among the rich. In Boston, it is a commonplace daily activity of the police to smash down the front doors of the homes of the poor with sledge hammers, steal anything worth stealing, and carry off the screaming urchins of any residents suspected of selling small quantities of hemp to one another, to respectable Sado-Judeo-Paulinian "foster homes," where they will be taught to bathe in the Blood of the Lamb, while their parents toil in a slave labor facility. But nothing of the sort has ever happened in any of the thousands of wealthy homes in New England where servants are employed, and a "phase" of "experimental" dealing in "recreational" substances among the kids is excused as a healthy indication of a budding entrepreneurial spirit.

What kind of "campaign donations" would Sieg and his masters have raised among the rich of Dutchess County if Sieg had sent out squads of semi-moronic goons with sledge hammers to batter down their mansion doors, seize their property, and carry off their male children to serve as catamites for Roman Catholic priests, while forcing their servants to recite before hand-picked "juries," composed of mindlessly conformist robots, everything they knew about the personal habits and finances of their employers?

Not much.

On the other hand, by assaulting the women and children of a religious minority with the full majesty of the law, he could reasonably expect to make points with the Pope and the Fish family, to get to wear a black robe like everyone else, and maybe to be anointed by the Sanhedrin of international bankers in New York as President Sieg Heilman some day,

He really had no choice. Sieg Heilmans never do.

Late in the summer of 1970, Bill Haines and I had to return from Arizona to Dutchess County for the final scenes of this disgusting farce, as prescribed by law. Billy invited us to stay with him in Clum's old house for the few days that it would take to go through the motions. I accepted, but Haines preferred to hole up in New York.

My case was last. Everyone else had pled guilty to this or that misdemeanor. The Hitchcock Cattle Company was fined a few grand, and Tim and Bill were put on probation for a year or two. The night before the day I was to be sentenced, Billy and I were sitting in the living room, smoking pot and listening to the Doors, when I had a grim thought. Maybe it was something in Billy's eyes, maybe it was the desolate spectacle of the almost barren house, maybe it was the Doors. Maybe it was moonlight madness.

During Priscilla's reign earlier in the year, I had occupied Jimmy's former residence up the road, but spent most of my waking hours with Billy and Priscilla in and around Clum's house, which had been nicely furnished with stuff she had bought in Sausalito with $20,000 worth of Orange Sunshine profits that Billy had forked over for that purpose.

She had taken everything with her when she left. Even the floor was bare. Yes, very grim compared to that interlude which had been a fairly fun time, everything considered, including lots of nitrous oxide.

"A grim apprehension is bothering me, Billy," I said.

"What's that?"

"Jiudice may not give me probation. I presume Tim's and Bill's lawyers made deals?"

(Jiudice was the actual name of the judge. Even stranger, Marco, Twain's chapter heading that popped up at the right place, was the actual person's name.) Billy nodded. I had been represented by the Public Defender's office, which means, in effect, I had not been represented at all.

Billy wasn't looking at me in his usual frank, open and jovial manner. Sullen would be more like it. There was a long pause.

"I'm not doing any time over this shit, Billy," I flatly stated.

"Well, if Jiudice gives you time, what can you do about it?" Billy responded.

"I can't do anything but you can. You paid to get taken off the indictments and you paid to make deals for Tim and Bill. I want the same."

This didn't go over very well. Why should Billy do what I was asking...

I interrupted. "I'm not asking," I said.

"Well, if you're not asking, what are you doing?"

"This is a hold-up," I said.

Billy was profoundly shocked. Although commonplace in the lives of the super-rich, extractions of this kind are normally accomplished by indirection and/or through intermediaries, usually lawyers.

"Let's go someplace and have a couple drinks," Billy finally said, breaking the tension.

We went outside and I think we both felt better immediately. It had been a muggy day, and the cool of the night was descending. Billy's million-dollar BMW awaited. It was all he had to show for an attempted hostile takeover of Armour by General Host in the Sausalito days. A German baron, who had gotten in and then gotten out, much to Billy's, Seymour Lazar's and Charlie's disgust, had ordered the cute convertible for Billy as a kind of tip for the tip, as it were.

It was late, and only the most prol bar in town was open. There were usually a few Bennett girls in the place, but on that evening it was occupied solely by young gentlemen of an African-American disposition. Within twenty minutes or so, Billy and

I were about as smashed as everyone else present and, Billy being Billy, we were swiftly engaged in general conversation about Vietnam, about the economy, and about this, that and the other thing. The other guys were mostly clustered around a couple of small tables, while Billy and I occupied the commanding heights of the thrones of human felicity at the bar in front of them.

When America's chronic race problems came up, I had reached the luminous, lucid and reckless stage of intoxication which had gotten me into and also out of the sugar-cube jam in Florida in '66, and I was ready to tell everyone about all kinds of stuff they had never heard before whether they wanted to hear it or not.

I drew two imaginary normal curves, with one overlapping the other, on an imaginary blackboard, to show why the difference in Negro and white representation in special classes and graduate schools was not evidence of discrimination but almost exactly what any knowledgeable tests and measurements psychologist, such as myself, would expect based on the test score statistics. The means of the two races' distributions of IQ scores were about one standard deviation apart, with the mean IQ of whites at about 101 and the Negro mean at about 86. That meant that at the extreme low end and extreme high end of the distributions, there would inevitably be differences of about ten-to-one in favor of whites, which was exactly what happened in practice.

Environmental factors cannot account for the difference. All the research studies I'm talking about match for parental socioeconomic status, and many are based on non-verbal, person-to-person test scores, not paper-pencil tests, which are less reliable. All of the many studies of identical twins reared apart have shown that 85 to 90 percent of the variance in intelligence must be attributed to heredity. The most likely IQ for any person picked at random is exactly midway between the mean of his parents' IQs and the mean of the racial group of which he is a member. These are the same kinds of probabilistic facts relied on by Resorts International to consistently make money at its crap tables, but the government insists on betting against the house.

Why? Well, who benefits?

There wasn't a murmur of protest. Intelligent questions were asked in a respectful manner. Two handsome gentlemen of color who had been playing pool in the back room put down their cues and came over to listen.

At closing time, as we rounded the corner out of earshot of the bar, Billy said, "My God, I didn't think we would get out of that place alive."

Pish posh. I have delivered the same lecture to mixed-race audiences in jails and prisons with the same absence of baleful consequences.

Although radical differences in intelligence are routinely observed between inbreeding populations within other species, like dogs, the mass media insists that all human races are about the same in average intelligence. This fantastic idea, contradicted by historical and everyday experience and mountains of scientific evidence, is none the less promoted by the oligarchy because it makes people with African ancestors think they are suffering from an incurable moral defect. "You can be anything you want to be, if you only try hard enough," is the text, but the subtext is "you lazy niggers." At the same time, the white working class is infuriated by "affirmative action," busing, and other forms of forced integration and propaganda on the tube that pictures miscegenation as a great idea.

This is a profoundly sinister and Machiavellian policy which deliberately stimulates racial antagonisms among working class people while pretending to deplore them.

The myth of intellectual equality among human inbreeding populations justifies the denial of genuine help to the poor: people with the mental ages of ten-year-olds, of all races, are told to go forth and become computer programmers and such like. It's either that, or live in a cardboard box under a bridge.

There is good reason to believe that the mean IQ of African blacks is closer to 70 than 86, which is exactly what hereditarians would expect.

IQ is race linked, but the Supreme Court of the United States has ruled that this is not so. All racial differences which appear in the occupational, educational and other statistics must therefore be ascribed to discrimination, or perhaps to the baleful cultural consequences of past mistreatment of the inferior population's ancestors.

Well-intentioned liberals and leftists in the United States are duped, as usual, and the working class divided, as usual, and the Right, which is usually wrong, can blame it all on the Left, which is usually right.

How wonderful can things get?

Read Jensen, Arthur, Ed.D., U. Cal. Berkeley, for the facts:
Educability and Group Differences
The Measurement of Intelligence
Bias in Mental Testing

All three books are models of superb empirical reasoning and analytical logic. They are clearly written and provide a wonderful introduction to statistics and the scientific method in general. You can then go on to *The g Factor*, also by Jensen, if you think you have the *g* to read it.

In the academic world, Jensen stands astride his subject like that mysterious colossus of old which, according to arcane history, once towered over the Aegean. Its balls were of brass, and clanged together and played "Stormy Weather," while lightning shot out of its ass. His critics, such as Steven Gould, are mere midges circulating at the feet of this imposing figure and of no interest to anyone except creatures even more diminutive and ephemeral than themselves, who dance to the music of the spheres without knowing it.

Like Tim and Bill, I got probation with no restrictions. According to Noel, it had been the most expensive misdemeanor case in the history of the State of New York. While preparing to leave the day after the formalities were concluded, I asked Billy how much my insurance policy had cost him. He squirmed a little. What difference did it make, and so forth and so on. For the first and last time in our bizarre relationship, I promised to never tell. Billy told me. He may have lied. Even so, the figure kept resounding in my memory for months thereafter. "What?" I would ask myself. "What???"

The last time I saw or talked to Billy was in Taos, in the fall of 1971. Joannie and I were living in Aldous Huxley's much renovated former quarters in San Cristobal while I worked on the first draft of this book in an almost identical bedroom, kitchenette and bathroom suite next door. There were five of these units altogether, and at the end of the row, our landlady Elmira's general store, post office and residence. The setting was ideal for writing. The event of the week would be a flock of sheep being driven past by shepherds whose costumes hadn't changed in two hundred years; or a request by Elmira that we babysit in the evening so that she and her married daughter could call on friends; or a visit from our patrons, Mike and Gai Duncan, who owned an entire mesa a few miles south. They needed to visit us if only to take showers, because in the approved primitivist fashion of the day, they lived in a hogan without electricity or running water, but with all the peyote one could eat in a month of Sundays.

One day the phone rang. It was Billy. He was on his way to Arizona with Aurora, from whom he was now divorced but still on good terms, and with her extremely comely seventeen-year-old daughter from her first marriage, who had always been carefully insulated from the scene at Millbrook. "I know Arthur," Aurora said, patting my hand on the dinner table after she reintroduced us, "just your type." She sure was. They were on their way to Arizona in the Mixmaster, and had to be in Tucson the next day, but had decided to stop over for the night in Taos in the hope of seeing me.

We drove to town in the diesel-powered, aluminum step van which Mike had donated to the Church. He had become bored with it, and had been using it as a chicken coop.

Our evening with the Hitchcocks at the hotel in Taos was just like old times. Despite a wide variety of grievances to choose from, not a cross word was said, although Aurora was a bit pissed off at a Latino hotel employee who had insisted on responding to her Spanish in English.

"Oh, it's just so stoooopid," she said, "but let's forget about it. I want to hear about your books, Arthur."

So did Billy. He offered to fly back from Arizona and help me sell the *Boo Hoo Bible*, an offer which I enthusiastically accepted. I had a list of people who appear in this book whose exact names I had forgotten, every one of which was on the tip of Billy's tongue. Neither Billy nor Aurora said a word about possible libel problems, the substitution of fake names for their own in my writings, or any other such stuff. Mike and Gai never brought up these matters either. In my experience, it's usually "the good men of the village" (roughly, "respectable" people) who want their names changed and their telephones unlisted, and generally skulk around under a cloak of anonymity. The "good men" of any and all "villages" are, as Confucius said, "the thieves of virtue."

Billy and Aurora, when they were in fine fettle, which was most of the time, were not ashamed of anything. While never for a moment denying their share of human failings and error, they were justly satisfied with the unique roles they had invented and played in the drama of their times, and now have more reason to feel that way, as this lunatic asylum of a country becomes crazier and more repressive and fascistic every year, showing how extraordinary it all had been.

Billy wanted to know what I thought he should "do next."

"Well, you two look like a good match to me, Billy," I said. "Why don't you buy a yacht and cruise around in the Caribbean for a while?" No, Billy thought he needed more action than that kind of life provided. It seemed to me all the action anyone might care for and possibly a lot more might be provided within this basic scenario but, since we were in a semi-public place, I didn't think I ought to go into details.

Did I make a pitch for a donation to the cause or for a retreat for the Neo-American Church? Nope. I didn't even ask Billy for the 5 or 10 grand, depending on how you figured it, which he owed me for collecting a bad debt for him in 1970. I was content with my lot at the time, and I had also come to feel pretty much about Billy as one would feel about a close friend who was phobic about shaking hands. Would I pursue the poor bastard with my hand out all the time? No, in both cases.

There was only one moment of tension. Billy asked me how I explained "doing all this writing and staying sober" now, when I hadn't been able to do it before. Aurora actually gasped and put a hand over her eyes. There was a pregnant pause.

"I've found someone who's willing to pay for it, Billy," I contented myself with saying, instead of leaping to my feet, screaming abusive epithets and recriminations and stamping out, vowing vengeance, which might have been great shock therapy for both Billy and me, come to think of it.

Billy never showed up to help sell and Mike and I did almost everything wrong that could be done wrong in advertising and distributing the book.

These were correctable errors, but there was nothing we could do about the cultural degradation of the spirit of the '60s that took place on all fronts in the '70s. Mass-market publishers flooded the "psychedelic" market in the early and mid '70s with brazenly fraudulent occultist, egalitarian-primitivist and "drug alternative" horseshit of all kinds, and the *Boo Hoo Bible* got lost in the blizzard of fakery, political infantilism, blithering idiocy and sinister lunacy that resulted. This, the media moguls declared, was the "New Age." Spoon benders and dolphins would lead us forward.

I think the following remarks about the "Christian" Greeks of Byzantium, taken from a famous subtitle called "The Decay of Taste," in Gibbon's *Decline and Fall of the Roman Empire,* sums up the situation very well:

> They held in their lifeless hands the riches of their fathers, without inheriting the spirit which had created and improved that sacred patrimony: they read, they praised, they compiled, but their languid souls seemed alike incapable of thought and action....In every page, our taste and reason are wounded by the choice of gigantic and obsolete words, a stiff and intricate phraseology, the discord of images, the childish play of false and or unseasonable ornament, and the painful attempt to involve a trivial meaning in the smoke of obscurity and exaggeration....The minds of the Greeks were bound in the fetters of a base and imperious superstition, which extends her domain round the circle of profane science. Their understandings were bewildered in metaphysical controversy; in the belief of visions and miracles they had lost all principles of moral evidence, and their taste was vitiated by the homilies of the monks, an absurd medley of declamation and scripture.

If anyone thinks I'm exaggerating, I suggest a visit to the reference room of a good library to scan the periodicals of those years. It was the old story of our being defined by our enemies, but in the '70s this trick was played in earnest. Every day and in every way, it seemed, Psychedelianism (or a genre vaguely associated with it, called "New Age") was represented in the media by a lower variety of infantile gibberish. Those assholes among us, or trailing behind us, as it were, who could be trusted to reliably deliver drivel and nothing but drivel to the public were given every opportunity to do so, and richly rewarded for the service they rendered to the cause of those who despised them.

Here's a quote from *Mind Games* (Viking, 1972) by Jean Houston and Robert Masters, complete with mock *King James* locutions, which is pretty typical of this kind of ideation:

> ... and understand now we can and must materialize the Group Spirit, endowing that entity with a sufficiently material being that it can appear to all of us ... and there is also believed to be a very great mystery surrounding the Egyptian pyramids ... the Mind Games are a means of advancing toward what must be the main goal of every person in our time; putting the first man on earth .... In the near future such Mind Games will be routine in education at all levels.

(This last prediction, I'm sorry to say, has come true in a lot of places, as what one might call the "idiot wing" of the Flower Power generation moved into teaching jobs in public education, much to the delight of the enemies thereof.)

In Fazzm terms, a stake was driven, not through the heart, but through the brains of the Psychedelian '60s in a kind of mass-media lobotomy intended to render the intellectual content of the previous period null and void.

Having taken an excursion down river, let us now return to the last days of '67 when yellow leaves, or none, or few, hung upon Millbrook's boughs; bare, ruined choirs, where once the sweet birds sang.

When Jackie spent the night of the December 9 raid in the can, Quinlan took the opportunity to have Jackie's hair fashioned in a way that conformed to Quinlan's personal tastes in boys' hair styles. This was widely interpreted as meaning Quinlan was queer, but I was told by an intelligent and well-educated African-American prisoner in Quinlan's jail that the

Sheriff required fat Negro women to crap on him in order to get off right, and paid a chosen few to perform this service. If that isn't heterosexuality, what is? Glad to have had this opportunity to clear his name. Fair is fair.

Tim threatened to sue, but didn't. The hyenas were growing confident. The emptiness of our various threats of civil rights suits and so on was becoming apparent to one and all. The Hitchcocks were doing absolutely nothing to retaliate. All we had going for us was unlimited bail money and good newspaper coverage.

Wendy and I stayed with Billy and Aurora in New York for a few days during the Christmas holidays. Billy was commuting regularly between coasts at this point.

Billy seemed genuinely outraged over the latest "outrages." Yes, by God, he was definitely going to bring suit. Those "miserable assholes" had "gone too far." We would keep them "so busy traveling to federal court in New York that they won't have time to hand out parking tickets in Dutchess County," and so forth.

I had heard this kind of talk before but we also had a new hand to play, maybe, if Billy could be persuaded to ante up. Tord Svenson had been busted in his garage laboratory in Boston for possession of grass and peyote, in small quantities, which made it look like a pretty good case for the religious argument.

A lawyer in Boston named Oteri had recently made a name for himself by coming close to getting a Supreme Court hearing in a pot case under the "pursuit of happiness" clause. If we could get a hearing before the Supreme Court with the same arguments in Tord's case, and add the First Amendment free exercise of religion and the Fourteenth Amendment equal protection arguments on the basis of Tord's membership in the Church, it wasn't inconceivable that the Court would rule in our favor. None of us really thought we had any chance of overturning the marijuana laws but even that aspect of Tord's case might be good because the court could turn thumbs down on the pot and thumbs up on the hairy little buttons and appear "balanced."

And if we lost, it seemed unlikely that Tord, who had no prior convictions or even arrests, would do any time for anything.

When I told Billy all about it, during a late supper with Sam, Martica, Aurora and Wendy at "21," he reacted in a positive way, and suggested that I invite Tord to a dinner we were to have at "Mummy's place" the following evening. Mummy was away, but didn't mind the kids raiding the icebox, as it were.

Once inside the old homestead, I could see how the surroundings had put egalitarian Tord in a state of shock. I was disconcerted myself when the finger bowls appeared on top of the dessert plates, a new one on me. I don't think his girlfriend said a word all evening.

Oteri, Tord informed us, wanted $25,000 up front to take it all the way. In those surroundings, a mere 25 grand sounded like the kind of loose change one might spend on tips between Christmas and New Year's. No flicker of emotion appeared on Billy's face when this sum was mentioned.

"OK," Billy said. "What I want you to do, Tord, is call Oteri and tell him to fly down tomorrow. We'll talk it over."

Tomorrow happened to be the day before Christmas. On Christmas, Billy was flying back to the West Coast. The next day, while Tord and I were on the way to visit a mutual friend in the Village, I asked him what Oteri had said. Tord hadn't called him at all.

"Oh, come on Art," Tord said by way of explanation, "Billy isn't going to do anything. Why should Oteri fly down here? If Billy's serious, he can see Oteri after the holidays."

Which was the end of that one.

Tord and his practically mute girlfriend went back to Boston where he copped a plea for probation.

Shortly thereafter the following paragraphs appeared in Lisa Bieberman's *Psychedelic Information Center Bulletin:*

> Despite comments in the previous Bulletins, on the futility of joining the Neo-American Church, I still get inquiries about it, and letters from kids who say they have been appointed "Boo Hoos," as if this entitled them to some special consideration. If there is any doubt left of the fact that the Neo-American

Church will not help anyone, legally or spiritually, consider the case of Tord Svenson. Tord joined Art Kleps' Church in 1965, shortly after it was founded, and was appointed to the "Board of Patriarchs" and given the title 'Keeper of the Divine Toad' by Kleps, who apparently considered this a high distinction. Tord helped Kleps with both money and labor, perhaps more than any other single individual, except for millionaire Hitchcock, who decided last year that Art would make a fine addition to his human zoo in Millbrook. When Art was jailed in Florida, Tord was one of the people who helped bail him out; with the money Art never repaid. He spent months with Art at Morning Glory Lodge and later at Millbrook, and was frequently urged to stay permanently. A few months ago, Tord's home was raided, and he was charged with possession of marijuana and peyote. If there ever was going to be a test of the legitimacy of the Neo-American Church and the right of its members to possess the 'true host,' which in Art Kleps' definition includes both marijuana and peyote, this would have been it. One could not name another member who had been more consistently active in the Church, or more deserving of help from its leader. But Tord did not get a penny from Kleps or from Hitchcock. Hitchcock showed a passing interest in a religious defense but abandoned the idea when he discovered the costs would not be tax deductible. Faced with the gap between reality and pleasant memories spun at lakeside, Tord realized that he could not win a religious defense on his own. How can you tell a judge you're the 'Keeper of the Divine Toad?' Tord pleaded guilty and was fined $200 and put on probation for three years. He will be a long time paying his legal expenses. When I returned with him from the courthouse, we found a piece of mail from Millbrook waiting at his house. It was a plea for contributions for legal defense of Millbrook's 'community,' signed by Leary, Kleps and Bill Haines. I understand this same plea for contributions has appeared in The Village Voice and other papers. Sending money to Millbrook makes about as much sense as sending it to the Mafia. Save your money, or give it to a cause where it will mean something.

I haven't seen Tord since.

My next TV interview, with Metromedia, was staged in the living room of Billy's apartment. I appeared on the screen with a Christmas tree to one side and a giant stuffed teddy bear on the other. I was smashed. I described the persecution that we were enduring on the estate and concluded my tirade against those responsible by threatening to fly over New York City and spray the place with a fog of acid and DMSO if we were not left in peace.

This got a rise out of the *Wall Street Journal*, which printed a "What's the world coming to?" commentary on the front page of the second section the next day, but the writer didn't really take me seriously, and neither did I, and neither did anyone else.

If a mist of the Supreme Sacrament had descended on Wall Street that winter most of the younger brokers and bankers would probably have said to themselves, "Well, stoned again," and swung right along with it. The flashier electronic issues might have enjoyed a mild rise, but I doubt if much else would have happened.

On Christmas Eve, Wendy, Aurora, Billy and I went to a party at Van Wolf's apartment which demonstrated how unconcerned with legality people had become in "cafe society" and show-biz circles in New York. Little cut glass salt dishes filled with cocaine sat on every table, complete with tiny salt spoons to lift the stuff up to your nose with for inhalation. A huge black man, dressed in full livery, sat behind another table rolling perfectly cylindrical double-length joints out of four standard-sized papers for the guests, a feat of dexterity I had never witnessed before and have never seen since. Some people who didn't indulge dropped by, but none of them seemed to regard the scene as exceptional.

Since Immanuel, my father's old church at 88th and Lexington, was only a block away, Wendy and I decided to attend the midnight service, which turned out to be a mistake. In the '30s and '40s the pews had been jammed during every Christmas service, the organist and choir had been first-rate, and the sermons sincerely celebratory. But now the choir was weak, the organist amateurish, the sermon flat, and attendance poor. The building itself seemed to have shrunk to half its original size.

"Well, Wendy..." I said, as we left.

"You can't go home again," she finished for me.

After Christmas, I proceeded to mop up Jesus Christ's favorite beverage for two or three days at Billy's apartment and was swiftly approaching that stage of the drunkard's progress which Tim had depicted in such picturesque detail in his "review" of the *Catechism*. I now know that the best remedy is to buy some cheap whiskey and start timing. I require a wall clock for this, a small shot glass, and relative peace and quiet, and I don't claim it will work for everyone. Two beers for starters, then one shot an hour on the first day of rationing, followed by one shot every two hours on the day after the day after. Then one shot every three hours. Then nothing, if you need to take a driver's test, or an oath of office, or whatever.

At the time, however, I had no inkling of any such means of extrication. I was keeping up a bold front, more or less, but I knew in my heart that I would soon be up half the night retching my guts out, followed by total abstinence for a week or two, and then yet one more attempt to behave like a normal "social" drinker, which might last for months, weeks, days, hours, or nanoseconds.

Billy suggested that we all go out for dinner at a new restaurant which had recently been recommended to him. It might help "lighten things up around here." Well, maybe. Wendy, Suzanne and Aurora were perked up by the prospect of an evening out, but we were far from being a happy group of people. None of us were able to kid ourselves about how things were going or how they were likely to go. Not only was this the end of an era, it would be an unpleasant end of an era as well, no matter what we did.

The Hitchcocks were entirely unfamiliar with feeling powerless as adults, and Wendy had little previous experience along those lines either. I did have, but I had sort of lost touch with it.

On our way downtown in the limo, Billy casually informed me that Little Billy had eaten one of Owsley's latest samples. The tablets were large and colored a bright orange, so they had probably looked like candy to him.

No, it wasn't STP, thank heavens. Only about 300 micrograms of LSD, that's all.

Yes, his pupils were dilated. Aurora said that he "seemed happy." Aurora did not seem happy, but was navigating on the general principle that all children were "naturally stoned" anyway. What difference did it make, really?

THE BATTLE OF THE SAND BELT

There is something in this. Aurora's mother was in attendance. So were one or two female servants from her side of the family.

The kid's first trip had commenced about an hour before we left the apartment, as best Billy and Aurora could calculate. Wendy seemed entirely unmoved by it all. Women who have spent most of the day preparing themselves for public appearance are not easily diverted from their charted courses. As for me, I needed a drink, which would presumably be supplied instantly on arrival, and now I needed it more than ever. I went along with the prevailing analysis but an enjoyable evening of tasty treats, witty repartee and hilarious anecdotage did not seem to fit the picture somehow.

I was not thinking at normal speed. I don't know when, but before we got to the restaurant it struck me that 300 micrograms for Little Billy was the equivalent of about 2,000 for me in terms of body weight, which is what really matters. And what if he did freak out? What would his grandmother do? Call her doctor? Call her priest? Call her astrologer? And what would he do? Call an ambulance? That's all we needed. A front page story in the *Daily News*.

We entered the restaurant and took off our coats. As a series of increasingly alarming visions of what might be happening back at the ranch continued to invade my soggy brain, we were suddenly plunged into a farcical miniature of the situation up in Dutchess County, from the constant unproductive contemplation of which we had hoped to find some respite with a pleasant evening out on the town.

It was not to be. To begin with, the restaurant, for all its expensive furnishings, might as well have had a big, neon sign out front reading EATS in looping letters. It was one of those establishments which fanatically insist, in the face of all contrary evidence, that food comes first, food comes second, and food comes third. There was no bar. There were no other customers. The place was brightly lit. (See, we have no need to occlude our food under the cloak of darkness. Why, it's just as bright out here as it is in the kitchen.)

We were not seated promptly. Instead, Tommy, Suzanne and some thug in an evening jacket who normally would have had the honor to perform this service, were engaged in an intense *sotto voce* discussion, with many head shakings and gestures, while the rest of us stood in a separate group attempting to look politely elsewhere, which was nowhere as far as I was concerned. Finally, it became clear what was going on.

The lackey who, according to Divine Law, ought to have been transformed with joy at the opportunity to serve beings so sublime as ourselves, had had the effrontery to ... WHAT? ... yes ... to OBJECT to the brevity of Suzanne Hitchcock's mini-skirt???

It appeared that the American Moronocracy was now dictating to gold-plated members of the ruling class not only what religious activities they could and could not practice in the privacy of their homes and what kinds of guests they could and could not have on their property but what they could and could not wear in public as well.

By the time I had absorbed this fact, almost inconceivable though it was, an even more inconceivable event was happening.

Suzanne was wrapping her ass in a SLEAZY SWEATER, or something, which the thug had extracted from his collection of discarded or forgotten garments???

In science fiction, there are "time warps." This incident, I suppose, might be called a Tom Wolfe Warp.

We were at last seated at a long table against the back wall of the joint, to hide Suzanne's shame, I guess. No restaurant should use such tables for anything other than banquets, in which case everyone seated at them should have his back to the wall. Now Billy, Wendy and I were looking straight at the wall, and at Tommy, Suzanne and Aurora, who at least had lots of stark white tablecloths with nothing on them to stare at over our shoulders.

I ordered a double martini from the surly waiter who handed out the menus, but this remedy, which I needed desperately, was never produced.

All written in French, longhand. No doubt the chef was considered a genius and everyone else who worked in the place was related to him by means of venereal congress between meals.

"Order for me, will you Billy?" I asked. "Something flammable ... couple bottles of Beaujolais ... something like that."

"I think I'll probably have the same," Billy replied. "This place is unbelievable."

That it was, particularly compared to "21," where booze came fast and first. Good old Van was frequently present and made sure we were treated right. Suzie, Van's wife, was one of the owners of the place. I had "baptized" their baby.

I exchanged glances with Aurora.

"You're worried about Leettle Beelly, aren't you, Arthur?"

"Yeah, this is no good. We can't do this."

Aurora didn't need any convincing.

I turned to Billy.

"Imprints, Billy. I mean, who's with him now? What are they saying?"

"Right," Billy said. Everyone else agreed. Six napkins and one sleazy garment came off laps and onto the table.

We had all been acting like goddamned fools and the sooner we terminated the bummer the better.

The limo arrived promptly but not promptly enough to get me out of the area without further incident. Fortunately, I was seated next to the right rear window, and it hummed down the way a good limo window should at the touch of the button.

SCHLAGORSCH! All over the street below but also on the door panel. Billy's chauffeur and the doorman managed to organize a bucket and a mop, while I subsided into a shuddering vestige. Wendy applied the Kleenex and Billy handed out hundred-dollar bills.

Leaving a pool of vomit in front of the restaurant was an appropriate gesture, like the threat to spray New York with acid and DMSO, but what good did it do?

Little Billy kept Aurora up all night but he didn't keep me up. Billy supplied the means to instant oblivion, and I took it. When Wendy and I returned to Millbrook the next day, it looked good, even if it was cold and falling into anarchic ruin. At least it meant something. What, I wasn't always sure, but something.

The balance of the winter passed like a slow train to nowhere. Before the eviction notices came in February all we did was talk about how we might put the place on a self-supporting basis in the spring, and after the eviction notices came, all we talked about was the case and how much we could hold the Hitchcocks up for and where we would go and what we would do after we left.

I made a couple speaking trips, one to a small college in West Virginia where I debated Sidney Cohen, and another to Cincinnati, where I debated my old adversary, Meat Hook Baird, on TV. On both occasions I was semi-drunk, tired, and ineffectual. The wind had gone out of my sails. There was nothing about the situation in which I found myself that made me feel either heroic or wise or a particularly good example for others.

I wasn't even getting stoned regularly, since it was too dangerous to keep anything in the house, and it was too cold to go outdoors in the snow for more than a brief stroll. The Meditation House was deserted. Everything we were doing was defensive and selfish and completely contrary to the emotions which had brought me to Millbrook in the first place. Have another drink, Kleps. Let's go over to the Ashram and watch television.

Evenings at the Ashram that winter, with everyone seated in the gloom of the press room, only moderately warmed by an enormous potbellied stove, watching a black and white TV, were usually grim and uninspiring occasions, Smothers Brothers or no Smothers Brothers. Appropriately, we would occasionally relieve the tedium by playing Monopoly and penny-ante poker.

Haines had perfected several standard routines which he would trot out whenever things threatened to get too morose. I must admit they worked, at least to the extent of preventing double binds among his followers from adding to the objective difficulties in which we were mired.

Self criticism was not permitted. Everything was Tim's and Billy's and Tommy's fault, not to mention the ruling class of Dutchess County in general. By constant repetition of this creed, punctuated with explosive outbursts of seemingly genuine anger at anyone impudent enough to offer a deviant analysis, Haines managed to produce an official doctrine on the subject which was as rigid as the Stalinist line of the '30s, complete with a mangled history of events which allowed the bad guys only bad moves and bad motives and the good guys only good moves and good motives.

When someone would ask, ritualistically, "How are we going to get out of this?" or some variant of that basic question, Bill would roar "Blackmail!" That's how we're going to get out of this. Do you know of any great religion that was founded on anything else?"

Before anyone could think of an exception, Bill would launch into one or more stories from his seemingly inexhaustible collection of anecdotes which vividly illustrated the ruthless perfidiousness of all the founders of all the established denominations.

These tales would cheer everyone up.

One gloomy evening, just as Wendy and I were about to turn in, we heard a car pull up in front of the portcullis below and then a knocking on the outside tower door, which was sealed shut. This was not a particularly unusual event. I uttered a routine "goddamit" and switched on the floodlights which Tord had expertly installed the previous summer. Wendy swiftly waddled to the tower bedroom, where the left front window gave us the best vantage point for reply to inquiries and the notation of license numbers.

Usually these nocturnal visits didn't amount to much more than a recitation of phone numbers or directions, so I remained at my desk. To look down from the front windows of the main room required climbing up on the portcullis enclosure which was so handy for the collation of *Divine Toad Sweat*s by naked girls and so forth, but even then the roof blocked the view of what was directly below.

"It's Michael Hollingshead," Wendy reported, somewhat wide-eyed, on her return. "He's got a girl with him and he wants to talk to you."

Wendy, who had a very retentive memory for such things, had instantly recalled every story she had ever heard involving Hollingshead's brief but notorious attempt to convert the Big House into a sleazy sideshow attraction in '65, while Tim was in Nepal. I hadn't heard his name mentioned in years. I looked out of the tower window. Sure enough. A big, old, battered, dirty sedan. Big, old, battered, dirty Hollingshead, standing at its side, squinting up against the lights. A pale and frightened female face peered up through a half-opened window of the car.

"Hi, Michael," I called. "Down in a minute." I considered turning off the lights, using the handy switch next to our bed, but thought better of it. Whatever this specter from the past was up to, he could damn well be up to it in full view.

"Prepare for the worst," I responded to Wendy's questions, as I put on my big, old, battered, dirty mackintosh and pocketed a flashlight.

"Are you going to let him in?"

"I hope not," I replied.

It was a dark and thundery night, but as yet no rain had fallen. Classic January thaw weather. I made my way across the flagstones under the arch to the pedestrian gate, where Hollingshead was waiting. He just wanted to get something he had stashed on the other side of the gate in days long gone. He seemed extremely strung out, as usual, but at least quasi-rational.

I made one or two attempts at conversation as we walked across the bridge, but Hollingshead wasn't having any of it. He was fixated on the subject at hand. Either something was under "that rock" or it wasn't.

It wasn't. Speedy, if not frantic, departure. Hollingshead didn't bother to thank me for my trouble, but then again, I hadn't asked him and his companion to come upstairs for some warm port and cold mutton or anything like that, either.

"His stash was not under the fucking rock, and maybe it never was under the fucking rock and maybe there never was any fucking stash," I concluded my report to Wendy.

In 1973, Hollingshead got a slim volume published by Blond and Briggs in London, and Abelard-Schuman in New York. He entitled it, with English diffidence, *The Man Who Turned on the World*.

It may be that this pretentious title was planted on him the way "With LSD I Saw God" was planted on me by *Pageant* magazine in '66, but I doubt it.

Acid Dreams (Lee and Shlain, Grove Press, 1985), which is not out of print, 1995, should also be examined with care by historians. Grove Press claims it is "social history." In fact, it is anti-history.

According to this farrago of truths, half-truths, blatant lies and rabid libels, many of which are clearly drawn from the mirthless lips of an embittered Hollingshead, our private world came to a close in the following manner:

> Roadblocks were set up around the estate, and anyone who wanted to visit had to submit to a lengthy, humiliating strip search. The state of siege grew more intense, until the commune was forced to disband in the spring of 1967. The golden age of anarchy at Millbrook had come to an end.

Wrong, wrong and wrong. There were no strip searches, it was not a commune and it was not disbanded in 1967. But, surely, that noble champion of all that is queer and wonderful, Barney Rosset, would not publish lies and libels as "social history?" George Weidenfeld and Ann Getty bought Grove from Rosset after *Acid Dreams* was published. Would Lord George "Geronimo" Weidenfeld and his simpering protégé stoop to shoveling shit to the public, despite repeated demands from me to desist?

Of course they would. Shit-shoveling is the name of the game in mass market publishing, as Tim always fully understood.

Millbrook and the *Boo Hoo Bible* are extensively quoted and misquoted in *Acid Dreams*, sometimes with attribution and sometimes without. The first quote from my writings takes up almost an entire page, but is attributed to a "resident." If the authors, who obviously had lots of technical help, had made any effort to contact me they would have found me. The current address of the Church is always listed in the *Encyclopedia of Associations*. If the listed address had been out of date, TRS or Equifax would have found my address and phone number in about three seconds and given this data to Grove Press for about $15.

The Bungalow is identified as "a four-bedroom, gardener's cottage with a Japanese bath in the basement."

This is either a slovenly error or intentional deception. (Both? I don't know. I suspect that the motivations of people in this line of work flit through their brains like bats.) The source for this particular absurdity must be a footnote in the *Boo Hoo Bible* (1971) in which I mentioned that Billy had moved into Clum's old house after selling his interest in the property to his brother. In the edition of *Millbrook* quoted by Lee and Shlain, the actual Bungalow is not only described at length but located on a map in the front of the book. Why did they relocate it? Who knows? Maybe my description of the farm manager's lavishly redecorated house sounded more interesting than my description of the Bungalow.

Lee and Shlain report, as if it was a matter of great importance, that Hollingshead "never fully trusted" Billy, which is something like saying that Fagin "never fully trusted" Queen Victoria. Nor should he have, but why bring it up?

In *Acid Dreams*, the meditations on mastication and digestion that Hollingshead devised in deadly earnest for his "seminars" (see his book, if you can find it) become "tongue-in-cheek affairs for the regular residents." Hollingshead had probably read the first two editions of *Millbrook* in the interval between the publication of *The Man Who Turned on the World* and his being invited by Lee and Shlain to participate in the confabulation of *Acid Dreams*. Having learned from *Millbrook* that his sermons were viewed with derision back in the kitchen, he retroactively made himself part of the fun instead of the butt of ridicule that he was in fact.

I am pictured as a "virtual unknown" to the presumably well-known residents of the estate, such as Hollingshead. I am described as being a "graduate student" in 1960, when, after five years of employment as a school and clinical psychologist, I take my first mescaline trip.

Acid Dreams says that, on my "first trip" at Millbrook (the Kundalini trip, I guess) I "wound up brandishing a gun." This particular libel may be Hollingshead's revenge for my telling the story about his boyfriend Ernie and his supposed non-suicide with his .45 pistol. I am then "thrown out" of the house by Hollingshead. Hollingshead, like most junkies, came as close to being a human scarecrow as one can get and still live. He could not have thrown Susan Leary six inches in a strong gale and he didn't throw me anywhere. He hid out, come to think of it.

"Later," I am "admitted" as "a resident of the Gatehouse." (I'm in a dormitory, I guess, where I am permitted to occupy a bunk in a corner, where the Hollingsheadian monks in charge can keep an eye on me and my weapon.)

The Church, which for motives unknown is always referred to as "the Neo-American Boohoo Church," is founded, according to Lee and Shlain, in 1966 instead of 1965. Since the community is falsely reported to have "disbanded" in the spring of 1967 instead of the spring of 1968, the Church is made to co-exist with the Millbrook community for less than a year. In fact, it was Hollingshead who was around for less than a year.

In "diploma-like" announcements, I am reported to "declare five hundred people across America" to be "Boohoos." This absurdity is taken from Tim's patently absurd "review" of the *Catechism*. I suppose Lee and Shlain could plead an inability to recognize raillery when they read it. Maybe they can't, but I think it's more probable that they just don't give a shit. A good line is a good line. Saying that their book is "social history," for example, is a good line.

Tim's episode of feeling somewhat melted in the upper story is made to appear chronic, if not everlasting.

Ironic justice is inadvertently (or, who knows, maybe advertently, maybe even vertently) administered when Tim's misquotations of me ("God's flesh," etc.) in his review of the *Catechism* are attributed to him as they ought to be.

Tim's "I am a charlatan" remark is reported as something he often said in public. He only said it once as far as I know.

Tim's Senate testimony and mine are combined, mangled and reversed to produce a fiction in which I am pictured as watching Tim's performance and, in sharp contrast to my actual reaction as reported in the book the authors presumably read, since they quote it, being "peeved" at the scorn and derision with which it was treated by the senators who heard it, rather than opposed to the thrust of the testimony itself (when I found out, later, what it was). Allen Ginsberg then materializes to "placate" the solons, who are said to be "infuriated" by my testimony in defense of Tim. As far as I know, the only senator who was infuriated was Bobby Kennedy, who wasn't there, and Bobby wasn't infuriated by the content of my speech but by the attention it diverted from his troupe of trained seals who were barking it up in a different ring under the big tent.

Hollingshead's banishment in September of 1965, after one summer of fucking the place up, is not alluded to in any way. The reader is left with the impression that he was a magisterial founder and fixture of the place from start to finish.

I am described as "always being on Hitchcock's case, trying to pump him for money or wheedle him out of it or steal it."

Never mind all of that continuous "pumping" and "wheedling," which is in absolute contrast to my actual conduct (and makes no sense in light of the fact that Billy, presumably without having a gun stuck in his back, hung around with me so much), but was probably something I should have done more of. Zero in on the announcement to the world at large by Grove Press and its hired scriveners that I was a determined, persistent thief, or tried to be, and that my target was my best friend at the time. Imagine that this is being said about you, dear reader.

For starters, who the hell says so? The authors do not attribute their generous contribution to my Interpol file to anyone, although the book is furnished with a large and detailed index, to give the impression that it is a work of scholarship.

"Scholarshit," is what I call this ancient and extensive genre.

I hereby notify everyone involved in any way in the publication and distribution of *Acid Dreams* that they are knowingly disseminating libel, which is a crime, and I demand that they desist at once. Will a team of British libel lawyers whose peckers are not in Lord Weidenfeld's pockets please come forward?

There is no reason to believe anything you read in this "social history" unless you have independent verification. The odds that any given statement is factual, on the one hand, or a slovenly error or an outright, malicious lie on the other hand, seem to be about 50/50. Clearly, if the record conflicted with their preconceived ideas, the author's standard practice was to change the record. Yet *Acid Dreams* is sold all over the world, and is believed, and its contents are taught as fact in American institutions of the Higher Learning.

And so we take our leave of Michael Hollingshead, with the fervent wish of the author that he should turn over a wet rock some day and find himself there, where he belongs, curling and uncurling in the slime with his fellow grubs, Lee, Shlain, Rosset, Getty and Geronimo Weidenfeld beside him.

Go get 'em, Swami! That's my bird!

Billy called shortly after the eviction notices arrived (Tim, in Berkeley, had gotten one too, Haines determined by phone as soon as he got his) and assured us that none of this was his doing even though his name was on the notices along with Tommy's. They had twisted his arm or something. He would "help" us relocate. Bill and I had learned through bitter experience not to assume that promises of "help" coming from Billy were anything more than expressions of sympathy, if not condolence. Haines and I solemnly agreed not to be taken in this time. Cash on the barrel head was to be our motto. We wouldn't budge an inch without it.

Wendy had her baby, a girl, whom we named Kristen. The problems which absorbed Haines and me and the rest of us on the estate ceased to have much emotional weight for her. She and her baby would survive quite well, no matter what happened. They did, I'm happy to say.

Tim didn't lose much time getting back after the eviction notices came. Our councils of war were usually held at the Gatehouse.

When Tim and Rosemary came over one evening, Tim had a lot of accumulated legal and business chores to take care of so the rest of us watched TV. The movie "Freud" was on, much to Rosemary's, Wendy's, and my amusement, but Tim's irritation with this evidence of his least favorite psychological theorist's mass-media success was undisguised.

"Tim hates Freud," Rosemary said.

"That's right," Tim sharply confirmed from his corner, and then abruptly returned to rattling my electronic prayer wheel.

"What do you think, Arthur?" Wendy asked.

"I'm ambivalent," I said, feeling like a Peter De Vries character.

Freud had a wedge of the human pie down pat, I would say, and anyone who thinks otherwise is a wishful thinker. Jung, on the other hand, had nothing down pat but he stuck his fingers in a lot of pies and identified a lot of stuff, including synchronicity, which, not being a solipsist, he didn't understand at all. The TV reception that evening was terrible.

In retrospect, I think Haines agreed to Tim's proposal to hold out and set a good example of passive resistance for the rest of the movement because Bill expected such a posture might raise the ante. It would convince Billy and Tommy we were acting together and meant business. Again in retrospect, I think Tim probably recognized Haines' motive and he didn't like it. It made Tim the ringleader and cast Bill and me in the role of two dummies operating under his hypnotic spell, who might claim afterwards we hadn't meant a word we had said, and reap the rewards of being Billy's friends, leaving Tim out in the cold.

Tim had probably expected that Bill and I would be too chicken to accept his plan to resist and that we would insist on selling out. Then Tim could have told his followers and the press that resistance was impossible because of our unprincipled conduct, taken his cut, and split. This would have secured his position with the egalitarian primitivists (he was involved with Hoffman and Rubin at the time, and making plans for a nudist parade at the Democratic Convention in Chicago), not hurt his relationship with Billy much, avoided any further legal problems and filled his pockets also.

At the time I wasn't even trying to follow the convoluted ramifications of it all. Haines freely admitted he lay awake nights attempting to anticipate every possible alternative and hatching one intricate scheme after another. I was amazed at Bill's agreement, and I sincerely believed Tim meant business.

As the events reported in the first chapter of this book demonstrate, I was wrong. When Tim saw that things weren't going his way because, so to speak, they were going his way, he solved the problem in characteristically Learian style. Suddenly, everything he had said or done earlier became "inoperative." If he didn't get his furniture back, he would go over to Tommy's side. If Tim found he was holding a low hand, he could always pull a blank card from his sleeve, with a crayon attached, and draw a new one.

Tim's and Rosemary's abrupt departure from Millbrook didn't seem to surprise Haines, but I was seriously pissed off. The credibility of any threats from Haines and me to offer passive resistance or to put anyone "in the cells right next to us," had been considerably reduced by Tim's defection. In order to correct any assumption that a vicious vendetta was no longer a possibility, I started making extremist statements to the press. In a statement to the *Millbrook Round Table*, I accused Tim of "turning tail" and compared his attitude towards the Hitchcocks with "the Irish peasants' veneration for the rich Englishman on the hill."

"That should show the furniture lover," I thought to myself on delivering this insult, which I knew would irritate Tim beyond measure, since it completely contradicted the image he wanted to produce with the egalitarians. It would also, I hoped, alarm the Hitchcocks, as a sample of the kind of brutal "realism" which I might be expected to express in court as well as to the press, if pushed too far.

Haines was delighted. I could almost sense a desire on his part to pat me on the head. Instead of behaving like some kind of "flower-power person," I was acting like a good, bullheaded German boy for a change. When, in another interview with the *Poughkeepsie Journal*, I suggested that a "deal" had been made between the Hitchcocks and the Dutchess County authorities, Haines' admiration knew no bounds. I was his fair-haired protector once again. He immediately put in a call to the West Coast and convinced Billy to send him a ticket and arrange a tour of Arizona to look at property for the Ashram. That didn't bother me a bit. I had finally decided that if we were going to play dirty rat games, I would be the filthiest rodent in town.

"When you see Billy," I told Haines as he prepared to leave, "tell him I have completely flipped my cork and you fear for the safety of one and all unless I am well taken care of."

When Billy called me from Arizona, he was most agreeable and came right to the point. He and Tommy were giving Haines $25,000 but since that sum had to provide for the entire Ashram, and I only had "Wendy and the baby to worry about," how about $10,000 for the Neo-American Church? If not, I could come out to Arizona and he and I could look for a little home on the range which would suit my tastes.

Screw Arizona. I wanted to go to Vermont. I took the $10,000 and Wendy and I drove up to North Hero Island on Lake Champlain where I quickly located a modest year-round house on the shore facing east over the small-mouth bass fishing grounds where I had spent many happy summer days as a child.

I decided to buy it, put the title in the name of the Church and start writing by night and fishing by day. It was not to be. The scene looked like heaven to me but the setting, and the prospective daily routine that went with it, looked like hell to Wendy, who proceeded to bitch about it from morning to night.

With her father's help, we bought a summer house, much closer to Burlington, on South Hero island instead. Ethan Allen, one of my heroes, had his last, fatal drunk on South Hero. Title was in Wendy's name. I didn't write anything worth reading all summer.

I must have been out of my mind.

I had ignored the *I Ching*. Like almost everyone at Millbrook since the raids started, I had thrown hexagram after hexagram directing me to the southwest which, besides the actual geographic orientation, represents, according to established Chingian doctrine, retreat, while the northeast represents advance. Had I taken up Billy on his offer to find a place in Arizona, I probably could have grown sinsemilla in relative safety, because I would not have had a mortgage to pay off, and thus no pressure to overproduce.

After our furniture had been trucked to Vermont, we drove back to Millbrook on May 23, exactly one day after the eviction notices had taken effect, to take care of some last-minute details. We came in through the east gate, drove past the barns and the Bungalow and stopped at Jimmy's house, which was next to the abandoned kennels on the road between the Bungalow and the Big House, because we spotted Jean's boys and Pat's girls playing behind it.

Jimmy had just moved out and Ed, Marshall, Pat, Jean and the kids were living in the house, having been given a few days' extension on the eviction order, since they had nowhere to go and no money to get there with, Tim having spent all of his essence friends' kiss-off money on New England Nuclear stock or promotion for his Chicago nudist parade, or whatever. Since they had all supported Tim in his effort to expel the Ashram, I think they were too embarrassed to ask Haines for sanctuary.

Oddly enough, Carl Perian and Bernie Tannenbaum, whom I hadn't seen or talked to since the day of my Senate testimony, were seated on the floor in the living room, looking gloomy. We discussed the situation in a desultory way. Carl said that my testimony had probably held up the enactment of the federal possession laws for two years. Bernie told about Meat Hook's candle and foreskin act with the little black boys entrusted to his loving care in Harlem. I didn't ask them how they came to be at Millbrook at that time, and they didn't volunteer any explanations. My curiosity about such matters was as close to zero as it had ever been.

The Ashram buildings were bare. We rumbled down to the Gatehouse over all the old potholes and that spring's new additions. A stained-glass window that I had installed was broken and swinging open. Inside, all was disorder. Our stereo was gone. Someone had exhausted our two fire extinguishers to spray foam around. Later I learned, on good authority, that these deeds had been done by "some kids from Woodstock" as long-haired and freaky-looking as ourselves.

It was a fitting end.

Chapter 44

A POSTSCRIPT BY CLARENCE

We were in a trap, you see—a trap of our own making.

I had further adventures at Millbrook, but that Millbrook never returned. It ended in 1968 as it had begun in 1963, in confusion and contradiction, a distillation of seemingly incompatible elements representing all the great motions of human nature from the top to about halfway down, from as many angles as one could tolerate.

As a place to live and learn, Millbrook was just fine. I enjoyed every minute of it, even when I was miserable. It was the only place where I've lived where I found it not only possible but easy to love my enemies. Hatred arose only when we were attacked from the outside by the Scum of the Earth. No matter how desperate things got internally, the place somehow almost never produced serious anxiety in anyone who didn't have a bad case to begin with, perhaps because everything that happened was either obvious or incomprehensible or both at the same time, just like the people who lived there. The big problems almost never lasted long enough to permit anyone to work up a real case of nerves over them, and you could almost always find someone willing to join you on whatever kick you happened to be on.

It's the only way to live.

In 1969, I distributed peyote to a band of the faithful on the

Washington Mall, not far from the famous art collection of Billy's famous ancestor (or of his famous ancestor's brother, to be more precise). When the police I had forewarned refused to arrest me, I went to the Justice Department with Joe Gross (stout fellow!) as a witness and plunked a bagful of peyote down on the desk of the Chief Counsel of the Justice Department, secure in the knowledge that "Bungalow Bill" had promised to see the thing through by getting me the money necessary for the case through a most cooperative (10 percent off the top) National Students' Association. With great reluctance, the Chief Counsel charged me with possession of peyote.

Tim, at that time engaged in an absurd attempt to become Governor of California, refused to help by word or deed. My effort, he said, was "premature." Sure enough, Billy welshed again, taking a trip to Europe at the crucial moment.

My consolation prize: Catherine Gordon, a seventeen-year-old blonde and brilliant beauty from the National Cathedral School knocked on my door in Washington to do an interview for a term paper.

Since the relationship which followed overwhelmed everything else in sight, almost all of which, including my marriage to Wendy, was going to hell anyway, I went to live with Kate in a cute apartment in South Hadley, Massachusetts because she was enrolled in nearby Smith College for the fall term. I even managed, much to my surprise, to get a job as a clinical psychologist at the local funny farm, but it was not to be, once again.

Nixon's mind police were out to get us all, with the enthusiastic cooperation of the "silent majority." First, I was fired because I tried to fill prescriptions from Joe Gross for small amounts of a variety of psychoactive drugs at a pharmacy in Northampton. Then a little creep named Paul Kane, who had been part of the Kuch-Mead-Malone axis in D.C., showed up at my door, asked to flop on my couch overnight and set me up for a grass and acid possession bust. While I was out on bail from that one, and while Kate and I were having lunch, the local cops broke our door down and arrested us on a charge of Lewd and Lascivious Cohabitation, a monstrous crime for the love of which the people of Massachusetts are justly famous.

Things became not only Kafkaesque but pathetic. I was arrested in Massachusetts thirteen separate times on different varieties of these same two charges. Eventually, I did six months of actual servitude and then took refuge first at Millbrook with Billy, who had become a mere tenant himself, living in Clum's old house, after selling out his half-interest to Tommy to cover the loss he suffered in the attempted takeover of Armour by General Host Corporation. Then, after Billy welshed on a couple more things, I went to live at the Ashram's ranch at the termination of Mescal Road, just a few miles northwest of Benson, Arizona, where the scorpions and the tarantulas roam.

Everything went to hell in 1969. On the issues important to Psychedelians, the mass media could not be expected to do better than the supposed counter-culture media, which was securely in the hands of the infantile communists and egalitarian primitivists. These "Maoists," as many called themselves, were willing to tolerate Tim's pseudo-scientific maunderings about higher consciousness as the lifestyle or women's-page side of what they firmly believed to be an old-fashioned political revolution of "the young" against "the old."

The understandable opposition of potential military slaves and many others, myself included, who were horrified by it, to the American invasion of Vietnam was converted by the media into a supposed general struggle to wipe out social injustice through mob action. This was universally pictured in the press and on the tube as the ruling passion of legions of American kids, most of whom were only seriously pissed off about two things: Vietnam and the drug laws.

The above narrative of post-Millbrook events sounds like fiction because everything is so neat and right as things generally are only in stories and scripts. The facts are available to anyone who wants to look them up. I hereby grant blanket permission to anyone to obtain copies of any and all records of my criminal history, which I confess to contemplating with a kind of balmy, mindless pride, from anyone who holds them.

The Ashram did end up in the desert at the termination of Mescal Road, where I eventually joined them, after spending my last night on the estate in a tent in the woods with three girl scouts. (A quiet little "sleep-in," believe it or not. Trixie Belden and friends were merely trying to cheer me up, bless their kind little hearts.) It was "General Host" against a slaughterhouse company. Billy did sell his interest in the estate to his twin brother and then moved into Clum's house as a tenant. Peggy married Walter Bowart, who then deteriorated into a "CIA mind control"-style paranoia case. I was in and out of Northampton's jail, which was built by Civil War prisoners, exactly thirteen times. I was declared innocent of lewd and lascivious cohabitation, of which I was guilty, but guilty of possession, of which I was innocent. And while all that was happening to me, Tim was being tried, convicted and imprisoned in California because Jackie left a joint in his father's car's ash tray. This happened right after Tim dumped on my peyote test case as an example of "bad timing" while I was bottoming out in D.C. because Billy welshed.

The fact was that the Supreme Court window was slightly open for a brief period at that time and has been firmly shut ever since.

When Tim escaped from prison, I escaped from Arizona, because Mike and Gai Duncan offered me a deal I couldn't refuse which restored me and the Church to a functioning public life.

"Those who are rich and great seem to know everything and own everything," Lao-tzu said to Confucius, "but they only serve to illustrate human folly."

To the unenlightened, such talk sounds like sour grapes, and nothing more. When life is understood as a dream, however, there is no reason not to think that the "rich" and the "great" serve to illustrate human folly. Who else could do it so well?

As for the many failings of Millbrook, I Snazzmly take all the blame. I didn't play my role well enough to justify the scenery. There's an endless list of things I did that I should not have done, and things I didn't do that I should have done.

But what the hell, I never claimed to be perfect. It was still a good show, an A- perhaps, and one can only resolve to do better next time.

When I look back on it I usually don't see profound lessons inscribed on the landscape in letters of fire, or anything like that, but rather a host of unconnected interludes, vignettes, snapshots, heads poked out of windows to offer a cheery greeting. In a word, scenes. People and places and deeds from '63 are mixed up with people and places and deeds from '70.

We are well-advanced out of the ooze of the booze age and into the warmth and light of the hemp age. The camel's nose is in the tent (1997) and the hump will follow. The acid age, in terms of tents and camels and humps and stuff like that, hasn't even started yet.

When Christopher Columbus was sent back to Spain in chains it didn't mean the exploration of the New World was over. When America was discovered, the imaginations of Europeans were liberated beyond any chance of cancellation. To merely believe in another world, as in the case of pie in the sky, is one thing. It is another thing entirely when you know you can get there by buying a ticket.

The extraordinary general harmlessness, as well as the enormity, of the revolution in consciousness which began on the day an obscure employee of Sandoz accidentally discovered LSD will someday be recognized by everyone. The bloodiest wars in history have not accomplished a thousandth as much genuine change in the general scheme of things as we have with our magic elixir.

Unlimited cheap power through cold fusion reactors and solar converters, super-conductivity, fully automated factories, houses grown from seeds, and chimp domestic servants who will love their work and behave like true Christians are all on the way.

A superior species is also on the way. The Goombahs are coming, right out of the test tube and into the White House in three generations. If the United States doesn't do it, the Chinese will. Can we tolerate a Goombah gap? Nay, I say.

The means to eliminate almost all diseases through eugenics and genetic engineering already exist or soon will and are only being resisted by the most primitive manifestations of the repetition compulsion.

Once these trifling problems have been taken care of, the human race, as we have known it, will cease to exist. Good riddance to bad rubbish. Why anyone should love the human race, as distinguished from particular human beings, is as much a mystery to me as it was to Mark Twain.

The social orders which presently bar the gates of Mr. MacGregor's garden to Peter Rabbit rest on the crumbling foundation of paranoiac systems of religious ideas which never had much joy to offer, and now have virtually nothing to offer except pie in the sky. They have only survived so long because those who profit from them have always and everywhere suppressed the facts about the psychedelic sacraments and savagely proscribed their use whenever the devices of censorship, slander and obfuscation failed.

These decrepit spook shows, and the megalomaniacal civil powers they support and which are supported by them, have become systems of institutionalized child abuse which must, to survive, systematically corrupt the education and sanity of children to create fresh hordes of crazed, bloody-minded slaves who will think only what they are told to think and do only what they are told to do, including bumping each other off when required.

Anyone who thinks America isn't crazy should thumb through the latest *TV Guide*.

Societies composed of lunatic killer robots, no matter how large and well-situated in terms of natural resources, are becoming increasingly non-competitive. During the times of Ghengis Khan, there may have been some group survival value in it, but things have changed.

High-technology civilizations can only be efficiently operated by people who think in an empirical way. Empirical thinkers do not derive truth from authority, but from experience and, in stark contrast to almost every other religion on Earth, it is experience, and experience only, and direct and personal experience at that, which we offer.

Money back if you're not satisfied.

Psychedelianism has already become the actual, living religion of the West. That most of its practitioners don't call it that only demonstrates its power. They don't need to.

The time is not far off when we will achieve victory over horseshit in these parts. We do not need force to do it because psychedelic experience and the religious philosophy which logically follows from it reduce and sometimes abolish the fear of death. Nothing that does this can be resisted for long.

Death cannot be viewed the same way by those who deny the externality of relations as it is by those who affirm it, supernaturalists or not.

The dream simile should never be forgotten. Death, a frequent occurrence in dreams, usually leads to an abrupt change from one dream to another, or, and the distinction is merely one of nomenclature, to an "awakening." It's not a "problem." It's an illusion like everything else.

There is no reason why the dreamer should not live on. In Snazzm terms there are no difficulties in seeing it this way and Snazzm terms are the only terms which apply. There are little trips and big trips. Sometimes scenes change, sometimes acts, sometimes entire dramas, but show business continues, as long as you want it to.

Nothing holds. All is transformation. I can't supply a soothing chaser of cosmic minds and oversouls (one per "multiverse"?) and such, because all of that is horseshit. It is your mind. It is not plural. If the truth is strange, it will sound strange also.

"The gods of the hills are not the gods of the valleys," said Ethan Allen. Neither are the idioms. Interesting that six movies have been made about Billy the Kid, a stupid murderer, and not one about Ethan, whom one might think would better fit the picture of an American hero.

True, I sometimes say it is my mind and I sometimes say it is your mind. I never say it is our mind. There is no contradiction in this because I believe I am talking to myself, and there would be no difficulty in it for you if you believed you were talking to yourself. You can only argue against my logic if you assume I assume what I deny.

"Let the dead bury the dead," said the founder of a great religion, which went wrong and stayed wrong as soon as he was no longer around to control it. The words of J.C., nevertheless, are frequently easy to understand as metaphors for Psychedelian facts.

It's all an illusion, but it's an illusion maintained with all the power of the mind, that is to say, with all the power.

To live with this fact fully realized is an almost unbearable ecstasy which most people cannot endure for more than a few hours every now and then; but one may recall and refer to it as needed while living a reasonably happy life.

The instrument for demonstrating the truth of these assertions ought to be available for about $5 a hit, adjusted for inflation, from Spanish Eddy around the block, and actually is in many places.

Much of the panic is due to this. LSD depresses the market for expensive and artificial substitutes: "drug alternatives" like supernaturalist religion and other forms of mass sedation. It is an outrageous insult to the Great American Established Church, which is an alliance of supernaturalists, that anyone should be able to purchase from Spanish Eddy for $5 a hit that which our glorious ancestors could not obtain for all the tea in China.

Tut, tut.

Vast libraries of ancient and venerated tomes are revealed to be 100 percent horseshit from A to Z.

Tish, tosh.

Heroic battles for control of education and public opinion come to nothing as all factions are overwhelmed by a "Higher Power."

Nothing new about that.

Terrible sacrifices to uphold various doctrines are shown to have been based on false assumptions and misunderstandings made by all involved.

Well, back to the old drawing board.

Yes, it's a blueberry pie in the face for many of our glorious ancestors, most of academic philosophy and vast realms of the Higher Learning.

In the *Mulamadhyamakakarika*, Nagarjuna says, "Nothing exists anywhere, whether we conceive of it as born of itself or of others or of both or of no cause whatever."

True.

If this world is an illusion, then this book is an illusion. I wrote it, but you made it up. You have to assume that if you want to follow me.

The external world is your "unconscious" mind. This book,

or whatever, is not a reflection, or a symbol, or an abstraction. Repression and manifestation are exactly the same thing, only held apart by an abstract system of categorization you keep trying to hang on to. There is nothing hydraulic about it. Nothing is pushed down or brought out. It's all right in front of your nose, all of it, always. It is in this that the relation between humility and Enlightenment consists. Swami Igapoo cannot see the world as already his, because it is filled with the very imperfections which, in his personality, he denies, in order to pretend to a moral superiority over others.

There is only one good argument, which is just as good against monotheistic supernaturalism, and that is to say:

"OK. So let us say that death is no problem. But what about suffering? What good does your philosophy do someone wishing for death because the pain is unbearable? Is the problem of suffering abolished because life is seen as a dream? So what if all relations are mental? You still have to go to the dentist when you have a toothache, don't you? What difference does it make?"

The answer to this is rarely heard. On those occasions when I have accomplished the necessary transformation, I have had nothing to say, for the simple reason there was nobody around to ask the question or listen to the answer.

Suffering? What suffering? Suffering and not suffering and not not suffering are all hallucinations.

This reply, understandably, will not satisfy supernaturalist metaphysicians and naive realists.

Solipsistic nihilists, on the other hand, shouldn't have any trouble seeing that the way to end a nightmare is to awaken from it.

FINAL P.S. BY M.T.

Hello—Central!

And if one doesn't want to end it all, what then? Is anything gained, entertainment aside, from reading this stuff? Let's assume the reader has never been exposed to genuine solipsist-nihilist philosophy before. This crippled intellectual condition is common, even among the erudite, in a culture in which such double-domes as Bertrand Russell and Edmund Wilson have consistently confused solipsism with subjectivism and introversion. Let's say one has reviewed one's own psychedelic experience and has come to the conclusion that, yeah, well, maybe there might be something to it after all.

If you are willing to give it a whirl, that is, learn how to see things this way, will you be any better off than you were before?

Probably.

You will be liberated from dualism and naive realism, and all the depression and neuroticism that flows therefrom, and from supernaturalism and occultism and all the paranoia and general mental derangement thereof.

On the positive side, you will have a capacity for synchronicity interpretation in the cheapest form it has ever been delivered, thanks to the marvels of modern technology. Another dimension of meaning will be added to your capacity to interpret experience.

The events of everyday life, what you see, hear, feel and think, should begin to fit together into new and surprising patterns and combinations, as you recall, when your next coincidence comes along, that it is all your dream, and look for the connection which, in the light of that hypothesis, must always exist between simultaneous or associated events in any dream.

Avoid syntactic rigidity. Remember that the relations you find are relations of meaning; not relations of physical cause and effect, power, or spatiality. It's psychological, and therefore everything is "over-determined"; loaded to the bulwarks with meaning and riding low in the water. You can read it this way and that way and the other way. You can read it in a hundred different ways. This isn't the pseudo-science of the occultists or science fiction. It's an art. As with all arts, doing it well requires practice and self-criticism.

You're free to see it any way you like and then you are also free to witness the necessary consequences, the corollaries, of your decision to see it that way. Every event, no matter how complex or accidental it may seem in McPozzm terms, can be seen in Snazzm terms as a commentary on the condition of your consciousness, and interpreted like an *I Ching* hexagram.

Take everything personally. It's your world, after all.

Ô saisons, ô châteaux,
Quelle âme est sans défauts?

Ô saisons, ô châteaux,

J'ai fait la magique étude
Du bonheur, que nul n'élude.

Ô vive lui, chaque fois
Que chante le coq gaulois.

Mais je n'aurai plus d'envie,
Il s'est chargé de ma vie.

Ce charme! Il prit âme et corps,
Et dispersa tous efforts.

Que comprendre à ma parole?
Il fait qu'elle fuie et vole!

Ô saisons, ô châteaux!

—Rimbaud

REVIEWS OF 1977 EDITION

This constantly entertaining, sometimes hilarious, occasionally libelous memoir of Leary and company in their headquarters in the early days of the psychedelic rebellion was written by a former prison psychologist who lived among them for several years. Kleps is the founder and chief Boo-Hoo of the Neo-American Church and the last of the psychedelic outlaws; he professes to regret nothing except the crushing of the revolution by straight society. Only Tom Wolfe conveys the essential aura of those years better, but Kleps is funnier. There are many colorful characters and anecdotes and several accounts of drug trips. Kleps' sardonic views on what he calls the "kid culture" and the West Coast scene may be surprising. He does not inspire confidence in his veracity (in the straight-world sense) and this tale has to be described as at best nonobjective (he is a philosophical solipsist, in any case). Nevertheless, for the moment, it stands as the definitive account of Millbrook.

Lester Grinspoon and James Bakalar,
Psychedelics Reconsidered

Dear Mr. Kleps: We did not intend the word "libelous" to be taken literally, and we are sorry if we have given offense. It was careless of us to use the word in that way. If we had it to do over, we would change it as you suggest. If the book is reprinted, we will advise Basic Books to make the change. We're glad you liked the book in spite of this. We also enjoyed your book.

Lester Grinspoon and James Bakalar, April 20, 1982

Kleps' 355-page paper-bound "True Story of the Early Years of the Psychedelic Revolution" is both hilariously funny and altogether different from the sort of myopic puffery so long favored by the Leary cult. The story wanders a bit. But on the whole, it is well paced, intellectually stimulating and delightfully irreverent.

John Bryan, *Berkeley Barb*

Kleps' rambling chronicle swings between stoned-out recollection and preachy manifesto as it conjures both the zanier moments and power struggles of a scene that broke down in mind-games, Senate hearings and eviction. Kleps splices the wisdom of Leary, Norman O. Brown, Lao Tse, Hume.

Publishers Weekly

Millbrook is both a lighthearted philosophical treatise and a hilarious look at the disparity between pretense and reality among the evolutionists.

Don Strachan, *Los Angeles Times*

The Millbrook story is typically American and could be about the inner power struggles within any large corporation. That everyone in the boardroom was dropping acid and tinkering with the American consciousness just adds immeasurable interest to the accounts....Readers looking for the "real" Leary and glimpses into the power struggles at Millbrook won't be disappointed, but I think *Millbrook* is more valuable for other qualities. As an exemplary story of how idealistic cooperative endeavors can fall apart, it is instructive. Kleps' insights into and descriptions of the acid experience are excellent. But what I will remember from his version of Millbrook are the ludic portrayals of human idealists.

Michael Perkins, *High Times*